DUELS AND THE ROOTS OF
VIOLENCE IN MISSOURI

DUELS
AND THE
ROOTS OF
VIOLENCE
IN
MISSOURI

DICK STEWARD

UNIVERSITY OF MISSOURI PRESS
COLUMBIA AND LONDON

Library of Congress Cataloging-in-Publication Data

Steward, Dick, 1942–
    Duels and the roots of violence in Missouri / Dick Steward.
        p.   cm.
    Includes bibliographical references and index.
    ISBN 0-8262-1284-0 (alk. paper)
    1. Dueling—Missouri. 2. Violence—Missouri—History. 3. Missouri—History. I. Title.
CR4595.U5 S78 2000
394'.8'09778—dc21

                                                                                    00-028669

∞ This paper meets the requirements of the
American National Standard for Permanence of Paper
for Printed Library Materials, Z39.48, 1984.

Text design: Stephanie Foley
Jacket design: Vickie Kersey DuBois
Typesetter: Crane Composition, Inc.
Printer and binder: Thomson-Shore, Inc.
Typefaces: Minion and Nueva

To Deb, Daniel, and Dwight

Contents

Acknowledgments

I T WILL BE up to each individual reader to determine the extent to which our violent heritage has contributed to contemporary social problems. This work will suggest, despite the controversy, that the link is indeed a strong one. What the author knows for certain, however, is the fact that this study could not have been completed without the help of a great many friends. Martha Hervey and Janice Muenks provided valuable insights. Leah Treadwell again proved to be a knight in shining armor. Without her tireless efforts and technical assistance the task would have proved hopeless. Finally, no husband and father could possibly have spent so much time and effort on a project without the patience, support, and good humor of his family. It also was invaluable to have an English professor, Deborah, my wife and mentor, in the house to correct my grammatical faux pas.

DUELS AND THE ROOTS OF
VIOLENCE IN MISSOURI

Introduction

VIOLENCE STALKS THE American landscape and haunts the minds and souls of our people. History, by documenting this specter of violence in our past, offers us an opportunity to understand our modern predicament. The roots of this social phenomena reach far back and extend into a myriad of diverse communities. Missouri, however, offers some unique insights. Regional and state histories such as this book are the building blocks of historical generalizations. Collectively, these case studies provide the inductive framework for greater constructs of historical causation.

Duels and the Roots of Violence in Missouri centers around a state's love affair with the code duello. Although this particular form of nineteenth-century violence was in some respects a unique phenomenon, it nevertheless provides additional evidence and documentation for those searching for the roots of contemporary violence. Modern social and behavioral scientists have long established a causal relationship between social class and violence. Poverty, far more than any other variable, produces aberrant behavior. Ironically, the churlish synergy of violence and class took a different twist in the nineteenth century. In an Orwellian inversion of epic proportions, acts of violence were orchestrated not so much by the downtrodden as by the elites. It was the upper class, using the dueling pistol as the weapon of choice, which defined the standards of social conduct. It was they, while engaged in this illegal pursuit, who conditioned and romanticized the efficacy of violence. In no area of the country was this process more apparent than in Missouri, with its brusque amalgam of southern and western heritages.

Violence, sadly enough, has played a far too important role in Missouri's past and present. Perhaps its frontier history, as well as its mixture of cultures and traditions, has contributed to this volatility. The statistics speak for themselves. In 1994, St. Louis witnessed 248 homicides. According to the Federal Bureau of Investigation, this high number contributed to St. Louis's ranking as the second most violent city in the nation. By 1995, with 110

1

killings in the first six months of the year, the city had fallen to third place in these unenviable ratings. Kansas City, although surpassed by St. Louis in murders, still recorded 140 homicides in 1994.[1] From January to June 1995 the death knell rang 76 times for murders in this western metropolis. But the scourge of violence was not confined to the large urban areas alone. Of the top ten stories for 1994 in central Missouri, as interpreted by the local press and television, seven pertained to violence and murder. Boone County, home to the University of Missouri–Columbia, accounted for 11 murders that year. Overall, the state suffered the needless loss of more than 600 lives in 1994. The numbers have decreased somewhat in the last years of the 1990s, but the coming millennium offers scant prospects for the permanent diminution of these travails.[2]

Duels and the Roots of Violence in Missouri, however, is not about the present. Rather, it explores the past to find the historical antecedents for the predicament we find ourselves in today. This book does not maintain that the contemporary malaise can be directly linked to dueling or to the power and imagery of institutionalized violence in the nineteenth century. Historical causation is a far more complex process than the actions of any single group or the perspectives provided in any single work. Nevertheless, implicit in the book is the author's belief that the stimulus of past violence has contributed, subliminally at least, to the aggressive actions and responses that we see today. Granted, the world of the nineteenth century is far removed from today's drugs, graphic media, racism, gangs, poverty, and other institutional dislocations, but the vestiges of that past martial spirit still haunt the land.

Before summarizing the major themes of this book, the author must offer a few caveats. Although an effort has been made throughout this work to keep the word "violence" from becoming too redundant, there is, however, no synonym in the English vocabulary for it. As a working definition for this overworked word, the author has chosen the one given by editors Hugh Davis Graham and Ted Robert Gurr in *The History of Violence in America: Historical and Comparative Perspectives—A Report Submitted to the National Commission on the Causes and Prevention of Violence.* Violence is a "behavior designed to inflict physical injury to people or damage to property." Force is defined in the same work as "the actual or threatened use of violence to compel others to do what they might not otherwise do."[3]

A second caveat: *Duels and the Roots of Violence in Missouri* does not catalog all forms of early violence such as assault and battery, rape, robbery, or arson. Nor is it concerned with the number of violent incidents so much as with the impact of violence on the collective consciousness of the citizenry. In addition, throughout this work an attempt has been made to balance the actions of dueling against the actors of dueling. Some individual affairs of honor, because of the importance of the characters and the consequences of the affairs, are rich in drama. In the majority of these confrontations, however, it is the connection of events and the symbols they conveyed—in other words, the actions and not the actors—that provide more meaningful insights into this peculiar form of decorum and death.

Nor does this work presume that Missouri's modern predicament is unique among her sister states. Other regions and areas of the country where the code duello hardly existed are quite obviously plagued by many of the same apprehensions that grip our denizens today. Perhaps we, as a nation, have traveled different cultural byways only to arrive at a perilous yet all too common destination. Missouri's social and intellectual road map is therefore both unique in itself as well as a part of a larger landscape of violence. This work will disclose the violent paths taken by many of the state's prominent and not so prominent citizens to achieve their goals. By studying the form, character, and social processes of institutionalized violence in early Missouri, we can unearth cultural antecedents that may provide valuable insights into our contemporary dilemma.

A number of themes run through this book. By virtue of its longevity and the way it categorized the rules and relationships among group members, the duel will be defined as an institution, i.e., a pattern of behavior, beliefs, and customs organized to meet a particular societal goal. These goals were often accomplished by individuals and groups playing their assigned roles through a structured environment. For the code of honor this structure included an elaborate set of symbols and icons (pistols, swords, etc.), rituals (punctilio and decorum), and rules (the terms of an engagement, the role played by seconds and surgeons, etc.). Institutions are further characterized by a variety of norms that are shared, sanctioned, and internalized by a majority of the members of a group. For the code these norms included honor, chivalry, and courage. Historically, institutions are philosophically and ideologically shaped by elites and designed to meet their needs. This latter point certainly held true for the Missouri duel.

Another theme is the uniqueness of the code duello in Missouri, for it was not entirely southern or western. Rather, it was a hybrid institution—an odd mixture of southern conformity and western individualism. On the Missouri frontier a variety of improvisations gave the duel its unique character. An examination of the historical circumstances and conditions that produced the nature of this institutionalized violence also reveal the resilient and adaptive qualities of the duel. This was especially true of its ability to captivate audiences by a variety of metaphors adapted to changing times.

In the early Missouri Territory, the roots of violence were nourished by duels that conveyed social status and defined hierarchy. A road map of opportunity can be discerned, one that took many an aspiring gentleman along a bloody road to achieve first status, then power, and finally wealth and fame. During the time of intense factional strife, political protagonism became the metaphor of choice for elites who were willing to resort to any measure to captivate the body politic. Fame and fortune were launched from dueling sites such as Bloody Island and Wolf Island for many of Missouri's upper class. This fascination with violence led to an adulation of the leaders who employed it. Missouri's nineteenth-century history was all too often constructed around the tales of "brave" men who employed the affair of honor to achieve their positions of power. This in turn lent respectability to the individuals and groups who likewise solved their problems by nonpeaceful remedies. This philosophy of violence, combined with the accepted belief that a gentleman was above the law when it came to the defense of honor, set dangerous precedents that are still with us today.

Contrary to some historical opinion, duels did more than merely reflect the penchant for problem solving by a resort to arms. The popularization of this bloodsport conditioned people into accepting a functional view of violence. The duel helped to define concepts of courage and cowardice, honor and shame, as well as muscularity and self-reliance. Firearms, which were commonplace among the pioneers, took on a new, symbolic meaning. A brace of pistols now became icons of status in the hands of frontier aristocrats. This obsession with weapons and the willingness to use them became another cultural legacy of the duel.

Institutional opposition from the press, bar, and pulpit did little to contain the deadly virus. By the period of Jacksonian democracy, the toxins of personalized combat had filtered down to the rank and file. Imitation, if not the sincerest form of flattery, nevertheless characterized the people's efforts not to discard upper-class behavior but to emulate it. Dueling, which had earlier exemplified hierarchy, became a means of achieving equality. Although much of the decorum of past years was lost in this age of leveling, the duel became a metaphor for civility and social maturity in the more rugged, western areas of the state.

By the 1850s slavery and sectional discord gave new meaning to the code as leaders journeyed to the field of honor to show their resolve and commitment to their respective causes. Even the destruction wrought by the Civil War and Reconstruction did not eliminate the glamour of the duel. Rather, virtually all types of grudge killings, blackguardings, and shootings-on-sight began to fall under the rubric of the code. Calling any kind of murder a "duel" became a time-honored method of avoiding criminal prosecution. In the changing world of violence the duel became both a metaphor of resistance to modernization and a transitional link between an older form of institutionalized combat and a newer, unrestrained type of physical mayhem. The best example of this jurisprudence of lawlessness was a 1908 duel between two Ozark women who battled with rocks (one little daughter served as a second and perhaps carried the missiles of harm). After expending their allotted number of stones, the women continued the "duel" with butcher knives until one collapsed in a pool of blood.

By the latter third of the nineteenth century, the southern, formal duel with its politeness and punctilio had generally given way to the western, improvised duel, better known as the gunfight. New myths and heroes superseded the fame of early duelists such as Thomas Hart Benton and John Smith T. The heroics of gunslingers such as Jesse James or Wild Bill Hickok, who enjoyed his first "duel" on the streets of Springfield, Missouri, captivated audiences not only in the state but across the nation. The roots of violence would be planted in a new generation by different techniques of killing, but their hold on the imagination would be as strong as ever.

Although numerous critics hoped to despoil this bitter sport of gentlemen in the same fashion that Cervantes had supposedly dispatched chivalry and knighthood, no literary pundit save Mark Twain ever came close to capturing on paper the code's full imprint on the culture of his times. Yet even this prodigal son of the South displayed an odd sense of nostalgia and ambivalence toward the code. Intellectually, he, like many of his generation and of generations to come, had difficulty in coming to grips with honor, manliness, courage, pride, and self-redemption. Yet the moral and ethical dilemma of how best to defend one's integrity when confronted by anger and hostility transcends the era. Although the actions of the nineteenth-century elites often provide a poor example for today's generation, we can, nevertheless, try to understand their world, their honor, their code—those cultural offshoots of the roots of violence.

1

The Transplantation of the Duel to the Frontier

A T FIRST GLANCE it would appear to be a historical anomaly that in an age of Andrew Jackson, Henry Clay, and Thomas Hart Benton such an aristocratic and medieval institution as dueling should graft itself to the very fibers of frontier Missouri. Yet this "one species of barbarism," lethally practiced by a small group that denominated themselves "the gentlemen," had, even before statehood, produced a weltanschauung replete with the most violent characteristics of the Middle Ages.[1] Ironically, the roots of violence in Missouri were nurtured by men espousing an extreme sense of individualism and were cultivated by statesmen ostensibly professing the best of democratic traditions. Rather than pragmatically discarding the code duello, a dysfunctional relic that had brought pain and death to so many families, Missouri's ruling class clung tenaciously to the past.

Like their counterparts in such regions as Mississippi, Alabama, Kentucky, and Tennessee, frontier Missourians exaggerated certain facets of the value system that they prized the most. Unable to replicate precisely their heritage, these western elites nevertheless constructed as best they could those practices they believed suited their social purpose. Dueling was one such institution that connoted upper-class status. Foreign observers of the American scene, such as Alexis de Tocqueville, also saw the historic importance of New World dueling. In his 1835 work, *Democracy in America,* he recognized the artful connection between representative government and dueling. Nearly thirty years later the British *Saturday Review* editorialized that the code duello flourished on the other side of the Atlantic precisely because of its adaptability to " 'demagogic' despotism."[2]

Violence in the promotion of upper-class interests had not been part of the traditional history of frontier political development. Frederick Jackson Turner, the dean of historians of the frontier, for example, had little to say on the subject of violence. Historical ethnologists traditionally stressed the egalitarian nature of frontier society, glorifying the common man and romanticizing the processes of social leveling that became the essential determinants of republicanism. In addition, folklore and folklife studies embellished the ordinary, day-to-day struggle for survival, while legends and myths sanctified a Manichean view of the wilderness as a savage place to be tamed by the enterprising yeoman farmer. From the seeds of this environmental dialectic sprang the flower of agrarian democracy, or so ran the argument.

This egalitarian perspective was part fiction, part fact, part romance, and part imagination. In reality, social and class distinctions were resistant to change. When encountering the frontier, Cavaliers and Yankees alike sought to perpetuate the old social hierarchies through a variety of complex political and cultural manipulations. One manifestation of this collective design was the duel. It was not only a symbol of upper-class respectability and gentility but also a furnace that forged the steely courage of natural aristocrats.

Even before the celebrated Thomas Hart Benton–Charles Lucas affairs of honor in 1817 on a Mississippi sandbar near St. Louis dubbed Bloody Island, the dueling pistol had become an icon of status, conferring not only reputation and courage but social prestige and public esteem as well. In Missouri's fluid frontier society, where rank and status were defined but still undergoing transition, a defense of honor by means of personal combat, especially the duel, solidified one's inclusion among the ranks of gentlemen. It was also an expeditious method of eliminating political adversaries, albeit not the only recourse.[3] Missourians of course were no more or no less violent than other frontier people. A resort to mortal combat as a means of personal redress is, of course, a remedy as old as humanity itself. Nonetheless, the adulation of violent deeds and the dramatization of bravery as epitomized by the duello held a particular allure to early Missourians.

The origins of this deadly institution lay in the medieval Germanic trial by ordeal and trial by combat. Chivalry and knighthood spread the culture of violence. By the time of the Renaissance the modern duel emerged as a popular sport among kings and princes. Ironically, technological advances during the early modern era contributed to individual combat. The most important was the widespread use of gunpowder. As warfare became more total, abetted by massive artillery barrages and large-scale employment of riflemen, it tended to depersonalize individual valor. Therefore, the corps of aristocrats, as a means of identifying and legitimatizing their class standing, instituted a dueling code.

This modern code was born in Ireland at Clonmel Summer Assizes in 1777. The code, with its twenty-six provisions, provided a set of rules that could be controlled and internalized by the European aristocrats. The growing popularity of the duel in early modern England was attested by William Pitt, Horace Walpole, Charles James Fox, Lord Canning, and the Duke of Wellington—all men of note who in their younger days graced the fields of honor. Others of note who later displayed their martial skills in the mensur (the German word for dueling) were Otto von Bismark and Karl Marx. Marx fought a duel over definitions of class status. As a result, the author of the *Communist Manifesto* carried an aristocratic scar over his left eye with uncharacteristic pride throughout the remainder of his life.[4]

The code crossed the Atlantic and became the basis of gentlemanly combat all the way to the Missouri frontier. The Irish code, however, was not a static institution. Refinements were made with the 1824 English dueling code. Other revisions were made by southerners in the New Orleans Covenants. The standard test for duelists in the late antebellum South was the set of twenty-six rules put forth by Governor John L. Wilson of South Carolina in 1838. In addition to Wilson's directives, Missourians in the late antebellum period relied heavily upon Lorenzo Sabine's "Notes on Duels and Duelling." Incongruously, Sabine hoped that his guide would lessen bloodshed and "advance the great cause of human brotherhood."[5]

Sabine's belief that civilized combat would lessen, not increase, the levels of societal violence was particularly chimeric in a frontier setting such as Missouri. Missouri was not like the Deep South. In Dixie many duels were "bloodless" or staged affairs, the events choreographed by principals, seconds, and surgeons acting out their parts with punctilio and grace. Missouri duels, on the other hand, were not "a pro forma exercise in etiquette." While southern duels often left both reputation and body undamaged, Missourians sought satisfaction with blood.[6]

Sabine and other dueling afficionados predicated their beliefs upon the good manners of southern gentlemen. It was unlikely, they reasoned, that one member of the upper class would respond to another with passion and outrage. Good manners, even when one gentleman sought the life of another, exemplified excellent pedigree. Nonstructural, noninstitutional outbursts of violence displayed a lack of personal control and were to be avoided at all costs. The code, with its social underpinnings of restrained violence, did not condone unorchestrated mayhem. Southerners hoped to sublimate passion and to keep it "within bounds" after honor had been called into question. The resolution of this moral and ethical dilemma between the natural man of passion and the social man of discipline was to be found in this convoluted form of controlled violence.[7]

Southern society, static by no means, still deferred to rank and class much more than did the societies of the northern states or the western territories. The mixture of southern individualism and honor was partly to blame. In other areas of the nation, the paradoxical nature of individualism had become increasingly apparent. Not so in the South. Southern individualism, nurtured by isolationism, provincialism, and suspicion of government and law, promoted a call to arms in defense of honor. "The harvest of individualism," wrote historians Jordan and Kaups, "all too often is license; its price, lawlessness."[8] But another side of individualism, this one more prevalent in the North, led to an existential resiliency that held self-esteem, self-restraint, and a healthy disregard for the opinions of others to be of equal or higher value than personal honor. Written law, self-control, and community tolerance were prized more highly in the northern states than the southern display of individual, extralegal passion. The court of public opinion, so venerated in the South, gave way in the North to the court of law. Paradoxically, southern individualism contributed to class deference.

Although dueling occasionally occurred among the lower strata of society, a resort to arms between men of unequal ranks was rare. As an integral part of the social system, the duel represented a "ritualistic expedient" to reinforce and to legitimize the social order. In another sense it symbolized southern devotion to hierarchy.[9] For young men of noble blood it was a rite of passage to manhood, and for aspiring gentlemen it was a sign of social respectability.

The code duello in the South was also characterized by its social pervasiveness and its longevity. It became "the most rationalized manifestation of a set of values accepted" throughout the antebellum South. From the Revolutionary War to Reconstruction, southerners paid homage to this sacred icon. Its sectional beatification was evidenced by the nonenforcement of the anti-dueling laws and by the host of politicians, editors, lawyers, and other professionals who supplanted the ranks of the planters and "maintained its ugly vigor."[10]

Dueling became the social craze of the southern upper class. Schools, replete with "teachers" of the deadly art, sprouted up in many large cities. College students, following the lead of their European counterparts, amused themselves and impressed the fairer sex with their acts of derring-do. The dueling fad also extended to the printed word. Since the "rhetoric of words" could easily escalate to the "logic of arms," a number of popular how-to books, brochures, and pamphlets, instructing the would-be duelist on the finer points of aiming and firing, surfaced throughout the region. Included in this list were John M. Taylor's *Twenty-six Commandments of the Duelling Code* and Joseph Hamilton's *The Only Approved Guide through All the Steps of a Quarrel.* Noted politicians and authors modified and elaborated upon the European dueling codes that had formed the basis of the American codes.[11]

Children, especially males, were not immune to the toxins of violence. The subculture of the duel began at an early age. Usually isolated from maternal socialization by age eight, these nascent duelists were indoctrinated by their fathers to uphold a concept of honor patrilineally passed down from one generation of gentlemen to the next. The martial skills necessary to guard that honor were also carefully taught.

In contrast to other parts of the nation, duels in the South also possessed a "classic" dimension. Notions of romanticism, gentility, and chivalry combined to make a volatile mixture. The cult of southern womanhood was at its apogee, and men venerated the ideal of feminine virtue. The duel made the objectification of women complete. As interpreted by the male gentry, virtue was passive and defenseless while honor assumed an active and defensive posture. Satisfaction normally required more than a mere apology; thus, honor dictated that a gentleman protect the good name and hence the virtue of a woman as vigorously as he defended his own reputation.

This heightened sense of family, womanhood, and personal honor meant that the most inconsequential of remarks or actions could lead to the exchange of shots. Only a few young men, such as Edgar Allan Poe, had the moral courage to walk away from a duel. A comment made in jest, a nuance, the slightest of faux pas, a prank, or any of a hundred trivial matters assumed heroic proportions. Two young men from Virginia, for example, burned powder over the pronunciation of a word. Two Georgia boys did battle over a recipe. A student of Stonewall Jackson's challenged his professor over a reprimand in class. Many a young man tested his mettle over the proper etiquette of greeting another gentleman's wife or girlfriend.[12]

On the other hand, the frontier elites, even if they possessed the southern mentality, did not have the South's heart and soul. In the first place, the southern planter class, unlike the upper class in Missouri, generally came from old, established families, and thus southerners were more secure in their rank and status in the community. Although most southerners who ventured to the dueling grounds came from the professional ranks of lawyers, military officers, and journalists, the imprint of the planter psyche was still deeply ingrained in their consciousness. Numbers, therefore, do not reveal the cultural dominance of the planters, especially as it pertained to the code. Missouri, however, never had a planter class that dominated its political economy.

Second, the milieu of the plantation centered around a peculiar sense of legitimacy and dominance over slaves, women, and lower-class whites that could not be reproduced in a frontier class structure. Southern provincialism with its matrix of myths, rituals, and ideals justified a hierarchical social system that trans-Mississippi elites could hardly ever obtain. The planter class defined and delineated an authoritarian social order and used many institutions to defend it. The duel was one such affirmation of this way of life. Moreover, it was one of the most powerful class institutions to generate this "collective meaning." Dueling represented a kind of conventionalism, sustained by forces of isolationism and provincialism, not to be found in Missouri, where the social order, while aristocratic in pretension, was still open to challenge. The southern planter, on the other hand, remained, if not an unchallenged figure, then at least an unvanquished and static fixture of antebellum life.[13]

Missouri elites, like their southern counterparts, employed the duel to justify hierarchy. Missourians too possessed honor, pride, and courage, but the western field of honor could not for matters of geography, culture, and demographics ever approximate the same fields of the South. Dueling in the Deep South represented the essence of a way of life and juxtaposed the symbolic with the real. Part ritual, part romance, and part theater, the duel reached the inner consciousness of the South. The Missouri duel, on the other hand, was about power. If this commingled with love, jealousy, or hate, so much the better, but its main purpose was to identify social rank, to justify political hierarchy, and to secure wealth and fame.

Another significant difference between these sectional duels applied to quantity. In sheer numbers, the Missouri duel paled in comparison to its counterpart in the Deep South.[14] Its relative spareness can best be understood by realizing that the social and economic underpinnings that sustained dueling underwent dramatic transformations in Missouri in the decades prior to the Civil War. By that time the duel had become little more than a caricature of life. Its significance therefore lay in the broader context of social and intellectual life in early Missouri. The southern business of dueling, replete with schools, courses, brochures, and instructors, would have looked strangely out of place in this western land. Likewise, the practice often lacked the "classic" quality that gave it an aura of romanticism and mystique in the South. Disputes over women seldom called a man to the field of honor. Also, southern etiquette demanded (in theory if not in practice) that a certain "studied etiquette," "touchy" punctilio, and sense of decorum accompany the duel. These "superficial," pro forma dictates were due to the fact that the duel's purposes were far greater than the mere elimination of life.[15] A southern gentleman might seek satisfaction without killing while a Missourian as often as not sought revenge through murder. In Missouri, dozens of years would elapse before jest and repartee would replace challenge and riposte.

In stark contrast to the formality of the southern duel, therefore, stood its more improvised counterpart in Missouri. Although the South later witnessed a rash of knifings, bushwackings, backshootings, quick-draws, fisticuffs, and other forms of noninstitutionalized violence, it remained a cardinal tenet of the ruling class that one avoided unrestrained passion or else suffered a temporary forfeiture of rank. No such social stigma awaited the mandarins of Missouri. Brawling, assault and battery, and other forms of mayhem were attributed to "hot blood" and noble courage. Consequently, when gentlemen from Missouri dueled, they were less inclined to pay respects to all of the formal trappings of the code duello and more likely to concentrate on the matter at hand, namely, the elimination of an adversary.

Although duelists from both sections of the country generally came from the ranks of young professionals, the code served to reinforce hierarchy and social caste in the South while it helped to define social status and to promote political success in Missouri. This was due in large measure to the fact that social classes were less defined in the western land. Of course, a variety of reasons for a journey to the field of honor existed in both sections of the country. Equally true was the fact that both societies articulated a militant sense of honor and had their share of parvenus and poseurs who played to the court of public opinion. But the southern duel was foremost a cultural rite of passage for the pubescent gentleman. In Missouri, dueling, often stripped of its civility, became a crass avenue of upward mobility. Moreover, it was a means of last resort among political protagonists.

In brief, the Missouri duel was an important sociocultural institution shaping the development of the state. And, like other southern ways and practices brought to this new and promising land, the duel underwent a winnowing experience. The code may never have affected Missouri's cultural life in the same manner as it did the culture of the Deep South; nevertheless, its imprint upon the psyche of Missouri citizens was both rapid and profound.

Those Europeans living in Missouri at the time of her transfer to the United States must have been surprised by the speed with which new forms of violence took hold. Missouri soil during the reigns of the French and Spanish monarchs had not been a particularly fertile ground for violence. The tight-knit social organization of the French and the harsh legal codes of the Spanish both provided differing degrees and forms of stability. All of this would change dramatically after Thomas Jefferson's purchase of the Louisiana Territory. No single factor can account for the increased social instability after 1803, but culture, economics, and geography all greatly contributed to a new and volatile situation. In 1807, less than three years after the formal transfer of Louisiana to the United States, Missouri witnessed its first formal duel between American citizens.

This new form of civilized violence, as well as the general level of mayhem throughout the territory, would have seemed strangely out of place for the early French inhabitants. Indian relations were far less contentious in the trans-Mississippi West before American rule, and random white-on-white violence was also rare. The same held true for the duello. On the frontier the formal trappings of controlled and polite violence held little social value. A majority of the early white settlers were miners, fur traders, hunters and trappers, missionaries, and soldiers. With the exception of the professional military class, few of the inhabitants seemed likely to adopt the aristocratic pretensions of the code. They had come from Canadian-French settlements in Illinois and usually settled on the Mississippi River banks opposite from their old haunts. Very little penetration of the Missouri interior occurred after the late 1720s, especially after Indian attacks at Fort Orleans, the first European fortification on the Missouri in what is today Carroll County. The sparseness of the population, the social and religious cohesion of the French Catholics, and the lack of large urban areas also contributed to the absence of institutionalized violence.[16] For those duelists who sought fame rather than revenge, the scattered rural settlements offered little chance for social recognition.

Even the cession of the Louisiana Territory in 1762 to Spain produced little social disruption. Over the next two generations, the Creole character of Missouri changed little, becoming Spanish in neither population nor spirit. Violence, the frequent offspring of greed, fame, or passion during Spanish rule, appeared to be rare. "There was," recalled Reverend Flint, "little to tempt the avarice" in this isolated station of a dying empire. While the Code of the Indies ruled the land, a draconian peace prevailed. "Perhaps in no country," recounted Amos Stoddard, "were aggravated crimes more rare than in Louisiana." A "dark and intricate policy" and a "frightful apprehension of the Mexico mines and the dungeons of Havana" deterred American immigration and "awed" the passive few into submission. Spanish governors welcomed no competition from social upstarts seeking to enhance their individual reputations. Consequently, little violence was recorded during most of the Spanish period.[17]

By the late 1790s the calm before the storm had all but ceased. Already Spain was questioning its immigration policy. In 1799, the population of Missouri stood at 6,028, nearly triple that of the previous decade. By the time of the Louisiana Purchase, one early-nineteenth-century chronicler estimated that only 10,120 non-native inhabitants peopled all of Upper Louisiana. By the end of the following year, 25,000 whites and blacks lived on the land called by the Indians "the land of the canoes." The "simple social democracy of the old French regions" and the regimentation of the Spanish regime had all but disappeared. It was replaced by a "distinction of classes" and increased lawlessness. "It was, perhaps," wrote one early-twentieth-century historian, "the natural feeling of reaction after the repression of the Spanish government."[18]

Geography as well as demographics played a leading role in the history of the Missouri duel.[19] From Marquette, Jolliet, and LaSalle to Boone and Lewis and Clark, explorers eyed the conduits of westward expansion running to and through Missouri. The great Ohio-Mississippi-Missouri waterway, and to a lesser extent the Cumberland Road, led pioneers to distribution points at Ste. Genevieve, St. Louis, and St. Charles. From there they traveled by river or by overland trail to the Boonslick and the Salt River. Others struck out on rivers such as the Gasconade, Osage, St. Francis, or Black, while still others followed the headwaters of the Meramec into the Southwest over the Kickapoo Indian trail or the Arkansas River system.[20]

Besides its claim as the gateway to the West, Missouri became the most logical outlet for proslavery expansion. The Ordinance of 1787 impeded the flow of slave owners into the Northwest Territories. Thus, Missouri became the logical outlet for their enterprise. Climate and topography attracted large num-

The large number of islands over which no territory or state held clear jurisdiction is illustrated by this map of one small section of the Mississippi River, adjacent to Randolph County, Illinois, and Ste. Genevieve and Perry Counties, Missouri. Such islands made ideal dueling grounds. Courtesy Illinois State Historical Society.

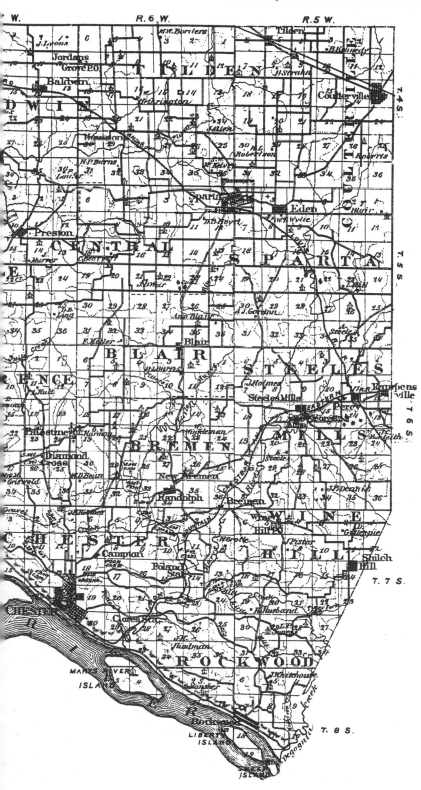

bers of southerners who culturally endorsed the practice of dueling. In addition, the two greatest river systems in the country influenced the culture of dueling. First, the rich alluvial soil and wide river valleys enhanced the chances of profitability from the slave system. This in turn sustained other institutions, such as dueling, which were symbiotically attached to slavery. Second, the Mississippi River, like no other river, formed numerous islands whose sovereignty remained largely in question. The most notorious of these deposits of sand and soil, later dubbed Bloody Island, was formed off the shoreline of St. Louis and claimed by Illinois. Other islands of note were Wolf Island, claimed by Kentucky, as well as Sny and Cypress Islands. Since title to these islands remained shrouded in doubt and tangled in litigation, they oftentimes became a virtual no-man's-land—an oasis of violence—immune from territorial, state, or federal prosecution. The islands, therefore, served as the killing fields for four generations of Missouri's finest citizens. Although they afforded gentlemen from other states and territories an opportunity to participate in the deadly sport of dueling, especially on Bloody Island, the *Missouri Republican* editorialized that Missourians were being stereotyped as unusually violent since they were given credit for almost all of the island altercations.[21]

Dueling and geography also became intertwined in 1763 when a young man, Auguste Chouteau, and his stepfather, Pierre Laclède Liguest, selected St. Louis as the site for a trading post. This elevated area on the west bank of the Mississippi River was about twelve miles below the mouth of the Missouri River, the great interior waterway of the territory. Because of its strategic position and the fact that it was not prone to flooding, St. Louis slowly but steadily emerged as the leading commercial center in the region. With its new economic power came political and cultural influence as well. Within a decade of the Louisiana Purchase, St. Louis had emerged as the cultural capital of Missouri. As such, it set the trends that would be followed by the rest of the state for the next century and a half. Unfortunately, dueling was one of the city's cultural legacies, for it was in St. Louis that the institutionalization of violence gained a powerful foothold. Since much of the populace associated dueling with fine gentlemen and refined manners, St. Louis became a trendsetter for the entire region.[22]

Even Missouri's great rivers, undoubtedly one of its major geographical features, abetted violence. The Mississippi, "twisting and turning as if it were a fugitive escaping from its own misdeeds," no doubt accounted for the greatest number of social problems. It was, as historian Philip Jordan has suggested, "a waterway down which coursed a flood of crime and sin." With so much of the economy geared to water transportation, it was a virtual certainty that social problems would accompany these infrastructural changes. The rivers lent themselves to drinking, gambling, and dueling. Violence characterized landlubbers as well as rivermen, but the waterways attracted a

higher proportion of daring men. Keelboatmen, river pirates, steamboat op-
erators, voyagers, riverboat gamblers, and others who plied their trade on the
rivers were never far from controversy and altercation. Reverend Timothy
Flint's *Western Monthly Review* chronicled a number of these river duels. The
Missouri Intelligencer also reported on September 24, 1819, how a Lieutenant
David Campbell, in an affair called a "riot," pulled a dirk and killed keelboatman Banks Finch about seven miles upriver from Ste. Genevieve. It appeared
that the killing was in response to Finch's drunken attacks on river passengers, especially Campbell's fellow officer, Captain I. D. Wilcox. On occasions,
military officers whiled away their time on the rivers by heavy drinking.
Drunkenness led to quarrels that were put to rest by rowing to shore and dueling it out.[23]

In 1817 the steamboat *Zebulon M. Pike* landed in St. Louis; it was followed
two years later by the *Constitution*. Although a decade would pass before regular service came to Missouri, the thirty-odd years of steamboat history were
turbulent indeed. The rivers served as major routes inland for rascality. Card
playing and drinking often made the gamblers' superstition a self-fulfilling
prophecy. The "dead man's hand" was two black jacks, two red sevens, plus
any fifth card, and usually, wrote historian Mary Alicia Owen, "the inevitable
tragedy occurred before it could be played." Steamboat dueling and other
forms of violence "enshrined under the name of chivalry" became an acceptable method of solving gambling disputes. Dr. John G. Bryan, a crack-shot
Missouri duelist, was one of many adventurers who enjoyed the fast life offered by steamboats. And, like many of his compatriots, he often found himself knee-deep in trouble. On one occasion the doctor quarreled with a
riverboat gambler, but had the politeness to refrain from killing him until
after they left the boat. Two other men, Bill Mitchell and Tom Woolnite, were
equally unfortunate. According to Dr. William T. Hord, medical director of
the U.S. Navy, Bryan killed both men on a riverboat and then went ashore
near Clarksville and shot Cameo Kirby in a duel. Even as late as 1856, T. H.
Gladstone woefully reported as he ascended the Missouri River that steamboats were "crammed with adventurers, who rush to the bar and mix threats
of violence against 'Yankee Blue-bellies' with offers of hospitality."[24]

The diaspora of southern culture created what historian Louis Hartz has
suggested, a "fragment tradition." People came to western outposts replete
with their traditions, values, and cultural baggage. But the uncertainty bred
by the wilderness forced the settlers to hold onto and to exaggerate those
traits most prized in their former communities.[25] Honor was no exception.
Neither was traditional loyalty for family, clan, and kinship.

Southern honor had always extended to the family, but on the early
Missouri frontier the "atomization" of group life led to local identity through
the matrices of strong kin relationships. Pride and survival forged the ex-

tended family structure. Family honor and tradition, therefore, were not abstractions or relics of their Appalachian past, but organic components of life itself. To challenge any aspect of this organic social order led to dysfunctional consequences. The social order, suggested Dickson Bruce, Jr., gave southerners an intellectual and cultural heritage from which they could build a sense of history. Not surprisingly, many early Missouri altercations and duels arose from matters of family honor.[26]

Culturally, the early arrivals to territorial Missouri also shared southern values of courage and cowardice.[27] Courage was at the apex of this system of values for townsmen and country folk, mechanics and farmers, keelboatmen and landlubbers, as well as gentlemen and crackers. Antithetical to courage, and the most loathsome character flaw, was cowardice. While the motives of honor and chivalry were designated chiefly to the aspiring class of gentlemen, courage came to be represented by self-reliance, individualism, economic achievement, and a host of manly bravados ranging from an expertise in shooting, hunting, and knife throwing through a variety of forms of personal combat. At the heart of courage was the visible manifestation of acts of violence and derring-do.[28]

The duel must be viewed in this cultural context. It, like other forms of violence, coexisted in an atmosphere where force of arms was not a means of last resort but often a means of first redress, and where serious bodily harm and even death lurked just below a surface of civility. Many nineteenth-century duelists and their critics mistakenly believed that the standards of gentlemanly conduct differed from those of the larger society and therefore compelled the duelist to fight in order to secure the approval of this small group. In fact, this facet of the subculture of the gentleman was only one part of a larger pattern of dysfunctional behavior in early Missouri.[29]

Class consciousness existed on the frontier but it was not as pronounced as in the towns and cities of the East or in the rural communities to the north of Missouri.[30] On the Missouri frontier there were fewer differences in terms of wealth and power. The basic necessities of life were derived from agricultural self-sufficiency and primitive barter. Goods were provided on the basis of need, and little surplus value existed. Yet the frontier was not egalitarian in social or political outlook. Differences in terms of social status emerged based not upon standards of power and wealth but upon how well an individual met group needs and personified the values cherished by the group. In other words, a man achieved status by displaying acts of self-reliance and courage that later could lead him down the path of political power. Many times group recognition was bestowed upon individuals who engaged in violent acts. This type of dysfunctional behavior abetted the cause of dueling. Ironically, status inequality existed on the frontier where professed notions of egalitarianism prevailed not because status was conferred on the basis of economics but because it was based upon abstract ideals.[31]

Political distinctions also existed. Although highly individualistic and self-reliant, the pioneer had yet to imbibe the spirit of Jacksonianism. Deference to elites, whether Spanish, French, or American, characterized his political behavior and made him easily manipulated by external symbols of the ruling class. One such cultural artifact was the duel, with its idolization of violence and its confirmation of status upon the very few. The code duello had always been a tool in the hands of elites. In the antebellum South it reinforced the old social order. In Missouri, on the other hand, the duel defined an emerging new social order. In traditional societies, wealth and family background quite logically led to a sense of noblesse oblige. Politics and power customarily emanated from ascriptively assigned roles. But in Missouri social roles were less defined, class lines more blurred, and social status less secure. Power, consequently, did not flow from wealth because great fortunes had yet to be achieved. That was, after all, why men risked everything to make the westward journey.

Power, therefore, was the second step on the ladder to wealth and fame, and it came to those in the towns who had first achieved higher social status. This was possible only after towns replaced the frontier as the focal point of economic activity. It was the towns that spurred the transition to a market economy. Towns also were the place where the drama of the duel was acted out. Here, too, attempts at class differentiation by emerging elites stood in marked contrast to a more simplified wilderness life. The problem for a transitional society, however, still remained: namely, that until great disparities of wealth emerged, elites searched for visual means to distinguish themselves from their lower-class counterparts. Since western towns displayed far fewer aristocratic trappings than their eastern counterparts, there were also less easily defined divisions of grade and rank in western communities. Various social devices, including the duel, became methods of class identification.[32]

Although relatively few in number, duels in early Missouri were played out with deadly intent. These sanguinary events were usually between gentlemen of some social prominence in the towns along the Mississippi River. As these frontier communities grew in size and social complexity, a host of newcomers vied for status, influence, and social respect, which they believed could be parlayed into political power. Power was the gateway to wealth and fame. It was within the matrix of this competition for social recognition that early Missouri duels were waged.

Violence, however, was by no means the only or even the most likely means of attaining class distinction. Ascriptively, a man might make "good connections" because of his family reputation, his class and educational background, or his "good breeding." He was also likely to achieve social status by his possession of land and slaves, military title, and occupation. The occupation most likely to attract attention was the profession of law. Lawyers would become, in the words of one historian, the "ruling class" in Missouri.[33] Nevertheless, in the first two decades after the Louisiana Purchase, fierce competition for lucrative contracts produced personal jealousies and factional animosities that made the legal profession a rather dangerous occupation. Many young aspirants, therefore, saw violence and the code duello as a shortcut to the legitimization of upper-class status and a convenient, albeit dangerous, means of eliminating potential rivals. Junior officers in the military also saw a "personal interview," as the duel was often called, as a means of reducing potential rivals for promotion. Preachers such as John Mason Peck and Timothy Flint many times complained about the officer corps around St. Louis, whose propensity for antisocial behavior menaced their missionary work.[34]

The social "chasm" in early Missouri emerged as the locus of economic activity shifted from the countryside to the towns.[35] "The gentlemen of the towns," remarked Flint, often spoke "with a certain contempt and horror of the backwoodsmen," but it was the former who were in fact, he reported, the "worthless people." Freed in his own mind from this social prejudice, Flint went on to vent his spleen on the social upstarts who purported to call themselves gentlemen. Here was a Christian tragedy of its own making based not upon the genesis of ignorance but the socialization of greed.

Flint, although fond of saying that one traveled "beyond the Sabbath" when he crossed the Mississippi, still believed in the redemptive qualities of reasoned and logical preaching. Hence a dichotomy between the pioneer and the town "gentleman," a pretender who put his own god above Flint's and worshiped at the false altar of honor. Yet one cultural characteristic, namely a "fierce and adventurous" spirit, which the good reverend mistakenly attributed mainly to that "small class that denominate themselves 'the gentlemen,' " was universally accepted among all classes. For Flint, these "new adventurers" of dubious social rank resorted to acts of institutionalized violence because they had "not yet had their place or standing assigned them in public opinion." Without benefit of character or education, these "gentlemen" found the "shortest road to settle their pretensions" was merely to fight a duel. Men such as these, Flint lamented, "are always ready for the combat." Dueling, he believed, was "the most horrible and savage relic of a barbarous age." The missionary no doubt exaggerated the number of "fatal duels" of which he had firsthand knowledge. Nevertheless, the utility of the duel, especially in the regions undergoing the most rapid Americanization, lent credence to his charges.[36]

The first official challenge between Missourians under the terms of the code duello occurred in 1806. The previous year Governor James Wilkinson had appointed a close friend, James L. Donaldson, as attorney general for the territory. Judges John B. C. Lucas and Rufus Easton, however, refused to accept his commission because the law incorporating the territory made no provision for such a position. Nevertheless, Donaldson persisted in prosecuting cases, perhaps in the hope that these continued activities would legitimize his claims. In 1806 he prosecuted a nephew of Colonel Samuel Hammond. The colonel was a prominent member of the community who would later run for the territorial seat in Congress. The elder Hammond also served subsequently as president of the Bank of St. Louis. The younger Hammond, according to Donaldson, had killed a Kickapoo Indian, but the colonel believed the charges were politically motivated. Enraged over the indictment, he swore that he would kill the attorney general. Toward that end he issued a challenge, which Donaldson refused to answer. Later, the two men nearly went to war during an accidental meeting on the streets of Cahokia, Illinois.[37]

The year 1807 witnessed the first recorded duel in Missouri history. It occurred near Cape Girardeau, a Mississippi River town that had made the transition from a European outpost to an American possession in rapid succession. In 1804 the population stood at nearly fifteen hundred, an incredible 20 percent increase from the year before. The French influence had by that time virtually disappeared, reported Amos Stoddard. Ironically, this first fatal encounter happened to be one of the very few whose principal cause was a woman. William Ogle, a native of Maryland who obtained the first hotel license in Cape Girardeau in 1806, was a merchant and the collector of internal revenue. Supposedly he had made a derogatory remark to the wife of Joseph McFerron. In 1806, shortly after they had arrived in Cape Girardeau, Ogle's wife died. Whether or not the Maryland transplant subsequently made overtures toward McFerron's wife, sexual or otherwise, no one can state for certain. McFerron, a former teacher and merchant, was a native of Ireland who had come to Upper Louisiana prior to its purchase by Jefferson. He had taught school at Mt. Tabor, a settlement west of Cape Girardeau, and had begun a political career that put him at odds with Ogle. At this point the details of the altercation become more sketchy. Ogle, who many considered the "town bully" (dead men found it difficult to defend themselves against character assassination during subsequent trials or hearings), may have been slapped in the face by McFerron, whereupon the former issued a challenge. Other accounts have maintained that Ogle's insult to Mrs. McFerron prompted her husband's delayed challenge. In any event, the men faced the wrong end of smooth-bore pistols on Cypress Island, opposite the banks of Cape Girardeau. McFerron supposedly had never fired a pistol, but the bitterness between the two men ran so deep that after the first fire, a second one soon followed, taking the life of Ogle.[38]

Although not arrested or charged with murder, McFerron felt compelled to tender his resignation as clerk of the common pleas court. His petition for reinstatement met with the sympathies of Frederick Bates, the acting governor. The case, Bates wrote, "is not a common case, and very few which have come under my observation can claim a similarity to it." The people of the county agreed with him. They continued to approve of McFerron's manly conduct, and he grew in political stature. Soon he was reinstated as clerk. While in his official capacity, he attended the first murder trial in Cape Girardeau in September 1808. Jeremiah Able had stabbed Neal Spear four times with a dirk; none too remarkably for that day and age, Able was acquitted.[39] As for McFerron, he later served as clerk of the Circuit Court of Cape Girardeau. From this position he moved on to become clerk of the Supreme Court of the Fourth Judicial District. He also attended the state's constitutional convention and served as a member of the first General Assembly. His political career was cut short on February 5, 1821, when, at the age of forty-one, he died of natural causes.

McFerron's duel in 1807 may well have prompted another citizen of the Cape Girardeau district to issue his challenge the following year. In October 1808, Charles Erasmus Ellis filed an arrest order in the Cape Girardeau Court of Quarter Sessions against Richard Davis for issuing a challenge to fight a duel. Davis's bail was a hefty five hundred dollars. This sizable amount of money plus the watchful eye of the authorities precluded a hostile encounter.[40]

Besides McFerron, two more prominent citizens of the region with dueling reputations were General Johnson Ranney and Alexander Buckner. Ranney was born in 1789 in Connecticut and had come to Cape Girardeau around 1814. In an environment usually hostile to "Yankees," Ranney was forced into "personal rencounters" that more than once tested his mettle. His courage and "pluck," however, soon won over his southern neighbors. Buckner had come to Missouri in 1818 after fleeing Indiana authorities for his involvement in a duel.[41] The good people of the Cape evidently did not object to his violent past, for in 1831, two years before his death, he was elected to the U.S. Senate.

Another duel that indirectly affected the inhabitants of the Missouri Territory was actually fought on British soil. According to the *Missouri Gazette*, Colonel John Campbell, a former Englishman, was "much esteemed" by the people of St. Louis. He had been appointed as the government's Indian agent and had moved to Prairie de Chien shortly after the Louisiana Purchase. Business had called him to Mackinaw on the upper Michigan peninsula where Louis Crawford, an agent of the British Mishillimackana Company, became the tool to destroy Campbell (the *Gazette* did not say by whom or why). Ironically, Campbell had previously saved his antagonist's life in a skirmish with the Indians, but the favor was not returned. The principals met on the British side of the border, and on first fire Campbell received Crawford's ball in his body and expired in a few minutes. The duel occurred in August 1808.[42]

In conclusion, no deterministic pattern, whether it be geographical, cultural, economic, class, or demographic, can explain the quantum leap in violence that occurred with Missouri's absorption into the Union. Nevertheless, compared to the previous periods of French and Spanish rule, the social changes were indeed dramatic. Although the atomization of pioneer life as well as the class structure of the early settlements militated against the more formal strictures of the code, the frontier nevertheless contained a fertile seedbed for violence. As St. Louis mourned a departed friend and as Cape Girardeau recovered from its only lethal duel, even greater social upheavals were transforming the quaint little Catholic village of Ste. Genevieve into the most dynamic and potentially hazardous area in the territory. As the following chapter will attest, there were many reasons why the roots of violence first took hold in the lead mining district of southern Missouri. Only later did the same type of social turbulence move with equal virulence farther north into the vicinity of St. Louis. In both areas, however, duels and various other forms of improvised violence were legitimized by the ruling class and countersigned by the lower class. Pistols in the hands of Missouri's new elites became hallmarks of status, helping to define class standing in these transitional communities. The duello was poised to make its first indelible mark on Missouri's social history.

2

Pistols

Icons of Status in Early Missouri

THE AMERICANIZATION OF the Missouri Territory produced a variety of sociocultural adaptations, including the duello. Like other institutions and conventions on the frontier, the code underwent many changes, and these changes provide valuable insights into how new arrivals adjusted to an alien environment. Initially, the influx of immigrants to Missouri soil accentuated the more conventional southern influences in this complex movement. But Creole community life, as well as southern conformity, clashed with northern independence to produce a heterogeneous and rancorous society. The offspring of this sectional miscegenation was the western hybrid we call Missouri.

At first the entrepreneurial impulses unleashed by the vast untapped resources of land and minerals seemed impossible to restrain. Greed, violence, inequality, slavery, excessive individualism, and social differentiation earmarked the advent of Americanization. Some areas such as St. Louis and Cape Girardeau weathered the storm better than others. Regions such as the Potosi–Ste. Genevieve lead mining district were not so fortunate. Ultimately, however, the new tides and currents of political, socioeconomic, and demographic change swept over all but the furthest outposts of civilization. The Missouri duel must be viewed within the context of this social cauldron, for it represented one important link in the transition from a traditional to a modern society.

The southeast area around Cape Girardeau remained relatively calm due to a minimum of land claims disputes. In St. Louis the old, established Creole or French families still exerted an inordinate amount of social influence. Their presence no doubt provided what Henry M. Brackenridge called "refinement and fashion."[1] Hence, dueling pistols had not yet become an icon of status in these two regions.

24

Rufus Easton, a congressman for the Missouri Territory, flirted with the code duello but ultimately resisted the temptation. Courtesy State Historical Society of Missouri.

Yet an illustration of the precocity of dueling as a social convention was Rufus Easton's flirtation with the code. An early arrival to St. Louis, this Connecticut-born gentleman, when tempted in 1806 to forsake "reason and philosophy" and obey "the fashion of society," was easily dissuaded by a fellow Yankee, Gideon Granger. Dueling, wrote Granger, was not courage: "I beg you to be more of a man," he implored, and "to partake more of the divinity, and not to be driven about by every blast of folly." The absence of a duel in his political résumé obviously did Easton's career no harm as he soon emerged as Missouri's second territorial representative to the U.S. Congress. Perhaps also the renunciation of dueling gave him the courage to refuse another encounter years later when John Scott, a hot-tempered Virginian and Easton's replacement as territorial delegate to Congress, challenged him to the field of honor. "I don't want to kill you," exclaimed Easton, "and if you were to kill me, I would die as a fool dieth."[2]

Violence, however, stalked Ste. Genevieve and the surrounding lead mining district. This area felt the shock waves of Americanization much sooner and much harder. Henry Brackenridge, born in the region in 1786, contrasted his placid youth with the vice and economic furor attendant to American rule. He lamented the loss of a young lawyer and friend, Mr. Allen (the author did not provide his first name), who, along with Brackenridge, traveled the country court route from Ste. Genevieve to New Madrid and was "compelled" to fight a duel that cost him his life.[3]

Stoking the coals of greed were not only the vast mineral resources found nowhere else in the territory but also a boom in land prices beginning around 1805.[4] Many of the more famous men of the state initially sought their for-

Governor James Wilkinson's policies delineated Missouri's early political factions and contributed to much violence. Courtesy State Historical Society of Missouri.

tunes in the lead mining region. Included in the list were John Scott, Henry Dodge, Moses Austin, Lewis Linn, John Smith T, Dr. John Bryan, Father James Maxwell, Ferdinand Rozier, Joseph Bogy, Auguste De Mun, George Jones, Thomas Crittenden, and Dr. Walter Fenwick. Three of these men went on to become U.S. senators and another fathered a senator, while most of the others served in various state and national capacities. There is also some evidence that Thomas Hart Benton first came to this area before migrating to St. Louis.[5]

Compounding an already volatile situation was President Thomas Jefferson's appointment of General James Wilkinson as territorial governor and Joseph Browne, Aaron Burr's brother-in-law, as territorial secretary. The president may have believed that the presence of the highest-ranking military officer in the army might have a calming effect on some of the more rancorous individuals who were pouring into the territory. If so, then Jefferson was badly mistaken, for Wilkinson's presence only made a bad situation worse. The general, who usually put his own interests ahead of his country's, immediately threw in with the ruling French Creole families of St. Louis headed by Charles Gratiot, Auguste Chouteau, Jacques Clamorgan, John Mullanphy, and Bernard Pratte. Most of these men had arrived prior to American rule and stood to gain handsomely if early and large Spanish land claims were awarded. They were dubbed the "Little Junto" by Joseph Charless, editor of the *Missouri Gazette*. The anti-French, anti-Wilkinson faction included Rufus Easton, William C. Carr, Edward Hempstead, James Bruff, William Russell, John B. C. Lucas, and Samuel Hammond.[6] They stood to gain if the large Spanish concessions were not validated and they were free to speculate on them. In the mining region Wilkinson also sided with the French families and those Americans such as John Smith T who had come to Missouri during the Spanish era.

American officials quickly recognized the potential for danger. Captain Amos Stoddard, who formally took possession of the territory for President Jefferson, ordered all public documents to be submitted to him for perusal. He hoped the order would obviate some of the confusion. It was to no avail. Soon, the enormity of the land-grant problem overwhelmed the frail and fragile political infrastructure. In one instance during 1806, Territorial Judge Rufus Easton caned a member of the board of land commissioners, James Donaldson, at least four or five times during a packed court session. Donaldson reached for his sword cane, which he always carried, but was restrained from using it.[7] Factional and personal jealousies, therefore, coincided with outright power struggles between lawyers, miners, farmers, and speculators throughout the territory.

Thus, the mining district promoted the factional strife engulfing Missouri. The leader of the anti-French, anti-Wilkinson faction was Moses Austin. Major Seth Hunt, commandant of the Ste. Genevieve district, also allied himself with Austin. Hunt had come to Missouri in the decade prior to the Louisiana Purchase and had obtained a large lead concession at Mine à Breton, near modern-day Potosi. Later he assumed the duties as chief justice of the region's Court of Common Pleas. His economic and political power afforded him the opportunity to reverse the Spanish custom that all mining property was held in common and unrestricted. This practice alienated many of the local French citizens.[8]

The man who challenged Austin's supremacy was John Smith T. He also arrived in Missouri during the twilight years of Spanish rule, probably with Wilkinson's encouragement. His modus operandi for acquiring land and lead was to purchase floating concessions and to jump claims. He has been called "the greatest of the speculators and claim-locators" in the mining area. To Austin and other established mining interests, he represented unscrupulousness, intimidation, thuggery, and the code duello in its most deadly form. Smith T's rather unorthodox approach to the acquisition of mines led in 1805 to Major Hunt's attempt to evict him from public lands and to arrest him if he did not comply. Instead, Wilkinson arrested Hunt and removed him as commandant. Next, he removed Austin from the Court of Common Pleas and Quarter Sessions and replaced him with Smith T. Smith T also was appointed lieutenant colonel in the militia.[9] The Wilkinson–Smith T alliance leveled the playing field against Austin, but it did not defeat him. Both sides continued to wage war by proxy armies loyal only to their respective leaders.

Smith T, a crack shot with both pistol and rifle, also challenged Major Seth Hunt to a duel and employed unsuccessfully a variety of tactics to tempt his arch rival Moses Austin to the field of honor. Austin refused the "invitation" and referred to the colonel as a "monster." They would meet, Austin warned Smith T, not on the field of honor but at the "Bar of Justice."[10]

While Smith T concentrated most of his attention on Austin, Governor Wilkinson saw Hunt as the most immediate threat to their schemes of a lead mining empire. On the pretext that Hunt had slandered his father, the governor's son, no doubt with the general's blessing, challenged the major to a duel. Hunt refused to fight an underling with whom he had no personal and direct quarrel. But Hunt was no coward. He agreed to "meet the governor on the other side of the Mississippi if it was his pleasure." The wily governor refused the offer to go to the field of honor against Hunt, but he instigated a series of physical beatings on the person of the major by officers loyal to him. Later the same officers publicly ridiculed Hunt as a "poltroon" and "a great scoundrel."[11] Hunt thereupon responded by issuing a challenge to the officers who had abused him. Wilkinson, believing he had sullied Hunt enough, issued orders against any duels. Within weeks, the major left the territory. By intimidating and disgracing Hunt, Wilkinson hoped to silence others from official criticisms.

Revenge, however, soon turned sweet for Austin and his allies. Spurred on by Wilkinson, Smith T and a number of cohorts had joined the ill-fated Aaron Burr conspiracy to wrest parts of the Southwest from Spain. When the filibustering scheme collapsed, Jefferson's newly appointed secretary and acting governor of the territory, Frederick Bates, stripped the conspirators of all their official duties in Missouri. Colonel John Smith T was particularly mortified. Such an "injustice" and act of dishonor could not go unheeded. On December 22, 1811, he challenged Bates to a duel. As the challenged party, Bates had the choice of weapons. Given Smith T's somewhat ferocious nature, it was likely that he would have met Bates with pistols, knives, rifles, or any combination of those weapons. But it was not to be. The acting governor promptly refused "the invitation." Two days later, after receiving the unsatisfactory reply from Bates, Smith T issued an even more forceful challenge. The secretary, he wrote, should not hide behind the cloak of his official duties. To "shrink from this test," he taunted, was a confession of guilt and a loss of "manhood." A gentleman, he argued, must be held accountable for all his words and deeds. "That monitor which the Supreme Being has placed in the breast of every man," he enjoined, "warns you of these injuries." Like trial by combat, a refusal to fight a duel was, in Smith T's mind, tantamount to culpability. Pistols, a fateful measure of divine ordination in the hands of two men of honor, he suggested, would prove guilt or innocence.[12]

Bates was not impressed with Smith T's reasoning. Only to the government, he replied, was he to be held accountable for his official conduct. The matter stood. Bates would live not only to see another day but also to become the second governor of the State of Missouri. Nor did his refusal to burn

Moses Austin, a prominent figure in the Missouri Territory, was nearly goaded into a duel with John Smith T. Courtesy State Historical Society of Missouri.

John Smith T was the most feared duelist in early Missouri. Courtesy Missouri Historical Society.

powder tarnish his political reputation, for the apparent reason that since he did not espouse the code duello, he was not accountable to it or to the men whom he aggrieved.

Bates had removed Smith T from all of his official duties, but he did not restore them to Moses Austin. His plans were twofold: first, to root out the last vestiges of Burrism; and second, to have a small measure of peace prevail in the mining district. On his first goal he did remarkably well. As to his second objective, he was only partially successful. Austin and Smith T continued to wage their battles, but they became more likely to do so in the courts of law and public opinion. Instances of organized violence gradually subsided as both protagonists, if not broken, were severely curtailed.[13]

During the mineral wars other duels were also waged. These contests were not fought over land and wealth per se but over family honor and community status. Ironically, in the first two deadly encounters after 1807, the intended principals never met. Rather, it was the second carrying the challenge who, with a proverbial twist, lent new meaning to the phrase "kill the messenger." To St. Louis attorney James Graham went the unhappy distinction of being the second Missourian since the Louisiana Purchase to fall in mortal combat. Like many similar meetings, this affair of honor was "a product of vanity goaded by scorn" and a consequence of emotional insecurities about standing and status in the community.[14]

In 1810, during a particularly heated card game where, one can only surmise, Bacchus, god of intoxication, reigned, Graham accused a young lieutenant, John Campbell, of cheating. At this time even gambling debts of gentlemen were perceived as "debts of honour." To lose in cards and then to renege on the payment was dishonorable enough, but a public accusation of false play usually required a call to the field of honor.[15] The accusation of cheating, next to "the lie direct," often provoked a challenge, especially if directed toward an insecure hothead.

True to form, Campbell challenged Graham, sending his challenge by way of Dr. Bernard G. Farrar, formerly of Virginia and the first American physician residing west of the Mississippi.[16] Farrar's loyalties were somewhat divided since he was personally acquainted with Graham and, according to one source at the time, was even on friendly terms. Yet Campbell had recently married the doctor's sister; thus Farrar obligingly carried the message. Graham, however, complicated the plot by refusing to engage the lieutenant on the grounds that, as a cheater and swindler, he had forfeited the right to fight in the style of a gentleman.

As was the custom, Farrar, with personal and family honor now at stake, immediately challenged Graham because, according to Henry Brackenridge, "the insult was, by a necessary inference, transferred to him, for if his friend was unworthy the notice of a gentleman, he must be no better for taking up the cause of such a person." Another account of this affair of honor suggested that Farrar consulted his friend, Thomas Hart Benton, a self-appointed authority on the code duello, on the proper course of action. Benton advised the physician that under the unrelenting terms of the code he had no alternative but to challenge Graham. This account, however, cannot be substantiated by other authorities, and it would predate Benton's supposed arrival in Missouri by nearly half a decade.[17]

Although Graham was reportedly a deadly shot, his hand was far less steady than his courage, and his shot was as flawed as his judgment. On three successive fires, on a Mississippi River sandbar later to be dubbed Bloody Island, he was struck in the side, the leg, and the hand, and finally he fell. Farrar was slightly wounded but, faithful to his Hippocratic oath, the physician attended to his adversary with "as much tenderness and solicitude as if he had been a brother."[18] Some time later, despite these "curious contradictions" by the doctor, Graham died of the wounds inflicted.

Before his death, Graham launched a spirited public defense of his old friend Farrar in the *Gazette*. There had been reports circulated, he wrote, that in "a late transaction between" the two of them "wherein General Clark was partially concerned," Clark and Farrar had engaged in "unfair and dishonorable conduct." These reports, he argued, were "malicious and false" and both men had acted as perfect "gentlemen." "Everything," on the occasion of the duel, he enjoined, "was conducted with the most honorable fairness and propriety."[19]

Graham's letter to the public offered some unusual insights into the workings of the code duello. These old friends had ventured to the field of honor propelled by forces they were unable to understand, much less to direct. Graham would soon die from the wounds inflicted in the duel. Yet he not only harbored no bitterness toward the perpetrator or his second but also defended their integrity as vigorously as his own. The sting of death was far less painful than the ignominy of dying at the hands of a dishonorable man.

In no small measure this element of fate, not only of the luck of the volley but also of the conditions that compelled combat, explained how, once the pistols blazed, animosity could quickly be displaced by friendship and mutual respect. This was the catharsis of shot and powder: a faint realization that as actors, they were part of a larger drama often beyond their ability to control. Another factor that led gentlemen who only moments before had engaged each other in mortal combat to embrace as comrades was their shared sense of social equality. Even though honor compelled them to the field, it was their sense of class cohesion and their belief that controlled violence was necessary and rational which bonded them together for life. By some strange psychological alchemy the victor and the vanquished mutually sealed a kinship forged by bonds formed in the shadow of death.

Dr. Bernard G. Farrar, one of the first physicians west of the Mississippi, killed his friend, James Graham, over a point of family honor. Courtesy State Historical Society of Missouri.

Recalling his firsthand knowledge of the Graham tragedy in his later years, Henry M. Brackenridge was not so kind. He fatalistically interpreted this sanguinary affair as due to "false honor" and a "barbarous and irrational morality" that "was in obedience to the public opinion of the place." The duelists, he wrote, were slaves to customs and conventions that demanded "the exhibition of mere animal courage." It was a land and time intolerant of cowardice, he lamented, but permissive of "immoral" and "disreputable" conduct so long as it was valorous. Gentlemen such as Graham and Farrar, he believed, were not responsible for this rubric of violence; they only reflected it.[20]

Like many of his contemporaries, Brackenridge curiously reversed the cause and effect of dueling and public opinion. Men like Graham and the doctor did not risk life and limb in order to win the respect of the populace so much as to keep it. Honor could not be won on the dueling ground, it could only be preserved. The loss of honor ensued when a gentleman refused to stand up for his family, his good name, or the social position he had already acquired in the community. Curiously, Brackenridge's affinity with the men who tamed the wilderness territory did not allow him to condemn in toto their furious ways. He exculpated both victor and vanquished and interpreted their actions not as dysfunctional, but as a consequence of an already "savage state of society" that forced them into a violent mode of behavior. Unwilling to resist the prevailing code of conduct, the duelists, like characters in a Greek drama, could not escape the inexorable fate determined perhaps by a single shot.

As for Farrar, compassion for a slain adversary aroused not an iota of self-criticism or introspective doubt concerning the code duello. In fact, he parlayed his affair of honor into a modicum of historical fame. Although he never again took to the field of honor as a principal, he participated as an attending surgeon in the Benton-Lucas duels. To show how indiscriminately ecumenical he could be, he delivered the challenge of Stephen Austin to Joshua Pilcher in June 1817.[21] He also carried the December 22, 1811, challenge of Colonel John Smith T to Frederick Bates, secretary and acting governor of the Territory of Louisiana. Not surprisingly, Bates refused on a number of grounds to meet the colonel, but he did not give as a reason for his disinclination the pretext that Smith T was not a gentleman. Thus he avoided the kind of insult that would have forced Farrar to challenge him. This strategy helped to avoid the previous year's tragedy between the doctor and Graham. Farrar's 1810 duel likewise did not harm his political career. In early 1812 he was elected territorial representative for St. Louis. Later he stood successfully for a seat in the General Assembly of the territory. Even the editor of the *Gazette,* who generally opposed the faction that supported the doctor, admitted that he exerted "himself in attention to the best interests of his constituents."[22] Farrar died a respected member of the state.

The year following the Farrar-Graham duel shared the stage with a great flood on the Mississippi River, the comet of 1811, the New Madrid earthquake, and a hunting party of Osage Indians thought to be on the warpath near Ste. Genevieve. It was also the year of the third fatal duel in the territory, which, like its predecessor, involved a physician and lawyer as well as points of family honor and definitions of social status.[23]

The culprit in this fatal duel was Ezekiel Fenwick, who, in 1809, had nearly gone to the field of honor. From most of the sources of that day it would appear that Ezekiel had a penchant for getting the good name of the Fenwick family called into question. In October 1809 he had challenged A. C. Dunn, also of Ste. Genevieve, to a duel for accusing him of stealing. In 1811 the character of this rather wayward member of the Fenwick family was again questioned. Embezzlement was the charge leveled against him this time. In late 1811, Ezekiel, who was reputedly associated with the healing arts but also the owner of "a house of amusement" in Ste. Genevieve, had been accused of embezzlement by a local merchant. The Fenwick family, with solid Kentucky roots, was one of the most prominent in the region. Ezekiel's older brother, Dr. Walter Fenwick, had an excellent medical reputation surpassed only by his economic preeminence in the community. This was attested by the fact that he owned ten thousand acres of land not far from the town. Rather than issuing a challenge to Dunn, which would have elevated his class standing and possibly impugned the integrity of the Fenwicks, the family decided upon the strategy of suing him on the grounds of slander. Dunn's lawyer was

Thomas T. Crittenden, appointed the preceding year as attorney general of the Territory of Louisiana by Governor Benjamin Howard. Crittenden also had excellent Kentucky breeding.[24]

The ensuing lawsuit was particularly heated. It may at times have even gone beyond the bounds of propriety due to the lack of legal knowledge and judicial restraint on the part of the presiding judge. In any event, the Fenwick strategy backfired. Crittenden, after repeatedly impugning the character and integrity of Ezekiel, won the case for his client. Ezekiel then challenged Crittenden, but the attorney declined the combat on the grounds that Ezekiel was not a gentleman. Crittenden's disinclination was a permissible action under the code because no one need fight an adversary beneath his social rank. But the refusal was an insult to the good name of the entire Fenwick family. At this point, Dr. Fenwick picked up the cudgel and challenged the derisive lawyer. Crittenden agreed to the terms since he "considered the alternative of fighting easier to encounter than the certain disgrace which would attend his refusal in the false judgement of public opinion."[25]

Duels of this nature attracted considerable attention, and each duelist, to enhance his own social status, invited notable individuals to serve as seconds and surgeons. John Scott, for example, the territorial delegate to the U.S. Congress and later Missouri's first congressman, served as Crittenden's second. Henry Dodge, the sheriff of the district of Ste. Genevieve, a general in the War of 1812, and later a U.S. senator from Wisconsin, was the second for Fenwick. The principals met on October 1, 1811, on Moreau Island, a short distance below Ste. Genevieve. Twelve-inch barrel pistols, made by two slave gunsmiths owned by John Smith T, were the weapons of choice. On the first volley, the proud doctor fell mortally wounded. He left a wife, Julie, the daughter of Don Francesco Valle, Jr., and seven children. But family honor had been vindicated!

The dueling focus next shifted to the ranks of the military. Laid to rest in these early years were many a young officer such as one Lieutenant John Clark, probably stationed at Fort Bellefontaine. While on a mission to the area near Council Bluffs he met death at the hands of another young officer over an affair of honor. The duel was held in such secrecy that the name of the victor as well as those of the surgeons and seconds were not recorded.[26]

Far less inimical to honor was the impromptu "duel" of Major Thomas F. Smith, husband of Auguste Chouteau's daughter Emilie, and Captain Bennet Riley, later promoted to major general during the Mexican War. While floating down the Mississippi River accompanied by two hundred soldiers, the two officers became intoxicated and quarrelsome. A dispute over the exact nature of an impediment in the river quickly led to a point of honor. Suddenly, Smith ordered the boat to be pulled around. The two men debarked, marked off a respectable distance for their pistols to bark, and commenced firing. Drunkenness, which no doubt caused the duel, undoubtedly contributed to its nonlethal resolution as well; both men were unable to steady their aim or to hit their mark. After the exchange of fire, each claimed satisfaction, boarded the boat, and continued amicably upon his way.[27]

On another occasion, Major Smith set out to kill Judge Luke E. Lawless. The judge, an Irishman whose name was certainly consistent with his character, had left his native country after being involved in a rebellion against the British. He next settled in France, but was wounded in a duel and fled to the United States. Later he would serve as Thomas Hart Benton's second in the Charles Lucas duel, and in 1837 he participated in the killing of Elijah P. Lovejoy, a St. Louis abolitionist. The exact nature of the dispute between Smith and Lawless remained a mystery, but Smith, who had purchased a pistol for the expressed purpose of killing Lawless, was finally persuaded by lawyer, friend, and future mayor of St. Louis John F. Darby to forgo the plan.[28]

Smith's difficulties with Lawless, which nearly led to bloodshed, were quite common among men of equal social rank. As for Smith's altercation with Captain Riley, it too was between men of nearly the same military rank. Very rarely did senior military officers allow themselves to engage in personal combat with junior officers. If such a breach of etiquette occurred, it was generally due to intoxication. Such appears to have been the case when in the summer of 1815 General William Bissell took umbrage at remarks made by an army captain whose name we know only as Hawkins. The affair took place at a tavern owned by the Austin family and resulted in a rencounter with sticks. Subsequent to the fight, Bissell provided a number of letters from eyewitnesses who substantiated his part of the story. At this juncture the matter was laid to rest and no personal interviews took place. Owing to the circumstances that sticks were used in the beating—a fact that usually imperiled honor and necessitated a duel—one can only surmise that further violence was abated due to the disparities of military rank.[29]

Professional military men were not the only ones who regularly took aim at each other during these turbulent years. In 1816, Maryland-born Henry S. Geyer, a captain in the Missouri militia, challenged Captain George H. Kennerly. Both principals had served in the War of 1812 and had become prominent citizens of St. Louis, Geyer as an established lawyer and Kennerly as an equally successful merchant. The parties agreed to terms quite within the parameters of the code: the place, a sandbar in the Mississippi, soon to be called Bloody Island; the weapons, smooth-bore pistols; the distance, ten paces. Their mutual hostility was evidenced by the fact that after first fire neither side was satisfied. This prompted a second exchange. On the second fire Kennerly suffered a debilitating wound in the leg and could not continue. Although his injury took years to heal and left him with a permanent limp, the bitterness between the two combatants dissipated as quickly as the summer dew. The catharsis of powder and shot solidified a new friendship that was to last a lifetime.[30]

The duel with Kennerly did no harm to Geyer's career, as his political star rose rapidly in the next few years. Elected in 1822 to the Missouri House of Representatives (Kennerly also ran for the house that year), he went on to serve as the speaker of that body. Geyer continued to be active in politics, and he also resorted to the code again when it suited his political purposes. In 1824 he twice unsuccessfully challenged Duff Green, editor of the *St. Louis Enquirer*. Throughout the next two decades Geyer's star continued to rise. In 1851 he succeeded Thomas Hart Benton in the U.S. Senate. Later, President Millard Fillmore offered him a cabinet post, but he declined.[31]

The Geyer-Kennerly foray, like so many duels in nineteenth-century Missouri, established a causal link between dueling and political advancement. But the exact nature of that connection still remained unclear. Obviously, some men burned powder to gain political recognition and to enhance their social status. Reverend Flint, for example, believed that many such social climbers bought a "new suit" of clothes, fought a duel, and declared themselves gentlemen while partisans "cried them up." The majority of early duelists, however, already possessed varying degrees of upper-class standing. The ever-present dilemma was a social milieu in which rank, status, and hence political advancement remained rather tenuous. Most politically motivated duels were fought by gentlemen who desired to climb higher on the ladder of success. Rarely did a prominent Missouri politician "fight down," that is, accept a challenge from a political underling. Political rank, like social rank, had its privileges. Dueling was a means, albeit not the one most widely used by young gentlemen on the political make, to silence an opponent. Even a challenge or the possibility of a challenge enhanced an aspiring politician's reputation among the populace. In essence, men who already held social respect in their communities engaged in the sport of gentlemen cognizant of both its potential benefits and its limited risks to their political careers.

The Geyer-Kennerly duel was one of the most talked about events in Missouri social life in 1816. It also happened to be the next to last military duel during the territorial years. The last such duel also took place on Bloody Island offshore from St. Louis. The island, which had received it sobriquet from the Benton-Lucas duels of 1817, again lived up to its reputation in August 1818. On this occasion two U.S. Army officers, Captain Thomas Ramsey and Captain Martin (the *Gazette* did not furnish his first name), made their way to its confines. Both men were stationed at the cantonment, Bellefontaine, on the Missouri River. The nature of their quarrel was not known nor were the names of seconds or surgeons. On what was believed to be the first fire, Ramsey was struck by a muzzle ball; he died a few days later. He was buried with full military honors as well as Masonic honors. The

Gazette on August 7 regretted his death, claiming his "character as an officer and a gentleman" made him stand tall in the annals of heroes who gave up the comforts of civilian life "to breast the storm of savage warfare, or the more savage British" in the recent war. Although military regulations called for Martin to be court-martialed, he "retained his command and was soon head of a cantonment on the Missouri river."[32]

In the wake of Ramsey's death the *Gazette* penned an editorial entitled "Important Article on Duelling and Politics." It appeared one week after the paper reported the captain's death. Murder, the *Gazette* believed, was "the most abominable crime," but in Missouri it had become "an honorable profession, a gentlemanly accomplishment, a SCIENCE." Libel and slander laws out on the frontier, the paper asserted, were haunted by a demon above the law, a demon called honor. This "boasting" concept of honor, the article continued, "rides in triumph over its prostrate majesty, openly defies its power and mocks its imbecility." A murderer, it suggested, should be driven from society and hunted down like "a wild beast of prey." But in Missouri, it concluded, the duelist had become "the favorite of the fair," and admired "by the multitude."[33]

All duelists, however, did not bask in the public limelight, nor were all duels fought with the punctilio of the military duels or of the Farrar-Graham and Fenwick-Crittenden affairs. Some rencounters legitimized not only social status but also murder. One such affair, which gave a new semantic twist to the word "duel," occurred in the highly charged atmosphere of St. Louis in 1817. On or about September 22 of that year, a merchant, William Smith, confronted William Tharp, a laborer, at the Missouri Bank of St. Louis. After a heated exchange of words and insults, the larger and stronger Smith proceeded to cane Tharp. It was a thorough beating, but under the code of honor of that day, it was the only remedy for Smith, since Tharp was below his social station and not entitled to give or receive satisfaction on the field of honor. Tharp, however, refused to see it that way.[34]

Within a week of his humiliation, Tharp had issued a challenge to Smith. Smith, however, refused to duel Tharp on the grounds that he was not a gentleman. At this juncture Tharp attempted to lure his adversary into any type of physical confrontation that would exact a blood price. On September 27 Tharp posted Smith and pronounced him to be a "most infamous scoundrel, rascal, and coward." The following day, Smith confronted Tharp while Tharp was putting up more handbills; Smith was killed. Tharp was arrested but "released on a combination of his own recognizance and bail as sureties for his appearance in court to stand trial." After what one contemporary account called "a very laborious trial," the Superior Court of the Territory of Missouri in August 1818 acquitted Tharp. He soon left for Kentucky.[35]

It was ironic both then and now that some called the Smith-Tharp incident a duel. The defendant, of course, certainly dubbed it so since it was a surer pass-

Flintlock pistols were a quick way to achieve status and power in territorial Missouri.
Courtesy State Historical Society of Missouri.

port to an acquittal and perhaps even higher social status. Most surely, as every murderer and his trial lawyer realized, juries were far more inclined to acquit if even the slightest pretense of a fair fight could be made. Under such circumstances, wishing could often make it so. Calling such affrays "duels" might very well prove convincing to a jury already predisposed toward acquittal.

More to the point, the Smith-Tharp "duel" highlighted the social turmoil prevalent in St. Louis during the late territorial period. It also revealed an improvisation of violence that set the tone for future affrays. In reality, the affair should have been called a shooting on sight and, as it unfolded throughout the history of this land, it gave a new meaning to the term "jurisprudence of lawlessness." The first step in the exoneration of murder was to make a personal quarrel public. Since Smith had caned Tharp in front of a St. Louis bank, the first requisite was easily met. The second requirement for a successful courtroom defense was for the killer to give notice to the offender and to the public at large that the offense given had justified the taking of life. By posting Smith, Tharp accomplished this requirement and put his antagonist on notice that he should be armed and ready to defend himself. If he was armed, then the killing could be called self-defense; if he was unarmed (a very unlikely event in early Missouri history), then he lacked vigilance and deserved his fate. An avenger, therefore, could simply instigate a fight.

These shootings on sight, commonly called getting "the drop" on someone or "snap shootings," were more akin to the quick draw gunfight of the Wild West than to the decorum of the duel. While the intent, namely the elimination of an adversary or rival, was the same, the methods were not. Tactically, the drop radically departed from the duel's "artistic principles of tragedy." Rather, it sought to kill as expeditiously as possible, with the minimum of risk to oneself and the maximum of risk to another. With the drop, one sought the utmost possible advantage against a foe (surprise, concealment, assorted weapons, etc.)

and the greatest certainty of his death.[36] Although the killing might appear spontaneous, the drop had a logic and structure all its own. It was a staged event, clothed by a rationale of self-defense, which held suasion for judge and jury as long as the carrying of weapons was legal. Small wonder that, in comparison to dueling, the drop was far more likely to be lethal.

These affrays also reversed the time-honored principle of English common law, which held that malice prepense must be established in order to gain a conviction of murder.[37] In other words, malice aforethought—in this case Tharp's deliberate intention to kill Smith—would not be held against him. Rather, his premeditated act of murder demonstrated that passion and impulse played no part in his decision. The perpetrator of a grave indignity must receive a day of reckoning, not by the law of the land but by the unwritten law that each man was the arbitrator of his own honor. This prescript was a personal obligation to which most developing communities subscribed.

After the killing, Tharp voluntarily surrendered to the authorities and stood trial. To flee or to resist arrest would have been an admission of wrongdoing. Pistol snappers, as compared to backstabbers, blackguards, or backshooters, could usually be exonerated by reversing the roles of victim and vanquished. Thus the deceased became the villain and his murderer the victim. An insult so degrading as Tharp's public whipping put the onus on Smith, who, lying peacefully six feet underground, could not defend himself.

Although the details of Tharp's trial are somewhat unclear, the transparencies of justice in this particular case appear to have followed a familiar pattern. The accused postponed a trial for as long as possible in hopes that hostile witnesses would be intimidated, die, move on, or otherwise forget the more salient facts of the case. It was in fact a territorial judge, J. B. C. Lucas, who had earlier called the trial "very laborious." Juries were then selected who generally shared the defendant's penchant for direct and violent methods of problem solving. Witnesses paraded forth bestowing the good character of the accused while assailing that of his slain adversary. Finally, the very stricture and severity of the law militated against conviction.[38] The charge of murder, as opposed to the lesser charge of manslaughter, carried with it the death penalty. Yet most juries were given no choice in the matter. Provided with no alternative between a murder conviction or acquittal, juries recoiled. Such was the case with Tharp. He was cleared of all charges. The jurisprudence of lawlessness prevailed.

William Bennett was not as fortunate as William Tharp. To Bennett fell the dubious honor of being the only man ever executed in the United States for dueling. As in Tharp's case, for Bennett the term "duel" was a misnomer. In February 1819 in Belleville, Illinois, a promising young attorney, Alonzo Stuart, called out Bennett. Apparently the two men quarrelled after Bennett's horse had reportedly broken into a cornfield owned by Stuart. The argument piqued the fancy of two of Bennett's friends, Jacob Short and Nat Fike. These two men urged Bennett to demand satisfaction for Stuart's remarks about Bennett's poor fences and his horse's lack of savoir faire.

Although Stuart was in good standing on both sides of the Mississippi, Short and Fike believed that a duel with them serving as seconds would elevate their social status and Bennett's in the community. It was of course somewhat difficult to get Stuart to agree to fight since Bennett, who many perceived to be a bully and ruffian, was below Stuart's social station and therefore rightfully deemed unworthy to participate in an affair of honor. But Stuart had no intention of actually exchanging fire with Bennett. He accepted only after Short and Fike agreed to load the rifles of both antagonists with powder but no shot. Believing Bennett to be a coward and braggart, Stuart was convinced that the abstract of bravado would turn to the reality of fear when the moment of truth arrived. The plan apparently took shape during "a drunken carousel." Bennett, however, discovered the ruse and either he or his seconds loaded his gun with ball. On the order to fire, he calmly shot the unsuspecting lawyer through the heart.[39]

Communities on both sides of the river were outraged, and Bennett and his seconds were arrested for murder.[40] Only a vigorous defense by attorney Thomas Hart Benton permitted the seconds to go free. Short and Fike maintained that it was Bennett and not they who tampered with the weapon. A ten-year-old girl corroborated their story. Bennett of course maintained his innocence. During the "duel" one of the seconds, perhaps on purpose, fired Stuart's rifle. It was therefore impossible at the trial to determine whether or not the dead man had lead in his weapon. In the meantime, Bennett broke out of jail and headed for Arkansas. His escape added to the deepening suspicions of his guilt. Nearly two years later he returned to Illinois and "by some sort of artifice" was apprehended. At his trial he denied any knowledge that the gun which killed Stuart was loaded. The jury, on the other hand, believed that the nature of his intent was indeed murder. Benton again served as his attorney, but to no avail. Bennett was sentenced to death by hanging.[41] Even on the scaffold, weeping, he professed his innocence. In retrospect, Bennett's real crime was not murder but the indecorous way he carried it out. He should perhaps have more closely followed the methods of William Tharp!

3

The Age of Political Dueling

EARLY MISSOURI DUELS revolved largely around social differentiation and definitions of class standing. Questions of status and honor were played out within the context of changing value systems, culture/behavior patterns, and character structures. By the late territorial period, however, the impetus behind dueling became more political as relatively small groups of elites, aware of the economic prizes at stake, intensified their efforts to promote their individual and factional causes while at the same time controlling the body politic. This was the essence of protagonism. The duelist, like the chief personage in a drama, became the champion of a cause. His role was that of a combatant—a militant defender of the interests he represented.[1] In these bitter power struggles, the protagonist might gain the admiration of the masses for his courage and coolness, but his immediate objective was more narrowly confined to the issue at hand, namely, the elimination of a political rival. The duel, therefore, became one upper-class tool in political clashes. From the territorial elections of 1816 through 1824 the code became legitimized as never before or after. The period was truly the age of the political duel.

Both consciously and unconsciously, duelists of the late territorial and early statehood years shared many common assumptions about the nature of politics and society.[2] These men of shot and sword were usually members of rival politico-economic factions called the junto and the anti-junto. Neither group had any recognizable ideology nor any clear sense of how to govern the territory. Since mass political parties had yet to appear on the frontier, the ruling factions had yet to make any real concessions to participatory government. Below the surface of incivility and contentiousness, however, lay a consensus that social turmoil must be confined as much as possible among the ranks of the elite. If conflict was unavoidable, then certain rules of the game had to be observed. Without some institutionalized restraints, conflicts could not be contained and might well spill over into the rank and file of Missourians, which might well endanger the somewhat tenuous political control of the upper strata of society.

Missouri's emerging elites no doubt were aware of the dangers of social leveling. Neither faction had any intention of either allowing their quarrels to become internecine or of having them filter down to the lesser social ranks. Regardless of the factional bitterness, neither side had yet made an appeal to the masses under the pretense of egalitarianism. Consequently, they continued to defend the duel as their exclusive purview. At the same time those groups not associated with the factional elites acquiesced in their less-than-equal status and generally remained on the sidelines of politics and dueling.

The *Missouri Intelligencer and Boon's Lick Advertiser* correctly observed the connection between dueling and privilege. Although the paper noted that the territory had no titled nobility in the European sense, it nonetheless believed that the direction of Missouri government was headed toward "aristocracy."[3] This reality was reflected in the upper class's ambivalence toward power. If the spirit and theory of territorial politics in Missouri was republican, then the letter and practice was decidedly the opposite. On the one hand, members of the ruling class evoked the rhetoric of democracy, while on the other hand they restrained the egalitarian spirit through the means of property, race, gender qualifications, stuffed ballots, voter intimidation, and bribery. Also, voting by *viva voce* (voice vote) controlled the temptation to deviate too far from political norms.[4] As a result, the privileged order differentiated itself largely by negating the power of others through definitions of class, race, age, education, money, and gender.

Taking a cue from leaders emerging in states west of the Appalachians, Missourians held to the notion of a "natural aristocracy" based not upon birth or special privilege but upon individual merit. This "open elite" system, however, needed built-in safeguards. One symbol that could simultaneously appeal to the populace while setting the natural aristocrat apart from the masses was the duel—the ability to kill with "an air of triumph." This was the class bias of the code duello—a point that was not lost on social critics who viewed duelists as "reputable *idlers*" who came from respectable families and who placed themselves above the rest of society. The duel was, as the *Missouri Intelligencer's* "Stiletto Pistoleer" rightly observed, "the cheapest and smallest capital upon which a man can possibly become a modern gentleman." It became an important way to understand what Henry M. Brackenridge called "a distinction in the classes of society." The role of dueling in the definition of hierarchy was not lost on those democratic elements who sought political leveling. Without such affairs of honor, remarked the *Missouri Intelligencer*, the duelist would bid "a long farewell to all his greatness" and "mingle for life among the common throng."[5]

Unlike in the Deep South, where theatrics often dictated a call to arms, Missouri square-offs were deadly serious. Few were staged or phony. Seldom bloodless and often lethal, the casus belli of the duel increasingly came to be political aggrandizement. Peter Burnett, who grew up on the Missouri frontier around 1820 and later became the first governor of California, also saw political "rivalship" as the key to dueling. "It becomes desirable," he lamented, "to kill off certain aspirants, to get them out of the way." "Each individual eliminated in a duel," wrote European historian V. G. Kiernan, "meant better chances for the others." His observation, true enough for the Old World aristocracy, equally applied to early Missouri. Thus, the duel historically functioned as an instrument of mobility within the ranks of a rather small ruling class. Reverend Timothy Flint aptly observed the fierce competitive spirit of Missouri politics when he wrote, "No new man can ascend to eminence, without displacing some one who is already there."[6]

Around the years 1816–1817 Flint witnessed many sanguinary encounters in and around the St. Louis region. Duels there, he noted, as compared to those in New England, "in proportion to the population, are as a hundred to one." He also observed their political nature. "There is," he recalled, "a continual chaos of the political elements" as "new adventurers" seek office. "All that fell were men in office, of standing and character."[7] Although Flint may have exaggerated the number of duels fought, he certainly recognized the connection between the duello and political aggrandizement.

Like their counterparts in the Deep South, the Missouri elites attempted to confine the practice of dueling to the ranks—however poorly defined—of the upper class. The duel was not for the constituency of the politically dispossessed. There were, of course, a variety of reasons for the exclusion of the lower classes. To challenge a man of lesser rank was tantamount to conferring upon him equal social recognition, which could easily translate into political equality. Political egalitarianism might well in turn lead to economic challenges and to even greater societal dislocations. What was perceived as political reality in the late territorial period apparently held true to form in the early 1820s as well. The "Stiletto Pistoleer," the 1823 Boonslick satirist and political commentator, understood full well the meaning and intent of the sport of gentlemen. Without dueling, he argued, "the barriers of just distinction between the high-blooded, honorable *gentry* of the land, and the base herd of *yeomanry,* or *commons* of the country" would be broken down.[8]

The exclusive club of the duelist placed him above the political crowd. No better illustration of the elite nature of the code could be found than in the remarks made by Abraham Byrd in the Missouri General Assembly during the 1822 debate requiring certain officials, officers, and lawyers of the state to take an oath forswearing dueling. Such a bill, he lamented, would deprive the state of much of its finest talent and "the effect would be to place the citizens of the community upon equal footing."[9] Both the duel's demise as well as its democratization were therefore perceived by this senator from New Madrid County as a harbinger of further social and economic displacement of the elite.

Flint likewise saw the connection between upper-class politics and violence. "Too many leading men," he claimed, "advocate duelling." A day would come, he wrote, when "instead of being blazoned, that a candidate for office has slain his man, it will operate as an impediment to his views, and this stain upon humanity will no longer disgrace the country." The *Jackson Independent Patriot* agreed. By dueling, "the rulers," decried the paper, practiced the "science of murder" and set a loathsome example for the people. Dueling crimes, it went on to recount, "are winked at by those even who affect to detest, and have the power of suppressing them."[10] The *Patriot's* condemnation was hardly surprising since most frontier newspapers abjured the science of murder. By associating the code exclusively with Missouri "rulers," however, the paper in no uncertain terms claimed that democracy and the code were incompatible.

Historically, the lower and middle strata have found social emancipation more in imitation of the ruling class than by independence from them. In this sense the duel wove a common thread with other forms of ritualized violence of the day. Some reformers and evangelists recognized the causal relationship between violence by those "polite and polished orders of society" and its dysfunctional consequences. In 1820 the *Missouri Intelligencer* noted that chivalry and false honor were taking deep root "among all classes" of society. It echoed the regret of another newspaper that "every 'puny whipster' thinks it necessary to fight a duel if you but stare at him a few seconds." Such critics may have been ambivalent as to whether the common man mimicked his leaders in order to assert a certain kind of equality or imitated them out of admiration and respect for their acts of derring-do. The St. Louis *Missouri Argus*, for example, noted as late as 1840 that dueling had a "pernicious moral influence . . . upon the mischievous."[11] The article suggested, in other words, that the notoriety and glamour associated with dueling influenced and encouraged other and more rowdy elements of society to engage also in acts of violence.

The epicenter of political violence shifted to St. Louis in 1816. That same year Missouri achieved third-class territorial status, and it was clear that she would soon be united in statehood with the Union. Both factions, the junto and anti-junto, intensified their efforts to gain political control of the territorial government by whatever means necessary. Thus, they would respectively situate themselves in key positions to determine future state policy. At the same time both sets of elites viewed political power as a stepping stone to greater wealth and fame. The atmosphere of "strife and discord" worsened with the coming 1816 election of a territorial delegate to the U.S. Congress.[12]

Edward Hempstead, the first delegate from 1812 to 1814 and a junto member, had declined to run again in 1814. This opened the field for the election of Rufus Easton, a bitter foe of the pro-Creole junto. The 1816 election was a maelstrom of political activity as each faction stepped up its efforts to control the body politic.

The political contest pitted incumbent Easton against the junto candidate, John Scott of Ste. Genevieve. The candidates agreed on most of the issues, including the end of government monopolies on mineral lands and the cessation of Indian purchases by government agents (called the factory system). They both advocated prompt admission to statehood, squatters' rights, and increased expenditures for internal improvements.[13] Agreement on most political issues, however, did not translate into social amity. Bribery, drunkenness, fraud, intimidation by armed troops, fistfights, and other assorted acts of mayhem attended the election.

One of the first rencounters, and a harbinger of tragedy, involved Captain Charles Lucas, a rising star in the anti-junto faction, lawyer, and son of Judge J. B. C. Lucas. The captain had written a handbill signed "A Farmer" that chastised John Scott and a number of his supporters. Joseph Charless, editor of the *Missouri Gazette*, had published the handbill, and Scott demanded and obtained from Charless the true identity of "A Farmer." Charless may have had little choice but to identify Lucas, as Scott was known to carry both pistol and dirk and had a penchant for using them. Scott and his friends next vilified the young attorney Lucas and his associates who had collaborated in the printed attacks. Through his friend Henry Dodge, Scott sent a challenge to all five men to meet him on the field of honor. Charles Lucas was the only one to accept the challenge. Charges and countercharges traveled back and forth across the political landscape, filling the newspapers with titillating details. A duel was set for August 19, 1816, with Frederick Bates and Colonel Eli B. Clemson as seconds for Lucas, and Doctor Joseph Walker and Captain Robert Price the seconds for Major Scott. Both sides called upon General William Rector as an impartial referee. Meanwhile, on August 10, 1816, Thomas Wright challenged Lucas. Wright chose as his second in the affair Major Taylor Berry.[14] The various and sundry challenges no doubt provided some high drama to the otherwise low political proceedings. In the end, however, more cautious minds prevailed, and no duels materialized.

The affairs were settled without powder being burned primarily through the good offices of mediators such as Henry Dodge, General William Clark, Bernard Pratte, and Auguste Chouteau. Lucas, however, was not satisfied. Evoking the rhetoric of western protagonism, he launched into a spirited defense of his hostile actions. Scott, reported the young captain, had earlier challenged Rufus Easton, knowing "that personal *interviews*" were against his principles, but when confronted by a heroic man, Scott backed down.

"Perhaps Mr. Scott thought it better that his honor should bleed, than that he should." His "show of arms," Lucas taunted, was "as contemptible as his boastings."[15]

The heated political rhetoric continued unabated throughout the closely contested election. When the dust settled, Governor Clark, who supported Scott's candidacy, declared that Scott had won the election for territorial representative by fifteen votes. Nevertheless, Congress doubted the fairness of the contest and called for new elections the following August. This of course only prolonged and exacerbated an already volatile situation.

Charles Lucas's cries of foul play and his taunting of Scott placed him at the head of the anti-junto faction. By 1816 he had employed the language of a protagonist and had articulated the vernacular of conflict. Consequently, he made it even more difficult for himself to escape future hostilities. His offer to meet John Scott on the field of honor proved that he possessed no moral or philosophical qualms about killing a political opponent. The engines of tragedy had started. Charles Lucas had cheated death in 1816, but not for long. His polemical talents, as well as his political influence, made him a lightning rod for the jealousies of the junto. During the October 1816 term of the St. Louis Circuit Court he clashed with a new apparatchik of the junto, Thomas H. Benton. In a heated legal exchange, both men questioned the veracity of the other. The jury decided the case in Lucas's favor. Benton, humiliated and angry, challenged Lucas. For reasons later explained, Lucas initially refused the invitation but eventually accepted the challenge and died at Benton's hand.

As for John Scott, always armed and ready, he never took to the field of honor. Elected in August 1817 as territorial representative, he went on to serve as the state's first congressman. Later he would successfully defend in the courtroom such noted duelists as John Smith T. Scott remained an ally of the junto until 1824 when he supported John Q. Adams for president. Again, a duel figured prominently in the deliberations. Scott had received assurances from Adams that, if elected president, he would not remove Scott's brother, Andrew, as a territorial judge in Arkansas. Andrew had been severely criticized for killing fellow lawyer Joseph Selden in a duel. The deal held. Andrew kept his judgeship, and John voted for Adams. Scott, however, lost the support of Thomas Hart Benton, who supported Jackson. In 1826 Scott was defeated in his bid for reelection by Edward Bates.[16]

The bitterness of the 1816 elections also prompted a bloodless encounter between political protagonists Thomas Hempstead, the brother of the first territorial representative, Edward Hempstead, and Joshua Barton, the brother of David Barton, the state's first U.S. senator. Thomas Hart Benton served as Hempstead's second while Edward Bates, a law partner of David Barton's, acted as Joshua Barton's second. The men met on what later came to be called Bloody Island on August 10, 1816.[17]

Missouri Congressman John Scott was always armed and rarely, if ever, ducked a challenge. Courtesy State Historical Society of Missouri.

Both sides realized the keen attention paid by the public to these affairs and how the duel set them apart from other ranks of the citizenry. Dueling, as Senator Abraham Byrd put it six years later, quite rightly kept the people from being "upon equal footing." It also, said Byrd, thwarted those who would "extend their leveling principles to the utmost limit of base-born republicanism, and subject *all* men to the dominion of law."[18] To underscore both the strict decorum of the affair and the exclusive club of the gentleman duelists, the seconds published the "Rules of the meeting between Mr. J. Barton demanding and Mr. T. Hempstead answering." Both parties followed all of the formalities of southern etiquette.

The Barton-Hempstead affair was a classic political duel. It was also unusual in the fact that neither party was hit on first fire nor was a second fire demanded. The duel originated from the harsh language and accusations that each political faction was wont to practice. Although both gentlemen were quite willing to kill each other, their animosity did not run deep. One harmless exchange of fire salvaged sullied honor and restored wounded pride. The punctilio and correctness of the duel, as well as the names of the principals and the seconds, was historically recorded.[19]

Meanwhile, farther down the Mississippi at Ste. Genevieve another political drama unfolded with deadly consequence. Auguste De Mun was the proud son of a former captain of dragoons of St. Domingo. William McArthur was a brother-in-law of future U.S. Senator Lewis F. Linn. The August

1816 elections found each man a candidate for the territorial legislature. During the campaign De Mun alleged that his opponent was involved with known counterfeiters and thereby was unsuited for political office. The insult prompted McArthur to challenge De Mun. De Mun, however, refused to duel on the grounds that McArthur was not a gentleman. This led to public charges by McArthur that De Mun was a coward and a poltroon.[20] The stage was set. Everything was in place for a killing. Both men only awaited the opportunity to get "the drop" on the other.

In antebellum Missouri the refusal to duel on the grounds that a challenger lacked the necessary social qualifications did not mean that the quarrel would end peacefully. Quite the contrary. The refusal often led to an improvisation of violence which, without the formalities and restraints of the code, increased the possibilities of bloodshed. Such was the case in the De Mun–McArthur affair.

The day of the shoot-out was August 28, 1816. De Mun and his brother apparently set out to find McArthur and kill him. At the time of the attack, McArthur was accompanied by Dr. Lewis Linn. The parties met near the courthouse square. At this juncture witnesses were not sure who fired the initial shot. John Scott later testified that McArthur and Linn instigated the shooting. Others believed it to be De Mun. In any event, pistols blazed, and McArthur beat a hasty retreat to a nearby inn, De Mun in fast pursuit. Other shots rang out. In short order McArthur emerged from the inn unscathed. His protagonist was not so fortunate. De Mun died shortly afterward and was buried in the Ste. Genevieve Catholic Cemetery. McArthur was never charged with any crime.[21] Although this was the only casualty of the 1816 elections, it boded ill for the elections of the following year.

The 1816 territorial elections, one must remember, had been marred by voter fraud and intimidation. These suspicious circumstances had prompted the federal government to call for a special election in August 1817 for the people to decide once again between Scott and Easton. The election was as hot as the weather, unfortunately bringing out the worst in both political factions. St. Louisans selected James Baird's Third Street blacksmith shop, the largest place in town, as the polling place. All the vices attendant to earlier elections occurred once more. Lieutenant Bennet Riley marched a contingent of troops up and down the street wearing caps labeled "John Scott." Later the young officer engaged in fisticuffs with a workman before John O'Fallon, a friend and nephew of William Clark, stabbed the workman with a dirk.[22] Next, O'Fallon pushed and insulted an Easton supporter, Dr. Robert Simpson. After further provocation, Simpson pulled a pistol and fired pointblank at O'Fallon. The powder only "flashed," and O'Fallon escaped harm. The doctor subsequently challenged O'Fallon to a duel, but they failed to make arrangements suitable to both parties.

General William Clark was a calming
influence in the Missouri Territory, but
he could not contain political violence.
Courtesy State Historical Society of
Missouri.

In the South the failure to achieve satisfaction would have led in all probability to a lengthy and public correspondence between the antagonists. Each
would have stated his perceived reasons for the hostile misunderstanding and
each would have attempted to vindicate his honor. In Missouri, however, letter writing often took a back seat to more direct action. Such was the case between Simpson and O'Fallon. Several days later when the two men met by
chance on the street, they engaged in a street brawl. Simpson again pulled a
pistol, but O'Fallon "pummeled" him before he could fire. Missourians all too
frequently did not stand on the punctilio of the duel. The 1817 elections also
precipitated the second and fatal rencounter between Benton and Lucas.[23]

Less than two years after the Lucas duel, Benton and political rival Richard
Venables brandished pistols on the streets of St. Louis in front of a crowd estimated at more than three hundred. Although no shots were fired, the two
men engaged in what one spectator called a "great fight." At roughly the same
time as this blustery affair, two duelists, apparently of opposite political persuasions and referred to only as Sullivan and Coons, met on Bloody Island in
September 1819. Sullivan was shot in the stomach but eventually recovered,
while Coons escaped having "had his whisker shot off."[24]

In the same year another duel pitted two political protagonists against each
other. They were Colonel John Smith T and Lionel Browne, the sheriff of
Washington County. "Everybody here," wrote Rufus Pettibone to Henry R.
Schoolcraft on September 26, 1819, "regrets that Smith was not killed"; it was
Browne, he lamented, who died instantaneously from a bullet to the brain.[25]

No single shot during the age of political dueling ever received such notoriety. With surgical precision Smith T successfully placed a ball where few if any men would dare to aim. This level of marksmanship made even the most intrepid of duelists reluctant to test their courage against Smith T.

In 1820 Luke Lawless, Benton's second in the Lucas affair, challenged Edward Bates. One might recall that Lawless helped lead a pro-slavery mob which killed Elijah P. Lovejoy, an abolitionist. Lawless was fortunate that he was still alive to challenge Bates since a few years earlier a former army officer, Thomas Smith, had set out to kill him on a St. Louis street. Smith had purchased a new pistol and mischievously wanted to try it out. John Darby, however, persuaded his impetuous friend to calm down, thus averting a potentially deadly rencounter.[26]

As for Bates, he refused Lawless's invitation because he did not believe that personal honor justified such a deadly recourse. Philosophically, Bates did not disavow dueling per se. Rather, he believed its utility lay in defending the higher honor of one's state. In 1829, as a member of the U.S. Congress, he unsuccessfully issued a challenge to Congressman George McDuffie of South Carolina for insults perceived to be directed at him but reflecting on the inferiority of western states such as Missouri. Duels to obtain personal satisfaction, so it seemed to Bates, were wrong, but vindication of state honor was another matter.

There were other challenges and duels in 1820 besides the Lawless-Bates affair. Near New Madrid Samuel G. Hopkins, captain of the forty-second regiment of the U.S. dragoons, killed on first fire a member of the Spanish nobility. The pistols in this affair were the same ones used by Aaron Burr and Alexander Hamilton. Folklore held that these pistols were used with "fatal effect" in eleven duels.[27]

Another 1820 duel that became part of Missouri folklore pertained to frontiersman and native Virginian Felix Scott. After a heated political argument, Scott was confronted with a challenge by his son-in-law. The son-in-law demanded a duel with shotguns. Scott accepted the invitation, and the two men met near Scott's St. Charles County home. He allowed the younger man first fire, and when he emerged from the volley unscathed, Scott then proceeded to give the upstart a beating with fisticuffs that the son-in-law never forgot. Felix's neighbors referred to him as "a great fighter" who never got whipped. He parlayed his rough-and-tumble reputation into political gold and subsequently served as justice of the peace for St. Charles County and as a state representative and state senator from the district.[28]

The first of the "western" duels in Missouri occurred in the Boonslick region in 1820. The Boonslick was the fastest-growing area in Missouri and a place where etiquette and formality were in short supply. In the spring of that

Acting Territorial Governor Frederick Bates, a fierce opponent of John Smith T and the junto faction, was challenged on several occasions but escaped injury. Courtesy State Historical Society of Missouri.

year a highly spirited military officer, Major Richard Gentry, rode swiftly out of the town of Franklin to overtake Henry Carroll, the twenty-eight-year-old son of Howard County's land registrar. Within minutes a pistol or pistols, depending upon which account one wanted to believe, flashed, and young Carroll fell from his horse mortally wounded. If one overlooked the lack of punctilio, then this rencounter was the only lethal duel on horseback recorded in Missouri history.

The improvised killing, termed a duel by Gentry supporters and a murder by the Carroll faction, stemmed from long-standing factional jealousies, land claim disputes, and disagreements over politics and slavery. In its wake, Carroll's murder set off a series of related controversies that could have cost many other lives. It also vividly depicted the twin aspects of vengeance and justice on the Missouri frontier.

Three aspects of the Gentry-Carroll affray deserve greater detail: first, the exact circumstances of the killing and the subsequent trial; second, the ancillary players who were engulfed in the controversy; and third, the long-term consequences of that fateful spring day. As to the "duel" itself, Charles Carroll believed his son had proven Gentry "a liar and a villain," and therefore to cover his "disgrace and cowardice," Gentry had taken the "wicked and diabolical" steps of shooting an unsuspecting, innocent man. Gentry, on the other hand, maintained it was a fair fight. The *Missouri Intelligencer,* under a March 4, 1820, headline entitled "AWFUL CATASTROPHE," described the public excitement concerning this "horrible transaction" and marveled at the many mourners who attended Carroll's funeral. But the paper refrained from drawing conclusions as to the guilt and innocence of the parties.[29]

A grand jury in Howard County indicted Gentry for murder, and in January 1821 the trial began in circuit court. Thomas H. Benton rode from St. Louis to head Gentry's defense team. Colonel George Strother also assisted in his legal defense and reportedly toured the county locating jurors favorable to their cause. The trial highlighted the hazards of frontier justice. Jurors sympathetic to Gentry were selected and an eyewitness, Jacob Varner, whose testimony might have been prejudicial to the defendant, was sent "out of the way" and never testified. Another potentially damaging witness, William O. Short, was hanged for murder before the trial. The Carroll faction later maintained that Short, hours before he faced the gallows, related how Gentry had plotted Carroll's murder at the condemned man's home. The Gentry team had little evidence to muster in his defense, although they did claim that a certain Robert Switzler had brought pistols to the Boonslick region from more than one hundred miles away with the expressed purpose of using them to kill the major. With the Carroll forces crying "intrigue" and "corruption," all charges against Gentry were dropped. The trial even made Gentry wince. On July 3, 1824, in the *Missouri Intelligencer,* he openly admitted that his "wicked attorneys" had thrown "many obstacles in the way of my persecutors." It was a remarkably candid admission to make, but he prefaced it by saying that it had been necessary to impede unjust "persecution."[30]

The affair, however, was far from settled. Thomas A. Smith, the receiver of public monies at the land office in Franklin, was aligned with Carroll. Smith reported that he had received incriminating information from William O. Rector about Judge David Todd, who was a friend of Gentry's. Smith believed Todd to have been with the major the evening before the murder and as a "civic officer" should have apprehended him before he set out to kill Henry Carroll. In addition, Smith intimated that the judge was also involved in a series of political irregularities that placed his judicial credibility in doubt. The judge responded with a blistering attack against Smith and the others who had resorted to "base calumnies" against his good name. The stage was set for more violence. Charles Carroll, the bereaved father of Henry, wrote to General Smith on September 21, 1820, that Gentry and Todd sought more bloodshed and warned Smith that he too had been "selected for further vengeance."[31]

The attending furor forced Gentry and his family to leave Franklin. Along with some other enterprising speculators, he helped to incorporate the town of Columbia. Undoubtedly, the Gentry trial exacerbated factional tensions and contributed to an 1824 duel between George Strother and Dr. Hardage Lane. Neither man on this occasion was seriously injured. Colonel Strother had helped defend Gentry, while Lane had accused the major of having "feelings even below the ordinary standard of human depravity." Another close

Major Richard Gentry was perhaps the only Missourian to kill his adversary while "dueling" on horseback. Courtesy State Historical Society of Missouri.

encounter occurred when Jonathan S. Findlay, an enemy of Gentry's, reportedly went looking for the major. According to Findlay, Gentry avoided the meeting for fear of "his valorous wrath." Gentry responded to the charge of cowardice the following month by suggesting that Findlay, "so hateful that a well bred dog would be ashamed to bark at him," got his pistols out and came looking for him only after he fully realized that Gentry was eighty miles away.[32]

Despite the Carroll killing and its verbal aftermath, Gentry's political career suffered no lasting ill effects. President Jackson appointed him postmaster of Columbia, and in 1821 Governor Alexander McNair gave him a promotion in the state militia. The following year he was commissioned a colonel. In 1826 the people of the Columbia district elected him state senator. By the time of the Black Hawk War in the early 1830s he had attained the rank of general. When the war against the Seminoles began, Senator Benton asked him to raise a regiment of volunteers and head for Florida. Gentry not only honored the request but also outfitted many of his men at his own expense and brought his son, Richard, along as his sergeant major. On Christmas Day in 1837, the general's promising career was cut short when he was killed in the battle of Okeechobee.[33]

The year 1823 also saw Samuel Perry, a prominent miner and business man in Washington County, kill J. D. Handy in a duel. Very few details of this affair have survived, and therefore it has been difficult to ascertain whether or not the duel was politically motivated. In March 1824 a grand jury bill of indictment,

State of Missouri v. Samuel Perry, was entered into the circuit court records of Washington County, but the charges were quickly dropped, the grand jury finding that it was "not a true bill."[34]

The last lethal duel in this period of intense political factionalism took place on June 30, 1823. It was a classic case of the inability of a newspaper, in this instance the *St. Louis Republican,* to juggle the conflicting demands of the rights of the press, the accused, and the accuser. Newspapers had contributed in part to many previous duels and hostile encounters, but the Barton-Rector affair was the first in which the press played the lead role in a killing. Oddly, too, this duel pitted two men who were not the principal protagonists in the controversy.

General William C. Rector was the surveyor-general of Illinois, Missouri, and Arkansas. It was a lucrative position, and Rector had close connections to powerful men such as Senator Thomas Hart Benton, John Scott, Thomas F. Riddick, and Governor Alexander McNair. His main critics were David Barton, Judge J. B. C. Lucas, and Rufus Easton. In addition to personal and factional animosities, Rector's enemies roundly condemned his practice of hiring relatives and cronies as deputy surveyors in the region under his jurisdiction.[35] Arkansas in fact was perceived as a personal fiefdom of the Rectors. The general's son, Henry, became one of its early governors. Specifically, Rector was charged with giving surveying contracts of three dollars a mile to twelve of these men who in turn sublet the work for as low as forty cents a mile and pocketed the difference. Initially, Senator Barton had supported Rector, but as the allegations mounted he became the most vocal critic of the general. The general in turn responded with a vigorous defense of his actions and went on the offensive with a spirited attack against the senator.[36] Since Rector's term of office was soon to expire, Senator Barton seized the opportunity to move against him. He enlisted the support of his brother, Joshua, the U.S. district attorney in St. Louis. The Bartons had come to St. Louis from Tennessee and fell in with the anti-junto faction. Joshua studied law under Rufus Easton and became the law partner of Edward Bates. David, one of the finest political minds in early Missouri, had become the state's first U.S. senator.

The Bartons realized that attacks on Rector might prove dangerous as he and his kin were known to be a rough and contentious lot, especially when it came to matters of money and family honor. But Joshua was no stranger to violence or the code duello. He had taken to the field of honor as both a second and a principal in earlier affairs, and knew the risks of this undertaking. With his brother David supplying the evidence and he publishing the results, the two men hoped to ruin Rector's public reputation and deny his reappointment. Since Rector was in Washington, D.C., lobbying to keep his job, Senator Barton returned to the nation's capital to oppose him. This left Joshua alone in St. Louis to keep up the political heat.

On June 25, 1823, there appeared in the *Republican* an article signed anonymously by "Philo" that outlined the charges of nepotism against Rector and his clan. The article further proclaimed that the surveyor had bilked the treasury by allowing his friends and relatives to receive the biggest and most lucrative surveying contracts. These individuals in turn sublet them to other incompetent surveyors, thus profiting at public expense without risk or labor.[37] The *Republican* had taken a forthright stand against corruption by publishing these allegations. Nevertheless, its commitment to freedom of the press and the right of the citizenry to criticize public officials was considerably greater than its determination to protect the confidentiality of its source. When Thomas C. Rector, William's brother, demanded the identity of "Philo," the editor of the *Republican* provided the name of Joshua Barton. To this extent, regardless of the nature of its civic duty to expose alleged corruption, the paper and its editor contributed to the tragedy that followed.

The Rector clan now pondered the proper recourse against the Bartons. A lawsuit had three disadvantages: first, the process itself would be drawn out and the delay could well prove disastrous to the Rectors' case; second, a court battle might expose many of the chicaneries the family desired to conceal; and third, litigation, even if successful, would prove unsatisfactory to family honor. The attack against the Rectors, although nonphysical, was still a personal affront, and the response must also be personal. An invitation to the dueling ground seemed a logical choice. Besides, it had the added advantage of possibly silencing other potentially hostile parties if they realized that they too might face the wrong end of a pistol barrel.

After concluding that a personal interview was the proper course of action, the Rectors next considered the target. Since David Barton was in Washington, D.C., and unlikely to accept a challenge, "Philo" became the best target of their distemper. They next decided that Thomas Rector should face Joshua Barton's fire. Of the different Rectors who would willingly fight, Thomas appeared to be the one most experienced in violence. The family had concluded that William Rector was too remote and far too valuable to risk in an exchange of shots. Without him, the entire business enterprise would collapse. Should Thomas fall, the Rectors planned to issue more challenges until they silenced Barton. They awaited a signal from Big Mound on the Missouri shore.[38] If or when a flag was waved in the air it would be a signal that another Rector must take up the cudgel. Gunshots and no flag would mean that Thomas was victorious.

The duelists met the evening of June 30, 1823, at six o'clock on Bloody Island. Joshua knew the place well since he had been there before as both a principal and a second. That evening a large crowd gathered by the banks of the river and eagerly awaited the outcome. The only terms of the encounter that can be ascertained were that the principals chose pistols at a reasonably close distance. The names of the seconds and surgeons have remained obscured,

Joshua Barton in 1823 died at the hands of Thomas Rector in one of the most celebrated political duels on Bloody Island. Courtesy State Historical Society of Missouri.

possibly because the authorities had gotten wind of the duel and no one wanted to be directly implicated. Rector, reported historian Charles van Ravenswaay, was "as cool as though he had been hunting rabbits." He may have even fired before the second gave the word. In any case, Barton fell, mortally wounded, and died on the island. Rector thereupon waved his hat in triumph to anxious members of the clan on Big Mound. No further sacrifices from the Rectors would be necessary. According to van Ravenswaay, "Gossips said that later in the evening the Rectors celebrated at a victory dinner and got so intoxicated that they were heard to holloa, as they pushed around the wine, 'This is Barton's blood.' " Barton was buried in St. Charles. The *Republican,* without one hint of its own culpability, lamented Missouri's loss of "one of her ablest and worthiest citizens."[39]

The Rectors' victory, however, was pyrrhic. The furor in Missouri traveled all the way to the doorstep of the White House. President James Monroe, who initially supported Rector's reappointment, reversed himself and denied him the position. Some years later the general died in his home state of Illinois an impoverished and broken man.[40] Fate was just as cruel to Thomas Rector. In 1825 he died in a violent altercation (more than likely a knife fight) in St. Louis. As for Senator Barton, bedeviled by drink and fits of mental instability, he never fully recovered from the shock of his brother's death. Increasingly he focused his wrath upon Governor McNair, first for not stopping the duel and second for making no effort to apprehend Thomas Rector after the killing. The battle of words between Barton and McNair escalated until finally on or about Christmas Day 1824, the senior senator from Missouri challenged the governor of the state to mortal combat. Failing to receive an adequate reply,

Barton challenged him again a week or so later. McNair also rejected this invitation.[41]

The Barton-McNair controversy illustrated how the penchant for settling personal and political differences by an affair of honor was ingrained in the psyches of many leaders in Missouri. It also demonstrated that elites had little if anything to fear politically from issuing challenges and threatening to kill their opponents for holding opinions different from their own. Nevertheless, McNair's refusal to accept the challenge marked a turning point in the duel's political utility. Over the next decade or two the temptation to resort to the code would wane. The diminution of politicized murder was in large measure due to the end of the era of intense factional discord. Conversely, the development of political parties provided the ruling class with less violent ways in which to compete for power. By 1825 the age of the political duel was nearing its end. But other metaphoric rationales, as well as new social and political justifications, would be found to sustain the institution.

4

Honor and Hubris

The Benton-Lucas Duel

T HE BENTON-LUCAS duel was not only one of the most celebrated duels in Western history but also one of the most complicated. Some violent acts are so egregious that they require explication. So it was with the Benton-Lucas appeal to arms. It pitted the aristocratic Charles Lucas against Thomas Hart Benton, a man of less than noble roots. Their battles, waged on an otherwise obscure island in the Mississippi River, gave that sandbar its sanguinary epithet, Bloody Island.

In many respects the killing of Lucas was no more tragic than a dozen or so other deaths of the same ilk. Both protagonists were bachelors, so that after the bark of pistols the victor was spared the cries of his adversary's widow and children. Still, each man stood as the champion of his respective faction, and each man, in the prime of life, appeared destined for greatness. In retrospect, the Benton-Lucas duel possessed the elements of tragedy; to this day, the memories of victor and vanquished call out for understanding and insight. Perhaps they should be given their ultimate satisfaction.

Tragedy in western culture has always worn two faces. The first face is Christian. Christian tragedy, with its emphasis upon free will, sheds considerable light upon honor. Honor, by its nature, is aggressive, self-assertive, and leaves nothing to chance or fate. Benton and Lucas were, after all, men who by their own volition made a conscious decision to wage personal war and were willing to pay the ultimate sacrifice.

Hubris, on the other hand, is honor's nemesis. It refers to a self-indulgent insolence, resulting from excessive pride and passion, which predetermines one's fate. This is the second face of tragedy, and it is Greek. Even with history's unerring hindsight, it is difficult to imagine a peaceful resolution between these two protagonists. Like actors in a Greek tragedy, they were pliantly cast in a political play and remained inexorably obedient to their roles.

At the time, of course, most citizens of the Missouri Territory did not perceive the Benton-Lucas duel in terms of Greek or Christian tragedy. For them, the affair was a frontier drama in which conflicting concepts and prescriptions of gentlemanly behavior could only be reconciled at the opposite ends of pistols. In hindsight, however, it was a story of honor and hubris on the raw edges of the Missouri border.

The duel has been recounted by such historians as William Stevens, Charles van Ravenswaay, and Walter Stevens with poetic beauty and visualization.[1] But beneath the real-life drama lay the hidden engines of tragedy that propelled the two men toward their destinies. It was true that in the violent world of the West, victory in combat was no longer perceived as a medieval ordination of God. But vengeance had yet to be sublimated by law. In the interim between divine ordination and the rule of law, the cult of honor cast a deadly shadow across the emerging society of Missouri. Inseparable from frontier honor was an exaggerated sense of individualism that held that institutional conformity was an admission of one's inability to assert control over personal problems. In fact, the law often inhibited the acquisition or maintenance of honor, especially for those who sought the appellation of gentlemen but were still unsure of their status in the community.

In a modern democratic society, honor and respect are equated more with mutual accommodation and tolerance of the opinions of others. But St. Louis in its territorial and early statehood days was anything but democratic. Considerable social tension existed between rival French and American settlers. The old Creole families were resistant to change and "determined to hold their all-embracing ancient titles." The newer American elites were just as eager to wrest these privileges away. Neither group was closely identified with "the masses of plain people." Those newcomers seeking recognition were very cognizant that reputations were greatly enhanced by feats of valor through personal combat. Social personality was commensurate to social rank and status. Leadership and prestige gravitated to those who exhibited this modal personality.[2] These social evaluations generally operated more persuasively in smaller, exclusive societies such as St. Louis's that were based upon personal contact rather than complex, impersonal activities.

In its early days, St. Louis was linked to the Indian trade as the established families of the city had derived great wealth from the exchange of clothes, arms, beads, paints, furs, skins, and lead. The primitiveness of the town was attested to by the fact that prairie chickens could be shot on the streets. Painted Indians armed with tomahawks and knives peopled the streets and establishments of the city. Joseph Charless, the editor of the *Missouri Gazette,* the first newspaper west of the Mississippi, entertained his Indian friends by politely allowing them to peruse his newspaper upside-down as they browsed around the press and sat in his waiting room. These encounters between native and white Missourians were far less unsettling than the influx of American emigrants, especially from the rough-and-ready states of Kentucky and Tennessee. Thomas Hart Benton fit well into this land of unbridled ambition. By his own account, he was "an adventurer ready to begin on a new theater" who sought to construct "some foundation of character and fortune." What better form of theatrics than dueling for one with such "a thirst for political life"?[3]

The world that Benton found in this gateway city was far different from the environs east of the Mississippi. Due in part to its Creole and Spanish heritage, the early-nineteenth-century social hierarchy of St. Louis, if not ascriptive, was at best rigid and reluctant to admit new members. Although a number of "would-be office seekers" came to the territory, little room for political advancement or social recognition existed.[4] In these twilight years of territorial government could be seen the dynamics of an emerging state. But for the time being, wealth and power beckoned to those elites who could hold onto power or to those who could wrest it from them.

Benton understood this political and social world of conflict. According to him and his biographers, he arrived in St. Louis in 1815 and fortuitously inquired from a perfect stranger the whereabouts of adequate sleeping quarters. This chance meeting was with Charles Gratiot, who just happened to have casually strolled down to the riverboat docks to inspect the newly arriving passengers. Gratiot was one of the most powerful men in the territory. He had married Victoria, a daughter of Auguste Chouteau, solidifying his station among the ruling Creole families. The Chouteau home and other structures occupied a whole square at the center of town and were meant to inspire, in even the most skeptical of nonbelievers, a sense of their social status in the town.[5] Benton's inquiry, so the accounts ran, was countered by an invitation from Gratiot that the American attorney stay at his home until suitable quarters could be found. Benton accepted the invitation and resided there for the next six weeks. Thus, as luck would have it, he fell in with the powerful junto faction.

Fate, however, is hardly that kind. A more likely scenario would appear to be that Benton's reputation preceded him. Although he spoke no French (he was later tutored by Bishop William DuBourg), his talents, both legal and pugilistic, were probably well known to the Creoles, who believed they could be put to considerable use by the junto. As to law, earlier Spanish and French settlers had brought with them the trappings of Latin civil law, but the Americans had yet to introduce English common law. Although in time this development would bring a sorely needed element of stability, jurisprudence in Missouri was still a highly uncertain enterprise. Such an environment was well suited for Benton's skills. Consequently, when he put out his shingle, he advertised his specialty as being in land claims and titles.[6]

The territorial bar in 1815, with less than a dozen lawyers, was no place for the faint of heart. Judges and barristers alike came armed to court, and pitched battles often erupted. Powerful and "violent" political and economic factions had developed, and the stakes in this wide-open game were immense.[7] Especially critical at this juncture was the status of the old Spanish land grants. The grants had already touched off a virtual war in the Ste. Genevieve mining district that for a time appeared to engulf the entire territory.

More than Benton's legal talents, however, piqued the interest of the Creoles. They were also impressed with his fire and ambition. His "fierce aggressiveness," which, even by the "untamed" standards of early Missouri, was "exaggerated," put him in good stead. It therefore was no coincidence that Gratiot met the thirty-five-year-old belligerent that autumn day at river's edge. Benton's job, as an apparatchik of the ruling class, was to popularize their cause, to defend their grants in court, and, if need be, to intimidate and silence their adversaries. The risks and rewards for such a task would be great. His most famous biographer, William N. Chambers, came close to making the same connection when he wrote, "Undoubtedly Gratiot and his associates saw in Benton a promising addition to their circle."[8]

Benton's formative years forged his fierce determination to make the Missouri venture his life's vindication. Born in 1782 in North Carolina, Thomas was not even ten years of age when his father, Jesse, died. The Bentons had claims to nearly twenty-four thousand acres of land, mostly in Cherokee country, but due to legal squabbles and Indian troubles most of it remained unpossessed. Nevertheless, Thomas's mother was determined, despite the lack of adequate funds, to work hard on the farm and to see to it that her son received a proper education. Toward that end, she enrolled him in the University of North Carolina in January 1798. By March of the following year he had been expelled from the university for stealing.[9]

Benton always maintained that he took money from four of his fellow students because he felt awkward about asking for a loan. He further maintained that he expected to pay it all back before the money was found missing. The explanation satisfied neither the students nor the administration. With his ruse discovered and his integrity questioned, Benton fell back upon the time-tested tradition of being prepared to duel anyone who directly challenged his honor. Expulsion, however, preceded confrontation. Nevertheless, according to his biographer, William N. Chambers, it "added humiliation to humiliation."[10] For Benton, honor had become a looking-glass self—a personality filtered through the prism of how he viewed what others thought of him.

Denied a university education, Benton became a self-taught man. In later life he bragged about his youthful reading of "solid books." Always sensitive, lest one equated the lack of formal education with the absence of classical knowledge, Benton extolled the quality of his speeches, which he claimed were more "literary" than political. The university dismissal, as Charles van Ravenswaay suggested, haunted his every move. His "sensitive pride had magnified the guilt" and led to "egotism" and "a rash fearlessness, and a lasting touchiness about his honor." Benton's perceptions of honor, like those of many southerners, were deeply rooted in "mythology, literature, history, and civilization." Unlike in the North, where honor was extended to every "moral, religious and sensible man in every station of life," southern honor was democratic only among the ranks of the elite. Although differences in social rank or economic power existed among southern gentlemen, honor was an indivisible commodity. In other words, one either had honor or did not. In this sense it conferred a leveling of virtue on those who possessed it. To lose any honor was to lose it all, and therefore one must guard against the slightest imputation.[11]

More than any other factor, the scandal at the university became the catalyst for his mother's decision to leave North Carolina and to move the family to Tennessee. Controversy, therefore, had forced the move to Tennessee. It would also enter into his decision to head for Missouri. He was determined never to be driven away in shame again. According to most of his biographers, Benton's decision to head west in 1815 resulted from an earlier affray with Andrew Jackson. In a Nashville hotel in 1813, Benton and his brother Jesse shot, fought, and clawed their way into infamy in one of the most sensational brawls in Tennessee history.

Benton had been a close ally of Jackson, but the two fell out when the general served in an adversarial role as William Carroll's second in a duel in which Jesse had been unceremoniously shot in the buttocks. As the story made the rounds of polite and not-so-polite Tennessee society, the Bentons became the brunt of many a salacious joke. Insulting and ribald laughter attended the Bentons everywhere they went. The humiliation of this episode prompted the classic confrontation in Nashville. Which party drew first or provoked the first hostile move has not been fully ascertained. Nevertheless, by the time the smoke cleared, Jackson had taken a slug in the shoulder, Jesse had sustained several nonmortal wounds, and Thomas had been knocked down a flight of stairs. Although the Bentons were the self-declared winners in the free-for-all, the altercation nevertheless ruined them politically. "I am," reflected Benton, "in the middle of hell; my life is in danger, and nothing but a decisive duel can save me or even give me a chance for my own existence."[12] Obviously, the skirmish with Jackson did not personally atone for Jesse's humiliation or salvage family honor. Thomas had brandished his masculinity in "the victory" against Jackson but he had not vindicated his honor. In addition, whatever social status he had gained by standing up to Old Hickory had been lost in political status. He had become a pariah in Tennessee politics.

This insecurity manifested itself in an 1813 challenge to William B. Lewis of Nashville. When Lewis demurred, Benton posted him "a cockade and gold-laced coward." To press him further, he exclaimed, would be "deemed un-

Thomas Hart Benton vindicated his
honor in a triumphal duel with Charles
Lucas. Courtesy State Historical Society
of Missouri.

Charles Lucas's promising career in politics
was cut short by his tragic death in a duel
with Thomas Hart Benton in 1817. Courtesy
Missouri Historical Society.

manly." This kind of bellicosity no doubt impressed the Missouri junto. The
junto also put Benton's editorial and legal talents to good use.[13]

As editor of the *St. Louis Enquirer*, Benton articulated the position of the
large Spanish land claimants. Unlike other legal "novices," he did not need to
advertise or to solicit cases from the populace as he had "all the business he
needed" from the Creole elites. These activities led to the accusation that he

served only "the interests of the tiny French aristocracy," a charge, which Chambers later admitted, was "to some extent" true. Benton detractors such as J. B. C. Lucas, father of Charles Lucas, needed no convincing. To them Benton had "become the executioner" of the junto's "nefarious schemes." Benton, they maintained, had "wedded himself" to the junto and had "organized a bloody faction" to eliminate their political rivals.[14]

The same years that witnessed Benton's arrival in Missouri also saw another aspiring gentleman from even more distant lands make his way toward the Missouri Territory. He was Charles Lucas. This young aristocrat, however, was not tainted by a questionable past nor burdened by self-doubt. He combined the trappings of eastern manners with the vitality of western ambition. And he, like his fellow sojourner from Tennessee, could never have imagined how destiny would intertwine their lives. Within a few short years of their westward journeys, they were fated to become the standard-bearers in a power struggle between two sets of elites for control of the territory.[15]

Young Charles Lucas was the favorite son of Judge J. B. C. Lucas, the patriarch of a proud family of Norman ancestry. The judge had arrived in the young nation in 1784. His "thorough and classical education," combined with his friendships with Benjamin Franklin and Albert Gallatin, abetted a short but successful political career in Pennsylvania. The judge once remarked that he came to the United States not as "a fugitive and an outcast" but "as a scholar and a gentleman." Upon Lucas's arrival in Missouri, President Jefferson appointed him a territorial judge of the superior court and one of three Upper Louisiana board members of the land commission. If there was any group with which the Lucas family should have had a rapport, it was the same established French families to which Benton had hitched his star. But it was not to be. Philosophy and profit quickly estranged Judge Lucas from the junto. Unlike the Creoles, the judge had drunken heavily from the well of republicanism and nationalism. Financially, however, that same well was nearly dry. For the Lucases were usually just a step or two ahead of their creditors. The move to Missouri from his adopted state of Pennsylvania offered not only a chance to serve his country but also an opportunity to enrich himself from land speculation. This ambition particularly concerned the French establishment. Many of the land claimants of French origin, Judge Lucas later wrote, "expected more kindness from me," but "many of these good people," he cautioned, "who act, mostly, with honor amongst themselves, seldom or perhaps never have acted with the national interests in mind."[16]

From 1807 to 1811, Judge Lucas and his youngest son unfailingly corresponded across the broad reaches of the Appalachians. Much of Charles Lucas's character was built around these letters of hope and misgivings. Charles had remained back east to acquire an education steeped in the classics, but the costs had been high. From their homeplace near Cannonsburgh, Pennsylvania, Charles wrote his father in June 1811 that he worried about the high price of his education and the lack of money for necessities like fine clothes. Two other features of this letter prophetically revealed a tragic side of his character. One was a desperate need to please his father and to prove his masculinity; the other was his equally disdainful attitude toward the self-proclaimed elites of the trans-Mississippi West. "I have," he confessed to the senior Lucas, "little regard" for the talents of St. Louis lawyers. By training as well as disposition, Charles found the impetuosity of these frontier barristers disagreeable and offensive. Yet the western environment with its compulsion toward greed and aggression beckoned the young Lucas to accept his challenge. "I can not come home like a boy now," he exclaimed to his father, "but as a young man."[17]

The elder Lucas shared the same lack of respect for most of the lawyers in early Missouri and no doubt influenced Charles's perception of them as well. In a letter to his son William, the judge disgustedly remarked on the number of untutored lawyers "flocking" to St. Louis. "The profession here," he lamented, "will soon be overstocked." In the years following Charles's death, he excoriated those lawyers unprepared by a "classical education" and whose minds were "shackled, falsified and artificial." Their abilities, he exclaimed, were "greatly over rated." Law to them was merely a trade and an opportunity for political intrigue.[18]

Despite his contempt for the social upstarts in the Missouri bar, Charles joined his father in St. Louis and began the practice of law. In his haste to succeed, he became within a few years one of the most respected attorneys in the territory, a captain in the militia, and a prosperous land speculator. He had also begun a promising political career that many believed would lead him to the U.S. Senate. Judge Lucas wrote to William that Charles "is getting rich fast," but his enemies were also "daily increasing."[19] In August 1816, Charles's boldness nearly led to duels with John Scott and Thomas Wright. By the age of twenty-four he had come to personify the determination of the anti-junto faction to wrest power from the Creoles.

Meanwhile, Thomas Hart Benton was busily establishing his reputation among the highly select circles of St. Louis. His ambition and hard work contributed greatly to his legal success. Benton's first exposure to public life was on the city's school board. There he sat amongst the likes of William Clark, William C. Carr, Bernard Pratte, Auguste Chouteau, Alexander McNair, and John P. Cabanne. In every respect Benton was a model citizen who displayed civic pride and responsibility in a variety of social endeavors.

During these formative years Benton took as his model and closest friend Edward Hempstead, an able attorney and territorial representative. When Hempstead's brother, Thomas, dueled Joshua Barton in 1816, Benton served as Hempstead's second. Edward Bates acted in the same capacity for Barton. The decorum and punctilio of the duel would have been the envy of any southern gentleman.[20] Although no blood was shed in the exchange of fire, all parties made it publicly clear that the affair was settled honorably among men of the upper class. No one could have been more pleased than Benton, for this was his rite of passage into the bitter sport of gentlemen.

History does not record the first meeting between Benton and Lucas, nor their feelings about the encounter. But one may surmise that it was not characterized by mutual admiration. To Benton, the mannerisms, social position, and erudition of Charles Lucas must have seemed "prim" and slightly effeminate— an affront to western manhood.[21] Yet for all this, the young Pennsylvanian possessed many of the attributes that Benton so longed to have. Small wonder that he chafed at the Lucas name and good connections. While they claimed breeding, he asserted prowess. While they claimed respect, he imparted a bravado conditioned by years of self-doubt and unclaimed honor.

Lucas, by temperament and background, no doubt saw in his rival's bold and brash style the epitome of frontier coarseness. Perhaps, as van Ravenswaay has suggested, he "felt repelled by the barbarism in his [Benton's] reputation as a brawler."[22] Whatever their personal perceptions, each man viewed with envy and suspicion the growing fame and fortune of the other. Both men, wrote historian James Neal Primm, were "self-confident, imperious ex-militia officers." It would not take much to set in motion a tragic train of events.

The spark that eventually ignited the fatal explosion on Bloody Island started in the St. Louis Circuit Court in October 1816. The two lawyers, holding contradictory opinions on a point of evidence, openly clashed in the courtroom. The argument quickly turned personal. Each held his interpretation of the evidence to be not only correct but abstractly true. The next assumption flowed logically. If one was the sole possessor of truth, then the other was the propagator of falsehood. In short, one man was a liar. Benton, however, could not countenance the slightest imputation of deceit. The memories of Chapel Hill still lingered dangerously close to the surface. According to the code of honor, two cardinal sins, "the blow" and "the lie direct," could be expunged only by the satisfaction of a duel. Perhaps Benton might have been mollified by a jury verdict in his favor. But Lucas won the case. Smarting from these twin rebuffs, Benton quickly sent his challenge. Lucas, however, was not to be goaded. He had performed his duty to his client, he told Benton, and the jury had sustained that verdict. Furthermore, he declared, "I will not for supporting the truth be in any way bound to give the redress or satisfaction you ask for, or to any person who may feel wounded by such exposure of the truth."[23]

Lucas's refusal to accept the challenge revealed some interesting facets of territorial life. First, he asserted the claim, long held by many members of the ruling class, that one's public duty to government, court, or citizenry should not be entangled with personal quarrels. Second, he refused to fight Benton and gave not the slightest hint of apology. Rather, he forcibly exclaimed his legal correctness and in his short reply twice used the word "truth" to identify that position. The note, therefore, sustained Benton's culpability in "the lie direct." Finally, the terseness of the reply suggested that his adversary was not worthy of a long, detailed explanation. This last point suggested the deeper reason why Lucas did not feel compelled at this time to face Benton. Benton did not possess the Lucas standard of honor. Shortly after Charles's death, his father summarized the Lucas position on honor. His son was a man who had "substantial honor." Words such as "good or bad" could do little to affect his reputation. As for dueling Benton, it was not fear of the man but fear of becoming like him that led his son to decline the invitation. Charles, he declared, "dreaded nothing more than the idea of sliding into the character which he most abhorred." Benton, the Lucas clan contended, was and could never be anything but "a common duelist."[24]

Before returning to the specifics of the duel, a few details about the nature of honor and hubris are in order. Although both men held differing views of honor, they shared a vice, common among elites of that time, which most aptly could be defined as hubris—an overweening pride and a boundless confidence in their ability to master any situation. Hubris was the negation of the social order and most often led to ruin, that is, nemesis.[25] But unlike the common folk, duelists placed life upon a higher altar, risking ruin and pitting themselves not against the gods but the luck or fate of a bullet's path. These men of hubris were attracted to dueling as much by the risk as by the gain. From the days of chivalry, those deeds most admired by the aristocracy were ones in which the ruling class manifested no fear of death. Two such examples would be the joust and the bullfight. The duel itself was therefore often anticlimactic, since the opportunity of proving one's courage was equal to the prize of killing one's opponent.

Over the past three centuries the duel had become the most dramatic form of institutionalized violence, partly because of this mystique. It was a display in symbolic form of the values and beliefs of a bygone age. Often waged in the mist of early morning or in the shades of twilight, obscured by tall willows on secluded islands, the duel had a mystical, almost surreal quality about it. It was in this vein that Peter H. Burnett wrote that the duel "is for effect, not reality, and prefers the shadow to the substance."[26] These were the unconscious and hubristic forces that motivated men such as Benton and Lucas to make the journey to Bloody Island.

One must also remember that the code duello did not require a man to fight below his social station. An important condition in the acceptance of a challenge pertained to the recognition of an adversary's equality of honor.

This equality Charles Lucas initially refused to countenance. The note's wording and its many implications were the most unkind cuts to Benton's pride. His thrust in the form of a challenge had been skillfully parried by a denial that cast further aspersions on his honor. These contrasting worlds of honor explained why Lucas felt little fear that an unanswered challenge would damage his career in politics. Nevertheless, it left unresolved the conflict that led to his calling out Benton less than a year later.

Benton's challenge and Lucas's refusal highlighted the dual nature of honor. For Lucas, his birth and aristocratic lineage were sufficient validations of honor. For the Lucas family, honor was deferred by group recognition. Although honor on the frontier was never completely secure, even when inherited, self-assertion through violence was less important to a family such as his. Charles Lucas was recognized as much for what he possessed—an aristocratic Norman ancestry, a classical education, refinement, and good breeding—as for who he was. His honor was derived as much from antecedence as from individual reputation, and it was secured by Old World definitions of inheritance and patrimony. It was in this ascriptive, self-validating context that Judge Lucas's words, "substantial honor," had meaning. It was a type of honor that precluded dishonor.[27]

Thomas Hart Benton did not possess and could not countenance this duality of honor. His was honor earned, not conferred. Insecure and self-assertive, he sought respect by achievement, not ascription. It was honor validated not by genealogy or birth, but gained by individual merit. The criteria for this conduct varied from one society to another depending upon its complexity, but in early St. Louis, where public opinion mirrored personal and factional relationships, violence was an acceptable tool for achieving group approval.

The next act in the Benton-Lucas drama began in August 1817 during the bitterly contested territorial elections. Property qualifications were a prerequisite for voting in these stormy days, as Charles Lucas knew so well. He therefore prepared to spring his trap. He suspected that Colonel Benton's three slaves, his only taxable property, had not been properly recorded in time to vote. Such an oversight would thereby render his ballot null and void. He publicly confronted Benton with the accusation just as Benton prepared to cast his vote. By questioning Benton's voting qualifications, Lucas aimed at an Achilles' heel that had festered since the incident at Chapel Hill many years before. Lucas's accusations therefore wounded Benton deeply. His intentions were unambiguous; the insult was clear, deliberate, and public, the humiliation perhaps politically lethal. Benton angrily responded with one of his favorite idioms: "Gentlemen, if you have any questions to ask, I am prepared to answer, but I do not propose to answer charges made by any puppy who may happen to run across my path."[28]

Lucas's words were a calculated insult, and Benton had responded in kind. Both men understood how and why the power of insult worked more persuasively among a coterie of elites, for only they and they alone could pronounce one deserving of membership in the exclusive club of gentlemen. Within a few days of the remark, Lucas sent his second, Joshua Barton, with an invitation for Benton to meet him on the field of honor.

His decision to challenge Benton over the "puppy" remark was multifaceted. The comment undoubtedly stung him to the quick. In fact, he could not, even in his own account of the meeting, broach the word "puppy." Instead he alluded to the "vehement, abusive and ungentlemanly language" used by Benton.[29] "Puppy" also suggested that the younger Lucas was little more than a lackey for his father. Furthermore, the term often connoted ill breeding as well as a mindless follower. Many statements of reproach could be found similar to one in an 1817 *Missouri Gazette* editorial that began, "Wise and well tempered men shun the ill bred puppy who carries" a dirk or pistol and who uses them at "the slightest irritation."[30] Although Benton had used the term many times before against his political foes, it struck a resounding chord in the ear of Lucas.

It was unlikely, however, that the epithet "puppy," even though it was pejorative, could have alone provoked a challenge. Lucas no doubt seethed with anger, but he was not completely blinded by it. The demand for satisfaction and the political calculus behind it stemmed from other circumstances as well. It came at a time when Benton was growing increasingly powerful. Earlier in 1817 Charles Gratiot had died. His demise, as well as the advanced age of many of the other members of the established Creole families, indicated that the old order was beginning to lose its firm grip on the St. Louis community. Soon the Americans would replace the French as territorial leaders, and Thomas Hart Benton intended to be in the forefront of this political change. In addition, Benton's mentor and close friend, Edward Hempstead, had just died from a fall from his horse. Hempstead by most accounts was in line to become one of Missouri's first U.S. senators. His death now elevated Benton to even greater political prominence. Benton's supporters later maintained that the anti-junto faction had already decided by 1817 that he must go. Only the time and the perpetrator had yet to be determined. It was at this juncture that Charles Lucas was chosen "by lot" to carry out their designs.[31]

Lucas's challenge likewise came at a very propitious time, as Benton was psychologically and physically vulnerable. He had sat up all night with the Hempstead family and had just ridden five miles to his office to change clothes and to prepare for the funeral at the Stephen Hempstead farm when the challenge arrived. He coldly read Lucas's note and agreed to accept the duel as soon as he discharged his duties to the Hempsteads. "I will fight," he exclaimed, "tonight, if possible; if not, tomorrow morning at daybreak."[32] Colonel Luke E. Lawless, he said, would serve as his second and arrange the details. Distraught and weary, he undoubtedly believed the timing of the challenge was calculated to give his protagonist every conceivable edge in the encounter. This was an important point for Benton and one he would always remember. Lucas's unmanly behavior, designed to give him a deadly advantage, "outraged" Benton and made him all the more determined to silence Lucas once and for all. In his mind it was Lucas who had first violated the unwritten prescriptions of honor. Whatever breaches of the code duello that followed, and there were many, Benton was convinced, at least in his own mind, that they were justified by Lucas's insensitivities.

On the morning of August 12, 1817, the two protagonists met on the field for the first time. On first fire Benton suffered a slight wound below his right knee. Lucas was not so fortunate. Benton's ball struck him obliquely on the left side of his windpipe and come out about an inch and a quarter below the point of entry. The wound was very close to the jugular vein. Benton had nearly scored a fatal shot. Dr. Pryor Quarles, Lucas's surgeon, determined that he could not take another fire.[33]

Although firsthand reports varied, it appeared that Lucas agreed to shorten the distance and to risk a second shot. After being persuaded by Quarles that he was in no condition to continue, the young captain replied that his honor was satisfied and he did not require a second meeting. Throughout the affair, Benton remained cool and confident, but he did not want the "interview" to end without another fire or the promise of a second meeting. According to the rules of the duello this was "a gross violation" of the code, for as the challenged party he was to give rather than to receive satisfaction.[34] In the years to come, no action on Benton's part would haunt him more than this breach of etiquette. He reluctantly agreed to postpone any future interviews only when it became obvious that Lucas could not stand for another fire and when he received assurances from his seconds, Luke Lawless and Joshua Pilcher, that another meeting would be forthcoming. At this juncture Joshua Barton, his second, and Quarles supported Lucas to an awaiting boat, whereupon he fainted and remained unconscious as they rowed him to the shores of St. Louis.[35]

Only six weeks separated the passage of time from the first to the second duel. Youthfulness and good health had speeded Lucas's remarkable recovery from his throat wound, and he had once again resumed his normal business routine. He had barely escaped death; that realization tempered his impetuosity. He genuinely did not want to meet his adversary again on the island retreat. Benton, on the other hand, appeared more intemperate. His badge of honor, worn with courage and assertiveness, was still fragile. Granted, Lucas had sought and received the satisfaction due "one gentleman to another," but

Benton still seemed uncertain of his social status. Of the two it was he who most needed to prove himself to his community of peers. Throughout the episode the colonel failed to recognize the unwritten but cardinal rule of affairs of honor, namely, that a duel could not confer honor, it could only restore it. Benton at times seemed to be pursuing both paths. Only he, however, could have said with any certainty whether he plotted the chain of events leading to Lucas's death or merely responded in the only way he knew.

During these hectic weeks of tangled emotions and twisted rumors, the two men were drawn as pawns as well as players into a drama enveloping them both. Each political faction wanted to put the most favorable spin to the August affair on Bloody Island. The anti-junto group, and in particular Judge Lucas, maintained that young Lucas, "perfectly cool and collected" on the field, would have killed Benton except for weak powder that caused the ball to lose its strength. Others maintained that after the first fire Lucas had suggested shortening the distance between the two protagonists and that it was Benton who fearfully retreated. These kinds of statements did nothing to defuse the situation. In fact, by accentuating young Charles's manhood, the anti-junto faction, especially his father, actually jeopardized it.[36]

The St. Louis citizenry was grandly and vicariously entertained by the accusations and insults that flowed back and forth between the two warring camps. Judge Lucas correctly assessed that the incident had "lost its original feature" and "ceased to be an affair of honor." He did not, however, admit his own complicity in the matter. Charles also professed his innocence and maintained that the reports had been "fabricated" by Benton's friends and not "circulated by any who call themselves mine."[37]

Correspondence exchanged during the six-week interval revealed that Charles Lucas, more than his father, the seconds and surgeons, and especially Benton, desired a peaceful end to the vendetta. On at least three occasions he disavowed any imputation of cowardice on Benton's part. As late as September 18, even Lawless believed that "in pursuing Mr. Lucas further his [Benton's] conduct would assume an aspect of vengeance foreign from his heart, and that the sympathies and opinions of his fellow-citizens would possibly be raised against him."[38]

Benton, however, made a mockery of those protestations. No sooner had Lucas met one set of demands for both a satisfactory explanation of the affair and its aftermath than another demand would quickly follow. Finally, on September 23 Benton issued a challenge that called for pistols at a "murderous" distance of ten feet. Lucas received the note upon his arrival from New Madrid three days later. He apparently decided that further appeasement was useless and agreed to fight. Even then he adjured responsibility for any false representations but, in resignation, wrote, "I shall give you an opportunity of gratifying your wishes and the wishes of your news-carries."[39]

Historian Charles van Ravenswaay vividly described the last morning of Lucas's life:

> The fateful morning was hot and close. The leaves of the willows and cottonwoods were beginning to yellow and drop into the eddies that swirled around the island; the heavy, still air drew from the river a faint smell of rotting driftwood. Through the morning quiet came the incessant shrill of late-summer insects. Mosquitoes rose from the foliage.[40]

Spectators lined the St. Louis shore to get a last glimpse of the entourage. In all probability the irony of the situation was lost on both principals as they somberly made their way to the island. Just the year before, young Lucas had recklessly boasted of his manly prowess during the altercation with John Scott. Now he had been hoisted by his own petard. The year 1816 had also witnessed Benton carefully establishing his credentials as a gentleman. The rules and decorum of dueling that he had so studiously adhered to in the Hempstead-Barton affair had been conveniently discarded in the heat of his own personal battle.

This September morning turned out to be the antithesis of honor. In the first place, the seconds badly misplayed their parts. They neither dispelled the rumors and innuendos pertaining to the first duel nor explored all paths of reconciliation to avoid the second. Their inaction therefore contributed to what Lucas had derisively called "the great expectations which have been excited." Lawless, in particular, must bear an inordinate amount of the blame for his part in the tragedy since he, more than anyone else, had the ear of Benton. Together, they could have reasoned their way out of the impasse.

Another failure on the part of the seconds concerned the mere ten-foot distance at which the duelists could take dead aim at each other. By acquiescing to such a shortened field of fire, the seconds contributed to the likelihood that one or both men would die. For his part, Benton had forsaken the customs and rules of dueling by demanding a second duel. As the challenged party he was to give, not receive, satisfaction, but he refused to stand on this formality. As the principals approached each other on the island, the seconds made a last-minute search of each man to see if they carried any concealed objects that would deflect a ball. No single aspect of the duel demonstrated the bitterness between the two protagonists so much as this inspection. It impugned the integrity of both men and implied that neither was above cheating, cowardice, and dishonor. It was also a tacit admission that the decorum of this particular duel had degenerated into little more than a blood feud. Unlike the duel, the feud required no formal equality, ceremonial setting, or rules of fairness.[41]

The sweltering heat that morning added to the discomfort and anxiety of the moment. As the seconds made their final preparations, Benton took off

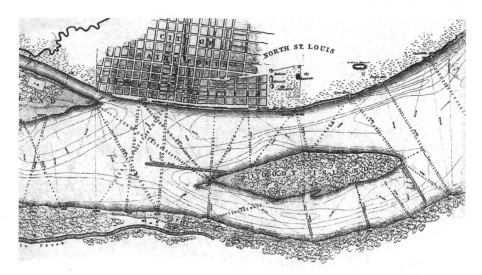

Bloody Island, just offshore from St. Louis in the Mississippi River, was the scene of many dueling tragedies. Courtesy State Historical Society of Missouri.

his coat and rolled up his sleeves. His flannel underwear, a bright red, was so visible that it "glowed like a signal across the water."[42] The dress of a duelist was emblematic of his class. It was part of the ritual and punctilio of the event, an external manifestation of class identity. By any gentleman's standard of good taste, Benton's red underwear was indecorous.

The most serious breach of etiquette concerned the count. Colonel Eli Clemson, one of Lucas's seconds, was selected to do the honors. He was to call, "fire-one, two, three." Neither principal could shoot before the count of one or after the count of three. Perhaps unnerved by the circumstances, he forgot to say "fire." Instead he began the call with "one, two, three." In this moment of hesitation, which must have seemed like an eternity to both principals and seconds, everyone nervously fingered their weapons. Then simultaneously the principals fired.[43] In a split second it was over and Benton stood silent, staring down at his ghastly handiwork. The bullet had entered Lucas's side just as he raised his pistol to shoot. The arm's outstretched position exposed his vital organs. The impact of the bullet at such a close range also misdirected Lucas's fire, and Benton came away unscathed. For the fallen young man, the end was mercifully quick. Later in life Benton wrote of the "pang which went through his heart when he saw the young man fall, and would have given the world to see him restored to life."[44] Stretching his hand out, he asked for Lucas's forgiveness, but at first his dying protagonist refused. "Colonel Benton," he decried, "you have persecuted me and murdered me. I cannot forgive you." Realizing, however, that he was soon to join the ages, Lucas recanted. "I can forgive you—I do forgive you." He reached his hand out to Benton and shortly expired.

Charles Lucas's promising career in politics was cut short by his tragic death in a duel with Thomas Hart Benton in 1817. Courtesy Missouri Historical Society.

As Lucas's body was taken back to St. Louis, Benton pondered the triumph and tragedy he had wrought. He had gained that equality of honor which for so long had eluded him. His personal attributes of courage and skill had prevailed. In the drama of honor earned, honor deferred, the Lucas sense of honor based upon European patriarchy had fallen victim to the raw ambitions of American individualism. The Lucas name had been held in high social recognition as a virtual right or due accorded men of such personage. This submission to ancestry Benton could not accept. For Thomas, honor had to be won by its own merit. For Charles, honor was woven within the collective fabric of his lineage.

But as much as Charles sought and expected deference, he also bowed to it. His father, the judge and family patriarch, had instilled in him not only ambition and strength of character, but the fatal need to please his elders and to defer to their judgment. That September morning young Lucas had fought history, culture, and tradition as much as Benton's wrath. While Benton sought to avenge and subconsciously to gain honor, Lucas had sought to uphold it. By upholding honor, Lucas bore the weight of family tradition. By avenging honor, Benton based his actions upon a personal sense of justice. But the quest for power, ingrained in the Lucas mentality for generations, had not taken leave on the Missouri frontier. Honor that had been bestowed upon the family by reputation and birthright in Europe could still be enhanced on the battlefields of American individualism. The old territorial order was indeed giving way to a new generation of political leadership. A Lucas victory in the duel with Benton might well have ensured the family's political favor with this ever-expanding populace. Democracy, a powerful antidote to the Lucas sense of honor, might still have been put to good advantage and republicanism could yet have bestowed upon noble lineage that which the rugged frontier environment might try to steal away. Whatever the expectations, they were not to be.

In the aftermath of the duel each side quickly affixed blame for the tragedy on the other. Judge Lucas, as expected, led the chorus of complaints against Benton. For its part the junto shifted the culpability for the duel from Charles to his father. A rumor circulated that it was Judge Lucas who forced the issue of a second meeting. Supposedly the judge was in a "rage" when he heard of the efforts at reconciliation. Amadee Soulard was the source of a quote that attributed to the elder Lucas the following remark: "You must fight him again." The judge further exclaimed that "the Lucas honor requires it!" Charles, according to this scenario, acquiesced. "Well, then, my dear father . . . well, then, I will be guided by you once more. If the Lucas honor, whatever it is, requires it, I will fight him again!" The Soulards, it must be noted, had a long-running feud with Judge Lucas dating back to his criticisms of Antoine Soulard, the surveyor-general who worked closely with junto associate General James Wilkinson. Their accusations were never corroborated and even Benton's biographer, William Chambers, wrote ambivalently about Judge Lucas's true deportment. On the other hand, few Benton biographers have exculpated his behavior in the death of Lucas, and even fewer of the colonel's detractors have seen redeeming qualities in his character. The duel, for Benton critics, turned out to be little more than a Manichean contest unfairly waged between villain and victim. J. Thomas Scharf believed Benton possessed "a bloodthirsty spirit." The second meeting in particular, he maintained, "was forced in spite of reason and humanity."[45]

For a short time, Lucas's death set back Benton's political ambitions. In January 1819, Joseph Charless felt confident enough to write what he thought was Benton's political obituary. In the last election of the town corporation, he boasted, Benton had received only thirty-four votes for the board of trustees. "Humane and peaceful farmers" would not, he added, vote for "professional duelists."[46] Charless's predictions, however, proved ill-founded. Popular "expectations" no doubt had played a prominent role in the duel, but this particular contest had always been more than an affair to curry favor with the populace or to build a political base. Rather, it was part of a struggle between two social orders, the old and the new.

Ironically, Benton, despite his alliance with the old Creole faction, emerged as the representative of a new social system based upon individualism, mobility, and opportunism. It was made up of new American immigrants seeking fame and fortune and whose impatience with the static, hierarchial order of old Missouri would soon become apparent. Equally ironic was the fact that

Lucas championed the interests of those in the anti-junto faction, who had arrived in the territory at a later date and could not countenance the Creole elite. Yet personally he symbolized what the old order stood for—ascription based upon family history and antecedence. This system was rooted in established customs and deference to class and rank determined by birth and social position. This pattern had functioned rather smoothly during French and Spanish rule, but with the transfer of power to the United States, another social perspective emerged to challenge the established order. The paradox, of course, was that Lucas opposed the very faction with which he most closely identified, and Benton worked for the same faction that he ultimately helped to undermine. Incongruous as it may seem, Lucas's death was symbolic of the nascent fall of the old order.

In 1817, however, matters seemed much less complex. Each group believed that the apex of power was so limited that only one faction could rule, and each equally resolved that they and they alone possessed the qualities of leadership. Both sides believed political concessions would inevitably lead to accusations of weakness, and weakness lurked close to the shoals of dishonor. Compromise and conciliation would be construed as deference to a social arrangement that would be tantamount to recognizing the inferiority of one's own group. Since very little room for political advancement existed, both sides used honor as a means of empowerment. Yet honor was only as abiding as its imputation by others. Thus, it must be defended by violence if necessary.

The altercation on Bloody Island must be seen against this backdrop. Any word or insinuation was perceived exactly as it was intended, as a means of limiting the advancement of a political foe by first dishonoring him. When Lucas accused Benton of voting without the proper qualifications, it was a calculated insult. The "jury" in this case, or as it was most conveniently called, "the court of public opinion," was a misnomer. Captivating the political imagination of the populace was as much the effect as the cause of this deadly encounter. The real jury was a social perception rooted in the personalities of a small coterie of men who defined exemplary conduct by courage and who used violence or the threat of violence to achieve power. The logic of the duel had come full circle. The cult of honor required an act of courage to vindicate honor; the action in turn solidified or conferred social status and reputation, which in turn became the conduit for even greater reward.

The career of Thomas Hart Benton exemplified this twisted logic. Benton was no moralist. He was, however, a conformist and a risk-taker. Risking death was a calculated gamble commensurate with the potential rewards, but it was also an admission that he deferred to a set of community sanctions which he was unable to recognize or unwilling to change. Benton's subsequent career was likewise characterized by opportunism and adjustment.[47] His remorse at the sight of the dying Lucas dampened his martial spirit but

Judge J. B. C. Lucas never forgave Benton for the murder of his son Charles and reportedly challenged the senator on a number of occasions. Courtesy State Historical Society of Missouri.

did not quell it. Throughout his public life, Benton held to his beliefs and was close to the center of many duels and bloody altercations. What changed was not so much Benton as the times. Yet he was perspicacious enough to recognize that the early consensus as to proper forms of institutionalized violence was changing, and that Missouri's evolution from a frontier community to a complex society required a different kind of bravado. Consequently, his intrigues were more of the cloakroom variety, but his advice to younger protagonists remained steadfastly that of the unrepentant duelist.[48]

Since St. Louis at the time of the duel was becoming the cultural and social center of the territory, fame won in the gateway city reverberated throughout the frontier lands. Benton's name, either cursed or praised, was on the lips of most inhabitants. Increasingly, he refrained from using the first-person pronoun and referred to himself in the third person. In his autobiography he claimed to have burned all of his personal papers concerning the duel so "that no future curiosity or industry should bring to light what he wishes had never happened."[49] The royal usage befitted one of such increased stature.

Remorse at the sight of his dying protagonist may have had something to do with Benton's refusal to duel again. But the overriding justification for his disinclination was the fact that he acquired reputation sufficient enough to turn the scales on his future opponents. Just as the Polynesian victor acquires the honor of his slaughtered enemy by taking his name, so too did Benton's momentous duels place him above the reproach of his detractors. Calumnies directed at the "gentleman" from Tennessee would only rebound to the discredit of the offender. As for Benton, he would gain in stature by stoically bearing the insults and rising above the level of his enemies. In this sense, he mirrored another Jackson protégé, Sam Houston, who, after having shot General William White in a duel that gave Houston added political stature in Tennessee, said that "he never fought down-hill." Once challenged after the battle of San Jacinto, Houston contemptuously filed the challenge as #14. "The angry gentleman," he mocked, "must wait his turn."[50]

Symbolically, honor deferred to Lucas, Benton now shared. Refusing to fight "down-hill" pragmatically shielded him from future duels and possible death, but increasingly it became a gesture of magnanimity toward his political foes. The champion retained his crown; the challenger kept his life. Thus when posted in a *Missouri Gazette Extra* by Richard Venables as a bully and coward, Benton remained calm and self-assured. Congressman Edward Bates in 1828 also tried to goad the senator into action. Bates mocked the "errors" of Chapel Hill, but once again Benton felt his honor and reputation were above reproach. His response to these philippics was in stark contrast to his earlier outbursts against Charles Lucas, a man who publicly vilified him far less than Venables or Bates. He also "paid no attention" to a dueling challenge in 1835 by former associate and political ally George F. Strother. Nor would Benton ever rise to the bait of Judge Lucas. The death of Charles, "the ornament of his father's family," left the elder Lucas obsessed with hatred and revenge. In 1820 he unsuccessfully ran for the U.S. Senate mainly to oppose Benton. On a number of occasions he taunted Benton and even once challenged him to a duel, but Benton would have nothing of it. Perhaps he was content that the old Roman curse, "May you bury your sons," had wrought enough suffering on the old man, as by 1837 he had lost sons Robert, Charles, Adrian, and William.[51] Perhaps too, Old Bullion realized the slow but inexorable drift from the code of honor to the code of law. Charles Lucas probably would have approved of these new changes in social conduct, but we shall never know. Today the two protagonists, Benton and Charles Lucas, lie in St. Louis graveyards, nearly within ear range of their flintlock pistols, their tombstones silent reminders of those turbulent years when honor and hubris cast their deadly shadows across the Missouri Territory.

5

The Press, Bar, and Pulpit

Institutional Opposition to the Code

A S DUELING GAINED a foothold on the Missouri frontier, forces emerged to oppose it. But the code oftentimes appeared more ingrained and resilient than the institutions favored by its opponents. The vices and "nakedness of the land," according to Reverend Samuel J. Mills, could only be extirpated by judges, editors, and clergymen who sought to instill some godliness among the "thousand ready to perish, their eyelids fast closed in spiritual slumber."[1] The Reverend Timothy Flint, an early Protestant missionary in the Missouri Territory, agreed. He noted in the *Western Monthly Review* that frontier institutions were likely to be as new and rugged as were the new homes and log cabins of the settlers themselves. Since educational institutions were primitive and family life often condoned violence, Missouri's transformation of character could best be accomplished, according to Flint, by the bar, pulpit, and press.[2]

The outlines of institutional opposition to this culture of violence became visible in 1808 with the appearance of the Fourth Estate. That year, the first crude hand-operated printing press crossed the Appalachians, floated down the Ohio River, and entered the wilds of Missouri. This object, mightier than any cannon or cavalry charge, was borne by the newspaperman and printer Joseph Charless. Within a dozen years of his arrival in St. Louis, he had duly earned the title "Father of Missouri Journalism."

Charless immediately went on the attack against dueling. His antipathy was part philosophical and part practical. First, he wanted to dispel many of the myths and misconceptions that might inhibit the less venturesome from migrating west.[3] A land of duels and gunfights was not the image of Missouri that Charless wanted to project. He also had a grander purpose. Since institutions designed to contain the reckless pioneer spirit such as law, education, and religion were generally fragile, Charless intended nothing less than the elevation of moral purpose on the frontier through the good offices of the press. According to historian Perry McCandless, frontier editors such as Charless "generally conceived of their function in the broadest possible terms."[4] Toward this end Charless used the fledgling power of the press to attack a number of social ills. Through print and type, he labored for rules of conduct and behavior that would attract a better clientele of emigrants to this western gateway.

Southern traditions, Charless realized, were deeply rooted in the Missouri psyche, and social and political reform, no matter which direction it took, was difficult to effect. Nevertheless, he stood his ground. Initially, his Jeffersonian principles pitted him against the powerful political faction represented by the St. Louis Creoles, the territorial governor, James Wilkinson, and the large Spanish land grant claimants. These groups he collectively labeled the "junto."[5]

The Benton-Lucas duels, more than any other violent rencounters, incited Charless into furious opposition, against not only the practice of dueling but also the perpetrator and victor of the final duel, Thomas Hart Benton. Throughout his tenure at the newspaper, he took every opportunity to portray the future senator as a man "crimsoned with the blood" of a young man "whose character and reputation" were spotless.[6] Although Charless frequently vilified Benton, his moral and philosophical opposition to dueling often led to inconsistency. While denouncing those members of the junto who burned powder, he remained more muted when someone of his own faction issued a challenge or brandished the rhetoric of heroic honor. His condemnation of the practice also had one unfortunate side effect for the historian. Convinced as he was that part of the fascination with the lethal practice stemmed from publicizing the events, he many times ignored them. On January 2, 1811, for example, Charless explained to an audience that it was "not a want of respect" that induced him to withhold information about this "barbarous custom," but in a civilized society, he added, dueling "should never be noticed by the journalist, but with the language of Cervantes, the inimitable author of *Don Quixote*."[7]

The notoriety thus gained by a duel, he believed, only emboldened others to seek the same type of social recognition. Weighing the public's right to know the facts versus the harm generated by documenting the events, the editor generally considered the latter course of action to be the most prudent choice.[8] Consequently, Charless purposely omitted a number of meetings on the field of honor, especially when they occurred between less prominent inhabitants of the community. Since journalism provided the first rough draft of history, these omissions unfortunately handicapped future generations of scholars.

On the other hand, frontier editors such as Charless did not shy away from controversy. They encouraged a vigorous dialogue on a variety of socioeconomic and political subjects. The unintended consequence of these lively debates, however, was the exacerbation of factional tensions with the resultant proliferation of violence. In their haste to reform, the newspapers many times blurred the distinctions between their own beliefs (what the press and its guest editorial writers accepted as fact) and public opinion (what the public thought to be the correct position on a controversial opinion). This ambiguity unwittingly contributed to some duels. When the philippics became too personal and infringed on the sensibilities of honor, the insulted individual often made a none-too-discrete inquiry to the editor as to the identity of the offending party. Charless and others, albeit reluctantly, usually obliged.

Charless's demand that anyone editorializing in the *Gazette* must be willing to identify himself may have been a sound publishing policy. For one thing, it curtailed some of the more reckless character assassination prevalent in frontier presses. For another, the policy ostensibly kept the editor somewhat above the fray. By having the name of the editorial guest at his disposal, Charless could always prove that he was not disguising his own penmanship under a pseudonym.

On the other hand, he knew that in such a highly charged atmosphere it would be difficult at best to protect the identity of anyone who antagonized a powerful member of either faction. This in turn, he must have realized, could likely produce bloodshed. Nevertheless, on August 17, 1816, he reiterated his position. "No man shall investigate the characters of claimants or office," he exclaimed in the *Gazette*, "and who use personalities effecting characters without leaving their names with me to be given up." Six months later Charless again expounded upon his duty as an editor by stating he would not "derogate from an established rule," that the real name of an author must be left with the editor. Divulging the name of the offending party in turn spawned many a challenge and sometimes a hostile rencounter. This was almost certainly the case in 1818 when Luke Lawless demanded of Charless the authorship of a derogatory article about him. When informed of the identity of the perpetrator, in this case, Judge John B. C. Lucas, Lawless replied that the judge's "age and station" prevented the issuance of a challenge.[9]

Another newspaper practice, which violated the spirit if not the letter of the anti-dueling campaign, pertained to the publishing of handbills detrimental to the character of a leading citizen. Under the nomenclature of the day, this practice was called posting. These denouncements publicly identified an individual by name and labeled him a "coward," "scoundrel," "poltroon," or some other equally offensive epithet. Posting was an original contribution by the United States to the institutionalization of dueling. The printing of these handbills was also remunerative. Even though managers and editors of the Fourth Estate realized full well that these postings were de-liberatively provocative, they continued to reap the financial reward under the aegis of a free press. Next to horsewhipping and cowhiding, postings were the most inflammatory practice that led to duels, and the press must share part of the blame for the ensuing violence.[10]

During his first years in Missouri, Charless had no immediate editorial rival. Even though he had no monopoly on virtue, he did have, for a while at least, a monopoly on print. This caused him to endure many physical indig-nities. He was assaulted, spat upon, shot at, and had his office burned nearly to the ground. On May 10, 1820, for example, Isaac Henry, an editor of the rival *Inquirer,* attacked him on the streets of St. Louis and cudgeled him badly. The beating was apparently due to Charless's defense of a number of Protestant ministers such as Joseph Piggot, the Reverends Walsh and Wright, and John M. Peck for some of their less than popular stands on social issues of the day.[11]

Personal danger should have been part of the job description of pioneer newspapermen. Publisher Duff Green, for example, was attacked on a series of occasions in the early 1820s by Andrew McGirk. These brawls led, accord-ing to historian Frances Lea McCurdy, to several duels. Half a decade later, an editorial in the *Missouri Intelligencer* entitled "Difficulties of Editors" summa-rized the precarious state of survival for frontier editors with the following quote: "Like Joab, they enquire, 'art thou in health, my brother,' while a deadly dagger is concealed beneath the cloak!" Undoubtedly, the personal health and well-being of St. Louis editors during these years of bitter factional strife was far from idyllic, but it was probably less dangerous than described by Judge John B. C. Lucas, a Charless ally. We have "never," he lamented, "enjoyed peace here. . . . Editors and other writers on public subject were awed into silence, and the press was muzzled by terror."[12] Like the proverbial Job, Charless and other frontier newspapermen were plagued by a sea of troubles that would have capsized many of a lesser spirit.

Some editors, such as Stephen Remington of the *Jackson Independent Patriot,* employed poetry and verse to vilify dueling. Nathaniel Patten, Jr., owner of the *Missouri Intelligencer and Boons Lick Advertiser,* linked dueling to aristocracy and believed democratic leveling was the best way to extirpate the practice. The *St. Charles Missourian* echoed Patten's views. The *Hannibal Gazette* portrayed duelists as guilt-ridden and likely to take their own lives.[13]

On the other hand, some papers became almost defensive about dueling. The *Missouri Republican,* for example, admitted that some duels had taken place on Bloody Island, but a few duels, even on as infamous a spot, did not indicate that Missourians were criminal or unruly. In an article entitled "Health of St. Louis," the paper stated that rumors about the scores of men killed in duels were false. These same men, it chided, were walking the streets of the city, and no one suspected them of being "ghosts" or "goblins." Other papers attacked the code by appealing to religion. Presses sometimes ran summations of sermons and exalted their readers to follow a more forthright path of brotherly love.[14]

Perhaps the most effective literary weapon employed against southern culture was sarcasm and humor. Charless, for example, had used ridicule as a literary device against dueling almost from the start. In 1810, his paper ran a very lengthy poem entitled "The Duelists" in which a frog and a mouse "in our western nation" went to the field of honor over a "lie direct." The poem reprinted in its entirety was forty-eight lines long and had to be one of the most hilarious and farcical tales in the history of the Missouri duel. On August 17, 1816, the *Gazette* ran an article published appropriately enough under the pen name "Peter Plughim." Peter gave notice to the "Don Quixote's" and their "Squires" who were "burning with martial fire and eager for mortal combat" that he had an Illinois field just suited for their purpose. In fact, he advertised, the grounds had just been "honored" a few days before by two "black gentlemen" who would have made "all knights of the pistol" quite proud.[15]

No paper, however, rivaled the *Missouri Intelligencer* for satirical humor. In 1820 an article appeared under the pseudonym "Plough Boy." The fictitious name was itself a mockery of the aristocratic notions of dueling, since no gentleman of the pistol or broadside would stoop to plowing a field or to allowing anyone to call him "boy." In January 1823 the same paper printed the most trenchant and sarcastic assault against the sport of gentlemen during the entire antebellum period. Masquerading as the "Steletto Pistoleer," this western democrat sullied the aristocratic pretenses of southern gentlemen. Obliquely, his attack against dueling became a call for more popular representation in government as well as greater leveling among the ranks of frontier society.[16]

In the southern part of the state the *Jackson Independent Patriot* also took up the reform spirit. It cited a poem by Dean Swift about a duelist named Thomas who "thrice ventur'd his life" only to return home to be "thresh'd by his wife." The *Salt River Journal* in the northern section of the state ran an 1837 article, no doubt penned by the editor, entitled "Advertisement." The author, "Cornelius O'Trigger," informed the "gentlemen" of the area that he would fight duels in either town or country. Humor, it appeared, had spread across the state. While the first generation of frontier editors mocked dueling and stayed clear of the fields of honor, the second and third generations had no such scruples. In the 1840s the publisher of the *St. Louis Argus*, Andrew J. Davis, was beaten to death by William Darnes. This incident spawned another duel by men closely attached to the Fourth Estate.[17]

By the 1850s, the fierce electoral partisanship in the press reflected the growing moral and philosophical divisions over slavery. In that decade alone, daily newspapers in circulation climbed from five to sixteen and reflected the widening divisions in the state over slavery. Overall, there were fifty-four Missouri newspapers in circulation including foreign language, religious, commercial, and other publications. These figures ranked the state fifth in the nation in terms of total number of newspapers. By 1860 the number of papers had nearly tripled. The bitter debates over sectionalism and slavery greatly contributed to this proliferation. Newspapers and their editors became more committed than ever to political parties and ideologies. Frank Blair, Jr., B. Gratz Brown, and Thomas Reynolds all reflected this new sense of militancy. It was a time that has been dubbed the awakening of Missouri journalism.[18]

With both a sense of history and a flare for histrionics, members of the Fourth Estate abandoned their earlier objections to dueling and ventured to the field of honor. Furthermore, they made little distinction between physical attacks, which necessitated a defense of one's person or property, and verbal and literary attacks, which impugned one's character. Rather than extirpating the roots of violence from the Missouri psyche, the press, sadly enough, had by the 1840s contributed to the prevailing attitude that they, like other elitist segments of society, were above the written law. Joseph Charless, among others, would not have been proud.

The *Gazette's* crusade against violence elicited little support from the legal profession. The shadow of this institution stretched far back into pathways of English law and was particularly cast in the likeness of William Blackstone, the most renowned jurist and legal scholar in English history. By 1771, more than twenty-five hundred copies of his *Commentaries on the Laws of England* circulated throughout the American colonies. No doubt every pioneer judge and lawyer on the Missouri frontier possessed or hoped soon to possess Blackstone's volumes on jurisprudence. For Missouri lawyers, especially those of a southern persuasion, the infatuation with Blackstone was understandable since his legal philosophy reinforced "a rural, hierarchical society that paid respect to communal feelings." One of the most important elements of law as interpreted by Blackstone was its power to sustain local autonomy. Since honor played an essential role in determining community respect, Blackstone's work was interpreted so loosely as to justify a variety of actions, both illegal and extralegal, which were sanctioned by the local community. Dueling certainly fit into this tradition in early Missouri. "A new country," wrote historian Philip Jordan, "bleeding from the cutting edge of the frontier, was a grim place and a hard one for the symbolic lady who held aloft the scales of justice." W. C. C. Claiborne perhaps expressed it best. Upon taking control of the Louisiana Territory for President Jefferson, he wrote James Madison that "the state in which I found the jurisprudence of the country embarrasses me extremely."[19]

Numerous factors lay behind the inability of early-nineteenth-century legal institutions to curtail violence in general and dueling in particular. Missouri was in many respects a microcosm of this jurisprudence of lawlessness. Some of the more important reasons for this sorry state of affairs were an absence of law for many offenses, a distrust of the judiciary, the slowness of legal procedures, unfamiliarity of American lawyers with Spanish and French laws, a lack of written statutes and legal references, and a wave of violence due to the confusion over land titles and mineral rights. These factors, along with others such as irregular court sessions, unskilled and corrupt officials, and a public tolerance of disorder, allowed men on the frontier generally to decide for themselves which laws would be enforced and which would not. Order, one western historian has suggested, generally came before law on the frontier.[20]

Early pioneers interpreted crime and various forms of physical redress not so much as violations of established law but as personal insults to the victim. These wrongs were generally to be righted by another violent rencounter such as a duel in order to achieve satisfaction. As David Brion Davis has suggested, the ideals of individualism led men, including those in the legal profession, to believe that they "possessed the powers of lawgiver, judge, and executioner." Judges and lawyers in particular were apt to interpret their power and responsibilities in a manner bespeaking ruling classes throughout various times in western culture when other forms of structure or order were lacking. Although they helped make and interpret the laws, these Missouri mandarins also believed that at times they were above them. Contemptuous of the masses, the men of the bar echoed the voice of democracy, but in reality they had very little respect for the will of the people.[21]

Another factor in the early nineteenth century contributed to the independence of legal practitioners. Missourians were deeply suspicious of their political leaders. This was a tradition solidly rooted in American culture. But law, with its theoretical underpinnings of equality and justice, had no such ideological stigmata. Justice was supposedly blind. Law, unlike politics, was not a feckless institution. While citizens of the Republic might be rightly skeptical of government, they still placed their faith in the equality of law. Historically, this fact may offer some explanation as to why the American legal system moved toward more independence from the other branches of government. The absence of both an active executive and legislative body in territorial Missouri likewise reinforced this sense of autonomy among the legal profession. Yet the formal education of judges and lawyers could best be described as shallow. They were usually tutored in the rudiments of jurisprudence by members of their own political faction or class. Cultural perspectives, suffice it to say, tended to be rather narrow. This provincialism served the cause of patrimony. In brief, the bar was a highly politicized institution where neither abstract moral nor philosophical vision prevailed over the temptations of personal gain and violence.[22]

Justice during these early years was also swift, harsh, and highly personal. The vast geography also helped produce a decentralization of the law. In 1807, for example, when Antoine Bissonnette fled from the mouth of the Osage River with goods stolen from Manuel Lisa, Lisa issued an order to bring him back "dead or alive." Within an hour Bissonnette was brought back, dead, by Lisa's employee George Druillard. A St. Louis district court jury took only fifteen minutes to render a not guilty verdict against Druillard and to exonerate the killing as "justified by the laws of God and man." The Bissonette case illustrated how lawlessness, especially during the territorial period, was contained in ways not intended "to increase respect for or fear of legislative enactments."[23]

Another manifestation of the highly personal and extralegal nature of early law enforcement pertained to the regulator movement. These unofficial gendarmes of law and order were generally men of the middle and professional classes who took it upon themselves to enforce the laws of the territory. It was their perception that law enforcement practices were too weak or too slow to contain the growing criminal element in Missouri society. Although the exact number of regulators was never determined, the evidence at the time suggested that some of them were lawyers and even members of the territorial legislature. The connection between taking the law into one's own hands, like the regulators, and upholding one's own honor, like the duelist, was made by at least one critic. An article appeared in the *Missouri Gazette* in 1816 signed by "A Friend of Liberty." The comparisons between a duelist and a regulator, he wrote, were accurate, since "Gentlemen who duel also argue that laws and authority cannot replace" what they termed honor. "They demand the right," he continued, "to answer a rude remark with an ounce of lead, instead of with laws." The fact that the territorial legislature punished neither regulator nor duelist, the critic further contended, revealed how little trust existed in law enforcement as well as in the American system of justice.[24]

As for the purveyors of justice, no single group in Missouri history journeyed to the field of honor with more frequency than lawyers. "By adopting the dueling code and adding *esquire* to his name," wrote Frances McCurdy, "the lawyer assumed status as a gentleman." More than any other profession, attorneys constituted the "ruling class." Since pioneer lawyers figured so prominently in most fields of endeavor including politics, business, education, military affairs, community leadership, agriculture, and social and religious life, they "exercised an influence in all fields out of proportion to their numbers."[25]

Ironically, lawyers more than any other group of professionals should have had a vested interest in litigation rather than violence. Nonetheless, as historian William F. English has pointed out, many western lawyers came from modest family backgrounds. This made them all the more sensitive to slights and insults that threatened their none-too-secure social standing in the community. "Participation in duels," wrote English, "and great scruple over their honor also registered their membership in the elite." It should also be noted that slander and libel laws were very vague and difficult to enforce. Libel cases usually required a trial by jury, which further complicated the adjudication process. In general, juries reflected public opinion and sided with the advocates of freedom over those of restraint. Slander and libel were both difficult to prove in a court of law. Even in cases where the plaintiff won, it was usually "too late" to change the public conception. Such was the case of George Shannon, a prominent political figure in southeast Missouri. In the early years of the nineteenth century, this man of self-proclaimed "spirit" wrote to the civil and military commandant of Cape Girardeau demanding that the law against "scornful and abusefull language" be put into force against a certain Robert Patterson. Shannon further wrote that he complained to Patterson but had received no satisfaction. It was especially "hard," he confessed, "for a man of spirit to be abused and get no satisfaction." For many such men of "spirit," the code became this extralegal means of redress.[26]

The militant defense of honor on the frontier departed radically from Blackstone's English common law dictum that a person threatened by an attack had the legal duty to retreat. Under the English statutes, only when every avenue of evasion was closed could a man who was physically threatened forcibly defend himself. The English law required the person assailed and in fear of death or bodily harm to retreat "to the wall" at one's back before killing in self-defense. Holmes, having perhaps less respect for precedent than many American judges, sarcastically wrote: "It is revolting to have no better reason for a rule of law than that so it was laid down in the time of Henry IV." Americans, however, long before Holmes's de jure pronouncement had in fact renounced the common law requirement of retreat. "Cowardice," wrote Richard Maxwell Brown, "was simply un-American." Standing one's ground became an accepted doctrine of U.S. courts in the West and the South, and, according to Brown, it was "enshrined" in the "ethics of the duelist." Duelists would obviously take good advantage of popular law. Furthermore, the principle of standing one's ground, combined with the proliferation of guns, spawned a quantum leap in deadly violence.[27]

Passion, revenge, and honor, as well as a very loose interpretation of self-defense, were usually sufficient justifications for a murder acquittal. This permissiveness helps to explain why more than four years of American rule elapsed before the first execution in the Territory of Louisiana took place on September 16, 1808. In this particular case a jury sentenced a young man to hang for the premeditated murder of his stepfather since there appeared to be no grounds for self-defense. Although no Missouri duelist ever faced a similar charge of first-degree murder, it would appear likely that the defense, using the self-defense argument, would have found a sympathetic jury. Conceptualizing any act of violence as a criminal infraction was obviously a relative rather than an absolute phenomenon.[28]

In most murder cases the assailant did not have to prove that he had tried to avert a hostile encounter. In fact, society tacitly accepted extralegal forms of violence as repayment for a variety of offenses, including rape, adultery, seduction, assault, the "lie direct," and opprobrious epithets. The right to defend one's person, honor, family name, or property usually had more sanction, even in the courtroom, than statute law. In brief, juries recognized certain rights forbidden by law, including the acquittal of the survivor of a duel, and denied other rights actually granted by law such as a fair and impartial jury, a speedy trial, and a competent court. It was not until the early 1850s that the state passed a uniform jury law which provided pay for jurors and their selection by commissioners appointed by the court in lieu of the local sheriff.[29]

The jury system also legitimized murder by giving an aura of legality and vindication to the accused. Law in essence sanctified murder. Since the culture of violence was so pervasive, each juror had no problem extrapolating a situation whereby he might well be on the other side of the courtroom. Many times jurors were selected who already had stood accused of the same crime. Nineteenth-century legal theory held that citizens (and therefore quite properly juries) should have a "sense of injustice" which would make "crime proportionate to guilt." In other words, jurists should be able to measure criminal guilt by the same common legal and ethical standards that had kept them from committing the same type of infraction. Frontier juries, however, possessed no such conscientious detachment.[30]

Other detriments to early courtroom justice were trial delays, jury intimidation, hung juries, and the fact that the charge of manslaughter had yet to be systematically employed. Another tactic used by Missouri defense attorneys was to find an all-southern jury. Whoever believed that the pen was mightier than the sword had not crossed paths with Palemon H. Winchester. In 1825, this young attorney from Tennessee was indicted for murder. He was accused of stabbing Daniel H. Smith, a northerner who was recognized as a fine artist and a great caricaturist, and who had drawn Winchester in a rather humorous and satirical fashion. Winchester's attorneys, Felix Grundy and Henry Staff, could hardly use the plea of self-defense since Smith was armed with only pen and paper at the scene of his murder. Consequently, they methodically rejected every prospective juror not from Tennessee. Throughout the three-day trial they frequently alluded to "cold-blooded Yankees" and "unfeeling, hard-hearted Yankees" who could conceive of no higher motive than money and had not the slightest regard for another man's reputation.

Disparaging glances were often cast in the direction of the assistant prosecuting attorney, who also happened to be from the North. As one might suspect, Winchester left the courtroom a free man. "The problems," wrote Professor English, "of administering justice and practicing law in a territory wherein the law was based on customs, and on poorly defined code was mostly difficult." The competency of judges was also a concern. In 1815 a group of St. Louis lawyers, for example, requested a circuit court system be established so that cases could be tried before men with legal erudition.[31]

In early Missouri courtrooms almost everyone, from the judges and lawyers to the defendants and plaintiffs, came armed with pistols and dirks. Many of these weapons were, according to the custom of the day, concealed.[32] Although the practice may have been prudent, it lent credence to the charge that justice took a back seat to violence. The constitutional right to bear arms, both concealed and open, became a hallowed tradition in the courtrooms of the Missouri frontier. In the hands of frontier elites, the Second Amendment became a license for mayhem. Candor forces one to the sad conclusion that the Missouri bar reflected the social attitudes of the times far more than it tried to change them. By their behavior or lack thereof, lawyers and judges often conditioned the public to the general level of violence. In all fairness, it should be noted that the courtroom was not always the safest of environments. William English, for example, noted that duelists "were often litigants and looked sharply for an opportunity to challenge an opposing lawyer or even one of the judges."

The penchant for arms, especially pistols; the publicity of duels; the respect given to duelists; and the impunity of law to deter dueling violations all nurtured the roots of violence. Former Missourian Peter Burnett, more than most of his early-nineteenth-century contemporaries, saw the connection between pistols, duels, and aggression. The more one carried and practiced with weapons, he argued, the more likely one would be to want to try his dueling skills. Otherwise, that skill was idle and useless. In this respect, Burnett argued, the duel did not act as a check on slander or as a civilizing agent. Rather, the effect of weapons was actually to instigate rudeness and to invite insult. In "proud men," he believed, there was "a sort of glory in defying consequences." Henry Brackenridge, who practiced law in the Missouri Territory, also left the region while still in good health. In a work entitled *Views of Louisiana*, he cited the practice of dueling and the need to be armed at all times as two of the principal reasons for leaving the Missouri bar.[33]

Brackenridge's move might have been prudent. The passage of laws prohibiting dueling were not only perfunctory in nature but also may well have been right for the wrong reasons. The institutionalization of dueling in the minds of many western elites was a sign that civilization was replacing barbarity on the frontier. The passage of the first bills to suppress the practice in

1814 and 1822 therefore indicated the territory's maturization. A sizable minority of the lawmakers never intended for the new laws to be enforced.[34] They were window dressing, intending to showcase the fact that a frontier class structure had replaced wilderness egalitarianism. After all, southern civility hypocritically required both laws against dueling and precedents for not punishing the lawbreakers. The same held true for Missouri's 1835 anti-dueling law. It was perhaps in this spirit that some members of the state's 1863 Constitutional Convention again provided for the disqualification from public office of anyone who served as a principal or a second in a duel. Even as late as 1907 most states called for the disqualification for political office of anyone participating in a duel. It was not until the 1943 Constitutional Convention that the anti-dueling edict was considered unnecessary and obsolete. With the ratification of the 1945 Constitution, dueling passed into legal memory.

The bench and bar, much like the Missouri press, had been relatively ineffective against the code. One other institution, however, appeared better suited to uproot institutionalized violence on the frontier. That institution was religion. Yet clerical groups and their leaders were also of no single mind on a variety of social problems and their remediation. These ethical and moral divisions were especially salient when it came to how best to expunge the land of the sins of honor. Organized religions in the territorial period were contentious, competitive, and fragmented. In brief, they reflected the growing trend toward pluralism that was taking place in other areas of Missouri life. Heterodoxy had not always been the rule. During the French and Spanish reigns, the Catholic Church exerted undisputed religious leadership. As previously suggested, the church contributed to the curtailment of various forms of violence, including the duello.[35]

After 1803, however, the Mississippi Valley became the seedbed for the time-honored manner of "civilized" dueling. Along with the American march of progress came secularism and multidenominationalism. Catholicism, the state religion for nearly a century, lost its hold, and Missouri soon became the battleground for a host of competing religions.[36] Each denomination in its own way struggled to establish its fragile identity on the frontier by leading in the crusade against moral imperfections, including the sins of honor. Religious diversity was at varying times both a source of strength and a weakness in the battle for moral and spiritual reform. Multiformity broadened the Christian gospel so that it could appeal to people of different social and economic ranks. Nevertheless, serious theological differences divided the faithful and in the end lessened the impact of religion in the reform process.

Anti-dueling, so far as it pertained to the churches, was only one of many issues to be addressed. Yet this matter, like so many other social problems, reflected deep divisions between Catholics and Protestants, evangelicals and established religions, as well as pacific and militant Christians. In short, if no consensus could be forged on dueling then certainly no solid, religious phalanx could be mustered on the larger and more divisive issues of slavery and racism. It is within this broader context of social reform that one must place the pulpit and the sins of honor.

In 1804 the first religious condemnation of dueling reached the Missouri frontier. In that year, as the territory began to surge in population, the most famous duel in American history was being waged on the heights of Weehawken, near Hoboken, New Jersey. There, on July 11, Aaron Burr stunned the nation with his deadly aim. His adversary was of course Alexander Hamilton. Hamilton was philosophically opposed to dueling and refused to fire at the vice president; nevertheless, he felt compelled to accept the challenge and to take his fire rather than risk the accusation of cowardice. Hamilton's death galvanized religious leaders across the country into condemning the practice. Many of these tracts, sermons, and treatises soon reached the Missouri frontier, where, according to Reverend Samuel Spring, the "evil" of dueling cast a "darkness" across the land.[37]

Missouri in 1804 was not for the faint of heart. Those few clergymen who ventured to the West were generally overwhelmed by the sheer primitiveness of the land and concentrated more upon survival than social criticism. Around the years 1815–1816, however, a number of ordained Presbyterian ministers left the eastern United States for the western territories. Some of these clergymen, such as Timothy Flint and Samuel Mills, were agents for the Connecticut and Massachusetts Missionary Societies. Others such as Daniel Smith received their instructions from the Philadelphia Bible and Missionary Society. Following shortly on the heels of the Presbyterians were Episcopal ministers such as John Ward. These clerics were prepared to do battle with evil no matter which ugly face it wore. Employing their rhetorical skills to uplift "the moral desolation" of Missourians, they quite naturally attacked what they believed to be the causes of spiritual deprivation.[38] Drunkenness, profanity, gambling, Sabbath breaking, prostitution, and of course dueling were some of the more pernicious vices they sought to expunge. Many of the more aggressive social reformers no doubt believed that dueling was particularly vulnerable to their moral exhortations. Perhaps they unconsciously assumed that a practice so aristocratic and illegal would be easy to destroy. If so, they were badly mistaken. Fifty years later the men of the cloth would still be engaged in battle against the sins of honor.

Ironically, it was not a clergyman from Missouri who most abetted the anti-dueling crusade in the territory. The most effective religious voice came from Mason L. Weems, author of the lives of noted Americans such as Marion and Washington, as well as the work entitled *Drunkard's Looking Glass*. To the literary world he was simply known as Parson Weems. In 1816, the minister published a forty-eight-page pamphlet entitled *God's Revenge*

Against Duelling, or the Duellist's Looking Glass. In the preface to the work, Weems set forth the style and manner of his attack against the institution of dueling by quoting Horace:

> For ridicule shall frequently prevail,
> To cut the knot, when graver reasons fail.[39]

Weems no doubt realized that political and moral exhortations, as well as legal condemnations, had little positive effect on curtailing the practice. His looking glass was motivated in part by the words of the poet Burns:

> Oh! for some power the git to gi'e us,
> To see ourself as others see us;
> Och! Frae what blunders it would free us!

Weems prayed that duelists would read his work and "no more dishonor reason nor stab humanity with their mad reveries." Therefore, he set out to expose those heinous practices with a combination of logic and satire. Within the space of months, his pamphlet made its way across the country to the wilds of Missouri.[40]

Unlike many critics in the legal and newspaper professions, Weems reversed the cause and effect of dueling. To the parson's way of thinking, dueling did not lead to other moral vices; rather, those vices led to dueling. Weems believed that a youthful indoctrination of temperance, industry, and truth would obviate the dueling passion. What destroyed these "imperishable pleasures" of the mind were "swinish drunkenness, thievish gambling, goatish lust, or satanic pride." A duelist, according to Weems, was not born; he was tempted by a variety of evils that made him susceptible to an even worse sin. Committing those moral crimes readied the individual to indulge in more heinous acts such as dueling.

Weems intensely hated the code duello and the duelists' twisted sense of honor. Accordingly, he placed them at the very top of his hierarchy of sin. They were, he argued, "the most unnatural and monstrous of all crimes."[41] While other theologians believed that certain gentlemen had fallen from grace and were therefore susceptible to a variety of moral vices including gambling, drinking, womanizing, and dueling, Weems believed that those who committed these sins developed a character flaw that led to dueling.

Weems's *Duellist's Looking Glass* revealed as much about the parson as it did about the subject at hand. Associating the code duello with the worst traits of southern whites, Weems sullied not only the master but the slave. Yet there was a ray of hope. If violence was a learned trait then it was possible through proper socialization to redeem even the most hardened of white southerners. Weems's view of the African slave, on the other hand, held forth no such reassurance. African passion, unlike white violence, was not an acquired vice but part of their brutal nature. Consequently, the animal instincts of blacks could not be ameliorated by social conditioning.

Weems's racial dilemma was all too common for many men of the western cloth. It was a theological predicament that they brought with them to the West. Their inability to transcend race, as it pertained to both Africans and Indians alike, handicapped the religious reform movement and divided Protestant against Catholic and old light Protestant clergymen against their fellow new light preachers. Race, therefore, defined the limits of reformation. This fracturing process, a none-too-unusual phenomenon in an increasingly diversified culture, allowed other social vices such as dueling to maintain a toehold on the Christian frontier.[42]

As the parson's pamphlet wound its way west, it no doubt profoundly influenced Timothy Flint, a missionary preacher in Missouri. Flint would have agreed that the code was a "diabolical delusion," although he might not have attributed the dueling spirit to "poor human nature" or man's natural "prejudice." In the *Western Monthly Review,* Flint wrote that in the animal world of teeth and talons, as in the world of the atheist duelist, a "callous indifference to pain and death" ruled the day. The solution to this "horrible infatuation," according to Flint, must come from the "triumph of reason." Reason, he argued, must overcome "the instinctive propensities and the physical tendencies of our nature." Two years before this article appeared, Flint published his recollections of life in the Mississippi Valley. Here, too, he excoriated the "horrid practice" of dueling but still maintained that the "progress of moral ideas" along with "knowledge" would curtail the abomination.[43]

Flint and Weems, by-products of the American Enlightenment, both expressed horror and contempt for the code of honor. Nonetheless, they arrived at their positions from different avenues of thought. Weems in his pamphlet suggested that dueling, like other anti-social behavior, was a learned experience. As such, it could be remedied by a variety of behavioral responses. Corporal punishment, a very powerful negative reinforcement, certainly would have been one behavioral tool. Flint, on the other hand, equated dueling and violence with man's fall from grace. Anti-social behavior therefore was part of human nature, but it too could be corrected and improved upon by using another natural resource, namely, reason. Neither clergymen tended to give much credence to antinomian doctrines of redemption through inner grace.

Nevertheless, other powerful religious forces were at work in the Missouri Territory that demanded more than a reasoned renunciation of vice. One group was the evangelicals. Their atomistic and more community-based religion stood in stark contrast to the beliefs held by the men of the Enlightenment. Opposition to dueling, therefore, was one part of a larger spiritual struggle evolving on the Missouri frontier. Shortly after the Louisiana Purchase, the land, as one historian has suggested, had become "a moral and spiritual battleground on which the Christian churches fought their common enemy—and one another." In earlier colonial times, an ecumenical spirit had often prevailed in pioneer communities. Even during and after the Revolutionary War, religious idealism had fostered a nondenominational type of utopianism. But the Missouri frontier was different. One factor was the century-old presence of Catholicism. These historical differences were often rooted more in political history than religious doctrine. To many Protestant clergymen, the Roman Church was a threat to republicanism. Lyman Beecher, for example, was especially fearful of the vast number of Catholics populating the area of St. Louis. Samuel Mills believed the Catholic Church opposed giving their people Bibles in order to keep them in a perpetual state of religious ignorance. French Catholics, he wrote, were "ignorant of almost everything except what relates to the increase of their property; destitute of schools, bibles, and religious instruction." As to the sorry state of affairs in Louisiana, Mills feared that "there are American families in this part of our country, who never saw a Bible, nor heard of Jesus Christ." In one respect, Mills was certainly right: the Catholic Church in the territory had fallen upon hard times. Nor had it attacked social evils such as dueling with any degree of alacrity. Religious life in Missouri, therefore, more closely resembled earlier southern denominationalism. Many of those churches, wrote Walter Posey, "shunned cooperation" and displayed "extreme antagonism" toward each other. "They found strength in exclusiveness, individualism, and eventually in divisiveness."[44]

Arrayed against Catholicism on the Missouri frontier, however, were forces far different from those of the established, eastern Protestant faiths. One organization philosophically opposed to both Catholicism and dueling was the Masons. Many of the Grand Lodges attempted to dissuade their members from engaging, both as principals and seconds, in affairs of honor. In some cases such as the Joshua Pilcher–Stephen Austin affair, they contributed to a peaceful resolution. However, many famous Missouri duelists such as Farrar, Benton, Captains Martin and Ramsey, Fenwick, Crittenden, McFerron, and Smith T all professed Masonry but placed its teachings below the altar of honor.[45]

Evangelicalism, a far broader and more powerful movement than the Masons, swept across the Missouri Territory and affected its participants' views of violence and dueling. At the core of this spiritual movement, represented largely by Baptists and Methodists, were concepts of free will and free grace. In addition, these groups had a deep personal commitment to salvation and inner faith. They further believed in divine intervention in ordinary living. Many evangelicals believed, as did one Baptist minister, that "I must let the Holy Ghost study my sermons for me." The Methodist ideal was the "creedless religion of the heart."[46] The term "evangelicalism" can be a useful broom for sweeping up a variety of religious ideas. The purveyors of these born-again, redemptive messages did not always walk in lockstep; but in contrast to the rancorous rivalries of the more established churches, evangelicals seemed less inclined to support one organized Protestant faith against another and more inclined toward a nondenominational way of life.

The Baptists, represented by the Reverend Luke Williams, arrived in Missouri in 1796, while Methodists such as Joseph Oglesby, Jesse Walker, and John Mason Peck came a little less than two decades later. Most of these itinerant clergymen were reluctant to preach in the larger towns and favored the byways and outreaches of civilization. Their sermons were emotional and the demands placed on their flocks were simple. They included conversion as a condition of church membership; in addition, each convert was to take individual responsibility for his salvation. They directed their animus toward unbelievers and scoffers against the true message. Like the established Protestant faiths, they too strongly disliked Catholicism. New Orleans, a Catholic city, was viewed by Peck as a "modern Sodom" with unholy aspects of "beastliness and degradation." Catholicism, to this man of the cloth, was a "fallacious system." "The Sabbath," he remarked, "was a day of hilarity, as in all Catholic countries."[47]

Besides Catholicism, another vice singled out for contempt was reason. This included those Christian elements they believed bordered too closely on Enlightenment doctrines. Voltaire, admonished one Methodist preacher, was "an intellect without a heart." Other evangelicals would also have questioned the utility of reason to achieve the moral condemnation of dueling. No doubt they would have taken issue with the Reverend Samuel Spring's belief that God in his "infinitude" had furnished man with reason to discover His laws and that public opinion would ultimately discard social vices such as dueling (through the influence of education).[48]

The conventional Protestant denominations clearly recognized the challenge posed by evangelicalism, but they along with the Catholic Church were less likely than the evangelicals to use their pulpits to condemn dueling. In a sermon entitled "Your Hands Are Full of Blood," delivered in St. Louis, John Mason Peck argued that the code was a crime against God, man, and society. The revelatory urgency that made the sermon a literary work of art, however, fell mainly upon deaf ears. Nevertheless, it was clear that evangelicalism had come to encompass a variety of reforms which challenged the established social and religious order. Democracy, wrote one prominent social historian, "found its alter ego in the romantic evangelical spirit of American religious life."[49]

Evangelical churches also took a more active role in conflict resolutions by policing the personal lives of their parishioners. The thrust of their spirituality for more than two decades after statehood was a perfect social order of harmony and peace. In some cases, when "outside temptations" became too great, the more committed of the flocks left Missouri for quieter if not greener pastures farther west. In other cases, when conflict arose that might have led the aggrieved to resort to the code duello, church leaders stepped in to mediate the quarrels. Their stern disapproval of fighting and bloodshed, along with their strict moral codes, often brought more than a modicum of peace to the community.[50]

Evangelicalism, since it sprang from indigenous forces on the frontier, was in many respects the most democratic of religious orientations. Having few if any Old World ties and no centralized administrative head, evangelical preachers answered directly to their constituents. Churches in many remote rural areas became the "moral courts" that regulated good conduct.

Grassroots evangelicalism also militated against the atomistic qualities of frontier life. As advocates of public order, the churches emphasized solidarity, conformity, and voluntarism. Their faith in the common man and their egalitarianism were strong antidotes to the aristocratic pretensions of both the gentlemen of the cities and the estates. Individualism for these Christian populists meant a personal striving for grace and perfection. It did not give one a license to uphold honor by violating the laws of either God or man.[51]

Missouri evangelicalism had another feature that gave it a democratic and anti-aristocratic quality. Unlike southern evangelicalism, the movement in Missouri did not become a wholehearted defense of slave society. While southern evangelicalism still clung to chivalry, the code of honor, and the duel, new-light Missourians were freer to reject southern conventions and to challenge the elites and their practices. In the South, slavery forced even the evangelicals toward a theological justification of the status quo. In Missouri, evangelicals skirted the moral quandary of abolitionism and concentrated on less controversial social issues.[52]

The early religious history of Missouri, therefore, reveals some sharp contrasts in how the churches viewed a variety of social problems including dueling and race relations. To the more established clergy, the code duello was part of a stage of frontier civilization that would eventually succumb to socialization and economic change. They interpreted dueling as an impediment to northern immigration, entrepreneurialism, and investment. Undoubtedly to these critics, public opinion and Christian reason would hasten the duel's demise. Although these critics did not interpret the rash of violence as "the fortuitous result of chance," they were less willing to place the blame squarely on individuals or collectively on the character of the people. It was the "times" and not people that were, according to the *Jeffersonian Republican*, "out of joint."[53] These religious critics strongly supported legislation that would hasten the day when the rough-hewn traits of the frontier gave way to economic development and social refinement. Statutory reform combined with moral suasion would lead to progressive, evolutionary change. The kingdom of heaven would be peopled by converted sinners.

To the evangelical, on the other hand, chivalry and the code of honor, although they defied moral codes, were nevertheless less susceptible to both cultural evolution and legal suasion. This was a battle waged for the soul of gentlemen and fought against an elitist and undemocratic institution that reason and discourse alone could not end. While the more entrenched religious figures might speak of shame and remorse, the evangelical emphasized sin, guilt, and ultimate redemption.

Not all frontier clerics, however, were as quick to condemn violence in general and the duel in particular as either the establishment clergy or the evangelicals. Some exponents of a more militant form of Christian theology saw a functional role for violence in the dialectics of civilization versus savagery. One purveyor of this form of reasoning was William Henry Milburn. This man of the cloth was born in Philadelphia in 1823. As a young man, he traveled west to ply his trade. His was the story of an intrepid and rough itinerant preacher. Although he condemned gambling, profanity, and drunkenness, he expressly shied away from condemning the code duello. Milburn's theological position on the nature of violence in many ways revealed certain similarities with the apologists of the duel whose profession of faith extended only as far as Deism. Milburn equated heroic action with the march of American civilization. "Cowards," he wrote, "shouldn't ride abreast with men." "We and the future," he argued, "owe the noblest domain upon which the sun now shines, to the valour, the patience, the fortitude, the zeal, and the Christian love of the heroes of the rifle, axe, and saddle-bags."[54]

Like many of the early duelists who saw a functional utility in dueling, these Christian soldiers presupposed a false cultural dialectic. In an imperfect society, they reasoned, honor must be defended; hence the duel was the least unacceptable form of violence. Without such a recourse, society would degenerate into incivility and blackguarding. Personal honor could not yet be replaced by community sanction. Courage must first be upheld before it was supplanted by virtue. Institutional violence, although wrong, was the lesser of two evils.

This form of crusading expansionist Christianity was also an expression of racism. Religious militants were predisposed toward a Manichean view of the frontier, a view of Anglo-Saxon virtue pitted against African-Indian vice. This misanthropic view of human nature could best be curtailed, according to the belligerents, by white civilization. Thus, they stripped the noble savage of his nobility and reduced the African—that "beast of passion"—to a beast of burden. Dueling, more a vice than a sin, was viewed from this militant perspective as a form of controlled violence that separated the emotional and uncontrollable African and Indian from their white superiors on the frontier.

Evangelical reformers challenged the notion of conquest and honor as exemplified by the militants, and they rejected the orthodox churches' more sanguine reliance on reason and progress. They instead looked beyond the conversion of sinners as manifested by the established churches. Evangelicals sought the Communion of Saints, stressing man's uniqueness and his individual choice to seek the Kingdom of God. These clergymen sought to build an egalitarian base for society through strong community involvement.[55] The evangelicals generally tended to promote their social agenda at the community level. Although opposed to dueling and other forms of violence, their voices were loud but not united. Rather than mobilizing opposition to a variety of social evils plaguing the frontier, they sought peace and harmony through personal mediation and local group sanctions. This type of individual involvement reflected the egalitarian thrust of the new-light Christians. Insofar as dueling, racism, and slavery were concerned, the fragmented and highly individualistic nature of pioneer religion obviated a united front against these social evils.

The anti-dueling spirit was perhaps best articulated by Peter H. Burnett. Burnett harkened back to a Shakespearian stage of illusion, in which the duelist was a player, a godless actor who sought affectation as much as import. The deadly sport of gentlemen epitomized a Shakespearian tragedy since the characters did not recognize that displays of "personal" courage actually reflected a "want" of true "moral" resolve. It was, as the *Missouri Gazette* had put it many years before, a "strange hallucination that must possess the mind." The duelist's stage, Burnett reminded his readers, was a hollow and shallow garden of pretense. Even the timing of most duels, either in the early morning mist or in the twilight of the evening's hues, enhanced "the shadow to the substance" of the issue. The duelist, he wrote, "is for effect, not reality," for he worshiped only "appearance." The duelist-turned-thespian might indeed play his part in the walking shadows of the mind, but he risked a far greater tragedy than what Shakespeare could ordain. Images of perdition were, of course, more biblical than literary for Burnett, as he likened the duelist's "animal" nature to the allegory of Lucifer's fall from grace. Any man who would risk his life for honor's sake, he believed, was a fool. But the man who would risk his soul and the soul of his antagonist for the sake of pride was a heathen. Like the devil himself, the duelist fell "victim to interest and pride." His "stony heart" could never hear the widow's cry nor have remorse for the "ruin" he produced. The man of shot and sword, he continued, was "a slave of the times" and could never rise above the "scorn and contempt of the wise." "Being contemptible himself," the governor added, the duelist "fears contempt." For Burnett, there was no place in the Christian psyche for institutionalized revenge. Thus he believed that the majority of duelists were "atheists" whose moral conduct was relative to the times and who believed in no "future state of rewards and punishments." It was the "fear" of what others might think of him that deprived the duelist of the "moral nerve to face a false public opinion." To Burnett, only a strong Christian faith could overcome the "more pliable consciences" that served "a vitiated public."[56] Although one suspects that Burnett was preaching to the choir and not to the guilty, it was, nevertheless, a most powerful and eloquent expression of social reform by a Christian evangelist.

In retrospect, Burnett and the evangelicals, as well as the other religious denominations, fought the good fight. Compared to the other political, educational, legal, and social institutions in early Missouri, the representatives of the pulpit remained the most vocal and steadfast opponents of the code of honor. Yet their inability to find united theological ground on a variety of social issues undermined the strength and vitality of the reform movement. Denominational conflicts and rivalries further split the ranks of the clergy. Nevertheless, the churches and missionary outposts across the land achieved some semblance of victory in the battle against the duel. More than any other group, they provided the leadership and idealism in the crusade to rid Missouri of the sins of honor.

6

Shame and Vengeance on the Missouri Frontier

EATH CAME EARLY in the events leading up to the Leonard-Berry
duel. On a rain-soaked evening in 1824, as Abiel Leonard hastened to
his appointed destiny, the shaft of his carriage impaled an intoxicated
Irishman who ventured into his path on a St. Louis street.[1] It was an inauspicious beginning for what was to become the most celebrated Missouri duel of
the 1820s—a duel that transformed Leonard into a virtual folk hero and cat-
apulted him within a few short years to statewide political prominence.
Leonard's affair of honor, more than any other on the Missouri frontier,
melded history and folklore into a blend of imagery and romance, myth and
legend, fiction and fact. As such, the career of Abiel Leonard offers for both
the folklorist and the historian a fertile field of study.

Arriving on the Missouri frontier three or four years after the Treaty of
Ghent, this diminutive Vermont gentleman possessed no trappings of natural
aristocracy to distinguish him from the hosts of immigrants swarming into
the territory. In fact, his very appearance worked to his disadvantage. A small,
frail man, barely five feet tall with poor eyesight and "so ugly as to attract attention," he hardly appeared to be the stuff of legends.[2] Many of the observers
of the western territories often remarked that the men of the Missouri frontier were tall, erect, and strong. These physical attributes commanded respect.
On the opposite pole of status recognition was the man of frail and sickly
body. As Professor Wyatt-Brown has suggested, "Poor health, small stature, or
any other physical defect carried special opprobrium" to southern men.[3] Yet
behind Leonard's deceptive physiognomy lay a bold and determined spirit
that would later prove to be an invaluable source of strength when he faced
death at ten paces in his duel with Major Taylor Berry.

Vengeance in the world of Abiel Leonard was the only recourse for a man
disgraced, and the code duello was the most commonly accepted method to
vent one's internal rage. Both shame and vengeance, like their counterparts

honor and satisfaction, were the cultural determinants in the history of dueling. Each particular affair, of course, had its own logic and internal dynamics that dictated the exact measure of violence. Honor and shame had always been at the opposite poles of social evaluation. But honor, unlike its opposite, shame, could be remedied by satisfaction alone. Satisfaction might entail bloodshed, but in many cases honor could be obtained by a variety of nonviolent means. On the other hand, shame, and the stigma attached to it, generally required blood and retribution. It was these fateful ingredients, shame and vengeance, therefore, that provided the engines of tragedy in the Leonard-Berry affair.

As in other frontier and developing societies, honor conditioned the patterns of social hierarchy in antebellum Missouri. It became the looking glass by which men defined themselves and others. Since honor epitomized an ideal and idealized personality, it was inherently juxtaposed with the duel. But shame was not. A gentleman might fight and even die on the field of honor and never know the haunting sting of shame. Honor was not so much gained or earned by the death of an opponent as by the act of facing death itself. A duel did not bestow honor; it could only preserve it. Technically, a man without honor had no right to challenge another man who possessed it. Points of honor, therefore, were usually laced with the finer points of logic, literary finesse, and a sense of the dramatic. But the distinctions so theoretically clear in the world of honor became blurred and distorted when applied to the real world where status anxiety and fear of self-worth were so prevalent.

Born in Vermont in 1797, Leonard faithfully attended to the rigors of a New England education. Upon leaving Dartmouth College in 1815, he joined a New York law firm for three years. Although moderately successful, Leonard sought the anonymity of the West to escape "the shadow of his father's dishonored name."[4] "Improvident and unstable," his father had been broken in rank and discharged from the Army for "gross neglect and inattention" in the fall of Fort Niagara to England on December 18, 1813. One must remember that the evolving American society nearly two hundred years ago offered little room for social maneuverability. Shame, like honor, was inherited, especially in communities where rank and privilege were ascriptively assigned. Family dishonor therefore played a motivating role in the young attorney's decision to find a new life and identity in the wilds of Missouri. Shame also dictated Leonard's actions as he pondered his future status after feeling the lash of Berry's whip.

Descending the Ohio River from Pittsburgh in a small skiff, Leonard made his way to St. Louis. It did not take him long to decide that his fortune beckoned him westward. After a brief stay in the Gateway City, he traveled to St. Charles, where he became extremely ill. He had always been a small man with fragile health, but he was determined not to allow this liability to cheat him

Abiel Leonard became a frontier legend when he killed Taylor Berry in a duel. Courtesy State Historical Society of Missouri.

out of an opportunity to practice law on the frontier. Glowing reports of the Boonslick region's growth potential enticed him to set out on foot from St. Charles and to walk the entire distance to the town of Franklin in Howard County, a trek of nearly 150 miles.[5]

This feat was in and of itself quite remarkable since the roads to the West were often infested with robbers and thieves. A man on foot was, of course, particularly vulnerable to outlaws, but Leonard, without any means of support, did not have the money to purchase a horse. What propelled him toward these distant and hostile lands was the promise of a lucrative law practice and the chance to put as much distance as possible between himself and his slightly tarnished past. Besides its reputation as "the best land in Western America for so great an area," the Boonslick country was awash in land claims disputes.[6] This kind of contentiousness, for a lawyer and future land speculator, was an ideal setting. After the 1811–1812 New Madrid earthquakes, settlers in that unfortunate region were awarded land certificates to settle anywhere else in the Missouri Territory. Nearly one-quarter of the claims, many of dubious validity, ended up in Howard County because its land values (nearly four dollars per acre) were the highest in the territory. Consequently, the Boonslick population grew by leaps and bounds. In 1824 the census reported a population of 3,076 free white males, 2,697 free white females, 698 slaves, and 12 free persons of color.[7]

In such a litigious country, one would expect a lawyer with Abiel Leonard's talent to prosper, but life on the Missouri frontier was hard and landing lucrative legal fees was even harder for this Yankee transplant. As historian William F. English noted nearly fifty years ago, Leonard's early days in

Missouri constituted "a period of bitter struggle." No doubt they were exacerbated, he continued, by his "cold New England manners, his dwarfed and sickly body, and the rude frontier conditions" he daily confronted.[8]

Leonard's problems were magnified by his Yankee origins. Southerners during the War of 1812 had developed a very hostile attitude toward New Englanders, because they believed their northern counterparts had shown cowardice in battle and in their talk of secession. For these reasons among others the people of the Boonslick felt they had every right to be suspicious of his patriotism as well as his personal qualities of truthfulness and loyalty. These feelings no doubt carried over into the courtroom.

In the meantime, however, the trials and tribulations of frontier life were taking their toll on Leonard.[9] Waiting "for cases that never came," he turned to Peyton R. Hayden, a southerner and one of Howard County's most successful lawyers. Hayden had encountered Leonard on his walk to the Boonslick region, and they had become friends. For a while they had ridden the old northwest circuit together. Later the two would fiercely compete for the prize as the best attorney in the Boonslick. But in these early and desperate years a future of fame and respect seemed remote. Now with his means "exhausted," the small, homely Yankee was given a trifling five-dollar legal case by Hayden. He lost. Thoroughly disillusioned, his life at a crossroads, Leonard walked to the nearby Missouri River.

The murky, churning waters of the Missouri River became more and more inviting. Death held little fear. Before he could make that irrevocable leap, however, he was persuaded to try again. Hayden had learned of his inauspicious legal debut and, having also heard that Leonard was on his way to the river, had ridden fast to overtake him. The men talked on the river bank and the two of them agreed that Leonard would try again to hone his legal talents.[10]

Still, success eluded hard work. Life as a circuit attorney was grueling and the pay was meager. Unmarried and isolated, a frail, struggling northerner in a southern land, the little Yankee had yet another cross to bear. Increasingly, the strain of reading and studying had led to the deterioration of his eyesight—a sometimes fatal infirmity in an age of dirk and pistol. With "the spectre of poverty" so very close, Leonard secured the position of prosecuting attorney for the First Judicial District of Missouri in Howard County in order to gain a modicum of financial stability.[11] Little did he know that the responsibilities of this office would alter the course of his entire life.

In his new official capacity, Leonard was charged with the responsibility of prosecuting Major Taylor Berry, a popular and well-known citizen of the county and one of the founding fathers of nearby Columbia. In the rough-and-tumble world of Missouri factional politics, good fortune bred envy and enmity. It also often led to political indictment as a means of character assassination. In 1824, the major was charged with forgery and perjury while in the discharge of his official duties. He was to be tried in Fayette. As the trial progressed throughout the early summer of 1824, it turned increasingly heated and ugly. Berry's friends none to subtly threatened bodily harm against those who falsely accused and, by implication, prosecuted Berry. The danger did not deter Leonard, who vigorously argued the case before a jury. In the end, he lost the case and Berry was acquitted.[12]

The major, not satisfied with legal exoneration, sought personal satisfaction. Not long after the trial Berry publicly accosted Leonard, denouncing him as a "damn Yankee." The much larger and muscular man proceeded to lash Leonard repeatedly with a rawhide whip. Due to the ever-changing nature of social judgments, honor on the frontier assumed an active rather than a passive role. Highly fragile and self-assertive, it continually sought vindication by acts of physical combat, a response referred to by anthropologist Pierre Bourdieu as the "dialectic of challenge and riposte."[13] While honor itself was socially conferred, the individual was the arbitrator of that honor; consequently, no legal verdict could rectify the dishonor Berry had suffered from Leonard's prosecution.

At the heart of the problem lay the contradictory nature of frontier law. Immanent law, "implanted in man and in society" by a higher force than civil legislation, bequeathed honor. Law adjudicated by man could not restore what had been violated at this higher sanctum. Without honor, no pride. Without pride, no status. The motto of the medieval aristocracy, *nemo me impune lacessit* (no man may harm me with impunity), equally applied to the frontier. Leonard, too, was a victim of this unwritten law. His humiliation could not be redeemed in court. A conviction on charges of assault and battery could not vindicate what Berry had taken from him.[14]

Of the myriad components of honor, the one which lay at the heart of Berry's grievance was that of integrity. Action must be taken to restore it if it had been betrayed or held in question. He assaulted Leonard because he could not or would not distinguish between the public actions of individuals as opposed to private actions. Frontier individualism placed honor and integrity above law, and Leonard, as the agent of law, became the perpetrator of his shame. Since Berry could hardly horsewhip the law, he beat Leonard, the personification of law.

There was another risk, one which Berry and the community believed slight, namely that the "little Yankee" would fight. Perhaps the major rested too much upon his past fighting laurels, however circumspect they might have been, to dissuade Leonard from issuing a challenge. Fatefully, Berry taunted Leonard: "I can whip you, but I am ready to receive any communication from you."[15] Unfortunately, the taunting proved fatal. Shame had haunted Leonard's past, but he was determined to exorcise it from his future.

The blows therefore were far more psychologically than physically damaging. Another miscalculation on Berry's part was his failure to understand the social transformation that occurred when Yankees, "educated in the land of steady habits," emigrated to the West. Perhaps Alfred Arrington, a sojourner through Missouri in the 1840s, had Leonard in mind when he suggested that these eastern men had "a touch of the savage in their nature" and wanted "to seek a more congenial climate, where the lion's blood in their veins may bound freer under the noons of a more fiery sun."[16]

Arrington's melodramatics aside, Leonard painfully realized that failure to respond to Berry's whip branded him a coward, "the most degrading" of social imputations. Furthermore, he understood the remorseless and homogeneous character of the region's people. Labeled a coward by the court of public opinion, his ability to practice in a court of law among the "ruling class" was rendered useless.[17]

Against this backdrop it was perhaps not surprising that shortly after the altercation Leonard sent a friend to call on Taylor Berry. General John B. Clark carried the challenge. According to Clark, he met Berry on a street corner in downtown Fayette and delivered the potentially lethal note. What was unique about the June 26, 1824, challenge, wrote historian Floyd Shoemaker, was its briefness, for it "gave Berry not even the alternative of an apology." "Sir," the note began, "I demand a personal interview with you. My friend, Mr. Boggs, will make the necessary arrangements."[18]

Berry's acceptance was firm but couched in delay. He would fight, but not until September 1, when his "many duties" would be completed. After that date, "any further delay will be asked from you only."[19] The dialectic of challenge and riposte was complete. Leonard agreed to the stipulations and the seconds, Thomas J. Boggs for the Yankee and Angus L. Langham for the major, arranged the terms. Each party would make its way from the Boonslick to St. Louis and there board a steamboat to Wolf Island, an island in the Mississippi River near New Madrid but under the sovereignty of Kentucky. There they would act out the final scene of their drama. The journey to Wolf Island would take nearly two weeks.

Every detail of the duel was carefully plotted, including the position of the sun, the count, the word, the choice of positions, and the dress (each man to wear a three-quartered coat). The pistols would be of each's choosing, the distance ten paces. According to legend, Leonard's poor eyesight and unfamiliarity with pistols prompted him to quit his law practice and to spend the next nine weeks consumed in the practice of the lethal art of dueling. For Leonard, Wolf Island was more than a field of honor; it was a killing field—a determination that one man and one man alone should leave the field alive. When Judge David Todd, an ardent Christian and adversary of dueling, heard of the impending duel he arrested Leonard in Howard County and forced him to post a five-thousand-dollar bond. "Name the amount of the bond," Leonard retorted, "for I am determined to keep my appointment with Major Berry."[20]

When the morning of the event arrived, Leonard was steeled and ready. On first fire, he grazed Berry. His opponent missed. Efforts at reconciliation failed, for Leonard was determined that night to hear the widow's cry. On second fire, the major again missed his target, but Leonard's bullet struck Berry in the lungs. Although not immediately fatal, the wound was clearly mortal. Yet even in victory, Leonard made no effort to reconcile with Berry. No remorse. No forgiveness.[21]

When the local newspaper heard of the duel, it reported that Berry had been seriously wounded but still held out hope that he would "survive and return once more to the bosom of his family and friends." Such was not to be the case. The major clung desperately to life for three painful and agonizing weeks before succumbing. Technically, the cause of death was pneumonia, so the Howard County Circuit Court, in its October 1824 term, indicted Leonard not for murder but for issuing a challenge to duel. The court also indicted his second, Boggs, for bearing the fatal challenge. Leonard pleaded not guilty as charged and put himself upon the mercy of the court. Although the jury could not agree on a verdict and the court adjourned, Leonard was subsequently found guilty under an 1822 Missouri statute. Acting under the rubric of this law, the Howard County Circuit Court imposed a $150 fine upon him. The court's harshest penalty, however, was that it also disbarred and disenfranchised him. At the same time there was an outpouring of sympathy for the slain Berry. His obituary alluded to a life of honor and an "enviable legacy" to his children. Those who "lamented their fellow-citizen," reported the *Missouri Intelligencer,* went beyond the "ties of consanguinity." "No good man," it added, "who knew him could be his enemy." With such pathos displayed for a fellow southerner, one might surmise that public opinion in the Boonslick had shifted decisively against the victorious Yankee. Remorse for Berry, however, did not mean contempt for Leonard. Southerners knew the code of honor gave Leonard little choice but to fight. Thus, at the same time that the people mourned Berry, some fourteen hundred of them also signed a petition to the Missouri General Assembly to restore all of Leonard's rights taken from him under the 1822 law.[22]

The 1822 law under which Leonard was convicted had been dubbed "An Act More Effectually to Prevent Duelling." It did nothing of the kind. Although it superseded the territorial statute of 1814—which set fines of two hundred dollars and barred from public office and the ballot box all duelists or those who challenged, or accepted or delivered a challenge—the 1822 law, as the debate on Leonard's duel proved, was even more unenforceable.[23] The preamble to the bill admitted that past efforts to curb dueling had proved ineffective, and therefore it prescribed that principals, seconds, abettors, and counsellors in a duel in which a person was killed or received wounds producing death within three months should be held accountable for murder. Furthermore, all such persons were to be barred from both civil and military office. To seal compliance, all elected and appointed officeholders were to take an oath to take no part in a duel while in their official capacity (Governor Frederick Bates refused to take the oath upon entering office in 1825). Judges of circuit courts were to instruct grand juries of these provisions for purposes of returning indictments against violators, and justices were to levy fines not to exceed five hundred dollars against persons suspected to be plotting such a crime. In addition, a provision for the extradition of fugitive duelists was added, as was a special oath to be taken by prosecuting attorneys that they would faithfully execute this law.[24]

The December 1824 debate on restoration of rights in fact became a debate on the common sense and the constitutionality of the law itself. Senator Martin Parmer from the western counties of Clay, Ray, and Chariton led the charge against the 1822 law. He spoke for many who believed the law to be unconstitutional and unenforceable. Abraham Byrd, also a member of the upper house of the Missouri General Assembly, added a different twist to the debate. He believed that only members of the gentry would recoil from an oath forswearing dueling. Their exclusion from the body politic, he argued, would not only create a void of talent but also would energize the forces of social leveling in the state. The dynamics of these social changes would be easy to predict. The "effect," he predicted, "would be to place the citizens of the community upon equal footing."[25]

"An Act for the Relief of Abiel Leonard" quickly, but narrowly, passed the house by a vote of 26 to 23; six members were absent. Senator Nicholas S. Burckhartt of Howard County then pushed the bill through the upper house in two days. Senator Alexander Buckner of Cape Girardeau believed Leonard was victimized by an unjust law, while Senator Biggs said that the petition of fourteen hundred came before the legislature "with the force of ten fold thunder."[26] On Christmas Eve, by a vote of 13 to 2, the more aristocratic senate passed the relief measure. Only Joseph Brown of St. Louis County and Abraham J. Williams of Boone County voted against the bill. A geographic breakdown of the vote in both houses revealed that the St. Louis and St. Charles districts divided equally on the issue, but the counties south of St. Louis on the Mississippi River—Jefferson, Ste. Genevieve, Perry, Cape Girardeau, Scott, and New Madrid—voted 10 to 2 against Leonard. The mining district of Washington, Madison, Franklin, and Gasconade Counties supported Leonard by a margin of two votes. What narrowly decided the matter in Leonard's favor was the overwhelming support of the western counties of Ray, Lillard, Chariton, Clay, Saline, Cooper, Howard, Cole, and Wayne, which supported the bill by a total of 14 to 1. The narrow margin of victory in the total vote was accounted for by the solid opposition of the representatives of Boone County, who voted 3 to 0 against the bill, and by Callaway County's Israel Grant, who also opposed the petition. Their opposition was motivated to some degree by the fact that Major Berry and Richard Gentry were key figures in the founding of Columbia.

Ironically, no legislator raised his voice against the duel as a form of murder. The entire debate revolved around the constitutionality of the 1822 law and which branch of government was proper for the appeal process. Senator Buckner observed that he believed the statute against dueling was inoperative from the start. The Leonard measure, therefore, was merely the pretext to reverse an unconstitutional act. Even the two senators who voted against the relief measure did so mainly because they believed it was the responsibility of the governor or the judiciary and not the legislature to grant such a pardon. Such was the outpouring of support for the Vermont Yankee.[27]

Yet inexplicably, the General Assembly, within a few weeks of the relief measure, reversed course and passed an act that required anyone heretofore engaged in a duel to be publicly flogged. Adding both heat and light to the whipping bill was the eruption of a long-smoldering controversy between Governor Alexander McNair and Senator David Barton. Barton held the governor accountable for the lack of prosecution of Thomas Rector, who in 1823 had killed his brother, Joshua Barton, in a duel on Bloody Island. As the war of words intensified, McNair accused Barton of drunkenness, debauchery, and insanity. The senator counterattacked by stating that McNair's misinformation had been obtained from Negroes. McNair, by then somewhat on the defensive, countered with the affirmation: "My information was derived from respectable white people."[28]

Barton, who sometime earlier had refused to duel H. W. Conway, the territorial delegate from Arkansas, on the grounds that truth could not be found in "the pistol of the desperado," now had H. R. Gamble carry a challenge to McNair.[29] The governor had already made it clear that he was "no duelist," but Barton challenged him not once, but also a second time seven days after the initial challenge. Each time McNair declined. His reasons for refusing to join in the sport of gentlemen, though sensible, were politically and cleverly calculated to appeal to the common man.

Hoping to turn the aristocratic impulse of the code duello against itself, McNair refused to fight on the grounds that he had come from "humble origins" and like his father was deficient in manners and "good education." Along with the intimation that modest roots protected him from the scourge of gentlemen "who are so contempt for poverty, and want of education," the governor sought refuge as "an aged man, never before concerned in a duel, and the father of a numerous family, dependent upon me" for daily support.

Alexander McNair, the first governor of the State of Missouri, was twice challenged to the field of honor by Senator David Barton. Courtesy State Historical Society of Missouri.

David Barton, Missouri's first U.S. senator, believed Governor McNair had not done enough to prevent the lethal duel between Joshua Barton and Thomas Rector. Courtesy State Historical Society of Missouri.

A large family "dependent" upon an "aged" father for "daily support" was not the stuff of the idle elite who could flaunt death but not risk financial ruin.

The spectacle of the senior senator twice challenging the governor to the field of honor reverberated through the halls of the state legislature and, along with the exoneration of Leonard, resulted in the most dramatic effort to save the politicians from themselves. If dueling served as a political weapon to eliminate or to disgrace an opponent, then it must be literally and figuratively scourged from the body politic.

The whipping bill, which Frederick Bates, McNair's successor as governor, referred to as "ignominious and stigmatizing violence," received a prompt veto and never again passed the legislature. General Stephen Trigg of Howard County, obviously with Leonard's ordeal fresh in his mind, defended Bates's veto and reminded his colleagues that sometimes a "gross insult" may give a man no alternative but to duel. As for himself, Trigg added, if required to duel, he would take up arms and fight his way out of the state before bearing "one of your lashes."[30]

A closer look at those in the Missouri House of Representatives who supported the whipping bill reveals them to be mainly from the less populated and newly formed counties of the state, while those members along the Mississippi from St. Charles to Cape Girardeau voted 13 to 6 to sustain Bates's veto. Although it cannot be confirmed, perhaps the spirit of evangelicalism and democratic leveling, more prevalent on the fringes of civilization, caused politicians to support a measure that struck a blow against aristocracy.[31] In any event, the whipping bill died aborning, and the quarrel between Barton and McNair remained only a war of words.

The vote to sustain Bates's veto of the whipping bill in the house revealed an interesting inconsistency when compared with the vote on the restoration of Leonard's rights. One might surmise that if an elected official felt that Leonard's killing of Berry did not warrant penalties such as the denial of citizenship under the 1822 law, then he would logically oppose the public flogging of an individual if such an incident occurred again. However, nine of twenty-six supporters of Leonard voted to override Bates's veto. Two Leonard advocates did not vote and the other fifteen, including duelists Henry Geyer and Spencer Pettis, remained consistent by supporting Leonard and opposing the whipping bill.

Those who had opposed the restoration of Leonard's rights were also divided on the whipping bill. Of the twenty-three nays on Leonard's relief bill, nine voted to sustain Bates's veto of the whipping bill, two opponents of Leonard did not vote, and twelve voted to override the veto and implement the whipping provision. Clearly, lines were drawn on these two issues on the basis of other factors than opposition to Leonard's relief and strong opposition to dueling by means of corporal punishment. It is instructive to note, for example, that only four representatives from Pike County in the northeast section of the state to Perry County in the east-central section (this area included most of the well-established towns on the Mississippi River) voted to override Bates's veto.

Frederick Bates had no love for dueling, and his veto message made that clear. He expressed his "utter" hatred of the "barbarous" and "impious" practice, but with Leonard's cowhiding fresh in mind, he also believed that whipping humiliated an individual "forever." Honor and shame transcended generations of the ruling class. Just as one could inherit honor, so too could a dishonorable act beget shame on the children's children of a whipped and beaten man. Noble blood could not be shed by the lash across the back of a gentleman, Bates argued, without attaching "a shameful reproach to his innocent offspring." Character, he reminded his legislative audience, had been built upon "manly enterprise—our *vices* are not of the mean and sordid order—even *they* have upon them the impress of a noble daring." To whip such a man, he further contended, would "destroy the germs of some of the sublimest virtues, with which these vices are in some instances very closely associated."[32]

Bates was more than using the lash as a metaphor of misguided justice. His insistence on the biological transference of honor and shame to the offspring of gentlemen and his admonition that the whipping bill would kill the "germs" of manly character reflected an organic view of the relationship between man and society. Society, like the human body, was not only a system of interdependent parts but a living, evolving biological entity. One could not amputate a vice like dueling without destroying a virtue like honor. The areas of the state closer to Wolf Island and Berry's demise had, as previously suggested, opposed restoring Leonard's rights by a ten-to-two vote. One of the more forceful opponents of the code in the southern part of the state was the judge of the fourth judicial circuit, Richard S. Thomas. The same year that Leonard dueled Berry, Thomas succeeded, by using every bit of power at his disposal, in averting a similar affair of honor between James Russell and Nathaniel Watkins, prominent landowners in Cape Girardeau County.[33]

Within months of Berry's death, Leonard's star began to rise. The news of the duel captivated Missouri audiences and "lent a certain magnetism to his name." His subsequent trial and the legislative petition brought to bear on his behalf only enhanced his notoriety. Soon such Missouri notables as David Barton began writing him confidential letters about political matters, and Rufus Easton, a former territorial delegate to Congress, sought Leonard's support in securing a position on the state supreme court. Others who employed him included John F. Darby, mayor of St. Louis. The State of Missouri paid him one thousand dollars for defending its title to the lands around Jefferson City that would serve as the site of the future capital. He was likewise paid handsomely to defend land claims and titles for the towns of Boonville and Hannibal. His practice also broadened to include suits over slaves, horses, steamboats, estates, and criminal defense. His legal breadth as well as depth made him an ideal student of law. In the early 1830s such notables as James R. Rollins and Thomas Shackelford studied law under him. Even political rivals such as Thomas Hart Benton and former governor John Miller, as well as Dr. John Sappington, employed his services and paid his ever-increasing fees.[34]

During these embryonic years, Leonard received much correspondence from a close personal friend, Dr. L. Cooper of Pulaski, Tennessee. One letter was particularly instructive for it contained insights into the multifaceted nineteenth-century world of duels, politics, marriage, fame, and fortune. Cooper, no doubt aware of Leonard's exploits, wrote his friend about the successes of another duelist, Sam Houston. Houston in an affair of honor had shot General William White and thus "silenced" one of his political adversaries. Although it would take a special act of the legislature to restore Houston's rights, the doctor believed the duel would help Houston become governor of Tennessee. Already, wrote Cooper, the duel had "greatly increased his popular support." The inference was clear. In these "days of chivalry," as Cooper so aptly put it, Leonard should capitalize upon his newly won fame. As a first step along this political journey, the doctor suggested that Leonard should marry and marry well.[35]

The advice was taken, and chivalry turned to affection. In October 1830 Leonard married Jeannette, the daughter of a highly respected man of steel and shot, Colonel B. H. Reeves. Shortly afterward the couple moved to Fayette. In 1834 he was elected to the Missouri legislature. In 1838 he challenged Benton for his Senate seat but lost. In 1855 he was named to the Missouri Supreme Court. During these years he amassed nearly sixty thousand acres of land. Much of this property was acquired as a result of the high legal fees he charged. The land enhanced his social status and contributed to his nomination and acceptance as a director of the Fayette branch of the Bank of the State of Missouri. He also became a leading political figure in the Boonslick and actively supported the candidacy of members of the Whig Party. To match his political and economic stature, Leonard undertook the construction of a magnificent home on the outskirts of Fayette. He named it Oakwood. It became a mansion infrastructurally symbolic of its time and an architectural and demonstrable representation of the man himself. By the time of his death in 1863, Leonard's stature and influence were such that the *Missouri Republican* could eulogize that "he has erected his own monument."[36]

Two incidents in his latter years, however, revealed that Leonard never forsook the code duello nor challenged the assumptions of its underpinning. Judge Thomas J. C. Fagg told the story of how two groups of three riders rode

Oakwood, Leonard's mansion, was a testimony to his fame and fortune in the years after the Berry duel. Courtesy James Denny, Missouri Department of Natural Resources.

stoically one evening in the late 1820s to Mann's Tavern in Bowling Green. They were destined to Sny Island, another geographical and legal refuge for Missouri duelists. Peyton R. Hayden of Boonville and Charles French of Lexington were the principals, and Leonard and Hamilton Gamble were to act as seconds. The surgeons' names were not revealed. After a supper of coffee, venison, and whiskey, one of the parties proposed a toast. The other party, silent and aloof, could not resist the temptation to imbibe just a little more of the liquid merriment. Soon, to the chagrin of none, the matter that had prompted the deadly sojourn was amicably settled, and the following morning both groups headed for their respective homes. Perhaps the most revealing part of the incident was Judge Fagg's afterthought, "that neither Hayden nor French ever sought political honors." Did the judge mean that the duel would have bestowed political rewards or that the gentlemen were denied political honor because they agreed not to fight? Subconsciously at least, Fagg had suggested a causal connection between political advancement and dueling.[37]

The other example of Leonard's lifelong attachment to the sport of gentlemen pertained to the Clark-Jackson affair. This event occurred in 1840 during one of the least enlightening presidential elections of all times. In the national debate of that year, Van Buren's aristocratic tastes were contrasted with Harrison's down-to-earth habits. While the nation indulged in vitriolics over hard cider and log cabins, Missourians were engaged in political debates of seemingly equal importance. General John Clark, while running for governor on the Whig Party slate, wrote an article critical of a political rival. In the piece, he misspelled the word "rascal." Claiborne Fox Jackson, his most bitter political foe, used the misspelling to mock the general and his inabilities to master the English language.

Acting upon the advice of his friend and would-be second, Abiel Leonard, Clark challenged Jackson to a duel. On or about September 15, Jackson agreed to fight. His second, Dr. Charles Scott, gave Leonard the terms. Apparently all parties concerned were cognizant of Missouri law, but neither principal believed the duel politically detrimental to his career. It would be on the Bonne Femme Creek near Fayette with rifles at seventy yards. Only the seconds and surgeons would be permitted to attend.

Leonard rejected the terms, calling them "brutal and barbarous," and the duel failed to materialize. Clark then posted Jackson as a coward. Subsequently, both men were arrested. The quarrel continued to brew, however, and only the fortuitous intervention of friends prevented a shooting-on-sight incident later on the streets of Fayette. Leonard always bristled at jokes that Clark had shown "the white feather" and defended his actions and the actions of Clark. On another occasion, Leonard nearly fought John Miller, at that time a state senator from Cooper County, for poking fun at his "coarse, ill-formed features."[38]

Leonard's spunk and pluck did not desert him even in the last years of his life. True to his Yankee roots, he could not condone secession even during the mayhem of the Civil War. Legend has it that during the war the notorious guerrilla leader "Bloody Bill" Anderson decided to attack Oakwood. Anderson had ridden with William Quantrill, Missouri's most famous bushwhacker. After his wife was killed in an accident caused by Union forces, "Bloody Bill" turned the Civil War in Missouri into a personal act of revenge. The massacres and atrocities attributed to him, as well as his singular trademark—human scalps tied to his saddle—made him the most feared and hated of the southern guerrillas. Leonard was not deterred. Rather than fleeing his beloved home, myth has it that he armed his family and slaves and, at the head of his small personal army, defied Anderson. The bushwhacker, for whatever reason, cut a wide swath around Oakwood. These stories, whether factual or not, also contributed to the legends and lore of Leonard. These stories were told by the *Sedalia Bazoo* and the *Moberly Enterprise-Monitor.*[39]

Leonard's duel no doubt was the defining moment of his life. It created a sense of self-identification that sustained him during the moments of danger and ultimate victory. Yet he never bragged or boasted of the killing. His personal papers, for example, produced few details of this particular tragedy. Facing death, overcoming shame, and reaping vengeance steeled his character and conquered any doubt as to the wisdom of that terse and fateful challenge.

Although memories of the duel resonated like the bark of his pistol through-out the remainder of his life, Berry's death neither haunted him nor forced him to second-guess the consequences.[40]

The nearly thirty years from the Wolf Island affair to his death mellowed Leonard very little. He remained the unrepentant duelist. Although he felt some personal remorse over Berry's death and, some say, financially aided his widow and provided legal services in looking over the deceased's estate, Leonard never regretted that fatal day. As to matters of guilt and salvation, Leonard never endorsed the evangelical movements that spread across the Missouri prairies. His God lay somewhere between the deism of Herbert of Cherbury and the strict Calvinism of his eastern roots; grace and catharsis by public repentance were spurned by this man of reason. He remained as he had come to Missouri, a crusty and indefatigable "compound of wrinkles, yellow jaundice, and jurisprudence."[41]

7

Dueling in Jacksonian Missouri

DEVOTION TO WESTERN interests and adherence to republican principles dominated the political landscape of Jacksonian Missouri. However, at the time of Old Hickory's election to the presidency, neither of the old factional cliques of the territorial period had "survived" in any discernible form.[1] The nucleus of the new party structure, therefore, had a much broader political base. Nevertheless, egalitarian impulses did not translate into a diminution of violence. Duels, although less lethal, became more frequent. In the three-and-a-half decades before the Civil War, the upper class still clung to outdated conventions of honor. Their cultural generalship, on the other hand, was augmented by the culture of violence. Rather than eliminating the code and its aristocratic pretensions, the empowerment of the people ironically only popularized it more. The democratization of dueling accompanied the democratization of politics. Punctilio, however, became a casualty of these new popular forces.

Theoretically, the genesis of participatory government should have signaled the demise of the southern customs and fashions of the elites. Increasingly, wrote historian Marie George Windell, the duelist was losing "his role as a man of honor," and was coming to be viewed by the public with ridicule or contempt.[2] The observation, obviously overstated by Windell, nevertheless reflected a number of social, demographic, religious, and economic forces that were changing the face of institutionalized violence. Enforcement of the legal statutes against dueling by officers of the law also reflected slow but inexorable changes in public opinion toward men of honor. On September 5, 1827, for example, William Webster of Madison County challenged Jesse Shelton to a duel with rifles. The authorities acted quickly with an indictment against Webster, and he was forced to flee the county.[3]

Political changes also put the duelists on the defensive. Hattie M. Anderson, in an article entitled "The Evolution of a Frontier Society in

Missouri, 1815–1828," attributed the ebb in the dueling spirit to the rise of Jacksonianism.[4] Historians naturally assumed that in the age of the common man, more men would be more likely to eschew the more aristocratic practices, including dueling. The men who formed "the backbone" of this new political party, Anderson wrote, were more apt to use their fists or other "primitive" methods than to resort to the duello.

Jacksonian politics, as Anderson suggested, was anything but demure. Sometimes the political feuds turned lethal. Two politicians in Jefferson City, for example, carried their feud to the streets of the capital city in a series of fisticuffs in early 1830. Pugilistic satisfaction in this case did not suffice, and the violence grew in magnitude until one of the men, Charles B. Rouse, killed his opponent, a young man by the name of John Purdham. In June of the same year, Rouse was killed while standing outside a tavern in New London. The killer was a sixty-year-old itinerant by the name of Samuel Earls, alias Sam Samuel. To the *Jeffersonian Republican,* Rouse's murder smacked of premeditation. The newspaper demanded that authorities interrogate Earls to find out who had put him up to the murder.[5] Unfortunately, Earls was hanged on or about July 8, 1831, and he never confessed.

Although duels in Missouri from the 1830s up to the Civil War were less often lethal than the duels of the 1820s, dueling was anything but muted. As the state entered into its second decade of statehood, the character of its people was changing and so too were its social institutions. In large part, the deadlier aspects of dueling were transplanted to the rough-and-tumble frontiers of Arkansas, Texas, and Colorado. Later the duel reaped a deadly harvest all the way to the Pacific shores of California.[6]

In Missouri, Jacksonian individualism, an expanding market economy, Protestant evangelicalism, and ethnic diversity all pulled the state into an orbit economically directed toward the North. These forces of maturation likewise counteracted the appeal of the code duello. Culturally, however, the southern influence remained powerful. The Missouri duel reflected the push and pull of these competing forces and underwent a number of social modifications. From the late 1820s until the slavery issue gave it a new symbolic meaning, dueling had both a western and a southern flavor. The 1828 duel between a certain Captain Harrison and a physician whose name was recorded only as Randolph was in the southern tradition. The altercation, as recorded in the April 14, 1828, notes of Mrs. William Clark, began when the practitioner of the healing arts struck the officer with a chair "in a trifling quarrel." Mrs. Clark reported that the duel occurred "on the Island," a reference no doubt to Bloody Island. The doctor had obviously not vented his spleen before the duel as on the first and second fire he shot and missed the captain. Harrison, even though he was the challenger and therefore entitled under the duello to give rather than receive satisfaction, did not fire on either occasion and calmly allowed Randolph two attempts to kill him. Neither party was injured in the affair.[7]

The duel of Lieutenant Charles May was also certainly in keeping with the more established traditions of the South. A native of Vermont and only twenty-one years of age, May had come west after his graduation from West Point. While in Missouri he was assigned to the Sixth Regiment of the U.S. Infantry. In early January 1830, this officer, who had, according to the *St. Louis Beacon,* "affable and engaging manners" and a "kind and ingenuous disposition," was mortally wounded in a duel. He died at Jefferson Barracks on the nineteenth of January. The paper regretted his death and did not name his adversary, but in all likelihood it was a fellow member of the officer corps.[8]

From a form of primitive justice individually meted out at the end of a flintlock, dueling also became a metaphor for southern urbanity. No longer perceived only as a device to redress frontier wrongs, the code during the Jacksonian age extended its violent roots from the towns along the Mississippi and Missouri Rivers to the heartland of the state. Typical of this widening field of honor was the 1858 indictment of James Boles by the Howell County Circuit Court for issuing a challenge to fight a duel. Boles sought and received a change of venue to Oregon County and was not prosecuted.[9] An 1854 bloodless duel between Samuel A. Lowe and D. D. Fear in the small community of Georgetown, Missouri, exemplified the changing nature of the duel. "This kind of sport," the *Central Missouri News* exclaimed, "was something new and pleasant, and the saloons did an extra amount of business the night previous." The duel ended when both principals became too drunk to step off the required eight paces.[10] The transformation of violence oftentimes made the duello a caricature of its former self. Some antagonists fought on moonlit nights. Others burned powder with rifles and pistols at ridiculously long distances. Both types of duels usually ensured that social recognition and satisfaction could be obtained with little chance of bodily harm. One affray was called an umbrella duel. Quite obviously it too proved to be nonlethal. Other antagonists battled with broadswords in the best traditions of the German mensur.

Caricature certainly epitomized the "duel" at Harmony Mission in Bates County. When two men resisted all attempts at reconciliation, the seconds, in exasperation, secretly loaded their respective shotguns with pokeberries. At five paces the men turned and fired. The guns exploded in mock fury and both the duelists fell to the ground, covered with "blood" and certain they were soon to die. Moments later, as the shock wore off and the ruse was evident, the parties enjoyed "a big drunk all around." The pokeberry duel occurred in the 1840s and became part of the legend and lore of the western counties of Missouri. The same type of merriment was played on two unsuspecting duelists, Mart Modrel and Pete McCool of Vernon County, in the fall of 1860. As in the case of the Bates County caper, these jokes were usually manufactured in rural areas where settlers paid less deference to the decorum and punctilio of the code duello than in the cities.[11]

An added dimension to the martial spirit was the introduction of women to the dueling equation. Earlier encounters were with few exceptions void of romantic overtones. Political duels revolved around power, not love. In Jacksonian Missouri, however, some young cavaliers went to the field of honor as an act of existential defiance, courting death to exalt life and love. Happily, most of these duels ended as bloodless charades with both antagonists maintaining the illusion of dignity. Many of these rencounters were reminiscent of an 1823 farcical duel fought between two St. Louisians, "Pompey" and "Prince." Here, as was the case in many southern affairs, the duel was a product of vanity goaded by scorn. The controversy was ignited when Pompey made disparaging remarks against Prince to a lady for whose attention they both vied. Pompey intimated that his fellow suitor was a drunkard and probably a bigamist. Whereupon Prince promptly issued his challenge. The terms were laughable. The duel would be held on Bloody Island at fifty paces! Obviously neither man hit their mark. Histrionics and history were playing a more salient role as the duel became choreographed for a different audience.[12]

It was just this type of subliminal appeal that kept the code duello alive in the 1830s and 1840s. Yet, the Missouri duel was changing. Although many challenges were still issued, fewer and fewer of the parties felt compelled for the sake of honor to burn powder. Even the nature of a hostile challenge was departing from its earlier norm. Some were couched in the most obtuse of language, designed more to impress posterity than an adversary. Such was the case with Ira P. Nash. This Virginian emigre arrived during Spanish rule and "ingratiated himself" with the authorities. He was one of only two Americans to receive a Spanish land grant in the Boonslick. He also was a physician and surveyor. In time, he amassed a fortune in land and slaves. In addition to fame and fortune, Nash had a flare for the dramatic. When, for example, in 1831 this "eccentric" Boone Countian challenged Gilpin S. Tuttle, he invited the latter "to take a short hunt" with him. He proposed that this chase, "perhaps my last," should take place near New Madrid on the Mississippi, "where the eye of Leonard flashed on Berry." Their "camp keepers" would make all the arrangements. Tuttle was not amused. The February 1831 note was turned over to Attorney General R. W. Wells, who signed an indictment against Nash. The trial was held before Judge David Todd of Columbia, a bitter foe of the duello, who fined Nash one hundred dollars. Thus Nash had the dubious honor of being the only man convicted of that offense in the county.[13] Nash also had the distinction of being one of the first slave owners in Boone County to manumit some of his slaves.

In resisting the gradual erosion of their southern heritage, the older Missouri guard launched a spirited defense of dueling. Senator George G. Vest, for example, once described the Missouri duel as an "institution." Senator Lewis F. Linn, commenting on the inability of law to curb dueling, believed that the institution was much like "getting married." "The more barriers erected against it," he remarked, "the surer are the interested parties to come together." Fair and equal combat did not make a man a murderer. And community standards, the doctor argued, would not sanction such an opprobrium. Linn further argued that dueling made for more decorum and fewer idle rumors when the threat of meeting one's maker at ten paces loomed so ominously close.[14]

No one during this period, however, acted as a lightning rod for political quarrels or defended the code duello like Thomas Hart Benton. Although he deplored a duel when "a young man, the hope of his father and mother" was "struck down in a duel" (an obvious reference to the deceased Charles Lucas), the practice was infinitely better than the mayhem of the Bowie knife or the revolver. Institutionalized violence, Benton maintained, offered a chance for reconciliation and "usually equality of terms" if the unpleasant event could not be avoided. The code, equated with "fairness and humanity," required men "to be free from ill will or grudge toward the adversary principal."[15]

For many bystanders, Benton's defense ran hollow. It was less a defense of the code and more an exculpation of his deeds some two decades before. His position juxtaposed two forms of violence, institutional and noninstitutional, as the only remedies available to civilized society. His honor, still blistered by the sting of hubris, he wore as an unrepentant badge of manhood. It could be adjudicated by no one except the offended party. His memory, jaded by the fading years since his trip to Bloody Island, conveniently forgot the "ill will" and recriminations that precipitated his meetings with Charles Lucas. With no sense of hypocrisy, he told his audience that he "expected" most duels would end "as soon as the point of honor is satisfied, and the less the injury so much the better."[16]

Benton penned these words despite his own participation in one of the most shocking episodes in the history of dueling in not only Missouri but all of America: the infamous 1831 Pettis-Biddle affair. Although generally referred to as a duel, it would be best characterized as a suicide pact. It was the most grotesque event ever to materialize in the state and, by the depth of the bitterness and the barbarity of the terms, it must be considered a historical anomaly. Spencer Pettis, born in Virginia of fine family stock, had been appointed by Governor John Miller in 1826 as Missouri's secretary of state. In 1829 he became the state's only representative to Congress. Major Thomas Biddle was also a man of repute. His family had served the nation with distinction since the days of the Revolution, and the major himself was a distinguished veteran of the War of 1812. He had proved himself especially valiant during the bloody battle of Lundy's Lane. On that occasion he captured a British artillery piece. Later he served with distinction during the siege of Fort Erie. After making St. Louis his home, he had married into the John Mullanphy family, an event that assured his continued social prominence in the city. At the time of the duel he was forty-one years of age and the army paymaster at Jefferson Barracks.[17]

In the summer of 1831, as Pettis stood for reelection to Congress, the hydra of war between President Jackson and the Bank of the United States had extended its tentacles deep into Missouri politics. Pettis, following the lead of Senator Benton, editorially supported Jackson's attack upon the bank and obliquely criticized Nicholas Biddle, bank president and brother of Thomas Biddle. Soon, both the congressman and the major were airing their personal differences in the *St. Louis Times* and the *Beacon*.[18] Biddle first responded in a St. Louis newspaper by calling Pettis "a dish of skimmed milk." Pettis retaliated in an editorial philippic by questioning Biddle's "manhood." Shortly before the August 2 election, Biddle proved him wrong. Early one summer morning the major went to the City Hotel in St. Louis and entered the room of the sleeping Pettis. He proceeded to beat Pettis with a rawhide whip. Pettis not only was caught completely off guard by the attack but also, suffering at the time from a bilious attack, was incapable of self-defense.[19] Fortunately for the humiliated congressman, residents of the hotel, upon hearing the uproar, rushed into the room and pulled Biddle off his nearly incapacitated victim.

After the attack Pettis made a sworn statement before Judge Peter Ferguson, whereupon a warrant for the arrest of Biddle was issued. While in court the major told Pettis that he was prepared to give him any kind of satisfaction that might be demanded. According to most sources it was Thomas Hart Benton who intervened at this juncture to delay a duel. The senior senator from Missouri tried neither to cool the passions of Pettis nor to prevent a duel. Rather, he reasoned from a cool and pragmatic position. Pettis's death before the election risked the congressional seat the Bentonites desperately needed. After his reelection, Benton argued, Pettis could vindicate his honor and, if he fell in combat, a suitable successor could be named.

Benton's logic prevailed, and Pettis postponed the day of reckoning with Biddle. The rancor worsened on the eve of the congressional election when Pettis, fearing another possible attack by Biddle, requested from Judge Ferguson a peace warrant against his former assailant. Although the judge complied, he also bound over Pettis. Once again each man felt his honor impugned. The next day the people of Missouri cleansed some of the stigma of the beating by rewarding Pettis with his second term to Congress. During these turbulent weeks as he recovered from his illness, Pettis also began practicing with both pistol and rifle in anticipation of his fateful meeting with Biddle. Retired Army Captain Martin Thomas, who would serve as his second, instructed him in the use of firearms. Less than a month after the August 2 election another verbal provocation by Biddle prompted a Pettis challenge. Biddle promptly accepted. He chose Major Ben O'Fallon as his second and Dr. Hardage Lane as his surgeon. Captain Thomas and Dr. Lewis Linn would perform the same duties for Pettis. As the challenged party, Biddle set the terms for the meeting.

Only in his most frenzied of nightmares could Pettis have imagined the suicidal conditions under which he would be forced to confront his adversary. The principals would meet on Bloody Island on Friday, August 27, with flintlock pistols as Biddle's choice of weapons. Ironically, the weapons had once belonged to Aaron Burr and had been used in his fatal duel with Hamilton. The former vice president later sold them to Captain Samuel Goode Hopkins around 1818 for five hundred dollars. Throughout their "blood-stained history" the pistols were used in eleven fatal duels, including one by Captain Hopkins near New Madrid. Because of his nearsightedness, Biddle demanded that the distance for the fire be shortened to a murderous five feet. Perhaps he believed that reason and common sense would prevail and that Pettis would not agree to such mortal terms. Perhaps in accepting, Pettis believed that the major would back down or that the seconds could find some way out of the dilemma. It was not to be. Once again, Benton might have been able to avert the tragedy. But history records no such attempt. Upon hearing the terms, he supposedly remarked only that "There will be no child's play in the meeting."[20]

As the appointed date approached, a fatalistic and melancholy mood pervaded both parties. But the duel electrified the St. Louis press and populace. The *Beacon* reported that nearly a thousand people lined the shore to get a glimpse of the parties as they shoved off for the island. Then they awaited the results. It did not take long. One account, most likely written by Benton and published in the *Beacon,* stated that the seconds loaded the cocked pistols and handed them to the principals, who stood five feet apart. The pistols measured between twelve or fifteen inches in length. The seconds, with their own pistols cocked, then stood at right angles between the duelists, keeping an eye on each other and on their principals. The words were pronounced, "Are you ready?" "We are," came the reply. The seconds then counted, "One-two-three." The duelists with outstretched arms simultaneously fired pistols which at that distance overlapped and nearly struck against each other. People on shore reportedly could hear only one shot. Both men collapsed, mortally wounded, in the burst of fire and powder. Pettis, in those last agonizing moments before the tragedy, had thought of a way perhaps to escape an almost certain death. On the word he suddenly stooped, hoping to inflict a mortal wound in his protagonist's abdomen while dodging his adversary's lethal shot. The tactic proved only partially successful as his bullet found its mark and lodged in Biddle's stomach. Pettis would die with the satisfaction of knowing that he had inflicted an excruciating and mortal wound on his adversary. Biddle's ball, however, also found its mark and passed entirely through the congressman's body.[21]

Although neither man expired on the island, the wounds of each proved fatal. As a last gesture of goodwill, the dying men forgave each other and expressed their sorrow over the whole affair. As Pettis's skiff neared the St. Louis shore, he saw Benton and asked him if he had acted as a poltroon. The senator replied, "No sir, you have shown yourself to be the bravest of the brave." On Saturday the twenty-eighth as Pettis lay dying, Judge Peck, an admiring political opponent of the young congressman, reportedly told him, "Mr. Pettis, you have proved yourself to be a great man; now, die like a man." Pettis replied, "Yes, sir," and momentarily expired.[22] He was buried the following day. He died, unmarried, at twenty-nine years of age.

Biddle fared little better. Although he lived past Pettis's funeral, it was by but a few days. On Wednesday, September 1, he was buried with full military honors at Jefferson Barracks, a victim, reported the *Beacon*, "to those false notions of honor." Years later after the death of his widow, his body was removed and reburied alongside his wife in a Catholic cemetery near St. Louis. Although the church had prohibited religious burials for duelists for hundreds of years, there seemed to be no clerical opposition to Biddle's final resting place. In the aftermath of the duel there was an outpouring of admiration for both of the slain. Encomiums citing their bravery and how they courted "death to avoid dishonor" resounded throughout the state. "I am proud of Pettis," wrote A. L. Langham to Thomas A. Smith; Pettis "acted nobly and died honorably—He is much lamented." A tempest of rain and wind reduced to some degree the size of the crowd at Biddle's funeral, but the Pettis rites were attended by the largest concourse of citizens for any such gathering in St. Louis history. Community standards, however, were changing. The reverence exhibited for Pettis and Biddle in the first days after the duel quickly began to ebb.[23] This affair of honor, more than any other in the state's history, galvanized public opinion against dueling. Newspapers such as the *Missouri Intelligencer*, as well as a number of politicians, distanced themselves from the duel.

Within a few years judges, police officers, and grand juries began to enforce anti-dueling laws more vigorously. In 1833, for example, Joseph Ferguson was indicted for killing Jacob Sigler. Although it appears that Ferguson escaped punishment, community standards were changing, especially in violent altercations that ended in the death of one of the parties. No longer was it possible to be completely confident of escaping all legal scrutiny. Cape Girardeau officials also stiffened the penalties against dueling. Patrick W. Davis on January 24, 1833, was arrested and fined five hundred dollars for is-

This nineteenth-century depiction of the Pettis-Biddle duel does not do justice to the murderous lack of distance between the protagonists. Courtesy State Historical Society of Missouri.

suing a challenge to Alfred P. Ellis. In 1834, a St. Louis court indicted Major William Gordon for bearing a challenge to fight a duel on behalf of *St. Louis Argus* editor James B. Bowlin. Bowlin had challenged James Brotherton for remarks derogatory to his character. The same year an impending duel between Major T. P. Moore and G. D. Prentice was averted by the authorities and the ridicule of the St. Louis press. In another celebrated case, a grand jury at the St. Louis Circuit Court in 1835 found a bill against George F. Strother for sending a challenge to Senator Benton.[24]

The state legislature, no doubt influenced by the Pettis-Biddle affair, passed a new law in 1835 that made dueling a felony regardless of whether anyone was killed or hurt. The legislature also made it a misdemeanor to send a challenge or to post one's adversary in the newspapers for refusing to accept a challenge. Acting in accordance with the new law, the sheriff of Polk County, Isreal W. Davis, charged in circuit court on April 13, 1840, that Robert F. Rogers had agreed to a duel with Joseph Young. Both were indicted under the new statute. Although the 1835 law reflected an increased social concern over dueling, it certainly did not come even remotely close to eliminating the practice. The following November, William Greenleaf Eliot, one of the founders of Washington University in St. Louis, wrote a letter to a friend stating that a duel had just occurred "between two young fools, lawyers." Neither of them was hurt, he stated, and they would probably fight again. In November 1837 two relatively obscure gentlemen, William C. Skinner and William S. Messervey, both of St. Louis, met "a little before sundown" on Bloody Island. On the first fire Messervey received a flesh wound below the knee. His antagonist escaped unharmed. Although many newspaper editors had earlier vowed to refrain from printing the names of the warring parties or the circumstances under which duels were held, both the *St. Louis Republic* and the *Missouri Argus* printed the details of the incident.[25]

In 1838, a difficulty between two little-known St. Louis businessmen, Mr. T. A. Le Lange and R. G. Tates, resulted in a duel fought near Alton, Illinois. The principals, armed with flintlocks, met at a distance of eight yards. Although the distance was treacherously short, there was a mitigating circumstance. The duel occurred by moonlight. It was the only one of its kind ever to be recorded in the state's history. Theatrics aside, Le Lange still suffered a wound in the arm. Satisfaction was thereupon acknowledged by both parties.[26] The encounter, like many of the other challenges and affairs of honor in the 1830s and 1840s, pointed to the inclusion of ever-growing numbers of middle-class gentlemen into the club of duelists. The democratization of the duel was also attested by the inclusion of different types of weapons as well as new social classes. In 1835 a tailor in Washington, Missouri, challenged Baron von Martels to a duel with sabers. The German aristocrat refused. In another Jacksonian duel fists became the weapons of choice. Augustus Jones, a U.S. marshall and a Democrat, battled it out in the belfry of the Herculaneum courthouse with Dr. John G. Bryan. Out in the Boonslick, General John B. Clark challenged Claiborne Fox Jackson to meet him near Fayette with rifles at seventy yards. Abiel Leonard, Clark's second, rejected the "brutal and barbarous" terms and the duel never materialized.[27]

The year 1840 also witnessed a spate of other hostile encounters, some of which did not turn out to be so harmless. It was a heated presidential election year, pitting the Whig challenger William H. Harrison against the Democratic incumbent Martin Van Buren, and Missourians easily succumbed to the rancor of the times. Rival newspaper editors in particular fanned the flames of political partisanship. Duels and challenges, especially in the city of St. Louis, became a way "to parry the thrusts of libel and zealous rhetoric" while seeking the greater prize of political dominance of the state.[28] One spark that ignited violence began when a Democrat and anti–National Bank editor referred to the St. Louis Whigs as a "dunghill breed" of Federalists. At least two formal challenges and one murder followed. The latter occurred when William P. Darnes bludgeoned to death the publisher of the *Argus,* Andrew J. Davis. The killing cost the victor a paltry fine of five hundred dollars. It also set in motion a duel on July 16, 1840, between Colonel A. B. Chambers, a supporter of Darnes, and Captain Thomas Hudson, who took up the cause of Davis. The two men, armed with rifles at forty paces, met on Bloody Island. After three exchanges of shots without effect, the seconds and friends intervened to settle the affair with no blood spilled. Afterward the principals, including their seconds, surgeons, and friends, retired to the Chambers residence where they "spent the day in song, merriment, and feasting." The attendants published a notice praising both men for their "coolness and brav-ery." Henceforth the two duelists remained "life-long friends." The *Republican* and the *Argus* then ran brief statements proclaiming the courage of both men and burying the difficulties that had led to the altercation.[29]

Out in the Boonslick, where rifles were perhaps a more familiar tool than in the streets of St. Louis, editors were not so kind to either Hudson or Chambers. Stemming in part from the geographical rivalry that existed be-tween the two regions, the *Boon's Lick Times* caustically wondered how at forty paces and three shots neither man could hit his mark. "They must have been very nervous, we think, not to be able to 'pop' each other at that short distance."[30] The inference was clear. Real men, tried and true, would not have flinched. Courage still required a vigorous defense of honor.

Even in Illinois during these years, the appearance of cowardice far out-weighed the political fallout from a duel. It was just this kind of fear that led Abraham Lincoln to a sandbar in the Mississippi River around 1842 to meet James Shields. Lincoln's strength and dexterity with a broadsword (his choice of weapons) convinced his much smaller and weaker opponent to reconsider the point of honor that was about to end his life. The decision was fortuitous, and Shields went on to serve Lincoln and his nation well during the Civil War.

Another example in the early 1840s of a man too proud to face the impu-tation of cowardice was J. B. Colt. This man, who was to become the youngest judge to sit on the bench of Missouri, was a native of Jefferson City. In 1840 he was admitted to the St. Louis bar. A few years later, Thomas Hart Benton proposed his name at Washington to be admitted to practice before the U.S. Supreme Court. According to the *Missouri Statesman,* Colt was a slender, handsome gentleman, well dressed and with an abundance of long silky hair. His persona, suffice it to say, made him quite the ladies' man in St. Louis. Shortly after his move to the city, Colt had an amorous relationship with a woman whose husband, a wealthy Kentuckian, was sick and bedridden with an incurable disease. The gentleman was Singleton H. Wilson, a prominent member of the bar.[31] The affair became common knowledge among the citi-zens of the city and thus provoked a challenge. The invitation to arms, how-ever, did not come from the ailing husband but from his wife's brother, William Barr, who sought to vindicate the family's honor. At first, Colt, who opposed dueling, declined the unfriendly invitation. Nonetheless, his friends and associates persuaded him that such a disinclination would most certainly be political suicide. Reluctantly, Colt met his opponent as prescribed by the rules of the code. The place was Bloody Island. An account of the duel in the *Jefferson City Inquirer* stated:

> When the parties met, Colt stood calmly and received his opponent's
> shot, which wounded him in the hip. He then had his man in his power

Even Abraham Lincoln was not immune to the dueling virus. In 1842 he challenged James Shields to meet him on a Mississippi River sandbar. The weapons would be broadswords. Courtesy State Historical Society of Missouri.

and could have shot him through, but did not. Raising his pistol in the air, he discharged his contents at the clouds showing at once his bravery and his magnanimity. He gained friends by his conduct on this occasion and rapidly grew in favor.[32]

Not long after the encounter Wilson died and Colt married the widow. Barr later married the only daughter of Senator Lewis F. Linn. Not all the Colt brothers were as fortunate as J. B., however. One of them killed a printer over money matters and cut the victim's body into pieces, packaging the body parts in a box mixed with salt. Mr. Colt then planned to ship the container on a vessel headed for St. Louis. The nature of the gruesome cargo, however, was discovered before sailing, and Colt's brother was arrested and hanged. As for J. B. Colt, he enforced the anti-dueling laws in his court with vigor. On September 4, 1849, authorities arrested two St. Louis Germans who were about to duel. The authorization was based on a bench warrant issued by the judge. Each antagonist was required to give bonds of one thousand dollars as sureties for their peaceful conduct for the next six months.[33]

The next spate of four duels and challenges occurred in the mid 1840s. All of them underscored the geographical dispersion and ethnic diversity of the Missouri duel. In May 1845, Dr. Robert A. Gray challenged Dr. J. Lawrence Page over remarks made by Page about Gray's professional reputation. Both resided in St. Joseph, and the town's constable carried the challenge. For nearly a month the *St. Joseph Gazette* carried details of the disagreement. The *Gazette* headlined its *affaire d'honneur* as "chivalry in the West." "Let not men suppose," it cautioned, "that chivalry is a plant that grows alone in the south and east, for there was a *beautiful sprig* of it exhibited in the town of St. Joseph." The editor was sure that it was because of the *"natural growth"* of the western climate. Ultimately, the newspaper sadly confessed that the duel had been averted but that it would have been a "delicious morsel" for the people of the town. The *Gazette's* mixed feelings of resignation and relief over the end of the affair highlighted once again the tacit desire of western cities to emulate the more refined practices of the eastern sections of the state. At approximately the same time as the Gray-Page challenge, two German American immigrants, Heisterhogen and Kibbe, met on Bloody Island and dueled with broadswords. The duel ended when Kibbe suffered a wound in the face.[34]

Other altercations did not end so fortunately. In September 1845, Colonel James Estill and Notley Young dueled near the town of Plattsburg in Clinton County. The difficulty arose out of a long-standing feud between the two men. The affair became even more heated when publications made by Young appeared in the *Platte Argus* defaming Colonel Estill and his friend Major James Woods. Estill was quick to challenge, and Young was just as quick to accept. Unfortunately for the historical record, neither the terms of the duel nor the names of the seconds or surgeons were recorded, only the fact that Young died, probably on the first fire.[35]

Another deathblow was struck in the small northeast town of Palmyra. The incident began in the winter of 1845–1846 when two prominent members of the community, who at one time had been the best of friends, addressed a literary society.[36] The men were Dr. John L. Taylor and attorney Henry C. Broaddus. After the session, Broaddus supposedly derided Taylor's speech and claimed that the physician used words and expressions out of context and with no syntax or proper understanding. Broaddus also criticized Samuel T. Glover, a fellow attorney and relative of Taylor's, as "narrow-minded, bigoted and illiberal."

Taylor was no man to cross. Before his sojourn to Missouri, he, along with his wife, had resided in Kentucky. The two eventually separated and Taylor claimed that it was his brother-in-law, John M. Harrison, who had precipitated the estrangement. Subsequently, the doctor challenged Harrison and killed him in a duel. This led directly to his westward departure. After coming to Missouri without a wife, he and Broaddus had for a while boarded together and even occupied the same room. Familiarity, however, must have bred contempt. By 1846, the ill will between them threatened to consume not only themselves but others as well.

In the middle of May 1846 Broaddus, for reasons unclear, decided to leave Palmyra for Kentucky. Taylor bragged that his departure was occasioned by fear of him. When this news reached Broaddus he postponed his journey and returned to challenge Taylor. The note on May 22 was borne by George W. Buckner, a young lawyer of considerable talent and a fine family background. Taylor agreed to the duel and set forth his terms by way of Joseph W. Glover, a relative and friend. The terms stipulated "double barrel shotguns, the parties two feet from the muzzles." The guns were to rest cocked upon a stretched cord and to be discharged at the word "fire." The parties were at liberty "to discharge one or both barrels as we may think best." The following day in a note to Glover, Buckner rejected Taylor's terms as "unusual, inhuman, brutal" and "without precedent in the code of honor." Meanwhile, the sheriff, William B. Phillips, had warrants for the arrest of both principals and seconds.

Nearly two weeks passed before the next development. From Quincy, Illinois, Broaddus and Buckner posted both Taylor and Glover. On June 5 the latter two retaliated with their own public handbill. The printed salvos inexorably paved the way toward disaster. At the bottom of the June 5 note, Glover indicated his true feelings for Broaddus and Buckner. "My first impression had given way," he wrote, "to a loathing sense of a pitiful cowardice and baseness of two of the most ignoble poltroons that ever disgraced the form of man." The postings now widened the scope of the quarrel and put the seconds, both young and impetuous men, at center stage. The four antagonists, all of them unmarried and lacking female counsel, turned to their male friends for support. (The sage and prudent advice of a wife was seldom solicited throughout the history of the Missouri duel, in any case.) According to a historian of the period, it was these mutual friends who "urged on the trouble, and contributed no little to the widening of the breach." The next evening at about 8:30 on Saturday, June 6, Glover and Buckner, armed with dirks and pistols, crossed paths. In the ensuing melee both men were killed. The tragic outcome of the Glover-Buckner affair may have had one positive result. The following summer in nearby Hannibal friends and relatives of two men, referred to only as Campbell and Pratt, prevented an impending duel. As for the original principals, they never met on the field of honor. Broaddus died in 1849 of cholera while making his way back to the state from Kentucky. Taylor served as a surgeon during the Civil War but was killed in Knox County in 1867 by a former Confederate surgeon. Ironically, Taylor was shot dead with a double-barreled shotgun. His murderer was convicted of the crime, but was ultimately pardoned by the governor.[37]

In early January 1847 another duel took place when former business associates John Burr and Dr. Albert McMannus, both of central Missouri, could not accommodate their conflicting monetary claims and proceeded to a sandbar opposite Ste. Genevieve. The choice of weapons was rifles at sixty paces. On the first fire Burr was wounded in the right shoulder, but Mc-Mannus escaped unharmed. The parties then reconciled and left the field as friends.[38] The Burr-McMannus affair was unusual in the sense that, by the decade of the late 1840s to the mid 1850s, few monetary disagreements led directly to duels. "Sir money," Spanish satirist Quevedo once wrote, "is a powerful knight."

Increasingly, business disputes were becoming points of law rather than points of honor. This was not the case, however, in a bizarre rencounter in the Missouri Bootheel. In the winter of 1855, Presley Phillips of New Madrid County informed his neighbor Judge Robert G. Watson that he possessed a county court order allowing him to cross the judge's land in order to reach the Mississippi River. Both men had built sizable plantations and had acquired a substantial number of slaves. Watson, who was in his seventies, had come to the region shortly after the New Madrid earthquakes. With financial backing and business acumen, he quickly took advantage of the confused state of affairs to amass a considerable degree of political and economic power. He had no intention of granting an easement on his property to Phillips.

With the situation at an impasse, the two men agreed to duel it out. On December 12, 1855, they met to discuss terms and weapons. Accompanying Phillips that day was a distant relative, Dr. John L. Ross, who may have been a designated surgeon in the affair. The doctor also had business interests in Pemiscot County. Also attending that day was Sullivan Phillips, the son of Presley. He was approximately fifteen years old. As the discussion between the parties intensified, young Sullivan drew a weapon and shot Judge Watson directly in the face. He quickly succumbed. The local authorities were just as quick to arrest the father, son, and doctor.

Passions ran so high in the Bootheel over the killing that the trial was moved to Madison County. The defense used the time-honored term "duelists" to describe the defendants, while the prosecution applied the appellation "murderers." The jury incongruously found Presley's son innocent of the charges but sentenced Presley and Dr. Ross to ten years in the state penitentiary. Their lawyer appealed the decision, and in 1859 the State Supreme Court overruled the lower court decision and freed both men. Thus ended one of the strangest affairs of honor in antebellum Missouri.[39]

By the time Phillips and Ross were exonerated for their part in the abortive duel with Watson, the emerging struggle over slavery was slowly but inexorably casting its pall across the state. Although the issue only obliquely affected the Missouri duel, it, like virtually every other institution, felt the impact of this coming storm. One protégé of Senator Benton whose career underscored the connection of slavery and dueling was Frank P. Blair, Jr.

Frank Blair, one of the early Republican leaders of the state, issued numerous challenges and had many hostile encounters. Courtesy State Historical Society of Missouri.

Blair's Jacksonian zeal for "egalitarian principles" and his growing opposition to the extension of slavery into the territories often led to violence. One man who particularly piqued Blair's ire was southern sympathizer Sterling Price. Their feud "under different conditions," wrote historian Walter B. Stevens, "would on two occasions have led to a duel." The first incident occurred in 1847 when the two men bitterly quarreled. As military governor of New Mexico, Price arrested Blair for insubordination. Although the details of Blair's incarceration are somewhat imprecise, the arrest precluded an almost certain duel. Ten years later while Price was governor, Blair excoriated him in the state legislature. Their personal and ideological differences had only become more intense over the course of a decade. According to Thomas C. Reynolds, Blair believed that Price "would have given his right hand to have been able, without violating his duty, to resign the governorship and challenge me."[40] Although the two adversaries never met on the field of honor, their quarrel would continue on a different level and a greater battlefield in the next decade.

Blair, however, did have one rather bizarre experience with the code duello. In 1849 he anonymously published a series of articles in the *Republican* defending Thomas Hart Benton and assailing the editor of the *Union,* Lorenzo Pickering. Pickering responded in kind, and Blair issued a challenge by way of his second, Thomas T. Gantt. Gantt later became judge of the court of appeals but apparently saw nothing professionally contradictory at this time in carrying an illegal challenge. Pickering's second, Franklin Ladew, accepted the invitation but stipulated that the choice of weapons would be bowie knives, the time high noon, and the place, the corner of Fourth and Pine in downtown St. Louis. Gantt and Blair saw the terms as nothing but an evasion and posted Pickering as "a contemptible poltroon." A few days passed before the two would-be principals accidentally met on the narrow sidewalk of Chestnut Street. As Pickering stepped off the street, one or both men made a threatening gesture and Blair subsequently plunged his umbrella into his opponent's face. Subsequently, Blair was indicted for issuing a challenge and pleaded guilty. He received a sentence of one minute in jail and a one-dollar fine. Although the director of the Missouri Historical Society in 1949 referred to Blair's encounter as the "ludicrous umbrella duel," the issues that precipitated the violence were anything but ridiculous. Only a few nights later, as Blair left a meeting in the Rotunda of the St. Louis courthouse where he had made a rousing speech supporting Free Soil, two conspirators, believed to be Pickering and Dr. Thomas Prefontaine, attempted to assassinate him. The parties fired three shots at Blair at a distance of ten feet and missed each time. Blair reportedly also fired at close range but missed his assailants.[41] Blair's resort to the code foreshadowed other instances where protagonists such as B. Gratz Brown would place the impenitent code of honor above the code of law. This defiance of statute assumed an added dimension as the battle over slavery gave dueling a new metaphoric purpose.

8

The Duel as a Changing Metaphor

ROM THE DAWN to the twilight of the Missouri duel, advocates of the code successfully evoked a variety of metaphors to justify violence. The duel's resiliency, especially in border states such as Missouri, must be interpreted not only against a backdrop of conflicting personalities and issues but also within the context of institutional adaptation. One aspect of this assimilation was the duel's ability to evoke powerful emotional responses and images that cushioned it against the forces of modernity.[1] In short, this chapter will examine the intellectual, political, social, and cultural metaphors of dueling and how they nourished the roots of violence.

Before the age of the political duel, social pressures and definitions of class standing compelled men to the dueling ground. The code served as a metaphor for civility and a measurement of social status. To many, it appeared to be a step up from the brawling of the early frontier. Gentlemen employed it as a means of expressing their conservative values against the forces of egalitarianism. In societies undergoing rapid socioeconomic change, elites have traditionally used various illegal and extralegal means to maintain their position. Vigilantism and lynching were two of the more sordid examples of this tradition.[2] Their use, however, was more to instill fear in the subordinate classes, while the code, on the other hand, operated mainly as a means of legitimizing one's place in the social hierarchy.

According to many standard theories of functionalism, wealth and power in western communities were symbols of achievement and therefore secondary to status. Wealth and power were not ascriptive qualities based upon one's title or position, but rather achieved characteristics resulting from one's striving for a higher social rank. In essence, it was not so much that status was conferred upon those who held wealth and power as that those material emoluments gravitated to men who had first gained the respect of their group or class. Status was in turn determined by how well one lived up to the predominant values of the community. Those values idealized courage and a vigorous defense of honor. Honor, unlike status, was self-ascriptive; that is, it was defined by an individual within the context of one's own moral and ethical standards of personal conduct.

In such an emerging society, however, both status and honor were continually in need of self-assertion. True, one's place in the social hierarchy was largely determined by how well one lived up to the predominant values of one's group or class. To that extent status was an achieved characteristic. Equally true, however, was the fact that communities placed a great deal of reliance upon deference to elites. Contrary to egalitarian social paradigms, most people did not start out equally in frontier communities. The elites, by nature of their family and educational backgrounds and their socioeconomic standing, preferred to keep it that way. Metaphors of violence in fluid, nonstatic societies were designed to control the democratic impulses.

For many of Missouri's early political leaders, dueling metaphors dovetailed with a functional theory of violence. In the first place, the duelist embodied cultural values through character traits which, they believed, all men should strive to obtain. Whether to impress a slave, an enlisted man in the militia, or a common citizen, the metaphor of the gentleman with cold nerve and a steady hand with the pistol conveyed a resolve and competence. Second, dueling served to maintain social equilibrium (if not necessarily social equality). Practically every defender of the code duello argued the legitimacy of this social function. Senators Benton and Linn, among others, even went so far as to argue that dueling militated against the worse scenarios of violence such as ambushes, blackguarding, knifings, and assassinations. Benton argued that duels even curbed violence because the requisite punctilio and coolness offered the principals time to collect their thoughts and passions before and during combat. Many of the early politicians and judges of Missouri such as William V. N. Bay echoed the same points. So, too, did jurist John W. Henry. "Fifty years ago," he wrote in the 1890s, "lawyers were more courteous to each other and to the court than they are now." An insult, he added, forced one to go to Bloody Island "or some other retired place, and look into the mouth of a duelling pistol or hide himself away in shame and disgrace." Colonel John C. Moore argued that the threat of a duel made men "courteous and respectful of the rights of others," including women. In duels, he said, innocent people were not hit. Many of these aficionados took their cue from Governor John L. Wilson of South Carolina.[3]

Dueling and its relationship to violence had another compelling function. Many of the lawyers of the day believed the possibility of a challenge led to greater decorum and less rancor not only in the world of law but also in the world of business. The duel was a metaphor for civility, since "the certainty of personal responsibility" for wrongs "closed the lips of the slanderer in social intercourse and checked the impulse of dishonesty in business transactions."[4]

Viewed from this functional perspective, the longevity of the code must be attributed in part to its ability to adapt to socioeconomic change.

Whatever the functional merits put forward by the proponents of the duel, they could not convince Peter H. Burnett that it brought equilibrium to the social order. He believed that duels, besides their immorality and the fact that they did not act as a check on slander or bad manners, were inherently unequal contests since they were "an acquired art" which necessitated years of practice. In addition, they required a "natural steadiness of nerve and quick accuracy of sight," qualities not universally shared by all men. Those with a "natural capacity" in the area of shooting, the instinct to kill, and the time for "habitual training" obviously had "an immense advantage" over the brave man with little or no experience. Once or twice successful on the field of honor, a duelist felt at liberty to insult, for he knew that, if challenged, he could dictate terms favorable to himself. The more he dueled, the more he killed and the greater his fame. This fame he could parlay into fear, which enhanced his success in his next hostile encounter. Only a "chance shot" stood between this kind of man and another slaying. In short, the duello, according to Burnett, exacerbated ill manners, for "proud men" reveled in "defying consequences."[5]

Burnett in his alacrity to condemn the institutionalization of the duello no doubt exaggerated the number of "professional" duelists who bullied the communities of the West. Nevertheless, he dispelled many dueling myths. He also demonstrated why the code had become a dysfunctional cultural artifact. By flaunting law and civilized authority, the duelist contributed to a disrespect for the legal and moral conventions of his day.[6]

The duel as a metaphor of courage, as Burnett knew so well, had such a broad dimension because it was so "recountable" and "identifiable." Danger, to paraphrase the eighteenth-century sage Samuel Johnson, dignified itself. Given the fame and social position of so many of these gentlemen, as well as the notoriety of their affairs, their kind of courage stood in marked contrast to the quiet and subdued resolve of everyday life. The ordinary struggles of living, working, loving, and dying did not have the same dramatic content as the existential defiance of death on the field of honor. As historian Joe B. Frantz has suggested, courage through violence left a "fixed moment" in one's life that could be used to "regale an audience" with the "dauntlessness" of one's deeds.[7]

The duel's poetic idealization of courage plus its metaphoric application as the epitome of polite society led to bizarre emulation by the "common folk." By the Jacksonian era, Missouri's more fluid social order contributed to different forms of interclass conflict. Pistols at ten paces or rifles at a respectable eighty degenerated into more and more common kinds of killings. The democratization of violence had begun in earnest. By the Civil War and

Reconstruction eras, even fewer individual social restraints were in place to curb the destructive and nihilistic forces of vengeance. The duel had kindled the spirit of vengeance, and the killing cult continued unabated long after its demise. According to a historian of the duel, one Missouri family feud alone left twenty-seven men dead by the year 1899. A code of the hills had supplanted the code of honor and manifested itself in bushwhackings, lynchings, maraudings, grudge wars, family feuds, and assassinations. "The Civil War," wrote historian Richard Maxwell Brown, "marked the replacement of the two-man personal duel by assassination as the main mortal hazard" in American political life. Bald Knobbers, vigilantes, regulators, rangers, and clansmen all perpetuated violence in ways that would have surprised early leaders.[8] The roots of violence had indeed burrowed deeply into the soil of Missouri.

One particularly interesting variation of semi-institutional violence was the slicking. This custom came to the Missouri Ozarks from the mountains of Tennessee. Slickings were severe whippings usually administered with a green hickory stick. Many misdemeanors and grudges, sometimes resulting from cheating in cards and horse races, were settled in this manner by the rugged pioneers in the Ozarks. Increasingly, however, land claims also became an issue. Since, as a general rule of thumb, a slicking called for the victim to leave the settlement, this custom created a "speculative spirit" that crept into the practice. If a man could be shamed into leaving his property, then that land might be obtained for little or nothing.[9]

In 1843, three western counties of the state, Benton, Hickory, and Polk, were involved in a Slicker War between the families of the Turks and the Hobbses.[10] One retaliation usually provoked another until the feud became so bitter that the governor called in the militia to preserve order. The following year two leaders of the feuding families, Ise Hobbs and Tom Turk, met to settle their difficulties with scythes. To dignify the combat, the protagonists and their families referred to this encounter as a "duel." Although neither man was killed, Hobbs eventually killed Turk in another encounter.

Slickings became a popular form of vigilantism and soon spread to other counties. In the mid-1840s, regulators in Lincoln County used the practice against suspected horse thieves. After one Troy citizen was slicked and did not leave the county, he was shot and killed. Other slickings provoked more killings. The practice also spread to St. Charles County, where various groups and factions used slickings to settle their feuds as well as to punish suspected thieves, counterfeiters, and other undesirables. By the 1850s slickings had subsided throughout the state, but vigilantism in other guises would plague Missouri well into the post–Civil War period.

In the taxonomy of violence, the formal duel resided at the apex of the pyramid. Next came semi-institutionalized combat at militia musters, court days, huskings, and celebration days. Slickings stood somewhere in the middle of the pyramid. Individual outbursts of rage such as cowhidings, horsewhippings, and canings were further down. These temper tantrums were generally regarded as legitimate acts of violence since the perpetrator usually employed them against individuals who had insulted a gentleman but who were not considered of a high enough social rank to warrant a challenge. The base of the pyramid of violence consisted of noninstitutional forms of mayhem such as knifings, back-alley brawls, blackguardings, and fisticuffs—the latter two being the common man's way of defending honor. They were also unfortunately replete with eye gouging and ear biting. Many "maimed faces," with mutilated ears and noses, bore witness to the general level of mayhem. A particularly dexterous fellow, for example, could pluck an opponent's eyeballs from their sockets with one good thrust of the thumbs. Blackguards, on the other hand, did their handy work with dirks, which were usually concealed until the propitious moment of insert.[11]

Court days, a carryover from the southern tradition, were a different form of violence. Families often traveled many miles to exchange gossip, sell their wares, and drink, gamble, and fight. These affairs became part of the unofficial court docket. Judges and lawyers who rode the circuit only visited outlying districts once or twice a year. Consequently, the sessions provided the pioneers with a good excuse for a gathering. Court days allowed the common man a chance to display his martial talents and to defend his honor. The term "up in arms" was more than rhetorical. At the end of the session, the judge dismissed court and encouraged the litigants to gain extralegal restitution by means of physical combat. These children of Cain continued to adjudicate matters by means of fisticuffs. It was, wrote historian William N. Chambers, "a favorite time to settle quarrels," and the "judges often found it pleasant if not necessary to adjourn legal proceedings" in order to watch the fights. In these fistfights there was a general rule that neither man was to hit below the belt until the word went round, "bite, kick and gouge"; then it was no holds barred. The judge and trial lawyers along with the expectant public waged bets on the outcome. These fights were a ritualized form of seeking personal satisfaction, in many ways similar to the gentleman's satisfaction of honor by means of the duel. The combat at these court days was accompanied by heavy drinking, oratorical outbursts, and many murders.[12] The judges and lawyers no doubt were wearied and bored by the long circuit rides that took them to the major towns along the Mississippi River. Yet by encouraging brawling, primarily for their own amusement, they showed a condescending if not contemptuous attitude toward the common folk.

Court days in the rural Ozarks continued in some fashion well into the twentieth century. Once in the spring and again in late autumn the inhabitants of the small county-seat towns turned out in droves for the circuit court sessions. Just as they had for nearly a century, Missourians of both genders and all ages and occupations traveled for many miles for these occasions. These judicial sessions were a time of games, horse racing, baseball, vending, and visiting. Juries were sometimes selected by the sheriff from the male citizens who happened to be on the streets at the time. By 1900, Missouri court days no longer served so much as an outlet of aggression as a source of amusement. Public hangings had sublimated that need.[13]

Executions remained public affairs in some areas of the Ozarks well into the twentieth century: the last public hanging in Missouri occurred in 1938. Typically, a third of the audience at these ghastly spectacles was composed of women and children. Picnics, story telling, and games accompanied the hanging. Even the condemned usually contributed to the festivities by giving a speech on the wages of sin and wishing the community no ill feelings. In 1906 one poor soul gave the sermon at his hanging and even sang a song.[14] Historians did not recall how the group judged his talents.

The poor man's duel occurred at the militia muster. These events were staged either four, six, or seven times per year. All able-bodied men from the age of eighteen to forty-five were required by law to be in the militia. After the so-called military exercise, referred to by one historian as a "carnival," the champion pugilist of the unit would mount a stump and issue a "challenge" to whip any man present. John Wilson of Clay County remembered how the champion bragged, strutted, and exhibited no fear. Historian William F. Switzler recalled that the challenges usually were issued late in the afternoon to those who formed "a wide and excited ring, which circled, hallooed, cheering and swearing, around neighborhood bullies who, on all such occasions, settled their personal differences with 'fist and skull.' "[15] By this time, many of the men were well on their way to being drunk and therefore inclined to fight. If a braveheart accepted the pugilist's challenge, the two "principals" selected their "seconds." It was their responsibility to keep everyone away from the fighting area and knock down anyone who tried to interfere or to aid one of the combatants. According to Burnett:

> The contests were governed by certain rules, according to which they were generally conducted. They arose, not from hatred or animosity as a general rule, but from pride and love of fame. It was simply a very severe trial of manhood, perseverance, and skill.[16]

Many times after the fight, the victor and vanquished "took a friendly drink together." "Most generally," Burnett went on to write, "the defeated hero had some complaint to make of foul play, or some plausible excuse to give, like an unsuccessful candidate for office."[17]

Burnett's observations highlighted the similarities between the common man's fights for fame and pride and the duelist's contests for fame and honor. Militiamen, like the duelists, could fight with impunity since they were immune from prosecution on muster day "for any civil process."[18] Each form of combat had a structure of violence that required adherence to certain conventions and restraints in order to make it a fair fight. Each had its own rules and seconds. And each had its own way of providing satisfaction. The muster fights, ritualized and choreographed on the rugged edges of the frontier, were every bit as much a rite of passage for the common man as was the duel for the man of class and rank. The duel, however, recognized physical equality between the principals while the militia muster duels, as well as the court fights, strove for physical superiority, that is, the clear identification of the best man. Within each realm of combat, social class and rank were clearly delineated.

Two other forms of violence that distinguished the best man were the husking fights and the brawls at celebration days. Husking was the removal by hand of the corn husk from the ear at harvest time. Pioneer families helped each other on these occasions and made certain "rules" to ensure that the huskings were not dull. According to folk tradition, any man who found a red ear of corn could kiss the girl of his choice. These kisses, especially the romantic kind, often provoked a challenge from a would-be suitor. Many of the ensuing fights were of the "rough and tumble" variety. This form of "crude combat," as historian Duane Meyer called it, left many a facial part missing.

Celebration brawls occurred on days such as the Fourth of July. Oratory and whiskey made for a volatile mixture at these events, and pugilists often settled the political debates with fists. These brawls were "dignified" somewhat by the fact that the contestants many times referred to them as "duels" and not as fistfights.

These physical struggles also pointed to a form of cultural indebtedness owed by the men of the frontier to the duelist. In brief, the democratization of institutionalized violence as evidenced by the poor man's duel had its antecedents in the code duello. Pugilists, following the lead of duelists, had rules of behavior that legitimized the brutality. These physical combats honored the code more in the breach than in the observance. Nevertheless, the code "covered them with its cloak."[19] These fisticuffs, with eyes, ears, and noses as frequent casualties, were anything but polite or civil, but they were avenues to increased social status and culturally influenced by the imagery projected by the duel.

The imagery of dueling survived in part by metaphoric adaptation. During the early days on the territorial frontier, the proponents of dueling interpreted the functional role of the institution as one of promoting civility, containing mayhem, and defining class standing. Its metaphoric power rested principally in the area of social symbolism. By the late territorial period, however, new political exigencies arose that called for new metaphors of leadership and self-sacrifice to justify the code. In the age of political violence, the duel, as a metaphor of protagonism, increasingly supplanted its social imagery.

By 1816 political passion and prejudice drew more and more men to the field of honor. Political aspirants far outnumbered the available political offices. Thus, to enhance their opportunities for gain and to eliminate potential rivals, some gentlemen resorted to the time-honored traditions of political violence. To justify their actions, these men of shot and sword often employed the values of chivalry and the rhetoric of protagonism. This new rationale for dueling enabled the duel to transcend personal gain and spite. It became, metaphorically, part of a larger battle for the people and their interests. Newspapers constantly reminded their readers of the functional rationale of violence. Fitness for political leadership, they urged, required fighting the common man's battles.[20]

Protagonism, of course, had its down side. If one employed heroic language and espoused the cause of protagonism, then it was politically dangerous to back down in a personal rencounter, since it stood to reason that the same white feather might be shown when it came time to defend the rights of the people. Frontiersmen saw life as a struggle for survival. Therefore, both a fight for personal as well as political survival seemed natural enough to them. Pioneers might not understand the gentleman's convoluted notions of honor, but they knew when a man said one thing and did another. And they knew when a man backed down, lost his nerve, and disgraced himself. Human vitality required boldly facing life and death. An inner strength was necessary to face a pistol at ten paces. This separated the fraternity of gentlemen from other social classes. By his ability to control fear, the duelist demonstrated his command over himself and his basic instincts. By inference, this type of control and command over fear indicated his worthiness to lead others. But the man who evoked the rhetoric of protagonism and then shirked a fight was not ready to defend the public good.[21]

Chivalry, sexism, and racism also fitted into this transitional world where past and present values commingled. One dispossessed class long championed by the protagonist was women. French women in Missouri, prior to the Louisiana Purchase, had played a more dominant role not only in the household but also in society at large. But the Americanization of the trans-Mississippi frontier did nothing to elevate their status. Women's roles, "a singular combination" of "fastidiousness" and "laxity," according to a British observer, were defined by the cults of domesticity and passivity.[22] This was especially true for those ladies married to the elites in the state. The duel became a metaphor for masculinity and the duelist became the knight-errant. By self-anointment he would be the guardian and protector of feminine virtue and the arbitrator of female rights.

Men of honor believed that the duel made gentlemen polite and discrete when it came to women and their seduction. Men were to take an active role and women were to have a passive role in social life. These social scripts were defined in literature as well as in actual life. Beverley Tucker, a southern novelist who spent nearly twenty years in Missouri, wrote a novel in 1836 called *George Balcombe*. In the book, Balcombe's wife reinforced the image of female passivity. Although she displayed "her domestic prowess" in a Missouri double log cabin, her decision-making abilities were limited by the standards of the day. Throughout the novel she generally remained in the background.[23]

Theoretically, the duel was a manifestation of the inferiority and powerlessness of the fairer sex, since their cause had to be championed by guardians of the chivalric code. Defense of women and their virtue did not automatically, however, translate into institutionalized violence. Duels fought over romantic love or the defense of feminine honor were rare. Unlike his counterparts in the South or in Europe, the Missouri duelist seldom engaged in mortal combat over women. Romantic notions were few when it came to western affairs of honor. In these affairs, women were not only expected to be passive but also were kept purposely uninformed. They were not consulted as to the nature of the conflict or the measures of redress. In many cases wives learned about a duel only after its conclusion. Perhaps this explained in part why the duel played such a small role in the emotional life of antebellum women in Missouri. Although silence cannot be equated with acceptance, a myriad of female diaries, letters, and manuscripts reveal practically no mention of the deadly art.

Women's passivity toward dueling was not lost on those publicists who labored in vain against its baneful influence. Perhaps in exasperation, perhaps in need of a transference of guilt, or perhaps for both of these reasons, the press struck a blow against women, the one group hardly in a position to defend itself before a chauvinistic press. On September 6, 1817, the *Missouri Gazette* editorialized with this oblique attack:

> The fair sex have it in their power to do much in affairs of this kind. Their frowns would tend greatly to put duelling out of fashion. In truth, we do not perceive how any lady of delicacy or sensibility can reconcile it to herself to take to her arms a duelist, who has, by successful shot, probably blasted the hopes of a family or covered a widow and children with mourning, and consigned them to wretchedness and despair.[24]

There was more than a little irony in the fact that the press, itself unable to effect more than a modicum of cultural amelioration, would heap scorn on one of the least empowered groups in Missouri society.

Racism also contributed to the protagonists' rhetoric. In all of nature and society, wrote John L. Wilson in 1838, there existed "a continual warfare for supremacy." In fighting the good fight, whether against each other, hostile Indians, abolitionists, foreigners, or Yankees, the protagonist believed that Anglo-Saxon blood would prove superior in this world of "perpetual" conflict. Missourians too believed in a natural aristocracy, and they employed the metaphor of race to justify it. Special, God-given endowments had been granted to the Anglo-Saxon gentlemen that entitled them to republican rule. Anglo-Saxons historically extrapolated their political superiority into a self-sanctifying struggle between superior and inferior people for land and natural resources as well. Unlike Old World ascriptions based on blood and lineage, this open elite system theoretically allowed natural talent to rise, but it believed those talents to be more distinctive in Anglo-Saxon blood.[25]

In time, the duel also became a metaphor for the heroic spirit of men destined to create a transcontinental empire. With a sense of history and a flare for histrionics, many duelists saw in themselves and their adversaries qualities that they hoped could be emulated by the developing nation. Duelists thus juxtaposed the content of their character with the national character. It was a time of "Young America," and the duel was not only a rite of passage for youthful elites but an idealized part of the ritual of national expansion and conquest. They were the archetypal figures of courage whose constellation of manly traits could be generalized to serve the national ideal. The centrality of this historic drama, of course, did not revolve simply around the duel, but for many a man of honor in search of a greater meaning, it helped rationalize their deeds.[26]

Dueling also acted as a social placebo for the masses. While it defined hierarchy and rationalized elite rule, it also served to distort and to deflect class antagonisms. In the transitional world of Missouri society, ethnic, religious, and class conflicts were momentarily subsumed in the clash of duelists. Many of the more sensationalized of these affairs were the main topic of conversation for weeks upon end. People from every walk of life gossiped and speculated upon the causes of the disagreements as well as their sanguinary effects. Lost among the hubbub was the fact that these sideshows were antithetical to democratic traditions. The elites had placed their personal honor above the rule of law, holding solely to themselves the right to determine the proper form of social conduct. Also lost upon the public was the fact that most elements of this drama were nonideological and immaterial; that is, they did not affect the distribution of power among economic and social groupings. Duels diverted people from their real-life struggles; in short, they substituted theatrics for the material base of conflict and sublimated class hostility. Someday, many an aspiring gentleman thought, he too might improve his social standing by taking part in a duel.

The duelist, on the other hand, was not a hypocrite. He operated in a world of idealization and heroic proportions. And he took politics very seriously.

Topics of local, state, and national importance were debated with both heat and light. Missouri leaders seldom questioned the right to differ on political matters. Unlike their neighbors to the South, Missourians did not become closed-minded. What produced a challenge, and a subsequent appearance on the field of honor, was a thin gray line between attacking the philosophy of an opponent and impugning his motives before the "tribunal" of the "public." Although skeptical of human nature, the duelist held an idealized version of all things dear to him, from personal honor, to womanhood, to family, to his state, and to his nation. Personal attacks, as opposed to philosophical disagreements, called into question one's character and convictions. A politician could be wrong, he could even admit his imperfections, but no one should challenge his motives. His world of a perfect social order could not countenance, within himself or others of equal social rank, the slightest suggestion of personal impropriety or selfish gain at the expense of the body politic.[27]

This mentality, with its penchant for social order, rank, privilege, and hierarchy, could easily magnify a personal insult into a threat to civility and community stability. Human nature must be restrained. If law, religion, or even education could not be counted upon to function in accordance with these precepts, then a resort to private codes of conduct must be sought. "Mistrusting themselves," wrote historian Dickson Bruce, "Southerners were even less sure of others' abilities to stay under control." Decorum, order, and control must be maintained at all times. Ultimate self-control came on the field of honor. Every relationship, from master to slave, husband to wife, and gentleman to cracker, had to be defined. Every personal attack on honor or family, which struck at a vital cord of the southern ethos, must be defended. The transcendental value of the duel was the rational, ritualistic part it played in sustaining the existing hierarchy. As the Reverend Timothy Flint suggested: "They throw away their lives, and the desperate indifference with which they do it creates a kind of respect in the minds of them that contemplate it." Other social commentators besides Flint tried to distinguish between honor and hierarchy on the one hand and virtue on the other. Men of honor, the *Missouri Intelligencer* argued in 1825, were profligates who falsely valued themselves. In reality, the paper exclaimed, these men were "spendthrifts" who "never pay a farthing." Men of honor, the paper added, indulged in numerous "shameful and dangerous vices" such as dueling. Unlike the industrious citizens of Missouri, who possessed character traits such as diligence, honesty, and virtue, men of honor were wrongly "received as gentlemen" and mistakenly treated with political and social deference.[28] The fires of democracy were slowly beginning to burn across the prairies of the Boonslick.

Although Missouri was moving toward political and intellectual pluralism, southern thinking still was predominant in the formative years of Missouri statehood. Southern culture had yet to be seriously challenged by any other viable system of thought. At the core of the southern concept of social order and decorum were ideas such as organism, which held that the social world, just like the world of nature, was a system consisting of mutually dependant parts. All parts—or to extrapolate, all classes, sexes, races, and occupations— might not be equal, but each was indispensable for survival. Organism implied a holistic but deferential approach to societal divisions. It implied a paternalistic relationship with elites ruling for the good of all. The dependency of slaves, women, children, and those Indians who had yet to be removed further West was explicit in this theory. Various symbols and icons of dueling enhanced this imagery of the elite's superiority over the disenfranchised and the disposed. All organisms, including social ones, operated under two universal laws: 1) Every organism had a life cycle of birth, adolescence, maturity, decay, and death; and 2) Every organism was in a struggle for survival against its own and other species.[29] From this crude evolutionary perspective, survival was nature's reward to the fittest social organism.

According to this theory, society, like any other biological organism, had various functions to perform. The duel functioned as both a civilizing agent and a means of allowing the bravest to rule. The protagonists, long predating Charles Darwin, carried the evolutionary analogy even a step or two further by suggesting that just as higher organisms developed a vertebra, then so too must civic leaders demonstrate their backbone by fighting for their own principles and the interests of the electorate. And just as an illness to the body needed quick attention, so too did an insult to honor demand a quick remedy. In each case a long delay might prove fatal.[30]

The duel inverted Darwinian logic. It was nature, as Governor Wilson suggested, that dictated "a continual warfare for supremacy." Therefore, it fell to the protagonist, born to fitness, to protect the interests of the weak and powerless. He assumed this paternalistic responsibility because of a reluctance to surrender power to those same underlings. Intellectually, it was easier to justify the duel on the grounds that it was a natural process and that all life went through a series of survival tests. This Darwinian worldview rationalized the violent aspects of the duel and gave it a pseudo-scientific basis.

Dueling and protagonism were also connected by another political dimension, namely paternalism. This pertained to the nature of elite rule. The roots of liberty that emerged from the heritage of Spain and France were indeed shallow in early Missouri. Jeffersonian principles were honored more in the breach than in the observance by the preponderance of southerners and proslavery men who dominated the territory. Rule by elites became the norm of early Missouri politics. If equality existed, it was among gentlemen only. Philosophically, this axiom of social power reflected the disparities of wealth and influence in the fledgling territory. The code of honor, historian Steven Stowe has suggested, acted as the "unspoken standards of class self-regulation" and depicted "an ideal society of upperclass males who band together to reinforce the most important linchpin of their power." This power, he further suggested, was the "freedom to act unilaterally because of their unquestioned unity."[31] This type of elitism fitted well into the scheme of paternalism. Henry M. Brackenridge, for example, reported:

> The lower class have never been in the habit of thinking beyond what immediately concern themselves; they cannot therefore be expected to foresee political consequences. They were formerly under a kind of dependence, or rather vassalage, to the great men of villages, to whom they looked up for their support and protection.[32]

Brackenridge's references to "vassalage" and "the great men of villages" harkened back to the feudal traditions of power, protagonism, land tenure, and military service. In Missouri, most men of power were lawyers and judges, that is, lawmakers and lawgivers. They were also men of military rank. Leadership abilities were normally clothed in the nomenclature of the military. A title of captain, major, or colonel demonstrated not only a gentleman's military bearing but also his ability to articulate the proposition that his battles were society's battles and that his personal glory resounded to the fame of his state or territory. "Commissions," reported Brackenridge, "make a man feel that he counts for something in his country." The penchant for military titles and the scramble to obtain them usually had political motives.[33] In 1824, for example, of nine candidates for statewide office, six had a military rank. In Howard County in that same year, ten of the nineteen candidates for local office held military titles.

Missouri's ruling class held another common southern value. They strongly believed that any physical abuse must be met by equal force. In 1817, for example, after being struck by Joshua Pilcher, a former friend and perhaps a rival for the attentions of a young lady, Stephen Austin exclaimed that a man of honor must seek out those who injure him. "I have spirit enough," he warned, "to chastise impertinence." A man of honor, Austin went on to say, must give an explanation for an injury or give satisfaction. Receiving no satisfactory reply, Austin proceeded with a challenge. For the protagonist, honor had to be actively, not passively, defended. Fortunately, the whole affair was settled amicably when the St. Louis Masonic Lodge, which both men attended, intervened. J. G. Brady, the Mason in charge, threatened to have them arrested in order to prevent bloodshed. In addition, after three weeks of pressure, Brady secured an apology from Pilcher that ended the matter.[34]

The man of honor was self-assertive and born to leadership. Whatever his professional role, whether it be lawyer, judge, sheriff, editor, or military officer, his ultimate objective was usually political power. As such, he operated in a closed circle of friend and foe. He firmly held that his ideas, values, motives,

Stephen Austin was prevented from taking to the field of honor by his Masonic lodge. The Masons, however, were less successful in preventing other members from dueling. Courtesy State Historical Society of Missouri.

and actions must stand above reproach. If an opponent questioned his integrity by either word or deed, then he must be willing to risk facing the barrel of a pistol. What reduced the potentially large number of hostile rencounters, given the heated rhetoric of the times, was the fact that some bold political figures refused to acknowledge the world of protagonism.

Contrary to prevailing opinion, many territorial and state leaders who refused to duel did not jeopardize their professional careers. A case in point was Edward Bates. "According to the age and spirit of the times," wrote John Darby, it was difficult for a man like Bates to "maintain his standing without acknowledging and often practically illustrating the code of honor." Yet, Darby went on to write, "Mr. Bates never fought a duel."[35] Generally speaking, it was only the protagonist, the metaphor of the man of action and virulent rhetoric, who spun a web of his own making from which it was impossible to escape without loss of honor and public esteem.

Also, contrary to beliefs held then and now, the protagonist did not operate outside the law—he only widened it to include both man-made and immanent law. He, however, would be the sole arbitrator of which law should be followed and toward whom it should be applied. Immanent law resembled natural law in that it was beyond the purview of statute. It could not be legislated or revoked. Consequently, it could be defended in courtrooms or legislatures only by the person directly affected. Although frontiersmen were generally suspicious of the efficacy of litigation, there was no social stigma incurred by solving problems under the umbrella of law. Many of the most vio-

Andrew Jackson was the quintessential protagonist. He was Thomas Hart Benton's political mentor but was almost killed in a Nashville shoot-out with Benton. Courtesy State Historical Society of Missouri.

lent and self-assertive political and social elites in early Missouri used the courtroom as well as the pistol. Circumstances and expediency dictated which means of redress best served their interests.

The model for Missouri protagonists was Andrew Jackson, who combined the egalitarian impulses of western passion with the deferential nature of southern authority. He also symbolized an elitism that sought adulation of the masses but frequently forsook the adjudication of democratic law. Jackson's mother summarized this extreme individualism in a piece of advice given to her son: "Never tell a lie, nor take what is not your own, nor sue anybody for slander or assault and battery. Always settle them cases yourself." Old Hickory heeded his mother's words. He also immortalized himself and Charles Dickinson when he killed the crack shot in a duel. Early in his career, when he backed down John Sevier with a challenge by such actions, Jackson gained considerable respect among the rough-and-ready populace.[36]

"Heroic spirits" such as Jackson became the prototype for Missouri duelists and the legends and lore created in the new West.[37] The duel as metaphor no doubt abetted this transformation. Over time, the declamations of protagonism projected the most powerful imagery. Yet this nineteenth-century progeny of medievalism has escaped modern historical investigation. Perhaps in part this was because the rules of the protagonist were largely unwritten, or perhaps it was because his world was such a strange mixture of existential defiance and conformity. He combined the rugged individualism of the frontier with the social conventions of the South. It was not that he was different from other members of his class, only that he exaggerated the code of honor and the prescriptions of violence to produce a cultural neurosis. Pride became hubris, the duel became nemesis. Courage turned to recklessness. Honor transmuted into eulogy. The more strident the rules of the code to which he subjected himself and others, the more absolute the punishment for transgression. The century was fortunate that more good men did not subscribe to this unwritten law.

Protagonism was not, however, the duel's only metaphoric representation. As this chapter has suggested, the duel was also a metaphor for social status and political hierarchy. In addition, it was distorted in order to justify organism, a sociological and scientific mode of thought prevalent in antebellum intellectual life. Adherents of the code duello also sought to legitimize it by arguing the duel's ability both to curtail spontaneous outbursts of violence and to preserve social equilibrium. Its metaphoric power was likewise attested to by the way numerous classes and groups in Missouri society tried, by their own violent deeds, to emulate the trappings of the duel. Few institutionalized forms of violence had deeper roots in Missouri than the duel, and fewer still had its resilient and adaptive qualities.

9

Sectionalism and Sacrifice

The Duel as a New Rationale for Old Violence

IN THE DECADE preceding the Civil War, the *ultima ratio* of the duelist was no longer confined to championing causes narrowly defined in individual or factional terms. Gone too were the early years when gentlemen risked death at ten paces in order to define their social status and to secure their standing in the community. The two instances which dramatized that protagonists journeyed to the dueling grounds for principles equal to, if not greater than, themselves were the 1856 Brown-Reynolds appeal to arms and the 1860 Pryor-Potter affair of honor. These encounters reflected a national tendency, apparent in the mounting violence of the late 1850s and early 1860s, to elevate the motives of the duelist to a higher plane of self-sacrifice. The cause that galvanized the new sentiment was slavery.[1] In short, the Missouri duel was swept up in a far greater conflict and, like other forms of violence across the country, it reflected the menacing stresses and strains of sectional controversy and disunion. B. Gratz Brown and Thomas C. Reynolds would become leaders of their political parties during Missouri's struggle over slavery, and both were ready to make the ultimate sacrifice to defend their sectional interests: Brown for the Union and Reynolds for the South. Pryor and Potter, although not Missourians, nevertheless influenced the philosophy of violence of one of Missouri's most prominent nineteenth-century statesmen, Carl Schurz. The dramas of 1856 and 1860, therefore, revealed a new dimension and a new utility for the code duello in Missouri. The duel had become a metaphor for sectional resolve and personal sacrifice in the months and years leading to the Civil War.

A portent of the sectional violence that would soon erupt across the land occurred in the 1838 duel between two congressmen, Jonathan Cilley and William J. Graves. The matter began when Graves, a Kentuckian, carried a challenge to Cilley of Maine. In a congressional debate, Cilley had sullied the good name of Colonel James W. Webb, editor of the *New York Courier and Enquirer.* Webb sent a challenge by way of Graves, which Cilley refused on the grounds that Webb was not a gentleman. The dictates of the code thereupon required Graves to issue his own challenge. Weeks of negotiations over language that might have prevented bloodshed proved futile. Eventually, both sides agreed to fight with rifles at a distance of eighty yards. The meeting place was not far from Washington, D.C.[2]

Although the confrontation did not directly revolve around issues of slavery or nullification, the duelists each chose consultants and seconds who shared many of their philosophical convictions. Thomas Hart Benton's advice, perhaps more than anyone else's, hardened Cilley's position and left little room for verbal maneuvers that might have prevented the altercation. Benton's motives were not altogether clear, but his evolving positions on matters of nullification and secession were making him suspect among the more ardent slavery supporters. Senator Henry S. Foote of Mississippi even pulled a weapon on Benton in the halls of Congress, but the pistol did not fire. That same year, George G. Vest wrote Atchison and lamented about a past time when "public men" (an obvious reference to Benton) "were honest and true." In this age, he further exclaimed, "thieves and adventurers" ruled the day.[3]

Whatever Benton's motives, the Cilley-Graves affair did not turn out as he planned. The first fire, inconclusive as it was, led to no reconciliation. Even a second fire did little to drain the cup of bitterness from their spirits. On third fire Cilley fell, mortally wounded. Following the duel, a majority report of a house committee recommended Graves's expulsion. Three of the four members of the committee were from Connecticut, New York, and Pennsylvania. The report, however, was rejected by the full House.[4]

Graves's victory did not make him a southern hero. He remained in Congress for only a few more years, and the sectional implications of the duel were temporarily lost in the rancor between Whigs and Democrats. Some years would pass before politicians would interpret violence between men of North and South as a test of sectional will. Nevertheless, the Graves-Cilley episode reflected the American absorption with questions of what constituted the national character. Southerners associated their character with "male effectiveness" as displayed by acts of manly bravado.[5] Cilley had shown northern courage but had died at the hands of a better shot. Would others from his section have the same strength of character when confronted either individually or collectively by southern resolve? The significance of the question was not lost on B. Gratz Brown. It was not coincidental that in accepting Reynolds's earlier challenge in 1855, he specified common American rifles with open sights and round balls with not over one ounce of shot, at a distance of eighty yards. These terms were identical to those in the Graves-Cilley duel.

Duels at midcentury were often fought with the punctilio of earlier times. Courtesy State Historical Society of Missouri.

Following the Graves-Cilley duel, the next score of years witnessed a changing standard of honor in the North that clearly proscribed the practice of dueling. The *New York Daily Times* in 1853 reprinted what it deemed a "model letter" on how and why to reject a dueling challenge. "The pen," it reported, "is mightier than the sword." Three years later, the same paper published what it considered to be the ten points of honor. None of them excused or condoned dueling. Northerners, although they still clung to cultural concepts of duty and honor, clearly were moving toward other institutionalized means of redressing personal difficulties.[6]

Southerners, on the other hand, defended their way of life and their peculiar institution. Many of them equated northern prescriptions of honor with the imputation of cowardice. Southern honor, on the other hand, immortalized valor and valued the opinions of others to the extent that it defined personal identification and self-worth. Graves defended his duel with Cilley by stating that "public opinion is practically the paramount law of the land; every other law, both human and divine, ceases to be observed, yea, withers and perishes, in contact with it."[7]

Southerners, like Graves, also exploited the histrionics of the duel to demonstrate their courage to the slave population.[8] With the approach of the Civil War, the duel was additionally employed as a metaphor of southern resolve to defend their way of life against the forces of democratic leveling and abolitionism.

A willingness to use violence was certainly in keeping with American traditions, but it became more pronounced in the later years of the antebellum South. It was, as historian Bertram Wyatt-Brown has suggested, a way of life that "pervaded all the white social classes." But the feature of the duel that distinguished it from other forms of violence was its symbolic and imaginative ability to define the essentials of southern character.[9] Southerners had rationalized other forms of institutionalized violence such as war and slave brutality as sanctified by the Bible and consistent with moral principles. As these and other practices came under increased attack, there was a growing tendency to justify the code duello with the same type of idealistic fervor. It was precisely this metaphoric element of the duel that northern intellectuals had come to loathe. They had rejected the code not only on moral and ethical grounds but also because it stood for an idealized world of antedated chivalry and false pride which masked a far different reality. Missourians too understood the duel's powerful, imaginative role in political life. It is within this context that the Brown-Reynolds duel, waged on an otherwise obscure island in the Mississippi, will be examined.

No affair of honor in Missouri history was so long in coming or as dramatized as the August 26, 1856, encounter between the two men. A period of nearly two-and-a-half years separated the initial controversy from the day of reckoning. The hiatus heightened the public's anticipation while it afforded both protagonists ample time for verbal heroics. In time, both men came to see their duel not only as making history but actually *as* history. The past had brought them to the island. The present would decide their individual fates. The future of their respective causes would hinge on their aim—the past present, and future all intertwined in the fury of a single fire. One commentator on Missouri duels, William V. Byars, aptly described the nature of this particular conflict as based upon a "constructive imagination, powerfully creative as a motive for self-sacrificing actions." The participants looked into the future and hoped that future generations would appreciate their mettle and understand their cause. Each man understood the metaphor of protagonism at work in his duel, and each was acutely aware of the verbal as well as the visual weaponry they wielded. Throughout the long and tortuous correspondence that culminated in the duel, both men constructed what Byars called "the artistic principles of tragedy." By education and training, each realized the transcendent value of words backed up by hostile actions. "Questions of language—of expression, form, motif—" historian Steven M. Stowe has written, "were at the center of what the duel meant as ritual." Brown and Reynolds each understood that language, as well as pistols, were weapons in their duel, and that victory might very well go to the one who best commanded both.[10]

Educationally, both men were prepared for the battle in which words would play a commanding role. Brown studied at Louisville and Transylvania

Universities and attended Yale University before launching his career in law, journalism, and politics. Reynolds had studied at the University of Virginia and completed a classical education at the University of Heidelberg in Germany. His fluency in German made him a formidable political foe.[11]

Both protagonists had come to Missouri at roughly the same period and both belonged to a Democratic Party, which at that time could accommodate men of varied philosophical persuasions. Brown quite naturally gravitated toward a free-soil position. His was a pedigree of abolitionism begotten by a Kentucky father, Mason, who may have fought three duels over his abhorrence of slavery. According to the ancestors of Dr. John G. Bryan, Mason dueled the doctor, who was a staunch supporter of slavery in Missouri. Judge Nathaniel W. Watkins, a judge, politician, and half-brother to Henry Clay, supposedly served as Bryan's second in their last encounter. Reynolds, on the other hand, was a true son of the South. Rumor had it that he had fled Virginia because of a duel.[12] By the early 1850s, Brown and Reynolds had established themselves as leaders respectively of the Benton and anti-Benton factions in the Democratic Party. In 1853 Reynolds had become U.S. district attorney for Missouri and had sided with the pro-slavery forces headed by David Rice Atchison and Claiborne F. Jackson.

Atchison and Jackson put to good use Reynolds's ability to converse in German and to make "inroads" into that all-important vote since, in hotly contested elections, the Germans often held the political balance of power. St. Louis Germans were a heterogeneous and divisive group. Intra-ethnic fragmentation, as well as ideological conflict, characterized these new immigrants. Their divisions by class, geographic origin, education, and religion were only exacerbated in a community such as St. Louis, with its dynamic economy and rapidly expanding population. The German vote had become a crucial element in the political calculus since the 1849 Jackson Resolutions had been introduced in the Missouri legislature. These resolutions opposed the doctrine of free soil and bore the stamp of the more extreme pro-slavery forces in the state. In addition, they split the Democratic Party and, when Thomas Benton openly condemned them, they brought to a close, in 1851, his thirty-year reign in the Senate. With the Benton and anti-Benton Democrats of near equal strength, the swing vote was often the Germans. Their vote, however, was largely unpredictable. Personalities as much as issues determined the outcome of elections. Between 1848 and 1850, 34,418 Germans migrated to St. Louis. Forty breweries, producing 23,000 barrels of beer a year (enough to provide 658 glasses per citizen of the city), testified to their new-found demographic strength.[13]

In April 1854, Brown courted the new immigrants. He weighed in against Reynolds in a series of editorials in the *Missouri Democrat* that were cleverly worded so as to discredit him in the eyes of German voters. Reynolds re-

B. Gratz Brown, an ally of Frank Blair, dueled Thomas C. Reynolds in a dispute stemming from the antislavery campaign in
Missouri. Courtesy State Historical Society
of Missouri.

Thomas C. Reynolds, Brown's opponent in
their famous duel of 1856. Courtesy State
Historical Society of Missouri.

sponded in a note inquiring whether or not Brown's intentions were "designed to be offensive." If so, he concluded, George W. Goode would receive his reply. The note avoided harsh and accusatory language and allowed the offending party ample room for maneuver. As such, it conformed quite nicely to the protocol of the duello. It was no accident that Goode, who had also been involved in an earlier duel in Virginia, was one of Brown's most ardent detractors.[14] Brown chose Colonel Robert M. Renick to deliver his reply to Reynolds. Pursuant to an exchange of notes and clarifications, the incident ended without bloodshed.

Another factor that may have militated against violence in round one of the feud was the possibility that Reynolds sought bigger game than Brown. He may have believed that the real author of the offending article was no less than Thomas Hart Benton. Acting upon that assumption, Reynolds made discreet inquiries to Brown that were designed to flush out the true identity of the author. This would afford him the opportunity to challenge the biggest name in Missouri politics. Upon learning that it was Brown, not Benton, who penned the criticism, Reynolds decided not to pursue the matter further.[15]

Brown's initial criticisms, on the other hand, were probably not intended to provoke a challenge. Nonetheless, political stridency was increasing dramatically. It was no aberration that the worst political riots in St. Louis history occurred during the elections of the mid-decade. The 1854–1855 joint session of the General Assembly fared little better. At times, wrote historian McCandless, it too "appeared to border on personal violence." The political rancor was so great that the legislature failed to elect a U.S. senator until 1857. The times were ripe for heroic, self-sacrificing action. "Politics in St. Louis, from 1850 to 1860," wrote Walter B. Stevens, "was a continuous performance."[16]

Brown understood this new dynamic. In 1855, at roughly the same time as the passage of the Kansas-Nebraska Act, he challenged Robert M. Stewart of Buchanan County, a state senator and political foe of the Benton faction, to a duel over remarks Stewart had made about Benton. The dispute became more heated when, in a verbal exchange before a joint session of the state legislature, each man called the other a liar. A time and place were set for the engagement and each principal, armed with horse pistols at ten paces, would be free to fire on the count. Brown, on the appointed date, journeyed to the dueling site. Stewart, who earlier said that he "didn't care a damn" whether or not there was a reconciliation, eventually withdrew his disparaging remark and the affair ended without powder being burned. Later Brown observed that had Stewart not apologized, "I should certainly have cut him down . . . as I was in most excellent practice and fully determined never to let him raise his arm." Another "arm" that was raised, however, pertained to the long arm of the law. Brown's part in the Stewart affair earned him the enmity of Cole County officials. He was indicted by the county but escaped punishment.[17]

Brown's resoluteness was equaled the following year on the bleeding Kansas frontier. Here, James Henry Lane, a delegate to the free-state constitutional convention, challenged pro-slavery advocate Grosvenor P. Lowrey. Lane's confidants tried to persuade him to forgo the duel, questioning how the "Eastern idealists" and "philanthropists" would react. The arguments fell on deaf ears as Lane intended to keep his appointment. Although the duel did not materialize, Lane was quite willing to meet fire with fire. He, like his Missouri counterpart, realized the symbolic importance of standing tall in a duel. Lane's "dramatics," one historian later wrote, "kept the prairie boys amused and inspired."[18]

Missouri politics in 1855, like those in Kansas, were very contentious. In the decade of the 1850s, for example, Missouri newspaper dailies increased from five to sixteen. It was proportionately a growth rate more rapid than that of any other area of the West and attested to the divisiveness of the slavery issue. Sectionalism even pervaded college life with deadly effect. In the early 1850s two separate killings were, according to historian Jonas Viles, related to state politics. In 1852 at the University of Missouri in Columbia, Robert Grant killed George Clarkson in part over a political quarrel. At the same institution the following year on December 19, two students, in what was termed a duel, met on the portico of Academic Hall. It was there that William W. Thorton of Shelby County, Illinois, shot and killed Benjamin F. Handy. Legend has it that because Handy's blood splattered onto one of the columns of the old administrative building, ivy would not grow there despite the best of efforts.[19]

During the 1850s Senator Benton was still the lightning rod for much of the political acrimony. Nevertheless, the storm that produced the fury lay in forces far greater and more powerful than mere politics. The Brown-Reynolds duel the following year may have been "the last political duel" in the state, but the shots fired that August morning were also the opening salvos of a far greater struggle that was soon to engage the state. The duel was, according to Stevens, "a glimmer, on the horizon, of the coming war storm." John N. Edwards, a compatriot of Reynolds during and after the Civil War, noted in a *Kansas City Times* report in 1872 that both duelists, "cool, brave, and daring, . . . represented a party, an idea, and a cause." The "cause," of course, concerned slavery. Slavery also contributed to another political phenomenon in the decade. Members of various parties, factions, and groups constantly shifted their allegiances as they groped their way toward a meaningful philosophy on the paramount issues of the day. This, too, was part of a "political evolution which was to become a revolution." A voter could be a "regular" Democrat, a Benton Democrat, a Whig, a Know-Nothing, a reform Republican, an Emancipationist, a Free-Soiler, or an Abolitionist.[20] Brown and Reynolds were aware of this added dimension. Their initial confrontation had occurred over the German vote, which both were determined not to lose.

In 1852 and again two years later, Brown had won a seat in the lower branch of the Missouri legislature. His victories, no doubt, could be attributed to the fact that his free-soil position reflected the majority of the St. Louis Germans and their republican sentiments. Reynolds and other members of the anti-Benton German faction were still poised to make inroads into that support. In 1855 Brown's editorial rhetoric again produced a menacing inquiry in the form of a note sent by Reynolds by way of St. Louis Collector of Customs W. A. Linn. Unlike the previous note, this one demanded an editorial withdrawal, "a disavowal and repudiation of the communication," and an "apology." In characteristic fashion, Brown refused all of the demands. He declared that he would not be browbeaten by Reynolds and awaited his protagonist's response. Reynolds promptly challenged, noting that Brown's reply was "not only insufficient, but offensive." Brown accepted the challenge, "constrained," as he put it, "to gratify your unjustifiable caprice." Captain D. M. Frost, he added, would serve as his second. Reynolds then named Linn to act in the same capacity for him.[21]

Frost informed Linn that Brown had chosen terms identical to those in the Cilley-Graves encounter. Reynolds objected to both choice of weapons and the length of fire. The American rifle, he argued, was "unusual and barbarous" and the distance of eighty yards, because of his nearsightedness, afforded Brown the invidious opportunity to "shoot me down with perfect safety." On March 25 Linn, in a note to Frost, proposed shortening the distance to twenty yards.[22]

What next followed was communication so voluminous and convoluted in nature that previous hostile encounters paled in comparison. Each principal published his interpretation of the code's precedents and prescriptions, and each was as concerned with achieving the utmost political advantage from the correspondence as he was with gaining the strategic advantage on the field. Frost, in a communication to Linn, also on March 25, asserted that Brown was completely within his rights to choose weapons and distance since this was a practice "sanctioned by the custom of the Anglo-Saxon race." According to Walter Stevens, a historian of this duel, "the effect upon politics was considered at every step taken in this correspondence." All rules of the code duello were respected, and every sentence carefully read and screened by "experts" of the code.[23]

One of the sources of expertise consulted was Lorenzo Sabine's *Notes on Duels and Duelling,* published that very year. In his notes, Sabine expressed the lofty hope that his ideas would lessen bloodshed and advance the cause of human brotherhood. Reynolds and Brown both carefully perused the *Notes,* especially the author's position on the distance of the fire. This was a particularly delicate issue because of Reynolds's nearsightedness. St. Louis historians who later examined Sabine's work also noted that both principals had outlined their respective positions on this matter in the margins of Sabine's text.[24]

Colonel T. P. Andrews brought still another mitigating circumstance concerning the weapons and distance to Reynolds's attention. Robert M. O'Blenis had just received a ten-year sentence in the penitentiary for killing a certain Mr. Brand who had refused to drink with him. Andrews cautioned Reynolds that killing Brown in a rifle duel might very well be defined as murder rather than as self-defense.[25]

After months of inconclusive wrangling, the principals postponed their fateful encounter. Although Brown had accepted Reynolds's challenge, it was he who ran afoul of the law. In June 1855, a writ was issued for Brown's arrest by authorities in St. Louis. Since he was still attending the legislative session in Jefferson City and courting a girl from the same city, the sheriff in St. Louis in turn notified the sheriff of Cole County to have him appear before the Cole County Circuit Court. Later in August, Brown was forced to post a bond for five hundred dollars in response to a grand jury indictment.[26] He was not, however, arrested.

The following year both men again waged heated political campaigns. Reynolds sought a seat in Congress, and Brown stood for reelection in the state legislature. The fires of bitterness between the two had smoldered but had not died out. The next time, Reynolds vowed, he would maneuver Brown into issuing the challenge, thereby giving him the opportunity to set the terms. The flare-up did not take long in coming. After Brown, in the *Democrat,* accused Reynolds of putting the Germans and Irish on par with Negroes, Reynolds responded to this "unmitigated lie" with an attack on "the notorious poltroonery of its editor." Brown's reply was the essence of protagonism. No gentleman need defend his honor on the field if it violated his moral or ethical principles. But Reynolds had used the heroic language of the code duello and was now subject to its rules. However, Brown contended, his opponent had already "backed out of a challenge" and could no longer be "viewed as within the pale of those who appeal to such modes for the adjustment of personal difficulties, or expect his effusions to be noticed in that light."[27] In short, Reynolds had forfeited his claim as a gentleman—his honor lost by default. For a free-soiler, even one from Kentucky who loathed many of the institutions and practices of the slave South, Brown's harsh interpretation of the code had a ring to it very reminiscent of that of the region against which he would soon take up arms.

Reynolds was clearly on the defensive. Nevertheless, he could still goad his opponent into issuing a challenge that would give him the strategic advantage on the field. He responded to Brown's philippics by posting him. Reynolds's attack appeared in the *Pilot* on July 29. The editor of the *Democrat,* he publicized, was a coward and a liar whose "object cravenness" allowed him to tolerate "insults of the most stinging and degrading kind." Furthermore, he exclaimed, Brown's earlier terms were a "farce." When pushed by Reynolds to fight "within a *visible* distance," Brown had shown the white feather. The posting accomplished its task. On August 18, 1856, with the elections completed, Brown issued his challenge. There was, however, something unusual in the wording of the note. Brown referred to it as a "peremptory challenge." Terse and demanding, it offered no maneuverability for the challenged party either to assess the nature of the insult or to find a way to defuse the situation. The note was highly offensive to Reynolds and his second, Ferdinand Kennett. They interpreted it as an imperious command, the essence of which precluded all debate and delay. A peremptory challenge admitted no refusal on the second party. It demanded an immediate journey to the field of honor in order to put a decisive and mortal end to their quarrel. On their objections Brown, after receiving assurances that the duel would be accepted, modified the original wording. Reynolds then promptly accepted the challenge with an equally terse two-line reply. Reynolds chose English dueling pistols at twelve paces. The combatants would meet on a small sandbar in the Mississippi River, outside the jurisdiction of Missouri and Illinois authorities. The site was about forty miles south of St. Louis and near the palatial estate of Ferdinand Kennett, an ardent pro-slavery politician and husband of Julia Deadrick Kennett, the granddaughter of John Smith T. The weapons of possible destruction had six-inch barrels, triggers, double-sights, and smooth-bores. Each pistol was to be leaded with a one-ounce ball. They were made of mahogany and had the word "London" engraved on the barrel.[28]

An unusual article of the duel originally provided for an interval of up to one minute during which time the second, who was to give the word, would say "fire" and "stop." After considerable discussion, the parties mutually agreed to cut the interval down to one second. The principals agreed to hold the pistols upright until the word "fire." At that time they would take aim and fire when the call reached "one." No firing would be allowed after the next word, "stop." This dueling technique was often referred to as the snap shot. Of the two principals, Reynolds was the most adept at this style of shooting as he had taken some time off to practice this rapid-fire technique. He also remarked, both before and after the affair, that he meant only to wound Brown and not kill him. Hence, the additional practice was necessary.[29]

Throughout these preliminaries, the public was fully informed as to the nature of the affair. Yet no one tried to stop it. The principals had waged meticulous public relations campaigns against each other, and reconciliation at this juncture would surely have been anticlimactic. Many of the state's leading citizens participated directly or indirectly in the affair. No one seemed concerned that their involvement might jeopardize their personal reputations or political careers. Brown chose Colonel David P. Mitchell and Leo

Walker as his seconds and Senator Benton and Frank B. Blair as his advisers. Reynolds chose Colonel Ferdinand Kennett and Captain Thomas B. Hudson as seconds and Colonel David H. Armstrong, Colonel W. A. Linn, and Isaac H. Sturgeon as his advisers. Dr. J. H. Shore served as his surgeon.

Since the journey from St. Louis to the sandbar was an arduous one, it required some rest and relaxation before the engagement. Southern etiquette, therefore, called for Brown and his entourage to be hosted by his adversary's second. According to John N. Edwards, who later served with Reynolds in the Confederacy, Kennett more than obliged. He received the group "with princely hospitality" and "surrounded" them "with every attention and luxury possible." "Nothing," Edwards later wrote, pleased Kennett "so well as a duel, if a duel had to be fought," and he was committed to giving "an air of elegance and aristocracy to the whole performance."[30] Reynolds arrived near Selma Hall on the twenty-fourth and stayed with G. W. Chadbourne, later president of the St. Louis Shot Tower Company. Brown was not married, but Reynolds had departed the city without even informing his wife of the impending duel. According to Edwards, however, she would have supported his decision:

> She believed in fighting duels when duels were necessary, and like the Spartan Matron would have buckled on her husband's armor and bidden him go forth to the fight and return on his shield or come not back dishonored.[31]

On August 26, the morning of the duel, Kennett prepared two skiffs that pushed off from Selma Hall toward the sandbar. To break the tension, he asked Brown's second, Mitchell: "Would you like to be shot today?" "As well one day as another," Mitchell curtly replied. "Why?" "It looks like tempting Providence," said Kennett. "It may be," retorted Mitchell, "but Providence blesses him who shoots first and pulls the steadiest trigger." From that point on the skiffs made their way in silence. When they reached the sandbar, it became apparent that Brown had made a strategic mistake. He wore a black suit that stood out distinctively against the sand. Reynolds, attired in gray, blended into the surroundings. Kennett then proceeded to win both coin tosses. Thus he was able to choose the best position and to call the word. The distance was stepped off and marked, and the principals took their positions. Kennett inquired if both gentlemen were ready, and receiving an affirmative, he cried, "Fire." Before he could call out the second word, "one," two shots rang out almost as one. Reynolds had gotten his shot off first and his ball struck Brown above the right knee. The impact threw the latter's aim off just enough that his bullet whistled harmlessly by his protagonist. Although in extreme pain and lamed for life, Brown insisted upon a second fire, but the sec-

Selma Hall was the palatial estate of Ferdinand Kennett. Brown stayed there the night before his duel with Reynolds. Courtesy Missouri Department of Natural Resources.

onds and surgeons would have none of it. Reynolds then approached his wounded victim and extended his hand in friendship. All of the rituals that pertained to reconciliation then occurred between the parties. Colonel Mitchell approached Kennett and suggested the propriety of the withdrawal of all communications between the parties of an offensive character. He further suggested that they should hereafter meet and recognize each other as gentlemen. Kennett, although he would later regret that Reynolds did not have the opportunity for a second fire, concurred. By chance, a passenger steamboat happened by. The parties hailed it and headed festively back to St. Louis.[32]

In the meantime, English, French, and German newspapers across the state tried to be the first to report the details. Some suggested that Brown had been killed. Others believed Reynolds to be seriously wounded in the shoulder. A rumor that the affair occurred on Bloody Island spread quickly, only to be squashed by other accounts that had it on an island near Selma. The *Morning Herald*, on August 27, echoed the sentiments of most papers. While it expressed its "disapprobation" to dueling, it went on to say that "we are convinced that *public sentiment* demanded it."[33]

Ironically, as the two gentlemen from this critical border state settled their affair of honor with coolness and bravery, the rest of the country was not following suit. Only a few months before, Preston Brooks had nearly bludgeoned Senator Charles Sumner to death in the halls of Congress. Bleeding Kansas was close to hemorrhaging as talk of a horrid civil war filled the hot summer air. It was as if the island sandbar had become a bastion of decorum in a sea of national turmoil. Both Brown and Reynolds hoped to express, in the finest traditions of the South, how violence could be structured and contained within the institutional limits prescribed by the code. The two men were, wrote historian William Byars, filled with hate and yet conformed "at every point to the punctiliousness of the code duello.[34] The *St. Louis Leader* on August 27, 1856, saw this dichotomy. It, too, perfunctorily condemned dueling but praised the "high spirit and chivalrous sentiment in the bosom" of both men. The paper then candidly confessed:

> We are free to confess that we see no *natural* alternative between admitting the duel and establishing a society of mean-spirited poltroons, insensible to the point of honor, and in which all personal protection being left to penury damages or the servile punishment of imprisonment, mercantile honor itself gradually disappears, and the name of gentleman becomes a myth. It is the supernatural grace of Christianity alone, that can solve this difficulty.[35]

The *Leader's* "confession," that neither money nor incarceration—no worldly remedy save the duel—could preserve the honor of a gentleman, went to the very roots of violence. The admission, if written half a century before, perhaps would seem less incongruous. Coming on the eve of the Civil War, however, it further demonstrated the cultural resiliency of the duel and how outer displays of violence revealed inner strengths of character. Unfortunately, as the coming decade and a half would attest, this type of controlled violence would seldom be emulated.

The duel had again served as a metaphor of civility, but it also symbolized something far more powerful. It was to be a Civil War in microcosm. "Every element of Civil War," wrote Byars, "was represented" in the St. Louis of 1856.[36] Reynolds and Brown both hoped that their resolve, self-sacrifice, and bravery would be emulated in the course of sectional struggle if and when it occurred. Their affair of honor represented a vain desire and desperate attempt to demonstrate that bitterness need not lapse into barbarity. Reynolds's outstretched hand of friendship to the fallen Brown dramatized the facility of personal reconciliation. Nonetheless, the example was all but lost within the maelstrom of guerrilla war and Reconstruction vengeance. Yet, at a very personal level, Reynolds's gesture began a long and stormy process that eventually led to a lifelong friendship with Brown. In 1860, Missourians elected Claiborne Fox Jackson and Reynolds to the two highest state offices. After the war began, the two of them fled to Confederate safety, taking with them the great seal of Missouri. Upon the death of Jackson in

1862, Reynolds assumed the office of Confederate Governor of Missouri. When the war ended, he retreated to Mexico with General Joe Shelby. After returning to Missouri, stripped of his civil rights, he presented, in 1869, the great seal to Governor Joseph W. McClurg.

Brown's career was even more distinguished. Within six months of the duel, Brown delivered a powerful speech in the Missouri House of Representatives calling for the gradual emancipation of slaves with compensation provided to the masters.[37] During the war, he served as a Union officer and a U.S. senator. In 1870, the people of Missouri elected him as their governor. It was in this capacity that he was able to reach out in political friendship and to restore Reynolds's civil rights. In 1874, the former Confederate was elected to the Missouri General Assembly. Two years before, Brown had been nominated for vice president on the Liberal Republic ticket. The two old protagonists retained their friendship until Reynolds's mysterious death in 1887. His body was discovered at the bottom of an elevator shaft in the St. Louis Federal Building. His wife, that "Spartan matron," had died a few years earlier and, increasingly, the old duelist had heard voices calling him from the grave. Eventually, he succumbed to the temptation in an apparent suicide.[38]

The Brown-Reynolds duel undoubtedly was the most important and sensationalized encounter in Missouri during the decade prior to the Civil War. But their affair of honor was not the only hostile challenge or exchange of fire in the years leading up to 1861. The details of these other encounters, however, were never spelled out. Therefore, it is unclear whether or not these affairs had political origins. One interesting facet of these Missouri duels and challenges was the interest they garnered from the eastern press. The *New York Times*, which received its information from the *St. Louis Democrat* and the *St. Louis Republican*, regularly published descriptions of violence from the border states. It was in the *Times* that the nation learned of two episodes in the summer of 1858. The first event was a challenge sent by St. Louis physician M. A. Pallen to another doctor in the city, Dr. Lane Walker. Dr. Drake McDowell served as Walker's second and arranged the details. The men would fight near Cahokia, Illinois, and therefore beyond the pale of authorities in Missouri. Each would be armed with a rifle and at fifty paces they would wheel and commence firing. For reasons unknown, the city authorities vigorously attempted to stop it. They first arrested McDowell, which had the effect of delaying the duel. Next, both principles were arrested and held for sums of two thousand dollars each. They were discharged only after they pledged to keep the peace.[39]

Civil authorities that same month, however, did not prevent a duel between two "well-known citizens" of St. Louis. The principles were John C. Moore, the challenger, and L. Bouvier. Illinois was also the scheduled meeting place for this affair. Bouvier's second was referred to only as Mr. Menard, while C. L. Richards acted for Moore. The terms were pistols at twelve paces. The city, reported the *St. Louis Democrat,* was filled "with much inquiry and speculation" regarding the duel. Menard won by toss of the coin both the right to give the word and the choice of position. On first fire, the shot of one of the parties (generally believed to be Bouvier's), cut the coat of his adversary across the breast but did no damage. Seeing no hits, both principals proceeded to reload, but Menard objected. No second shot, he argued, had been stipulated in the initial agreement and, therefore, the affair should be called off. Moore, he maintained, had received satisfaction and, "on the score of conscience," Menard declined to participate further. Although the episode in and of itself was of little lasting consequence and ended without any further dramatics, it was significant that the *Democrat* reported on it with great seriousness. Far from holding the parties up to ridicule or making a caricature of the duel, the newspaper wrote that both principals "behaved with great coolness and courage." Historians of the code duello in the United States have documented that dueling "increased rather than decreased" in the South on the eve of the Civil War. These late 1850s rencounters in Missouri also attested to the duel's longevity there as well.[40]

As for the Brown-Reynolds duel itself, southern sympathizers quite naturally applauded the coolness of Reynolds while St. Louis Germans in particular admired Brown's courage and resolve.[41] It fell, however, to another German immigrant and transplanted Missourian, Carl Schurz, to discover within the moral framework of the duel the conflicting elements of personal tragedy and collective reclamation. With the growing realization of a pending sectional cataclysm, the duel acquired a new, operative significance. Schurz, who in 1860 had yet to embrace Missouri as his adopted state, also understood the powerful imagery projected by the duel and how it juxtaposed southern bravery and European romanticism. Now, in the desperate efforts of desperate men to avert the impending crisis, the duel assumed the strange, perverse character of peacemaker.

In an earlier day as a university student in Germany, Schurz had eschewed the practice of dueling, believing that no civilized people, "except, perhaps, the French," saw the institution as anything but a "remnant of medieval barbarity." His aversion to dueling, however, did not translate into a philosophical opposition to violence. As a university student, pro-democracy activist, and officer of the Franconia Student Society, he had thrown himself into the fray against the Prussian aristocracy with the same fervor he would later display in the causes of antislavery and unionism in the United States. Although the Germanic battle against overwhelming odds was "futile," he later wrote, it was an exciting "baptism of fire." Schurz, like many an embattled and disheartened 1848 revolutionary, fled the fatherland and made his way to a new continent and toward a new and vastly different kind of political struggle.

Carl Schurz, later a U.S. senator from Missouri, personally disliked dueling, but believed northerners might be forced to fight in order to show southerners their resolve on issues such as slavery. Courtesy State Historical Society of Missouri.

Soon he, too, was caught up in the exhilaration of democracy. Freedom, however, appeared to be checkmated by a southern plutocracy determined to suppress through violence the unlimited potential of a democratic society. Schurz no doubt had in mind the acts of intimidation that had become hallmarks of the southerners' closed society. The civil war in Kansas was no doubt fresh in his mind.[42]

In 1859, a duel that was applauded throughout the South occurred in California. This, too, may have influenced Schurz's thinking. The principals in this affair were D. C. Broderick, U.S. senator from that state, and D. S. Terry, Chief Justice of the California Supreme Court. Although certain personal issues divided the two men, it was generally assumed that the senator's abolitionist philosophy and Terry's staunch defense of slavery led to the duel which ended Broderick's life.

Perhaps an even more important event to influence Schurz was the Sumner-Brooks episode. Few political events in the half dozen years before the attack on Fort Sumter highlighted the cultural rift between North and South like the 1856 assault. Charles Sumner had referred to his senatorial colleague, Andrew Butler of South Carolina, as the Don Quixote of slavery. The speech in turn prompted Preston "Bully" Brooks, a relative of Butler's, to cane the Massachusetts senator thirty times in the course of a minute or so, leaving Sumner an invalid for several years. Chivalry required, of course, that Brooks wait until all ladies had left the Senate Chamber before he proceeded with the beating. Brooks, who was no stranger to the code duello, never entertained the notion of challenging Sumner since the latter, he believed, lacked courage as well as honor. Besides, Sumner was not his social equal.[43]

Throughout the North, politicians, intellectuals, and editors railed at the Sumner "outrage." When southerners cannot answer by reason, Emerson exclaimed, they try to kill. But they aim to kill only the best of their opponents. A man's bodily strength and his skill with a gun or knife, he added, are usually in opposite proportion to his intelligence and wit. Southerners, on the other hand, believed Brooks had vindicated family and sectional honor. Yet the general sentiment on both sides of the Mason-Dixon line ruled out the feasibility of a duel as a means of satisfaction. At approximately this juncture, Schurz began a philosophically painful reassessment of the duello. No matter how well-intentioned or valid, critics of southern behavior, he believed, were simply talking past their pro-slavery counterparts. Yankee opponents to dueling, wrote one northern observer, had "the canker of peace" upon them. Schurz was prone to agree. Southerners, he now reasoned, had traditionally employed a variety of tactics and techniques, including the duel, to prove their manliness and sectional resolve in the face of northern criticism. It was now time to fight fire with fire. The incident that rekindled this renewed sense of militancy in Schurz was the Pryor-Potter affair of honor, which occurred in April 1860. More than any other single political event, this encounter convinced Schurz that the adversary must be met on his own terms.[44]

Roger A. Pryor was a congressman from Virginia who challenged northern Congressman J. F. Potter to a duel over differing personal opinions concerning slavery. The argument had occurred in open debate on the floor of the House of Representatives and therefore the quarrel had been made a matter of public concern. Potter accepted Pryor's challenge and named bowie knives as his choice of weapons. When Schurz heard of the duel and its terms, he wrote from Milwaukee to a friend, saying, "God grant that all goes well." "I feel so anxious about our brave friend Potter," he confessed, "that I can hardly think of anything else."[45]

Pryor, in the meantime, had already reacted in horror to the barbarity of the terms set by Potter and declined to fight. Upon hearing of Pryor's disinclination, Schurz jubilantly wrote to Potter. The congressman's constituency, he exclaimed, believed him to be a "devil of a fellow" and had thrown "up their hats" when Pryor backed down. "Your fate," he went on to add, "is sealed. You have done the right thing at the right time and in the right place." By showing the southerners "your teeth" and having done so in such an "emphatic way," Schurz exclaimed, Potter had taught them a lesson about northern courage. A Republican hero had driven them "to the walls." Potter's heroics for Schurz transcended mere partisan politics. Many southerners equated a disinclination on the part of a northerner to duel as cowardice. It was symptomatic, he believed, of how the South had come to view the entire region north of the Mason-Dixon line. To refuse a duel "on the ground of conscientious scruples" only confirmed the North's lack of fighting resolve. Most southerners, wrote historian Grady McWhiney, scorned "such pacifism" and considered Yankees "too business-minded and dishonorable to fight." Although Schurz did not try to explain in depth the nature of southern character, it logically followed that, since southerners romanticized violence and looked upon war and other collective forms of aggression as aggregates of individual affairs of honor, then it might become necessary, he reasoned, to sacrifice personal principles "for the public benefit." Potter's bravado symbolized northern determination. If emulated by others it just might serve as a reminder to southern hotheads that it was a dangerous mistake to underestimate the Yankee fighting spirit. In a letter to Potter on November 30, 1860, Schurz described the nation's "firmness" against southern obduracy. "He could not have entertained any real fear," wrote historian Chester V. Easum, "as to the firmness of the man who had earned the sobriquet of 'Bowie knife Potter' in his encounter with Pryor."[46] The duel, as a metaphor of ennobling self-sacrifice, courage, and sectional resolve, had found a new, if perhaps uncomfortable, convert.

The nation, Schurz believed, would, in the months and years to come, issue many calls for personal acts of self-sacrifice. The dueling ground, an icon of southern privilege, might appear to be a strange place for acts of immolation, but if a single death could help dramatize a northern willingness to meet violence with violence, then an individual wrong might be righted by its collective import. Schurz knew the risk implied. "That such a state of public sentiment is not healthy," he later mused, "will be readily admitted. But we lived then in a feverish atmosphere which dangerously upset the normal standards of human conduct."[47] Schurz had appealed to a higher law than honor in his condemnation of dueling: he had appealed to conscience. But then he placed an even higher object above it. That was the "public benefit." The duel, magnified into a test of wills between slave and free societies, functioned for this latter-day Missourian as an idealization of Yankee resolve that might, in a perverse way, help to preserve the Union. B. Gratz Brown no doubt would have agreed.

10

Myths and Legends of Dueling

UNLIKE ITS COUNTERPART in the Deep South, the Missouri duel was a hybrid institution that seldom evoked the same nostalgia or romance. Nevertheless, during its bloodstained tenure the code spawned some unique and fascinating characters who contributed to the legends and myths of Missouri history. Every age has its heroes, and each age serves as a reference point for succeeding generations. So it was for the duelist. His exploits, especially during the antebellum years of Missouri, foreshadowed the latter-day hero, the gunfighter. Legendary figures such as John Smith T, the Missouri colonel who reportedly killed fourteen men in duels, served as transitional links from one form of violence to another. The code duello, as Kathryn C. Esselman acutely observed, "served as the basic model for the dramatic presentation of the gunfight." Men of honor such as Dr. John G. Bryan, who, as legend has it, backed down Smith T, belonged to a different fraternity of fast-shooting gentry than the gunfighter.[1]

Duelists, however, shared center stage in the formative years of the nineteenth century with other types of legendary figures. As the gateway to the West, Missouri was geographically situated as the jumping-off point for new genres of legendary heroes. One type was the mountain man, characterized by Kit Carson. Another type was the desperado, represented by men such as Frank and Jesse James. Culturally, the state also served as the link between earlier types of folk heroes such as keelboatman Mike Fink and frontiersman Daniel Boone on the one hand and gunfighters like Wild Bill Hickok on the other. Between these two time periods, the duelist personified the archetypal hero figure. All of these legendary genres were by-products of transitional societies struggling for cultural identification.[2]

By the early stages of the Industrial Revolution new metaphors of violence for a modern mass culture were necessary. Dueling still symbolized in this age of expansion the recurrent themes of brinkmanship and risk taking, but different myths and legends in new narrative forms were becoming more popular. This manner of interpreting historical experience through selective memory helped to fill, as Richard Maxwell Brown has suggested, the public's need for "a heroic ideal."[3] By the late nineteenth century, despite the best efforts of Missouri's myth makers, the legendary figures of dueling had been replaced in popular culture by a new type of western hero. This chapter is not only an examination of heroic figures of the code duello but also a study of how and why the myths and legends of violent men evolved during the 1800s in the way they did.

Early popularizers of bourgeois culture divided their attention between two kinds of heroes: the duelist and the folk hero. Of the former group, no one eclipsed the fame of Smith T. The folk hero was represented by the hardy frontiersmen, keelboatmen, and mountain men. These common men with uncommon qualities, so went the lore, were the shock troops of civilization. As previously noted, a third type of hero emerged after the Civil War that would in time eclipse both the pathfinders and the duelists. By nomenclature he would be typecast as the cowboy; in the vernacular he would be known as the gunfighter. While earlier heroic figures survived in somewhat muted form, these western archetypes lent credence to different myths created by new social exigencies. In one sense this unique breed of bad men represented the continuation of frontier pragmatism and self-reliance. In another respect they became a metaphor of western romanticism. And lastly, the cowboy mythology fulfilled the American need for a new hero—one that fused the earlier escapades of the western scout with the traditions of the antebellum gentleman. The ranch became the embodiment of the plantation minus the slaves as the cowboy version of democracy merged with the southern gentleman's penchant for honor.[4]

The cowboy mythology, focused as it was on men of simple ways and basic concepts of right and wrong, captivated later generations of Missourians precisely because the state's western roots proved to be deeper and more enduring in the long run than the more aristocratic traditions of the South. Each type of hero, the pathfinder like Boone, the duelist like Smith T, and the gunfighter like Hickok, generated a myriad of tales and lore. The gunfighter myth eventually eclipsed the other two by virtue of its versatility. The gunfighter came to encompass a variety of archetypes. He could be the lawman such as Hickok or Wyatt Earp, or the highly individualistic cowboy, or the outlaw. Each hero epitomized a distinct facet of western lore. Moreover, the Wild West expressed for modern America its "need for recognition" and equal status with Europe. The western hero, in short, became the American "parallel" of the medieval knight. He also could appeal to the dialects of good overcoming bad on the western frontier.[5] He personified those exaggerated character traits of rugged individualism and egalitarianism that were part of the ongoing process of democratization.

Earlier myth makers, however, had concentrated on the duelist and the common folk hero as they created civilization from savagery. They quoted a number of primary sources that supported Reverend Timothy Flint's assertion that when one crossed the Mississippi, one "travel[ed] beyond the Sabbath." Some settlers, like early-nineteenth-century historian Firmin Rozier, applauded the type of "bold, brave and adventurous" men who, filled with a "spirit" of venture and gambling, came to the wilds of Missouri. Others were not so kind. Henry R. Schoolcraft believed the land to be beyond "the pale of civilized society." Henry M. Brackenridge agreed. The status of society in territorial Missouri was so "savage," he concluded, that it was impossible for him to make it his lifelong home.[6]

Such an environment, the myth makers argued, reduced men to a common denominator of survival. It also bred heroes and legends. Folk heroes were generally men who assimilated to the rugged, natural habitat. Theirs was an escape to nature's arms and a rejection of quit rents, routine, taxes, debts, wages, and laws. One gained status and recognition on these outermost fringes of the wilderness not by rising above primeval instincts but by becoming the very best at those skills deemed essential for survival. Shooting, trapping, hunting, knife throwing, wrestling, fistfighting, running, and horsemanship were ways of gaining social stature in frontier communities. These manly pursuits were indelibly stamped into the frontier character. Governor Frederick Bates said as much when in 1825 he remarked that the character of the state was built upon "manly enterprise," and that "our vices . . . have upon them the impress of a noble daring." Even laws, he confessed, would not be able to suppress some of the violence "so interwoven with our habits." Only the passage of time and "other reformations," he added, would sublimate these basic instincts. Bates was undoubtedly correct. For its day and time, Missouri played out the dialectic of civilization and savagery with as much fury and deadly intent as any frontier before or after.[7] This was the world that early chroniclers of epic heroes described. Imbued with a spirit of democratic leveling, these writers interpreted the wilderness hero as the harbinger of grassroots democracy. L. U. Reavis, a historian in the 1870s, wrote of these legendary figures; their "habits," he said,

> were formed in the camp and in the forests; and their sense of justice was never blunted by those habits of guile which the complex relations of purely commercial communities engender. They were sensitive to insult, and summary in their manner of settlement of all quarrels.[8]

It was a harsh and hostile land populated, as General James Wilkinson, the territorial governor, lamented, by Indians and "pettifoggers" who swarmed like "locusts."[9] The resourcefulness of these folk and epic heroes as they confronted adversity contributed to hero mythology in which violence was condoned at best and idealized at worst. The frontier, however, always stood for more than a rugged environment where a man could test his metal and trust his powder. It was a geographic metaphor that embodied an etiology of entrepreneurialism and economic expansion.[10] Violence, which often accompanied the development of this capitalist ethos, thus served as an unwitting tool to shape many of the myths, heroes, and legends of the times.

Unlike the typical folk hero, who generally employed the same savage tactics as his adversary, the duelist took on a different persona. The stylistic context of the duel, mixing decorum with death and punctilio with principle, carried with it overtones of a higher social order. These social and ideological distinctions also dictated that distinctions be made in the topology of violence employed by members of the gentleman class. The duelist represented not the wilderness, but the arrival of civilization. He and others of his ilk operated in the backwaters and bayous of the wilderness. Technically, he was more of a pioneer than a frontiersman. By the time he arrived in an area, he had often been preceded by hunters, trappers, military scouts, squatters, and small, self-sufficient farmers. His type of speculative farming and mining activities required a more sophisticated infrastructure of food, supplies, equipment, and transportation than could be sustained in atavistic wilderness communities. A man such as John Smith T was not so much in harmony with nature as he was out to tame it and harness it to his designs. Nor was his life the story of a solitary wilderness figure cut off from the mainstream of civilization. Contrary to one historian who "ranked" him alongside Daniel Boone as an explorer, his isolation was always more symbolic than real.[11]

Smith T's appetite for land had been whetted by ownership of extensive landholdings east of the Appalachians. This was not uncommon among many of his contemporaries who possessed the same educational and family background.[12] But the possibilities of almost unlimited western lands drove him forward with a fervor matched by few men of ambition. It fell to men of his ilk to become the militia officers, land speculators, the founders of settlements, and later the political elites of these new communities. The commonly held assumption was that greed, speculation, and violence were the by-products of this kind of frontier entrepreneurialism.

Although the idealization of violence characterized both types of heroes, many important differences existed. While the frontiersman symbolized western independence and unconventionalism, the duelist stood for southern breeding and good manners. While the former became part of the wilderness, the latter proved that it had been overcome and subdued. Each tradition, replete with a set of social and political implications, competed for ideological influence with the masses. Each tradition also developed a set of myths, constructed through narrative, that metaphorically linked idealized conduct to certain symbolic forms of violence. Since myths are expressed through narrative form rather than discursive or argumentative structure, their mode is metaphorical. They do not, therefore, have to stand the tests of logic and analysis. Myths, especially in the trans-Missouri West, became a blending of fiction, fact, and folklore. Literary and folkloric, these myths established a "pattern of anecdote and characterization" oftentimes expressed through metaphor.[13]

Metaphors reinforced myths through historical imagination and memory. It was through this process that myths abetted the historical transformation of dueling into legend. Myths also confirmed the structural underpinnings of a society and were part of a social and psychological process that transformed knowledge into power through the creative force of the imagination. Myths have the capacity to change as societies change. Their utility can be found in diverse ways. They can be a valuable tool in a state's or in a community's search for a "usable past." They can lend credence to the prevailing customs, traditions, and values of a people by interpreting the past so that it becomes a prescription for future action. In frontier Missouri, myths played a vital role in socialization and the culture-making process.[14] Behind the code of honor and the cult of shame lay the functionalization of myth.

Arguably, the United States has been more myth-laden than most western societies because of its lack of a feudal tradition and its relative newness upon the world's stage. Missouri in the early nineteenth century was a microcosm of this historical void. As a frontier land with Spanish, French, and Indian heritages, Missourians looked for ways to bind themselves together. They sought something distinctively American and uniquely southern with which to identify. History, legends, and myths served these ends. In the age of the great man theory of history, the idea that the duelist stood alone on a solitary field of honor, above the morality and courage of the ordinary citizen, became a vital element in this mythology. For many Missouri citizens, sites such as Bloody Island evoked memories of valor and sacrifice.

By the age of enterprise, however, dueling had less metaphoric utility for the new capitalist upper class. Although they respected the content of the duelist's character, the new economic mandarins were less inclined to support the violent methods employed by the old elites. Nevertheless, the code represented for the men of venture capital one idealized aspect of the American spirit. Dueling, therefore, served as a historical link, albeit a weak one, between one form of physical recklessness and a later form of economic risk taking. In the final analysis, however, it was the cowboy who rode through the pages of history while the duelist walked into a footnote. As the latter part of this chapter will explain, the demise was to some extent caused by American literary romantics' fascination with the dialectics of nationalism versus disunity, civilization versus wilderness, and hero versus villain. American historians were also indebted to literature. They too examined the march of history as the triumph of the common man—of reformer over reactionary; of yeoman farmer over tidewater aristocrat; of frontiersman over mercantile hydras such as the Bank of the United States; of manual laborer over self-serving capitalist.

Dueling played an uncomfortable role in this panegyric scheme. It was sectional rather than national, aristocratic rather than democratic, and egotistical rather than altruistic; but above all, it was difficult to fit into the "usable past" of American history. Good can triumph over evil only in the context of visualizations that are simple, symbolic, and ideological.[15] Dueling in the antebellum period may have possessed these taxonomic qualities, but in the postbellum age of industrialization, new myths and symbols were necessary. For post–Civil War generations, therefore, new meanings had to be given to old experiences. New heroes and legends would be forged from the rubrics of the past, but they would serve new masters and meet new social agendas. Industrial democracy was not an ideal environment for the myths and legends of dueling.

It was not, however, for want of effort that nineteenth-century historians and popularizers of the duel failed to keep alive the names of men like John Smith T. No duelist ever captivated Missouri audiences in the last century like the infamous colonel. The myths and legends that surrounded his name appeared to ensure his notoriety in tales and textbooks long into the twentieth century. But surprisingly, this "savage fighter" with fifteen kills, as so described by historian Floyd Shoemaker, has hardly merited a footnote in many of the state histories.[16]

The lost legends and myths of Smith T developed from a variety of sources throughout the nineteenth century. The first source originated from oral and folk tradition passed on during his early career in Tennessee and Missouri, when "only the boldest pioneers would hurdle a pathless wilderness to seek such distant lands." The histories written by the Goodspeed Publishing Company during the 1880s cited anonymous sources back in Tennessee in depicting Smith T as a feared duelist who had killed many men in personalized combat. In 1910 historian William B. Napton wrote that "in the town of Nashville alone, Smith T had participated in a number of duels and other hostile encounters."[17] A perusal of the Tennessee court records, however, revealed not one duel, lethal or otherwise, in which he fought. Yet Smith T did not attempt to quell the stories that were even then beginning to take on the proportions of legends. Undoubtedly, he believed the accounts of his unerring aim deterred many unauthorized squatters who might otherwise have settled on his vast landholdings.

After his arrival in Missouri, he again put to good use the tall tales that had originated in Tennessee. During the turbulent decade following the American possession of Missouri he became embroiled in his bitter war with Moses Austin for supremacy in the mineral district from Potosi to Ste. Genevieve. His crimsoned past once again served to give him an aura of invincibility that caused many a wavering miner to side ultimately with him. Even Austin wrote that Smith T was a man of "daring" who, according to his sources, had wreaked more havoc in Tennessee than any forty men. Some may give him godlike qualities, he wrote to Rufus Easton, for "truly he is a God but a god of Darkness."[18]

The next set of tales were derived from Smith T contemporaries such as Henry M. Brackenridge, John Darby, and Firmin Rozier. These authors belonged to the school of Young America. Highly nationalistic, they glorified American expansion and applauded the men of the heroic age who made it happen. The evolution of the nation's political economy, replete with literary hyperbole about its legendary heroes, conferred an epic dignity to this march of progress.

These purveyors of myth bestowed upon duelists and adventurers a higher social status than was granted to the wilderness pioneer. The functionalization of myth conferred legitimacy upon both violent codes of conduct and economic risk-taking. In their memoirs, reminiscences, and personal recollections, they exaggerated many historical facts to promote their book sales. Also, by magnifying the stature of the famous men they knew, they likewise enhanced their own sense of self-importance.[19] Association with powerful and violent men bolstered the authors' egos while they cashed in on the hero's fame. Writers of this genre were proponents of an atavistic, highly individualistic sense of history. They idolized the men of the heroic age and tried to put their figures on a par with the likes of Jackson, Bowie, Crockett, and Houston. Since Smith T had in fact challenged both Houston and Jackson to duels, his stature was secured in their eyes.

Besides courage and daring, the lions of the heroic age were usually men of business acumen and classical education. They were generally nonconformists whose success was achieved in spite of their disregard for convention and precedent.[20] Their character reflected the energy and belligerence of the frontier. These environmental influences shaped the hero as he in turn helped to change it. From his exploits could be gleaned the seeds of pragmatism and ambition that would blossom forth in the twentieth century. According to the myth makers, the hero's demeanor toward the poor and downtrodden, as well as toward his defeated foes, was marked by kindness and generosity. Normally, men such as Smith T displayed handsome physical features that were rewarded by the affection of a devoted woman. This commitment, how-

John Darby, lawyer and mayor of St. Louis, popularized the Smith T legend. Courtesy State Historical Society of Missouri.

ever, was sometimes disrupted by long and perilous journeys that required great tenacity and self-sacrifice.

Firmin A. Rozier, who as a youth knew Smith T, described him as a man of undaunted courage who killed fourteen men, mainly in duels.[21] Rozier consummated the marriage of myth and history already conceived by Darby and Brackenridge. Brackenridge, an attorney for many large landowners, believed that "kindness and benevolence appeared to be the natural growth" of the colonel's "heart." Yet it was a deceptive physiognomy. The same author told of watching Smith T track a bear into a cave, shoot it, and then lie quietly on the ground as the bear crawled over his body to die outside the cave. Brackenridge, however, was less inclined to stress his natural side than the rational. To amplify the point that the frontier had not degraded his hero, he told how Smith T had a falling out with old friend Samuel Perry over a mining dispute. One day, he overtook Perry as he was riding toward Ste. Genevieve. He told his friend that he regretted their differences but, referring to a brace of pistols he was carrying, suggested that the two settle the problem in a "rational manner" by dueling it out on the spot. When Perry sensibly declined, Smith T cordially accepted the verdict and continued to ride with Perry for some distance. They conversed on a variety of subjects, and the colonel did not broach the subject of a duel again. Brackenridge believed that his hero's fame in the "western states and territories" was "unrivaled." "Nothing," he exclaimed, "was wanting but a more extended sphere of action to have equaled or surpassed the fame of Marion or Putnam."[22]

John Darby, later mayor of St. Louis and another early exponent of the Smith T legends, also served as the colonel's attorney. More than any of the early popularizers of the Smith T myth, it was he who best portrayed the dual nature of his character. He described the dialectics of savagery and politeness that became the essence of Smith T's persona. This swashbuckler had come to the frontier—a primeval world of violence—where he established his legend. "It was said," wrote Darby, "he had killed fifteen men, mostly in duels, where his life was in danger." Although "every person seemed to have a dread and fear of him," his tales of courage and derring-do were "in the mouth of every-body." As he seized the economic possibilities afforded him and confronted adversity, he gained strength from his hardships rather than being overcome by them. As such he developed a kind of "courage, self-reliance, and determi-nation possessed by few men." To his eulogist, Smith T was not outside the law, albeit fragile as it was, as much as he stood above it. His extreme sense of individualism allowed him to establish his own jurisdictional parameters. Yet his fights were fair, "honorable, open, manly warfare." Even though he often sought justice by his own hand, he "always stood his trial" and was never con-victed. His oft-quoted remark summarized the contradictions in the life and legend of this remarkable pioneer. He was, said Darby, "as polished and cour-teous a gentleman as ever lived in the State of Missouri" and as "mild a man-nered man as ever put a bullet into the human body."[23]

Following the eulogists came the sensationalizers. These were antebellum writers who had few causes save their pocketbooks. One of the more notable was Alfred Arrington, alias Charles Summerfield. From 1847 to 1849 he published three books that expressed his "sincere admiration" for the "high heroic courage" of these "chivalrous sons of the fiery south." For Arrington, John Smith T stood "at the head of the whole class," for no man except him had killed eight men in a single combat. This "Ajax" in both "size and in courage" was the most savage product ever produced on the Missouri frontier. Despite his numerous killings, no jury ever found him guilty of murder because he was "the idol of the lower class." The "memory of his goodness to the poor," Arrington mused, still lived in the hearts of humble widows and orphans, "who forgetting all his cruel-ties," believed him to be "a steadfast benefactor" to all of them.[24]

Throughout the narrative, Arrington emphasized Smith T's affection for the poor and their reciprocity toward him. The aristocratic trappings of the duelist were giving way to a new type of western hero, the desperado. Arrington hoped that the colonel, although rich and famous, could be identi-fied with a larger mass audience. This "meanly clad" individual, "though rich, hated the rich," wrote Arrington. "I have sworn," said the hero, "to slay every d____d speculator that dares to set foot in the state of Missouri!" Not until after the Civil War would the transition from duelist to gunfighter be complete, but the outlines of a new type of western lore with heroes such as Jesse James were clearly visible.[25]

One of the last serious revisions of the life and legends of Smith T took place in the latter part of the nineteenth century. In 1888, *Goodspeed's History of Southeast Missouri* recounted a number of his adventures, including a disastrous foray against the Indians at the Galena mines in Iowa. The *History of Saline County,* published in 1881, began stretching the historical record by reporting on "three or four duels, in all of which he killed his man." It inaccurately reported that he fought at least one of these affairs of honor on Bloody Island. In an effort to make the subject larger than life and to inject some panache, the book told of his ability to instill fear. "His commands," it stressed, "were always obeyed, or there was a funeral if they were not." Another historian of Saline County recorded that he may have been the "most singular and remarkable man in some respects who ever lived" in the county.[26]

Twentieth-century historians, however, were not so impressed by the colonel's exploits. By the Progressive period, a certain amount of healthy debunking of popular myths was well underway. Walter B. Stevens, in his volumes called *Missouri: The Center State 1821–1915,* for example, spared Smith T only one page. The contradictory elements of his character that had given marrow to his life were all but neglected. Robert S. Douglass and Floyd C. Shoemaker likewise gave him short shrift. The multifaceted and conflicting facets of his personality, that is, the polished gentleman versus the intrepid duelist as well as the ruthless entrepreneur versus the benevolent patriarch, had all but disappeared.[27] In most respects, the myths and legends of John Smith T have been frozen in time since the days of the Progressive historians. Modern scholarship has either reinforced the earlier caricatures with only a fleeting remark or ignored altogether the career of this remarkable pioneer and his single duel.

Even less has been revealed about another unusual character of early Missouri, Dr. John E. Bryan. Bryan, an ardent foe of Smith T but one who reportedly shared the same constellation of heroic traits as his antagonist, has virtually disappeared from the legends and lore of the state. We know little about shadowy Bryan except that he arrived in the Ste. Genevieve region from Kentucky sometime before the Louisiana Purchase. He was ardently pro-slavery. His business activities included mining, medicine, journalism, politics, farming, and industry. He likewise indulged in many social, political, civic, and religious activities in the mining region and later in St. Louis. However, the doctor was, according to most of his friends, averse to publicity.[28]

In addition, he left no manuscript collection, public writings, or private papers. His exploits were recounted by his grandson, Bryan Obear, who collected testimonials written by prominent men acquainted with the reclusive physician. The record reads as a Who's Who of antebellum Missouri history. Unfortunately, the original letters were omitted from the file submitted to the Western Historical Manuscripts Collection in Columbia. What remained were typed, second-hand notes whose authenticity cannot be substantiated. The lack of primary source material creates an interesting methodological problem for the historian. The objectivity of the collection must also be questioned, as its purpose as stated by Obear was to demonstrate that Dr. Bryan's "example of high manhood is worthy of emulation, and his deeds and memory of preservation."[29] The following accounts of Bryan's life, therefore, must be interpreted against this backdrop.

In a brief narrative of his grandfather's life, Obear contended that in 1822 the doctor shot Kentuckian Mason Brown in a duel. The wound was nearly fatal. Judge Nathaniel W. Watkins, a circuit judge and onetime speaker of the Missouri House of Representatives, also verified the Brown duel. However, he maintained the wound was inflicted on the "third encounter" between the two protagonists and that he [Watkins] had served as Bryan's second on that occasion. The nature of the quarrel was supposedly the anti-slavery position held by Brown. George M. Wilson, a mayor of Farmington, Missouri, believed it to be this duel that ran Brown out of the state. Confederate sympathizer and Boonslick politician John B. Clark, Sr., wrote that Brown was hit in each of the three duels but that only the last was near-fatal. Scattered throughout the various testimonials to Bryan are quotes that corroborated his skills as a duelist. Colonel Thomas L. Snead, an adjutant of General Sterling Price, quoted General John Marmaduke as saying that Bryan had fought "many duels." Dr. William T. Hord, a medical director in the U.S. Navy, testified that the doctor killed Bill Mitchell and Tom Woolhite in duels on a riverboat and shot Cameo Kirby in a duel near Clarksville. Other writers stepped forward to verify these and other rencounters.[30]

The attempt to resurrect myths and images on the order of those of John Smith T was also evident in a letter attributed to former Governor Thomas Fletcher. Bryan, he noted, had killed a gambler and reprobate (Fletcher could not recall his name), but "not a Marshall or Sheriff west of the Mississippi River" would dare arrest him. Even if they had, Fletcher went on to say, the people would have "risen up and torn down the Courthouse before he could have been tried." Judge Watkins wrote that "his liberality knew no bounds" and he was "idolized" by his slaves. Thomas Wiley, a newspaper employee of Bryan's, wrote of the doctor's traveling across Missouri, "laying down the law to evil doers." Good people "were on his side and the bad men got out of his way." Edward Bredell, a merchant, miner, and lawyer in the Potosi–Ste. Genevieve region, wrote: "To fight the doctor meant to be defeated or killed."[31] William H. Swift, editor of the *St. Louis Dispatch,* wrote the following eulogy:

> He lived in a time that produced great men, wise and chivalrous, in a time when men had to fight to preserve respect, honor and property, and he fought fairly—out in the open and he was never defeated.

He reminded one, Swift said, of "knights and grand princes," and he was the "standard of morality and refinement." Judge John S. Brickey, who referred to Dr. Bryan as "Black Jack," said of him, "One after the other they went down before him, like wheat straws before a scythe . . . for as he was in single combat, so he was in everything else to the highest pinnacle of human endeavor."[32]

Bryan's mythical image contained violent and symbolic qualities; yet, because his story was rarely retold, he has faded from our collective memory to a greater extent even than John Smith T. Encomiums of such superhuman fighting ability attributed to Bryan would tend to place him alongside legendary figures of the Missouri frontier such as Smith T. There were other similarities in the lore about the two men: both Bryan and Smith T were said to have "compassion for poor people," and the breadth and depth of their knowledge of the classics was magnified. In essence, the tone and style in which the Obear Collection presented Bryan would make one wonder how the mineral area could have contained the likes of the doctor and the infamous colonel at the same time. In point of fact, at least according to the Bryan camp, it did not. Constructing a legendary edifice for their hero, many of the writers set out to destroy the myths surrounding the invincibility of John Smith T. George M. Wilson, for example, was one of those who held to the belief that it was the doctor who ran Smith T out of the state shortly before the colonel died in Tennessee.[33]

It was left, however, to William Hyde and Howard L. Conard, the editors of the 1899 *Encyclopedia of the History of St. Louis,* to provide the last and most complete revivification of the Bryan myth. This "gallant cavalier" with a "phlegmatic temperament" was nevertheless, they reported, "mild and gentle of nature" and a learned man. Although he philosophically opposed the institution of slavery, the authors added that he owned many slaves and was "an ideal master." He allowed his slaves to work for their freedom, but many, they added with a straight face, resold themselves back into slavery to the doctor, preferring to be "Dr. Bryan's nigger than a free nigger." Besides this benevolence, Bryan was said to be a philanthropist and civic leader who headed a large family and vassalage in southeast Missouri and acquired "the patriarchal diadem" for that region of the state.

Hyde and Conard likened Bryan to Smith T but suggested that the former was a more "courageous" individual. Because of the doctor's skill as a duelist, he instructed many young men in the deadly art. "Opponents," they declared, "were loth to challenge" him. The legend of Dr. Bryan was nearly complete. It required one magic episode that would establish his reputation among the ages, namely, a confrontation with that most "famous" of duelists, John Smith T. According to the authors, the event occurred when the two men clashed in court over conflicting land claims. Smith T, who "took a short road to wealth," had tied up in court a legitimate claim of the doctor's. After the trial had been continued for the seventh time, Bryan followed the colonel from the courthouse and confronted him on a Ste. Genevieve street. After an exchange of unpleasantries, the doctor struck Smith T across the face. Townspeople waited for Smith T's second to arrange details for the duel since it was "thought certain." If the account is true, then it was the first and only time in his bloodstained career that the colonel showed the white feather. Hyde and Conard left no doubt that it was Bryan's unanswered insult which prompted Smith T to take his "trusted slave" and leave the state. Shortly afterward he died "on the east bank of the Mississippi, in Tennessee."[34]

The *Encyclopedia*'s attempt at the dawn of the twentieth century to revive a new dueling legend occurred at a very unpropitious moment in the history of this bitter sport of gentlemen. A transmutation of the dueling myths had already begun, primarily because they appeared less relevant to new industrial and intellectual elites. The lives and legends of duelists personified less and less the essence of a changing American character. The influence of Frederick Jackson Turner no doubt played a pivotal role in this transformation. Despite the power of corporate America, Turner believed the pioneer experience could help regenerate republican values in an urban age. But his scheme of history interpreted the frontier environment as conditioning the individual more than the individual changing the environment. Consequently, Turner downplayed both the roots of violence and the elites who institutionalized such practices as the code duello. Nor did the deeds and actions of the duelists relate well to the needs of an evolving industrial society. In brief, one set of myths, legends, and heroes was overshadowed and replaced by another. Although both duelist and gunfighter espoused attributes of fair play and chivalry, the duelist represented a moral leadership that could be exerted only by the elites. The cowboy and the outlaw, on the other hand, acted out the dialectics of good and evil on an egalitarian stage before an emerging audience called a mass popular culture. These new "giants" became the archetypal figures of western history. The new hero was "the product of primitive, chaotic, elemental forces, rough, barbarous, and strong." He was, according to a late-nineteenth-century cowboy historian, "the most gallant modern representative of a human industry second to very few in antiquity."[35] No western figure better epitomized the transition from duelist to gunslinger than William "Wild Bill" Hickok. Not surprisingly, Hickok's mythic career also began in Missouri, the gateway to the West.

The date was July 20, 1865, the place Springfield, Missouri, an unlikely birthplace for mythogenesis. On that day when tempers flared as hot as the noon sun, two former friends, now mortal enemies, confronted each other near the Greene County Courthouse Square. At seventy-five yards they drew their pistols and fired simultaneously. When the smoke cleared, David Tutt had fallen to the ground with a bullet in the heart and William Hickok stepped forth into the pages of western history. Within a year and a half, *Harper's New Monthly Magazine* had published details of his "Date with Destiny," and Wild Bill had become a nationally recognized figure.[36]

The "duel" in the street not only launched a legend but also marked a transition from the punctilio of the code duello to a new and far more lethal form of personalized combat. It also witnessed the emergence of a new and more lasting type of mythic hero, the gunfighter. But Wild Bill Hickok's heroics that day would undoubtedly have been remembered by only a handful of folklorists and historians save for one salient point. He and other transplants such as Calamity Jane and Belle Starr were not immortalized until they left Missouri and made their mark in the West. Springfield in 1865, however, was still by western standards a border outpost. During and after the war it was a veritable cauldron of sectional conflict. It was, according to one historian, "the liveliest" and "the deadliest" place on the border. To another, Springfield was "the rendezvous of the most desperate and depraved" on both sides of the Civil War. Tensions between Rebels and Yankees ran exceedingly high in the summer of 1865. Hickok, who served as a sharpshooter, spy, and scout for the Union Army, had made more than his share of enemies. One was David Tutt, a gunman and gambler from Yellville, Arkansas. During the war Tutt had served as a Confederate sharpshooter for General Sterling Price.[37] Rumor had it that he deserted and joined the Union side late in the war. It was also alleged that he and Wild Bill were friends until a pro-Union woman by the name of Susanna Moore came between them. Moore's claim to fame, other than her affair with Hickok, was her "duel" with Agnes Masterson, a Confederate sympathizer. The two women fired single-shot pistols at one another, but both missed. They next engaged in brutal hand-to-hand combat. Moore's fighting spirit must have impressed Wild Bill, but much to his chagrin, Moore took up with Tutt after the war. This liaison, combined with the fact that each man wanted to be known as the best gambler and pistol shot in the Ozarks, exacerbated matters between the two men. The spark that eventually ignited the shoot-out came from a dispute over Hickok's watch.

In a high-stakes poker game, Tutt had cleaned Hickok out. At that point, Hickok either put up his watch for collateral or Tutt, realizing that Wild Bill

Wild Bill Hickok's "duel" on the streets of Springfield launched a new type of western hero. Courtesy State Historical Society of Missouri.

might renege on a fifty-dollar gambling debt, snatched it from him. Derisively, Tutt bragged about his intention to wear it the following day. The watch, which Hickok claimed was a family heirloom, now became a point of honor. Accordingly, Hickok warned Tutt that if he wore the watch he would kill him. The following day at high noon, Tutt walked down the main street and toward the town square of Springfield wearing the watch. Wild Bill was there to meet him. No pleasantries were exchanged. Both men knew the task at hand. Almost as one they drew, but only one fell dead. Without even waiting to see if he had hit his mark, Hickok wheeled around, leveled his revolver on Tutt's friends, and warned them to take no part in the feud. When they dispersed, he turned himself over to the Greene County sheriff. A jury quickly acquitted him. Within a few months, his star rising and his fame assured, Hickok left Springfield to become a deputy marshall and later a scout for William T. Sherman and George A. Custer.

No one popularized the Hickok myth more than Colonel George Ward Nichols. In *Harper's New Monthly Magazine,* Nichols graphically detailed the Tutt-Hickok duel. Adding to the legend was J. W. Buel of the *Kansas City Journal,* who in 1881 published *Heroes of the Plains,* and Colonel Prentiss

Ingraham, who wrote *Wild Bill, the Pistol Deadshot* in 1882. Collectively, these tales established Wild Bill's deadly shooting skills as well as his affability. It was hard for many "respectable people to believe," wrote historian Richard O'Connor, "that the Hickok they knew could be the Wild Bill of the gunfights and bushwhackings."[38]

Although duelists and gunfighters both subscribed to violence, there were many traits that distinguished the new western hero from his southern antebellum counterpart. In cowboy mythology, the hero was usually not tied too closely to a woman (Hickok's liaison with Moore notwithstanding). Dueling myths, on the other hand, often linked gentlemen of the Deep South to the undying affections of a lover (Missouri duels rarely fit this pattern). Typically, the cowboy's only possessions were his horse, gun, and saddle. This lack of property was due to his affinity to nature. Duelists, to the contrary, were men of property and aristocracy whose links were to civilization more than to the wilderness. While the cowboy's individualism was achieved by and through nature, the individualism of the duelist had to be recognized through the conventional framework of society. The cowboy shunned these formal conventions, but the duelist placed credence on etiquette and punctilio.[39] The cowboy's roots were plebeian, and intellectualism had little place in his world. The duelist prided himself on his patrician background and his classical education. It was, therefore, not surprising that, in the end, the cowboy/gunfighter legend had the greater mass appeal.

The emergence of this new type of hero in the postbellum era was not by chance. It corresponded to one of the greatest periods of economic and social change in the history of the Republic. One of the culture conflicts was between the old, established, preindustrial families of the East and the brash, new capitalist elites who were prepared to challenge their status and leadership. Both groups, however, were deeply suspicious of the urban working class. In addition, both feared a rising tide of "mongrelization" (the influx of non-Anglo-Saxon immigrants) that threatened the homogeneity of eastern bloodlines. Each elite group, operating with a different set of assumptions, nevertheless embellished the cowboy/gunfighter mythology. The parvenus, skeptical of the deferential social position and lineage ascribed to the families of old wealth, saw in the western hero those attributes of strength and assertiveness which they saw in themselves. Their heroes could also serve as role models and symbols of success for the urban poor. The functionalization of this myth was perhaps best exemplified by the image of the cowboy's rugged individualism. The inference was clear. The industrial working class did not need unionization, collectivism, or government assistance as a pathway to success. Rather, all that was required was the vision of the frontier.[40]

Their leadership challenged, the older, established elites responded in a variety of ways. Typically, they prided themselves on their scholarly and artistic endeavors as well as their dedication to public service and philanthropy. Even their style of leisure and sense of confidence contrasted markedly from the moneyed class derided by Thorstein Veblen for its conspicuous consumption. At first glance, it would seem incongruous that the old-line aristocracy would have identified with the emerging mythology of the West. Yet eastern intellectuals had always held a fascination for the frontier. For example, antebellum writers such as Washington Irving, James Fenimore Cooper, and Francis Parkman had interpreted frontier history in the dialectical framework of civilization versus barbarity. Their heroes, the likes of Daniel Boone and Natty Bumppo, were relatively free of social and institutional restraints and possessed few trappings of culture and refinement. On the other hand, establishment figures such as Owen Wister, Theodore Roosevelt, and Frederick Remington endowed their new heroes with ennobling virtues of culture and refinement.[41]

Replacing the conflicting dynamics of savagery and conquest, the turn-of-the-century writers interpreted the West as a unifying force in the march of American civilization. Hence the functionalization of myth surrounding the cowboy. To many members of the eastern establishment, industrial progress would advance westward, bringing with it the creation of a new social order. In this sense the West was symbolic of the catharsis of both body and soul of the East. To intellectuals as diverse as Wister, Roosevelt, and Remington, the westerner's pragmatic ability to succeed in the face of an ever-changing environment held valuable lessons for the upper class. Ironically, all three of these men had gone west for personal reasons of health, and all had found renewed strength and determination.

Of the three men, Roosevelt came the closest to juxtaposing the feats of gunfighters and duelists. His visualization of the West was strictly Darwinian, and violence, especially "privileged violence," according to Richard Slotkin, was a subject of great fascination.[42] He was particularly impressed with Senator Thomas Hart Benton, whom he believed embodied the spirit and dynamism of the West. This personal hero, like many of the others Roosevelt held in esteem, was a gentleman of an "aristocratic character" who defended his honor to the utmost.

By identifying with past frontier heroes, eastern elites hoped to legitimize their present privileged positions of power. By identifying with contemporary cowboy/gunfighter heroes, they hoped to regenerate "the lost manliness and vigor" of their class. This was the cornerstone of Roosevelt's philosophy, which he incorporated into a speech entitled *The Strenuous Life.* Heroic nations, like heroic individuals, Roosevelt exclaimed, do not "live in the gray twilight that knows not victory nor defeat." The "lessons" of war and the keys to victory could be found in the examples of men such as himself and the rugged individualists of the West. In his monumental work, *The Winning of the West,* Roosevelt quoted members of an earlier eastern elite who encouraged their sons to travel west to avoid the "dissipation" of easy living and the "scenes of idleness" that too often afflicted the upper class. Roosevelt no doubt took to heart those brandishments. Later they were personified in Cuba by his volunteer regiment, the Rough Riders. This odd combination of cowboys and aristocrats had become, in his words, a group of "hardy and self-reliant" men, the best the West and East could produce. It was only fitting that his troop presented him with Remington's bronze "The Bronco-buster" as a farewell gift.[43]

The eastern establishment, one must remember, did not monopolize western mythology. Self-made capitalists of the new industrial order likewise recognized in the cowboy those Darwinian qualities that they most admired in themselves. For them, the new type of hero was in the vanguard in taming a different frontier. With some social extrapolation and plenty of wishful thinking, they argued that if entrepreneurial westerners such as Wild Bill could subdue a frontier, then so too could they tame American cities on the urban frontier. The metaphor of conquest was also employed by eastern intellectuals. In a novel entitled *The Breadwinners,* John Hay, secretary of state under both McKinley and Roosevelt, had his hero Captain Arthur Farnham use his military skills to put down labor unrest among the railroad union. A Charles King novel written in 1893, *Foes in Ambush,* featured Indian fighters doing battle with industrial strikers. The following year Frederic Remington, who covered the West for *Century Magazine* and *Harper's Weekly,* described the Pullman strikers as savages to be tamed. Wister and Roosevelt had also become equally dismayed at urban violence. Roosevelt in fact believed that western heroes could regenerate "the lost manliness and vigor" of his aristocratic class. The example of the gunfighter/cowboy, especially when it came to taming uncivilized towns, he argued, could be put to good use in the struggle against domestic and international foes. The Rough Riders, as previously suggested, were the logical extension of this way of thinking.[44]

Another type of cowboy, namely the outlaw, also sublimated the drab effects of industrialization and urbanization. As such, this other western hero provided vicarious pleasure to the working classes of the city. No outlaw captured the American imagination quite like Jesse James. His exploits were first brought to life by Major John N. Edwards, a major in the Confederate army and a post–Civil War journalist. Edwards, more than any other postbellum Missourian, articulated the "lost cause" of the South. Both as a duelist and as a writer, he incorporated the twin elements of cultural resistance to Missouri's new economic order. Ironically, the legacy that he bestowed upon his state and nation was less about himself and more about a famous outlaw, Jesse James. Edwards was one of the first to sensationalize the desperado and to create the mythology of resistance. He created a powerful image of southern right and Reconstruction wrong through the life of a heroic figure who resisted authority, aided the poor, and defied the legal sanctions of a corrupt and repressive society. To a large extent the groups in Missouri who lionized this outlaw were the same ones who romanticized the past and interpreted dueling as part of the nobler traditions of a bygone age. Jesse James as the modern gunfighter was certainly no aristocrat, but his roots were southern, rural, and traditional.[45]

Outlaws such as Jesse James operated in one of the most turbulent periods of the state's history. Since it was simpler to condense the general level of societal barbarity into the actions of a single individual, James's career helped to define the cultural life of late-nineteenth-century Missouri. His historical importance, nevertheless, quite obviously stemmed less from his deeds and more from the form and content of the legends he spawned. Among the literary figures who took liberties with history, few surpassed Edwards.[46] By popularizing the myth of James's social banditry and broadening his appeal to a mass audience, writers such as Edwards dignified aggressive behavior and kept the roots of violence alive and flourishing into the twentieth century.

The outlaw drama also marked another transitional phase in Missouri violence. Because the outlaw embodied traits of chivalry, honor, and fairness in his gunfights, he became the extension of the duelist. Professor David Brion Davis perhaps put it best:

> Even after western gunmen had surrendered their sawed-off shotguns and six-shooters, Americans continued to glorify the memory of grim-faced duelists, who drew blood when a remark was made without a smile, who walked stiff-legged toward each other at high noon, their gloved hands poised above the curving handles of revolvers in oiled holsters.[47]

In most books, weeklies, and dime novels popular in this age, the gunfighter/outlaw duels were perceived as "chivalric affairs" and the "code duello was punctiliously observed." In fact, because the exploits of desperadoes were marketed for the first time to a mass culture, they eclipsed the fame of their more restrained predecessors, the duelists.[48]

Like the myths and legends of the cowboy/gunfighter, the outlaw mythology struck a vital and responsive chord in the American psyche. Perhaps, as some social behavioralists believe, the appeal of outlaws and rebels has "suppressed meaning" and is therefore the "most suitable to this process" of myth making. It also may reflect in modern life "a subconscious yearning for escape from the constraints of civilization." "There still exists in many people," wrote historian Joseph G. Rosa, "a sympathy and vicarious identification with the man with a gun." In any event, fascination with outlaws both then and now provide some useful insights into the roots of violence. Heroes, as evidenced

Jesse James provided the working class with a new type of outlaw-hero. Courtesy State Historical Society of Missouri.

by Edwards's characterizations, vary with social times, political and economic conditions, and cultural attitudes. These dichotomies between good and bad character traits in heroes are generally more pronounced when one set of elites, as in the case of postbellum Missouri, imposes its value system upon another. This altering of power relationships, as Frank Prassel has shown, increases "the tendency for diverse interpretations of crime and justice." "Thus," he argued, "one group's hero becomes another's villain."[49]

Outlaws such as Jesse James and gunfighters such as Wild Bill Hickok became heroes of the new proletariat, whose lives of organization, poverty, conformity, and standardization stood in stark contrast to their "blazing" individualism. Cowboy mythology appealed to the egalitarian nature of the common man and best typified that aspect of the American character. What added to the fascination with the Wild West was the fact that it was a living drama played to a mass audience. Yet in the personal triumphs of these mythic heroes was an underlying sense of tragedy. For this was the first time in history that a living culture and way of life could be seen vanishing before the public eye.[50] The 1890 census that marked the closing of the frontier and Frederick Jackson Turner's work in 1893 brought home to the intellectual class what the public inchoately sensed. From both intellectual and middle-brow observers, however, came a nostalgic and romantic revivification of the West, even as the last act of the drama unfolded.

The functionalization of the gunfighter myth also had another effect. Cowboy violence, "somewhat sugar-coated and sentimentalized ... helped

Americans taper off from the excitement of the Civil War years." Sectional prejudices were also less pronounced in the West. After the war, as a new type of national consciousness emerged, the cowboy became a new kind of sectional hero with whom both sides of the Mason-Dixon line could identify. He became "the most durable and prolific of all American legends." "Few mythologies," wrote O'Connor, have had so "vivid a life." Since this western drama was "broad in space but narrow in time," it was easy to see how "legends overlapped each other" and "myths ran together."[51]

Myths and legends, as O'Connor observed, have indeed become intertwined in history. Nevertheless, a discernible pattern of prototypical heroes emerged from the pages of Missouri's past. Tales of the early explorers, keelboatmen, and pioneers were supplanted in time by the deeds of duelists such as John Smith T and Dr. John Bryan. They in turn were transitional figures leading to the emergence of Hickok the gunfighter and James the outlaw. Each set of myths and legends, reinforced by powerful metaphors of energy and mettle, provided fertile ground for the roots of violence. What etched these legends in stone were, of course, the ultimate acts of violence, Hickok's assassination by Jack McCall in 1876 and Bob Ford's murder of James in 1882. The memory and lore of Hickok holding his dead man's hand and James straightening the picture "Home Sweet Home" immortalized the tragedies and the heroes.

11

Dueling and Transitional Violence

ISTORIANS OF THE post–Civil War era have been far too quick in dismissing the code duello. They have generally assumed that with the defeat of the South, the institutions which identified and defended its way of life fell as well. Historians have also suggested that in the wake of such human and material devastation, few men of valor would need or care to defend their honor by a resort to the code. David Brion Davis, for example, credited Mark Twain with the code's demise. It was his "ridicule," Davis wrote, that "is generally considered to have given the death blow to an institution already debilitated by the unexpected grimness of war."[1] In essence, the duel, according to this line of reasoning, had become a cultural casualty of the greatest conflict in American history.

Twain's literary attacks on dueling were no doubt impressive. After a brief and inglorious stint in the Missouri Confederate Army, he headed west. His affectation of southern culture, however, embroiled him in controversy once again. In May 1864 he challenged a Virginia City editor, James Laird, to a duel. Although in later life Twain lampooned the entire episode, Nevada authorities were not amused. Before the violence could be consummated on the field of honor, Twain was run out of the territory with "four horse-whippings and two duels" still owed to him. In his autobiography this errant son of the South stated that he was "inflexibly opposed to the dreadful custom."[2] On the other hand this rejoinder was somewhat tempered by a semi-comic caveat:

> I have never had anything to do with duels since. I thoroughly disapprove of duels. I consider them unwise and I know they are dangerous. Also, sinful. If a man should challenge me now I would go to that man and take him kindly and forgivingly by the hand and lead him to a quiet spot and kill him. Still, I have always taken a great interest in other people's duels. One always feels an abiding interest in any heroic thing which has entered into his own experience.[3]

Twain's remarks intimated that the code at last had become a caricature of southern chivalry and a distorted relic of heroic honor. It was in such a mode that in 1878 he jotted down in his notebook the finer points of dueling:

> How to kill your man in a duel. Take a rusty old gun which you think is not loaded—let it go off accidentally in the direction of the other man with the distinct intention and desire to miss him. This will fetch him, sure.[4]

Humor also characterized the duello in the Missouri River Valley. One episode, caricatured as the "brick" duel, took place in Callaway County. This good-natured and humorous affair has been the most retold story of the period. The principals later became very prominent figures in the state. They were Judge Thomas Buckner of Kansas City and Colonel R. M. White of Mexico, Missouri. Some time during the 1870s, the two young men attended Westminster College in Fulton, Missouri. During the course of their matriculation at the college, they developed a deep friendship. It was strained to the breaking point, however, by their mutual courtship of a handsome young lass in the local community. Buckner, with a fire in his belly (and perhaps in his heart as well) saw no alternative but to end the contest for her affection in the best traditions of the South. Romance in the wilds of Callaway County, it appeared, was finally going to ennoble the Missouri duel with a "classic quality" that would have been the envy of even Sir Walter Scott himself.

The impending duel became the talk of the campus. Classmates of the two antagonists drew vicarious thrills from the prospects of being part of a historic drama. (History does not record the sentiments or expectations of the faculty.) Attention was focused on the young White as everyone awaited his response to Buckner's challenge to mortal combat. White, however, was not to be seduced by the temptation to eliminate his rival by dueling, no matter how enticing the prize. His family had moved to Missouri shortly after the Civil War, so he was less familiar with this type of problem-solving. Consequently, he could muster only two cheers for the code.

White realized that an outright refusal to fight might be interpreted as a sign of weakness by many of his colleagues as well as the beautiful girl who was the object of his affections. His extrication from this dilemma lay in the fact that, as the challenged party, he had the right to name the time, place, and choice of weapons. When Buckner's second and several other classmates arrived to receive his terms at the notification ceremony, the atmosphere was termed "grim and real." White then handed Buckner's second the following terse note. "The site will be the dry well on the college campus, with Buckner at the bottom and myself at the top. The weapons will be bricks."

The temptation for laughter now overpowered the bewilderment of Buckner and his friends. White had fired a literary volley, not at Buckner, but

Mark Twain ridiculed dueling but could not quite escape the concepts of honor, courage, and violence. Courtesy State Historical Society of Missouri.

at the code, which was far more devastating than the bark of a pistol. Anxiety and hostility quickly made room for merriment as both parties shared a good laugh at themselves and the code. The antagonists renewed their friendship on the spot. Perhaps the only person not reconciled by the antics was the young lady whose beauty had nearly launched a ship of disasters. "Legend has it," wrote historian James Moss, "that she spurned both 'combatants' and married someone else."[5]

Buckner and White literally made a mockery of the code. Twain, figuratively, had done the same. They were not, however, the only ones to step forward and to combat the pathologies of the past. Eugene Field was another individual who undermined the glamour of violence. More than any other Missourian, he justly earned the title of "a poet of humanity." The mutually destructive connection between dueling and society at large was evidenced in one of Field's poems. Born in 1850 in St. Louis and educated at the University of Missouri, Field later served on newspapers in Kansas City, St. Joseph, and St. Louis before moving on to the *Chicago Daily News.* In the last stanza of his children's poem "The Duel," he wrote the following:

> But the truth about the cat and pup, Is this:
> They ate each other up![6]

Field's great love of children and his admiration for their simplicity and imagination was perhaps one reason he sought to dispel the mystique of violence. In his "Auto-Analysis," the newspaperman/poet reaffirmed his traditional faith in "churches and schools" but abjured the instruments of savagery. "I hate," he added, "wars, armies, soldiers, guns and fireworks."[7] Nevertheless, Field was no pacifist. He had grown to respect the "rugged" Yankee character that had put to rest the lost cause of the Confederacy. Yet he also realized the internecine nature of the battle to preserve the Union and to end slavery. Returning to Missouri in early manhood, Field was appalled by the wanton destruction of the war and its aftermath. "Life and property," he wrote, "were held of slight consequence, violence obtained to a preposterous degree, crime actually ran riot."[8] "The Duel" therefore parodied not only individual destruction but sectional and national immolation as well.

Shifting societal attitudes like those expressed by Twain and Field were reinforced by technological changes that began in the late 1830s and early 1840s. Percussion pistols were replacing flintlocks, and this added an even more dangerous element to the art of dueling. Moreover, many of the newer pistols were rifled—an innovation that increased their accuracy. In theory, these alterations should have hastened the end of dueling. Even though most dueling codes specifically stated that the pistols were to be smoothbores, the temptation to kill an adversary was often overwhelming. Smoothbore flintlock weapons had hardly ever been instruments of exactitude, but with the rifled-bore Colt revolver, pistols at ten paces now took a lethal quantum leap. Many of the Civil War duels were fought with revolvers and reflected this new and dangerous dimension.

The changing nature of violence was not limited to weapons alone. The duel itself was in transition. Increasingly, it was becoming a thinly disguised excuse for gunfights, street murders, revenge killings, and family feuds. All of these improvised responses were much more emotional and intense in areas devastated by guerrilla warfare.[9] In brief, the Missouri duel, despite the holograms of destruction wrought by the Civil War and Reconstruction, displayed remarkable resiliency. And it continued to prove resistant to social change well into the onset of modernity.

The Missouri duels of the early 1860s harkened back to a time when questions of honor rather than ideology or self-sacrifice ruled the day. On December 19, 1860, for example, a duel occurred at the rear of Harlem House on Bellefontaine Road, a few miles north of St. Louis.[10] The principals were Brigadier General D. M. Frost of the Missouri militia and E. B. Sayers, a civil engineer in the City of St. Louis, who had earlier laid out Camp Jackson. Sayers had recently served as quartermaster in an expedition to the Southwest and had criticized Frost's official conduct during this period. The charges, published in a letter to the *Missouri Democrat*, were personal and had nothing to do with the secessionist issues that were wracking the state and country. Frost was absent from the city when the paper ran the attack. Upon his return,

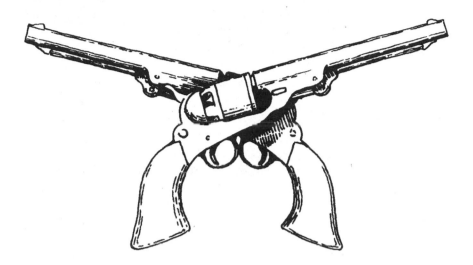

Colt revolvers provided a quantum leap in the likelihood of fatalities in duels.

he promptly went to Sayers's office and horsewhipped him. Sayers challenged, and Frost quickly accepted. The weapons were pistols at twelve paces.[11]

The ignominy of being horsewhipped no doubt heightened the enmity of Sayers more than that of his opponent. Frost, in fact, was said to have told his second, Captain Wade, that he was inclined not to fire at all. The general, however, did insist that Wade examine the person of Sayers to see if there were any impediments such as a watch or pocket knife that might deflect a ball. Sayers, on the other hand, declined any examination of Frost. The *Jefferson City Inquirer* rebuked the general for his ungentlemanly conduct. It referred to the "whole affair" as a badly played "farce." Although the newspaper did not elaborate, the very fact that it took such a heated interest in the affair leads to the speculation that the duel had some kind of political or factional overtone.[12]

As for the duel itself, it ended as a bloodless affair after the first exchange of shots. Sayers, some have said, was very nervous and fired quickly. Frost then "magnanimously" fired in the air. The principals thereupon "amicably" settled their difficulties. An indictment, however, was issued against the parties in the St. Louis Circuit Court, but neither was prosecuted.[13] What made this particular affair noteworthy was the fact that it was the only Missouri duel precipitated by an act of physical violence such as a caning or a horsewhipping that did not end in death or serious injury to one or both of the participants.

The Sayers-Frost affair of honor was one of the very few Missouri duels during the Civil War era. Those duels and hostile challenges that did occur usually pertained to questions of either personal honor and integrity or character and courage. The potential for increased mortality among these combatants was heightened by the fact that most Civil War officers did not carry the standard smoothbore flintlock pistols with them in the field. Therefore, if a controversy arose that demanded satisfaction, the principals usually resorted to Colt revolvers, a far more lethal weapon. One such Civil War duel took place near Independence, Missouri. The only reference for this affair was an article published in 1904 by historian W. R. Smith. He stated only that a Major Rapley fought a certain Captain Belden. He did not give their first names, or identify their seconds, or even mention under which army they served. The terms of the duel were that each man would be armed with a revolver. At a distance of fifteen paces, each man would advance and fire at will. Early in the exchange of fire, Smith reported, Rapley's bullet struck Belden, but Belden continued to advance and to fire until finally he collapsed at Rapley's feet. The captain's courage and tenacity must have impressed Rapley as he refused to kill his adversary. Remarkably, Smith claimed, Belden eventually recovered from his wounds.[14]

The most celebrated of the Civil War duels involved a Missouri military officer and occurred in Arkansas on September 6, 1863. The belligerents were Confederate generals John S. Marmaduke and Lucien Marsh Walker.[15] Both served under General Sterling Price. The nature of the dispute revolved around the imputation that Walker had shown cowardice during a battle near Helena. When Colonel R. H. Crockett, Walker's second, sought a clarification from Marmaduke, the latter sent a note detailing the "more than scrupulous care with which General Walker avoided all positions of danger" during the military engagement. The note immediately prompted a challenge. Captain John C. Moore volunteered to serve as Marmaduke's second. They agreed to fight at the Le Fevre Plantation with Colt Navy revolvers at fifteen paces.

General Price, upon hearing of the impending affair, ordered both officers to remain at their headquarters for the next twenty-four hours. Marmaduke ignored the order, and Walker did not receive it before he left for the plantation. The night before the duel, both men stayed at the Le Fevre home, thus avoiding detection and possible military arrest. Each member of the two parties realized that the terms of the engagement would likely bring death or serious injury the next morning to one or both of the principals.

Fifteen paces was extremely close, given the fact that the weapons were Colt revolvers with six shots. Nevertheless, Walker had agreed to the terms. Perhaps Marmaduke had proposed the closeness because of his nearsightedness, which, even at this distance, blurred the image of his adversary. According to Captain Price, as the duelists stepped off their paces and faced one another, a "little gray weed" appeared directly in Marmaduke's line of fire. Marmaduke used the weed to sight in on General Walker. On the first

John S. Marmaduke killed a fellow Confederate general in a duel in 1863. He later became governor of Missouri. Courtesy State Historical Society of Missouri.

fire, both principals missed their human marks, but on the second fire, the "little gray weed" spun its magic. Walker collapsed, mortally wounded. Marmaduke approached his victim and knelt beside him. When asked about the extent of his wound, Walker replied that he was a dead man. The ball had passed through the right kidney and lodged in his spine; thus, he was paralyzed from the waist down. The dying general then told his second, Colonel Crockett, to inform his wife that the duel was unavoidable and he had been forced to defend his honor. Next, Walker forgave Marmaduke and told the parties that his antagonist should not be prosecuted. According to Davy Crockett's grandson, "Not a moan escaped his lips but a smile so sad, so sweet played on his lips." Walker was carried from the field and died a day or so later. Upon returning from the duel, Marmaduke and his second were arrested by General Price, who had little stomach for these affairs. During the war, southerners had an "unwritten rule" that personal honor should not take precedence over the honor of the Confederacy. Soon, however, Marmaduke resumed his command to meet any impending Union attack. No charges were brought against him, and he never stood trial.[16]

In retrospect, the duel appeared to have had no adverse political repercussions for Marmaduke. Despite his father's earlier admonitions against dueling, he was not tainted by the affair. In 1884, the people of Missouri elected him governor. It was a position he held until his death in December 1887.

As Marmaduke defended his honor in the traditional southern mode, his native state was witnessing unparalleled paroxysms of violence. The Civil War in Missouri, as historian Michael Fellman has aptly described, degenerated into the worst guerrilla war in U.S. history.[17] If political elites of the antebellum age such as B. Gratz Brown or Thomas Reynolds had any hope that the conflict could be contained within the bounds of gentlemanly conduct, then they were sadly mistaken. The example of the duelist, confident, collected and, above all else, in complete control of his passions, offered no model of conduct in a guerrilla war. War without borders and vengeance without compassion sullied the honor of all concerned. Perhaps out of nostalgia, or in part out of desperation, both sides in this gruesome struggle longed for the bygone days of civilized conflict. Although no duels materialized in the state between opposing forces during the war, there were occasions when the duel as a metaphor of civility was echoed. One such event occurred when guerrilla leader William Coleman challenged Colonel S. N. Boyd. It was a rather unique message in that Coleman suggested that each bring "an equal number of men" to the field and that all engage in combat. He did not spell out the terms. In 1864, near Kansas City, the metaphor of civility was again evoked by Charles P. Taylor. Writing to a Union captain by the name of Kemper, the guerrilla officer asked to fight him "like two barons," man to man.[18]

Not surprisingly, in both of the preceding instances, it was the Confederate side that personalized and romanticized combat. Union soldiers, on the other hand, looked upon the war as a job, albeit an unpleasant one. They, more than their southern counterparts, distinguished more clearly the differences between collective and personal violence. Those who survived the war and its bloody aftermath had less need to prove their manhood. The defense of honor under the code appeared inconsequential in light of the past carnage. General U. S. Grant, who lived in Missouri from 1854 to 1860 and unsuccessfully ran for political office in St. Louis in 1858, summarized the prevailing attitude of the times. In his memoirs he wrote:

> I do not believe I would ever have the courage to fight a duel. If any man should wrong me to extent of being willing to kill him, I would not be willing to give him the choice of weapons with which it should be done, and of the time, place and distance separating us, when I executed him. If I should do another such a wrong as to justify him in killing me, I would make any reasonable atonement within my power, if convinced of the wrong done. I place my opposition to dueling on higher grounds than any here stated. No doubt a majority of the duels fought have been for want of moral courage on the part of the engaged to decline.[19]

Grant no doubt echoed the sentiments of a vast number of Civil War veterans both in Missouri and across the nation. Yet the heroic language of olden days died hard.[20] Missourians also pointed with pride to what they mistakenly believed to be their own unique contribution to the code. After the Civil

War, Joe Shelby's Missouri legion crossed the Rio Grande to aid Maximilian, the Austrian puppet placed on the Mexican throne by Napoleon III of France. It was here in late 1865 that Shelby's men introduced the "Missouri duel." The terms of engagement were simple. Both antagonists stripped to the waist and armed themselves with nine-inch bowie knives. Each gripped the corner of a red bandanna handkerchief by their teeth. The man who first let go of the handkerchief lost the duel. The *Kansas City Times* reported that it was "not of record that any man ever released the bandanna alive, and not infrequently, both adversaries died." General Shelby, the paper noted, subscribed to the code and allowed the knife duels to continue because of his sense of honor.[21]

Bowie knives, a common accoutrement on the frontier, were used in a variety of hostile rencounters about the same time Shelby's men employed them in Mexico. One dueling book, for instance, depicted two 1865 women in Venice, Missouri (in the south-central Ozarks) engaged in a bowie knife duel. Although the scene was quite violent, the book did not provide any information on casualties.

Another duel, and certainly one of the most novel dramas ever to be labeled as such, unfolded in late 1865. This affair also took place in Mexico between two men under Shelby's command. The warring parties were John Thrailkill, a former Quantrill Raider, and John West. While encamped near Linares, Mexico, the two men quarreled bitterly. West questioned Thrailkill's veracity, and the latter struck him twice across the face. At dawn's light, Captain James H. Gillette, West's second, delivered a challenge. Thrailkill appointed Isaac Berry to serve as his second. The terms set forth called for each man to pick a Colt revolver from underneath a blanket. One pistol would be loaded with six bullets; the other would be blank. The unarmed man would then be compelled to stand and accept the fire of the other. Thrailkill's luck prevailed. It was he who obtained the loaded pistol. Since he was a dead shot, it was almost a certainty that West shortly would no longer be among the ranks of the living. In the interim, however, Thrailkill had taken another kind of gamble. It pertained to a cock fight. As he continued to lose heavily on the fights, he wagered another officer that if he lost one more bet, he would spare West's life in order to pay off his debts. He then proceeded to once again lose badly. West had not learned of the wager and, the morning of the duel, stood stoically facing a loaded revolver. Thrailkill, true to his word, spared his life. With each of his six shots, he harmlessly picked off twigs of the tree under which West stood. West would live to see his beloved state again.[22]

A number of postwar engagements also occurred within the state. Sensitivity to defeat, as well as feelings of inferiority and insecurity, prompted some men to resort once again to the code.[23] On July 13, 1870, for example, Major H. Keith, formerly of the Thirty-first New York Regiment, dueled Captain L. P. Van. At the time of the affair, Keith worked for the *St. Louis Times.* Van, who once served in the French army and later for the Confederacy, accepted Keith's challenge and chose cavalry sabers. The duel occurred near St. Louis. The major received a slight wound on his forehead and another cut on his head. Van was not as fortunate. He sustained a wound that put out his eye. "The whole affair," reported one newspaper, "is involved in mystery" as both principals and seconds "are extremely reticent." As to the nature of the quarrel, the paper speculated that it may "have grown out of reflections cast on the fighting qualities of the Yankees."[24]

Major John N. Edwards was another veteran stung by northern victory. He was acclaimed by many newspapermen as one of the greatest western journalists in the post–Civil War era. In his earlier days, he had been appointed in 1863 as a major in General Joe Shelby's Confederate regiment of Lafayette County. After the war, he traveled with Shelby to Mexico and tended his services to the helpless Maximilian and his wife, Carlotta. In 1867, Edwards returned to Missouri and soon found employment; writing for the *St. Louis Times,* Edwards became embroiled in a controversy with Colonel Emory S. Foster that led to a duel. It was a duel resulting from the memoirs and rancor of the war.[25] It began innocuously enough when a committee of the Winnebago, Illinois, County Fair invited Jefferson Davis to speak to their organization. Many in the community, especially the women, vigorously protested the presence of the former president of the Confederacy, and his address was canceled. Edwards took umbrage; in a *Times* editorial he wrote that the invitation was rescinded because the women of Winnebago County were afraid that Davis would see pieces of furniture and heirlooms stolen from southern homes by William T. Sherman on his march to the sea.

The remark stung Colonel Foster. Perhaps he was oversensitive owing to the fact that on August 16, 1862, he had been defeated by Missouri guerrillas at Lone Jack and forced to surrender. Here was a golden opportunity to uphold his honor and the honor of his country. He responded in a blistering editorial in the *St. Louis Evening Journal,* calling Edwards a liar who had sullied the good name of women whose loved ones had served in the cause of the North. Foster believed that such slanders were "contemptible curs, unworthy of respect or recognition." Edwards immediately demanded a retraction or the satisfaction due a gentleman. Although Foster "disavowed any personal allusion" to Edwards, he declined to retract the statement. After considerable correspondence that was in the finest tradition of antebellum chivalry, Edwards issued his challenge. Colonel Harrison B. Branch would serve as his second. Foster accepted the challenge and named Colonel W. D. W. Barnard as his second. The surgeons were Dr. Morrison Munford for Edwards and Dr. P. S. O'Reilly for Foster. He proposed, fittingly, a site six miles north of Rockford, Illinois, in Winnebago County as the site of the duel. His choice of weapons was rifles at twenty paces. The two parties met at Chicago and traveled by train to the dueling grounds. At 5 P.M., September 4, 1875, the rifle shots rang out. One fire sufficed. The parties quickly reconciled and fled the scene to avoid arrest. Indictments and extradition papers were prepared by Illinois authorities but were never issued. Although two historians of the Missouri duel have suggested that times had changed so much by 1875 "that the whole affair produced ridicule rather than anger or regret on the part of the public," it does not appear all that clear that the affair was taken so lightly.[26] The *Kansas City Times* reported the results of the duel the following day and called it a "bad practice." Nevertheless, the paper went on to add that dueling was

> No worse than abusing each other in types, or fighting it out on the streets. If two men must fight, it is better to do it in a retired place, without alarming outsiders and in accordance with rules previously agreed upon by the parties.[27]

Edwards, for his part, did not feel humiliated enough to avoid a near repeat some seven years later. This time his antagonist was a fellow journalist, J. H. Payne. The *Columbia Herald* believed that a duel between the two men was quite possible and cited, without any ridicule or derision, Edwards's earlier affray with Foster.[28]

The need to idealize the past, as illustrated in the life of Edwards, intensified in the latter part of the century. Defenders of the duello had been right, but for the wrong reasons. These traditionalists had correctly predicted that with the demise of dueling would come a subsequent leap in violence. They had, however, mistakenly drawn a false causal relationship between the fall of one form of violence and the rise of another. They also erred in not realizing their own real and symbolic contributions to lawlessness, murder, and mayhem. This was part of their legacy to the post–Civil War era. In the process they had sown the seeds of ferment, albeit not the only ones planted in those years, which would later reap a bitter harvest. Placing themselves above their communities' moral and legal prescripts, they unwittingly nurtured the very roots of violence they hoped to extract. Violent behavior legitimized by institutional hauteur, as previously noted, rested upon a sense of relativism, that is, that what was permissible among the ranks of gentlemen was not an acceptable form of conduct for the rest of the populace.

But the gentlemen of shot and sword had done their work too well. They had tried to instill honor, control, courage, and self-reliance into the body politic by their acts of valor. Even though they sought respect more than emulation by those they believed to be socially inferior, their methods had nevertheless captivated a mass audience. The impunity with which the duelists killed and maimed provided the pretext for even greater social turbulence in the decades after the Civil War. The gunfighter and outlaw mystique was a logical extension of the duelists' nonconformance to law.

The working classes also understood the changing nature of violence. They remembered how the roots of violence extended back to the militia musters, celebration days, huskings, and court days. They recalled, too, that redress for wrongs, especially if they involved questions of honor, family, or self-respect, had generally been solved on the spot without recourse to courts or law. Many post–Civil War encounters harkened back to the traditional means employed by frontiersmen for settling their problems. The decades following the war also witnessed, as Professor Philip Jordan has suggested, "an upsurge in criminal activities of every variety." Much of this violence emanated from former Union and Confederate troops who stalked the countryside seeking revenge and retribution. The war "gave opportunity to the ignorant to learn the heady lesson of murder and to be instructed in the finer arts of vice." "Lynchings," wrote Jordan, "were more numerous than before the war." Clark County, Missouri, he added, "during the 1870s was an unbelievable area of violence." Sadly enough, Clark County was not unique.[29] Accounts of atrocities and grudge killings were common throughout the state. One eyewitness described how not one barn or house stood standing on the road from Rolla to Salem. Even piracy on the Missouri and Mississippi Rivers became once again a scourge upon the state.

Dueling also had a resurrection of sorts. Typical of this new genre of violence was a *Jefferson City Peoples' Tribune* article dated November 5, 1873. It was entitled "How Plain Missourians Settle a Difficulty." The newspaper related how two men, John Goforth and Simon Melville, were out hunting near Forsythe in Taney County and took time out for a "duel." Each carried an old-fashioned squirrel gun. The conversation quickly turned to subjects other than deer. "I hear that you've been lying on me," Goforth stated. "What do you hear?" asked Melville. "That I had been beating my wife." "And so you have," shot back Melville. Goforth then laid down the gauntlet. "Those who told you lied," he exclaimed, "and when you repeated it you also lied and you knew at the time you were lying." Under the code of the hills, the accusation, he realized, meant a fight. The two men agreed to step off thirty yards each, wheel at the word and fire immediately after wheeling. Thereupon, each simultaneously fired, according to the rules. There were no infractions. Melville's bullet struck Goforth in the right arm while Goforth's shot winged his antagonist's right shoulder. When the smoke cleared, the two then walked back to Forsythe. A surgeon extracted the balls but reported to the Jefferson City newspaper that Goforth would more than likely lose his arm.[30]

Duels between gentlemen may have had a more formal structure than the Melville-Goforth affair, but each class of Missourians ultimately achieved satisfaction. Johann Bauer, a German immigrant farmer in Adair County, wrote to his mother back in the fatherland in 1875 that the local newspapers sometimes carried news about mensurs in places like Heidelberg. As for Missouri duels, he cautioned, they were "strictly forbidden here, yet it does happen sometimes, but only in secret."[31]

One of the last affairs of honor in Missouri that had the trappings of a formal duel took place near Mount Vernon in Lawrence County in 1881. Like most of the postbellum affrays that cloaked themselves in the garments of the code duello, this episode again revealed that the axis of institutionalized violence had shifted away from the eastern centers of commerce and toward the western fringes of the state. The duel was between a Doctor McBride and a physician known only by his last name, Montgomery. Owing to the fact that little information about the affair survived, it can safely be assumed that there was no serious injury or loss of life to either party.[32]

Affairs of honor settled without bloodshed but still under the strict decorum of the code duello, though rare, still existed. Politics usually played a large role in these affairs. A number of county court indictments in this period reveal challenges and rencounters revolving around the disenfranchisement of former Confederates. Many of these men took their public rebuke as a personal insult and were willing to fight to restore their honor. Other affairs during the era harkened back to the bygone days of chivalry. In January 1883, for example, two St. Louis gentlemen by the names of Gebbard and Cunningham vied for the affections of a certain Mrs. Langtry. Gebbard challenged Cunningham, but Cunningham refused the invitation, whereupon Gebbard posted his antagonist in the finest traditions of southern chivalry.[33] This kind of affair was the exception rather than the rule. Missouri society was changing, and so too were many of its traditions and customs.

The changing role of the duel was reflected in a number of ways. In each case, however, one can see the roots of modern violence. First, by defining an altercation as a duel, the participants were likely to escape prosecution. The duel became the metaphor of choice for murderers. This semantic device had been a time-honored recipe for murder without punishment and dated back to the infamous Smith-Tharp affair in 1817. It continued to be employed with even more deadly effect after the war. Second, improvised killings under the rubric of the code escalated. The autonomy of both local law and enforcement agencies allowed personalized forms of retribution, especially in the rural areas of the state, to persist well into the twentieth century.

Similarly, labeling as a duel a stabbing, shooting on sight, or gunfight dignified both the winner and the loser. Dueling with its aristocratic lineage evoked a sophisticated image of bravery. Consequently, it elevated the common man engaged in personal combat to a status higher than he otherwise could have achieved. Henry R. Schoolcraft very early in the nineteenth century grasped the role played by the duello in connecting upper- and lower-class violence. Dueling, he wrote, "is prevalent in Missouri" and "continues to receive the sanction of men occupying the first rank in society." What most disturbed this keen observer, however, was how the duel continued "to extend its baneful influence over other classes of community."[34]

Schoolcraft keenly understood how the duel was so deeply embedded in the psyche of the common man. He would hardly have been surprised by the report nearly a hundred years later of an 1892 knife fight between Missourians Joseph Paxton and Billy Tankersley. This rencounter, in which Tankersley was most likely killed, was dignified as a "duel" by the north-central Missouri newspaper the *Milan Republican*. Duels that were nothing more than "unrestrained personal combat" provided "the professional killer, the bully, and the psychopath with an opportunity to win reputation and honor from cold-blooded murder," wrote David Brion Davis.[35] Missouri's heritage of violence most aptly verified Davis's observation.

African American newspapers also displayed a penchant for elevating common criminal behavior into the vernacular of chivalry. One newspaper particularly fascinated with the code duello was the *Kansas City Call*. As late as the 1920s it placed a variety of violent encounters under the rubric of the code. On the front page of its September 15, 1922, edition the paper headlined a "Regular Duel" on the streets of Chicago. This "death duel" ended after two antagonists "emptied their revolvers into each other's body and then staggered together in a final grapple that ended with the death of both." The following year the *Call* headlined Mrs. Blanche Stevenson of Kansas City, who warded off two would-be robbers with three shots from her pistol. The paper marqueed this incident as a "Midnight Pistol Duel." Later the same year the paper ran a front-page article entitled "Two Killed in Gun and Knife Duel," in which John Giles of Kansas City shot and fatally wounded John White, "who in turn cut Giles so badly that he died" not long after the fight. In January 1927 the same newspaper headlined a "Duel in Snow" in which the deceased, Milton Smith of Kansas City, was shot five times in the chest by an "assailent" [*sic*] who was also wounded.[36]

Classifying as duels a bloody shoot-out that nearly resulted in a riot, a botched robbery and pistol exchange, and numerous gun-knife fights was certainly no different from the white journalistic traditions in the state. It was not, however, the *Call's* categorization per se but the timing that made the observation noteworthy. By the 1920s the metaphor of the duel had become a veiled attempt to legitimize street violence in urban cities. The *Call* unwittingly made another connection between past and present violence. The code with its inflated sum of honor can also be linked to other manifestations of transitional violence. The modern game referred to as "dozens" in the African American community was reminiscent of a sport called "bulldozing" in the 1920s. Both forms of amusement began with multiple or "dozens" of verbal insults designed to measure one's ability to handle escalating abuses without resorting to physical redress. In many instances it did not take long before the effrontery resulted in violent retribution. The *Call,* for example, reported two men dead and two seriously wounded in a 1927 Kansas City game of "bulldozing."[37]

If imitation is in fact the sincerest form of flattery, then black urban mayhem, like many other forms of contemporary violence, is rooted in the aristocratic institutions of the past. The desperate need for peer respect, the exaggerated sense of honor, the inflated ego, the quick resort to hostile actions, and the belief that satisfaction must come from personal acts of retribution could describe the modern black practice of "dissing" or the traditional white ritual of dueling.

White Missourians, lest one forgets, remained equally adept at embellishing violence. Undoubtedly, one of the most bizarre incidents that might be construed as a duel, if for no other reason than to exonerate the killer, occurred in Ralls County in 1886. Americus Wood Farmer shot and killed his son, William, who was also armed and intent on murdering his father.[38] On or about July 8 of that year, the men began drinking heavily and soon started to quarrel. Both lived near New London, Missouri. The *Carthage Evening Press,* under a headline that read, "Duel between Father and Son Caused by Whisky," reported that nearly twenty pistol shots were exchanged. William, the paper continued, hit A. W. six times while taking three balls in the abdomen. The wounds, the paper believed, were "fatal ones" for both parties. Both men, it explained, were farmers "in good circumstances, and good citizens when sober."[39] Like so many of these so-called contests, they resembled the drop, snap shot, or quick draw more than a duel. Labeling them as duels, however, provided both an aura of respectability and a better legal defense in case one party was seriously hurt or killed.

As late as 1893, an improvised shooting in Brunswick, Missouri, was termed a "duel" by the newspapers of the day. On or about June 17 the mayor of the town, John H. Heisel, shot and killed the city marshall, Richard Ashby, outside Finch's Saloon. Each man emptied his revolver but Heisel, although struck in the abdomen and lungs, survived. Ashby did not. The origin of their difficulties dated back a few years to when Heisel, a married man, took Ashby's daughter, Hattie, to Chicago for a romantic interlude. The pair was arrested by Chicago authorities and the scandal ended the mayor's marriage. His wife, upon hearing of the tryst, headed to California. Years later the mayor's brother, W. J. Heisel, cursed and allegedly struck Hattie on the streets of Brunswick. Ashby and his son Joseph responded in kind, attacking and beating W. J. Tensions mounted throughout the day as the townfolk awaited the mayor's response. That evening at the saloon, the two men met and agreed to step out into the street and shoot it out.[40]

Perhaps more culturally instructive than the gunfight itself was the way it was reported by the press. The news accounts harkened back to the heroic age: Missouri newspapers dubbed the spontaneous outburst a "duel" rather than a murder. This literary nuance vindicated not only gunfighters but also the community at large. A "duel" perversely signified that a community had come of age—that rural violence had inexorably given way to civilized violence. Altercations termed duels, either with fists, revolvers, knives, axes, rocks, or pitchforks, conveyed a distorted sense of southern gentility and refinement. Although the newspapers did not overly sensationalize or romanticize many of these affairs, they still wrote with admiration about the courage and honor of the participants. Nor did they condemn this kind of violence or even suggest that it should be contained. The style, tone, and tenor of these pieces were distinctly more antebellum than modern.

Dueling was also kept alive in one instance by an insurance company. On July 3, 1901, in Vernon County, Missouri, a shoot-out between John W. Davis and L. E. Bryan resulted in the death of Davis and serious injury to Bryan. Davis had a life insurance policy for three thousand dollars that his wife and children tried to collect. The company, Modern Woodmen of America, contended that the death resulted from either a duel or a premeditated act to cause bodily harm. In either case, Davis had violated the law and his family was therefore not entitled to the money. H. C. Timmonds, the judge of the Circuit Court of Vernon County, did not agree and awarded the Davis family the benefit certificate. The Court of Appeals at Kansas City on April 6, 1903, reversed Timmonds's decision and found merit with the company's arguments. Although the court did not establish conclusively that the Davis-Bryan affair was a duel, it did believe that some kind of "prearrangement" had occurred which made it an unlawful act.[41]

Brawls and gunfights loosely interpreted as "duels" therefore kept alive the memories of the code even into the twentieth century. Both the rhetoric and the deeds of Missourians illustrated how hard the cultural patterns of the past died. The *Joplin Daily Globe* on November 16, 1902, for example, reported that Colonel John I. Martin, inspector general of rifle practice of the Missouri National Guard, had challenged Peter Arlund of Louisville "to mortal combat" in defense of his friend Colonel Wetmore. Arlund, the paper said, assaulted Colonel Wetmore in the St. Louis Planter's Hotel. It was a result of a quarrel over a woman. Colonel Martin had offered to act as a substitute for his friend "on the field of honor." The *Globe*, having discovered a good story, decided to capitalize on it. In view of the fact that Colonel Martin was somewhat of a sharpshooter and fighter, the *Globe* contended, he had no fear of Arlund. The challenge, the paper went on to add, had been sent the day before, stating that the Missourian would meet Arlund any time, any place, and with any weapons. "Arlund," the paper reminded its readers, "is also known as an expert with rifle and pistol. There is some though [*sic*] of having the affair pulled off at St. Joseph, but it is feared that duel will be as transitory as a cloud of smoke."[42]

Six years after Martin's challenge to Arlund, the *Higbee Weekly News* reported a duel in Decatur, Alabama, between Arthur Owens and Tomie Mayer. It headlined the duel as "Chops off Rival's Head" and went on to state that it was poor Owens who had been decapitated. "If the chivalric code, with its cold indignation and pompous self-consciousness, was finally deflated by ridicule," Professor Davis keenly observed, "personal combat was more deeply embedded in American mores." The following year, under a headline reading "Fatal Missouri Duel," the same paper revealed that on February 7, 1909, near Desloge, Missouri, John Hughes and George Ketcherside had shot it out with deadly effect. The *Weekly News,* however, failed to say which man was killed in this improvised duel.[43]

One of the last and most poignant reminders of the duel's transitional nature occurred in 1908. On November 27 of that year the *Branson Echo* reported a duel between two women, Mrs. Frank Graham and Mrs. James Crabtree.[44] The paper's only criteria for referring to this event as a duel was the fact that it had been prearranged. The dispute began when the women quarreled over their husbands' shares in a joint agricultural arrangement. The *Echo* gave no reason why the men did not settle their own affair.

Originally, Mrs. Graham and Mrs. Crabtree consented to meet on a lonely spot in the Ozark hills. The only witness to the duel was ten-year-old Fannie Graham. She may very well have carried the weapons. The antagonists further agreed that their choice of weapons would be rocks. Their affair of honor escalated, however, when, after dispensing their allotted number of missiles, they proceeded to use knives. Mrs. Graham, the paper reported, fainted after she had been slashed in the shoulder and the hand. Neither was Mrs. Crabtree unscathed. She was cut across the face, breast, and hands. After the rencounter, both women were arrested and released on bond. The *Echo,* however, warned that more trouble could be expected. Satisfaction had obviously not been given or received.[45]

Ozark vengeance under the umbrella of the code did not end in the early years of the twentieth century. Residents of Branson remember that as late as the mid-1950s two local residents nearly shot it out on Main Street. The quarrel between the two men escalated when one of them killed the other's hound dog. This prompted the owner of the dead canine to challenge the killer to mortal combat under the terms of the code duello. The antagonists were to meet on the street and proceed to empty their weapons. Branson authorities, however, got wind of the "duel" and halted it.

The Graham-Crabtree affair underscored the democratization and ultimate perversion of the code duello. Two women battling with rocks and knives, probably in defense of their sharecropper husbands' meager rewards, and calling themselves duelists revealed how the roots of violence had begun to spread across an ever-expanding landscape. These twisted definitions also illustrated how the code had become a useful metaphor in the transition from the theory of controlled passion to the reality of unmitigated rage. The sinews and fibers of social restraint had broken down under the pressures of Reconstruction feuds, Klan intimidation, vigilante justice, and outlaw roguery. It would be a long time before they would be restored. The two farmers willing to duel and to die over a dead hound dog forty years later underscored the powerful symbolisms of violence created some 150 years before by the architects of the code. The supplicants of the old order, if not perplexed by this lawlessness, would surely have been dismayed. Not only had a new capitalist elite come to challenge and eventually to undermine their chivalric world, but a new wave of plebeian mayhem—the very antithesis of the code—had begun to mount across the land. Ironically, the roots of this new violence were nurtured by the very men who earlier believed that they, and they alone, could stand above the law.

Postscript and Conclusion

The dueling islands, just like the gentlemen who strode upon their sands, have all but vanished, alluvial memories sacrificed to the murky waters of the Mississippi. The pistols too are muted now— silent rejoinders of a chivalric world quickly slipping from our collective consciousness. Yet the silence of the pistols and other assorted weapons of honor still echo with resounding fury across the streets and thoroughfares of our land. Violence, shorn of honor, has become our civic karma.

The roots of violence, as sadly noted, were nurtured by the blood of some of the most prominent figures in Missouri history. The institution that cultivated many of these roots was the duello. For well over a century the code cast a deadly shadow across the state and in the process helped to condition its citizens to the utility of violence. But this study is, after all, more than a history of self-inflicted class wounds. It suggests that there were victims beyond the few who actually fell on the field of honor. In analyzing the code duello, therefore, one must not take a single binary conflict, no matter how sensational its consequences, out of a broader contextual meaning. The duel must be interpreted as part of a larger structure of societal violence. The number of duels, challenges, and hostile rencounters were, as noted throughout this work, quantitatively low compared to the general level of lawlessness. What is most significant is not the number of encounters but their import. In the hierarchy of violence, the duel stood at the apex and reflected the societal norms of that day and age. On the other hand, dueling represented more than a mere reflection of Missouri's cultural values; it romanticized the martial spirit and indoctrinated the populace into believing that violence was an acceptable means of problem solving.

Placing themselves above the law, the duelists presented to themselves and to the public a false dialectic of violence and cowardice. Unrestrained by legal formalities, they set dangerous precedents for future generations who also took the law into their own hands. Missouri's sanguinary past may well serve as a none-too-distant mirror reflecting images of ourselves but refracting our vision of ethical behavior. In time it became difficult to distinguish the killer from his victim.

Apologists for the duel interpreted it as a choreographed act of aesthetic violence. They insisted that it (and they) exhibited no marks of pathology. Rarely if ever did they raise the question of what needs and gratifications the duel fulfilled both for themselves and the public. Rather than questioning whether dueling contributed to aggressive behavior, the practitioners of this deadly sport continued for nearly a century to maintain that hostility was displaced, not reinforced, by the regenerative forces of personal combat. But the continuum of bloodshed requires historians to seek out and to analyze the shared images and collective meanings that make up the conventions of violence—what J. Cawelti has called "an ongoing continuity of value."

Certainly a part of this value system was an adulation of dueling heroes, who took on almost mythic proportions. Although the vast majority of Missourians never believed that they would journey to the field, there was nonetheless a certain identification with the duelist and a mystique surrounding his code. Even ancients such as Aristotle had observed the power of imitation through various forms of literature and art. The duel, choreographed with principals, seconds, and surgeons playing their assigned roles in the shades and hues of twilight or sunset, certainly was a macabre art form. To be aware of this phenomenon is of course not the same as subscribing to some kind of psychological determinism. Freud never ventured to the dueling grounds; Marx, however, did. Nevertheless, the duelists, as testified by the newspapers that popularized them and the people who lined the river shores to get a glimpse of them, may have vicariously appealed either to the public's unfulfilled impulses and needs or to some symbolic form of fantasy.

Perhaps too the duelists appealed to a psychic conflict that rages within us all, that is, the wish-fulfillment concept of ordinary citizens identifying with acts of courage and revenge. The fascination of the populace with dueling, of course, still provides little insight into the personality mechanisms of the duelists themselves. Yet they too were not immune from the same cultural and psychological motivations. Neurotic behavior may after all be reflected in both the perpetrator and the victim of violence as well as in those who vicariously watch it. Methodologically, however, it may be easier to examine the stimulus behind dueling than to explicate the response. Missourians responded to dueling in a variety of ways, and not all of them increased the tendency to resort to violence. In brief, historical reductionism, that is, reducing causation to a single explanatory agent, must quite obviously be avoided. Antebellum elites, for their part, reversed violence and its causes. For them, dueling was an effect rather than a cause of social disequilibrium. They argued that the institutionalization of dueling stemmed largely in part from its functional consequences; duelists thus saw themselves and their particular brand of personalized justice and honor as agents of civilization, not barbarity.

Another aspect of the dueling culture pertained to the upper-class belief in the functionalization of controlled violence. The gentlemen of shot and sword tacitly believed that the cultural polarities which existed between themselves and the rugged pioneers could be bridged by paternal conditioning. The duello with its control, politeness, and punctilio became one form of socialization. The duel accomplished this objective by its adaptive and metaphoric powers to fascinate large audiences while it sustained hierarchy. Individual duels, therefore, become items of historical curiosity, significant within a personalized context of sociopolitical power. Collectively, however, the institutionalization of dueling provides historical insights into how and why the roots of violence have grown so deep and remained so resistant to social melioration.

The elites betrayed the future not by their dishonesty but by their hubris. As natural aristocrats they trusted in their ability to lead by heroic acts, but they adhered to standards of honor soon to be transmuted by war, Reconstruction, and modernization. The duelist became an anachronism in the last decades of the nineteenth century and was replaced in popular lore by the cowboy/gunfighter mythology. Here was a dialectic of good versus evil that the duelist could not approximate. In many ways this new genre of violence captivated mass audiences by its pure simplicity. Both types of heroes, however, used the pistol to rectify perceived injustices. For the duelist the injustices were personal. For the gunslinger the injustices he might suffer could be either societal or personal. In any event, it was the duelist who served as the transitional link from an earlier form of violence to the new.

The gunslinger's hostility could now be vented under personal codes of honor that only remotely resembled those of Governor John L. Wilson or the Irish Dueling Code. It was not long in coming when the gunfighter, as represented by legendary lawmen such as Wild Bill Hickok and Wyatt Earp, was rivaled in importance by the outlaw, personified by the likes of Billy the Kid and Jesse James. This latter form of hero was of course a victim of societal injustice. The anti-establishment, anti-authority figure, the sole arbitrator of when to use deadly force, presaged the random and wanton violence of contemporary life.

Even the imagery of the duel has ironically remained a metaphor of today's struggles and competitive travails. In essence, the duel has become a metaphor of modern life. But the conflicts represented by the duel are no longer historically interpreted in the same ways. Violence within the bounds of honor has been replaced by personal confrontations void of civility and intent. Lacking consensus in our lives and our communities and absent an ideology to structure purpose, the duel has become episodic. From dueling banjoes, to a pitcher's duel, to a duel in the desert against Saddam Hussein, we convey through the roots of violence a disturbing image of our character.

Notes

Introduction

1. State of Missouri, Department of Public Safety, *Missouri Crime Summary, 1994,* 3–15.

2. United States, Department of Justice, *FBI Uniform Crime Report, January–June, 1995,* Table 4.

3. Hugh Davis Graham and Ted Robert Gurr, eds., *The History of Violence in America: Historical and Comparative Perspectives—A Report Submitted to the National Commission on the Causes and Prevention of Violence,* xxxii.

1. The Transplantation of the Duel to the Frontier

1. Timothy Flint, *Recollections of the Last Ten Years,* 178. For unusual anthropological insights into the nature of violence, see Pierre Bourdieu, "The Sentiment of Honour in Kabyle Society," 202. Robert Baldick, *The Duel: A History of Duelling,* 12–13. For another early observer of frontier violence see James Logan, *Notes of a Journey through Canada, the United States of America, and the West Indies,* 187. Timothy Flint, "Duelling," 458.

2. David H. Fischer and James C. Kelly, *Away I'm Bound Away: Virginia and the Westward Movement,* 116–17; J. Winston Coleman, Jr., *Famous Kentucky Duels,* 3–4. For the European perspective see V. G. Kiernan, *The Duel in European History: Honour and the Reign of Aristocracy,* 51–52; John Cockburn, *The History and Examination of Duels,* vi–vii; Peter Gay, *The Cultivation of Hatred: The Bourgeois Experience Victoria to Freud,* 10; E. L. Godkin, "The Probative Force of the Duel," 306–7; Julian Pitt-Rivers, "Honour and Social Status," 29. Sir Jonah Barrington was called "the Father" of the code duello. See Notes and Vignettes, W. C. Breckenridge Papers, 1752–1927, collection 1036, vol. 10, no. 132, Joint Collection, University of Missouri, Western Historical Manuscript Collection, Columbia, Mo., and State

Historical Society of Missouri Manuscripts. Hereafter cited as WHMC. Ben C. Truman, *The Field of Honor,* 9–10.

3. W. R. Smith, "History of Dueling in the State of Missouri," paper read before the State Historical Society, December 9, 1904, 1. Located in the State Historical Society, Columbia, Mo. James E. Moss, "Dueling in Missouri History: The Age of Dirk Drawing and Pistol Snapping," 3–4; Howard L. Conard, ed., *Encyclopedia of the History of Missouri,* vol. 2, 328; William Hyde and Howard L. Conard, eds., *Encyclopedia of the History of St. Louis,* vol. 1, 611; Notes and Vignettes, V. E. Phillips Papers, collection 25, folder 21, WHMC; Baldick, *The Duel,* 55; William O. Stevens, *Pistols at Ten Paces: The Story of the Code of Honor in America,* 2–5. Hereafter cited as Stevens, *Pistols.* Observation and Notes, William V. Byars Papers, Duels File, Missouri Historical Society, St. Louis, 142. Hereafter cited as MHS.

4. Gay, *The Cultivation of Hatred,* 20–21. Religious leaders were not so enamored. See Mason L. Weems, "God's Revenge against Duelling, or the Duellist's Looking Glass," 40; James Kendrick, "Dueling: A Sermon Preached at the First Baptist Church, Charleston, South Carolina, August 7, 1853," 13; W. C. Dana, "The Sense of Honor: A Discourse," 9–11; Lyman Beecher, "Remedy for Duelling," 7. This sermon is located in the Duels Files, MHS.

5. Hamilton Cochran, *Noted American Duels and Hostile Encounters,* 16–19. Sabine is quoted in Walter B. Stevens, ed., *The Brown-Reynolds Duel: A Complete Documentary Chronicle of the Last Bloodshed under the Code between St. Louisians,* 61. Lorenzo Sabine, *Notes on Duels and Duelling,* 280–81.

6. Dickson D. Bruce, Jr., *Violence and Culture in the Antebellum South,* 36–37. Also see Bertram Wyatt-Brown, *Honor and Violence in the Old South,* especially chaps. 2 and 3, for an excellent account of southern honor and shame. Virginius Dabney, *Pistols and Pointed Pens: The Dueling Editors of Old Virginia,* xvi; Edward L. Ayers, *Vengeance and Justice: Crime and Punishment in the 19th Century American South,* 19–21; Thomas Gamble, *Savannah Duels and Duelists, 1733–1877,* 49, 116; *Missouri Gazette,* December 27, 1817. Excellent descriptions on the southern duels are found in Jack K. Williams, *Dueling in the Old South: Vignettes of Social History,* 53–54. Also see Stevens, *Pistols,* 45–46; WPA, *Federal Writers' Project,* "Early Days in Arkansas," chap. 2, Arkansas History Commission, Little Rock, Ark. Hereafter cited as AHC. *Harper's New Monthly Magazine* 16, no. 94 (March 1858): 473; Joseph Holt Ingraham, *The South-West by a Yankee,* vol. 1, 95, 190, and vol. 2, 16.

7. Bruce, Jr., *Violence and Culture,* 38–39; Don C. Seitz, *Famous American Duels,* 176–226; Ellen N. Murray, *The Code of Honor: Dueling in America,* 10–17.

8. Drew Gilpin Faust, *A Sacred Circle: The Dilemma of the Intellectual in the Old South, 1840–1860,* 144; Terry G. Jordan and Matti Kaups, *The American Backwoods Frontier: An Ethnic and Ecological Interpretation,* 68.

9. Bruce, Jr., *Violence and Culture,* 41; E. L. Godkin, "Southern and Other Duelling"; Stevens, *Pistols,* 78–79; Truman, *The Field,* 29. The duel no doubt pervaded many economic classes other than the planters and to a greater degree than historians such as John Hope Franklin suggested. See John Hope Franklin, *The Militant South, 1800–1861,* 33–51; Jack K. Williams, *Vogues in Villainy,* chap. 2; Bertram Wyatt-Brown, ed., *The American People in the Antebellum South,* chap. 5.

10. Ayers, *Vengeance and Justice,* 15; *Southern Literary Messenger* 1, no. 11 (July 1835): 641–44; Clement Eaton, "Mob Violence in the Old South," 353; Harnett T. Kane, *Gentlemen, Swords and Pistols,* 99–100. Williams, *Dueling in the Old South,* 7. For anti-dueling laws see Legislative Material, 1813, record group 60, folder 19, Tennessee State Library and Archives, Nashville. An 1814 order can be found in the St. Louis *Missouri Gazette,* July 9, 1814. See also Myra C. Glenn, *Campaigns against Corporal Punishment: Prisoners, Sailors, Women, and Children in Antebellum America,* 40.

11. Cochran, *Noted American Duels,* 232–33; Stevens, *Pistols,* 31–32; *Harper's New Monthly Magazine* 16, no. 94 (March 1858): 472; Williams, *Dueling in the Old South,* 41–43; John Lyde Wilson, *The Code of Honor or, Rules for the Government of Principals and Seconds in Duelling.*

12. Steven M. Stowe, "The Touchiness of the Gentleman Planter: The Sense of Esteem and Continuity in the Ante-Bellum South," 6–11; Williams, *Dueling in the Old South,* chaps. 1–2; Stevens, *Pistols,* 245.

13. Steven M. Stowe, *Intimacy and Power in the Old South: Ritual in the Lives of the Planters,* 5; James C. Ballagh, ed., *The South in the Building of the Nation,* 207; Faust, *A Sacred Circle,* 144.

14. McCune Gill, *St. Louis Duels,* 1–9. This rare book is located in the Mercantile Library, St. Louis, Missouri.

15. Dabney, *Pistols and Pointed Pens,* xvii; Kendrick, "Dueling: A Sermon," 7; Kenneth S. Greenberg, "The Nose, the Lie, and the Duel in the Antebellum South," vol. 95, 58, 62.

16. Amos Stoddard, *Sketches, Historical and Descriptive, of Louisiana,* 244; E. M. Violette, "Early Settlements in Missouri," 41; William E. Parrish et al., *Missouri: The Heart of the Nation,* 21–22. The church held "brutality" to a minimum and there was "no evidence of a single duel." Cited in Gregory M. Franzwa, *The Story of Old Ste. Genevieve,* 43–45; Carl J. Ekberg and William E. Foley, *An Account of Upper Louisiana by Nicolas de Finiels,* 111; James A. Robertson, ed., *Louisiana under the Rule of Spain, France, and the United States 1785–1807,* 137, 212–13. Much of the primary source material in this work came from the 1803–1804 writings of Dr. Paul Alliut and Berquin-Duvallon.

17. Charels E. Peterson, *Colonial St. Louis: Building a Creole Capital,* 1–3; E. M. Violette, *A History of Missouri,* 43; Flint, *Recollections,* 203–14; Stoddard, *Sketches,* 282. The same picture applied to the Arkansas Territory. See Morris S. Arnold, *Unequal Laws unto a Savage Race: European Legal Traditions in Arkansas, 1686–1836,* 44–45, 283; U.S. Congress, *American State Papers, Documents, Legislative and Executive, of the Congress of the United States in Relation to the Public Lands,* vol. 2, 373; John Bradbury, *Travels, 1809,* 269; Walter B. Stevens, *St. Louis: The Fourth City 1764–1909,* 57. Hereafter cited as Stevens, *St. Louis.* The author is indebted to fellow historian Ana Price for her insights into Spanish colonial policy during this period.

18. Stoddard, *Sketches,* 249; Violette, *A History of Missouri,* 45–47; Gilbert C. Din, "The Immigration Policy of Governor Esteban Miró in Spanish Louisiana," 155–65; Gilbert C. Din, "Spain's Immigration Policy in Louisiana and the American Penetration, 1792–1803," 266–76; James H. Perkins, *Annals of the West: Embracing a Concise Account of Principal Events Which Have Occurred in the Western States and Territories,* 543; Robert S. Douglass, *History of Southeast Missouri,* 189.

19. For the best description of early ecology in Missouri see Henry C. Hart, *The Dark Missouri*, chaps. 1–2.

20. Jonas Viles, "Missouri in 1820," 36–52.

21. Harrison A. Trexler, "Slavery in Missouri Territory," 197–98. For an excellent description of early geography and topography see Robert A. Campbell, *Campbell's Gazetteer of Missouri*, chaps. 1–5. On the Missouri-Kentucky dispute over Wolf Island see Allen Anthony, *River at the Door: Unusual Experiences in Isolated Areas*, 37; Logan, *Notes of a Journey*, 114; *Missouri Republican*, September 3, 17, 1823.

22. For a description of an early French citizen see John F. McDermott, "Auguste Chouteau: First Citizen of Upper Louisiana," in John F. McDermott, ed., *Frenchmen and French Ways in the Mississippi Valley*, 1–13; John F. McDermott, "The Confines of a Wilderness," 3–12; R. L. Kirkpatrick, "Professional, Religious, and Social Aspects of St. Louis Life, 1804–1816," 373–81. St. Joseph followed St. Louis's lead. See *St. Joseph Gazette*, May 16, 18, June 6, 13, 1845. This may have been as close to a duel as this town, with "good morals" and few drunks, came. See Sheridan A. Logan, *Old Saint Jo: Gateway to the West, 1799–1932*, 31–32, 44–45.

23. Alexander Marjoribanks, *Travels in South and North America*, 395–400; George H. Devol, *Forty Years a Gambler on the Mississippi*, 27–30, 51–52, 86–87, 112–13, 135–36; Philip Jordan, *Frontier Law and Order*, 23, 65. For a bibliography of Missouri rivers see William E. Foley, "Antebellum Missouri in Historical Perspective," 186; Leland D. Baldwin, *The Keelboat Age on Western Waters*, 118; *Missouri Intelligencer*, September 24, 1819; Charles van Ravenswaay, "Bloody Island: Honor and Violence in Early Nineteenth-Century St. Louis," 7; Jordan, *Frontier*, 101.

24. Jordan, *Frontier*, 101; Mary Alicia Owen, "Social Customs and Usages in Missouri during the Last Century," 188; Edward J. White, "A Century of Transportation in Missouri," 137–41; T. H. Gladstone, *The Englishman in Kansas*, xvii, xiv; Note, Thomas C. Fletcher, n.d., Bryan O'Bear Collection, collection no. 1387, folder 6, WHMC; Note, Dr. William T. Hord, n.d., ibid., folder 8.

25. Frank L. Owsley, *Plain Folk of the Old South*, 57–58; Violette, *A History of Missouri*, 46; John W. Monette, *History of the Discovery and Settlement of the Valley of the Mississippi*, 547; Louis Hartz, *The Founding of New Societies*, 6–10. Hartz's fragmentation model sees a "mechanistic process" at work in transplanted societies that places the people as objects rather than subjects of historical change. From this perspective, external environmental factors in the development of sociocultural change, such as the frontier, are "to be discredited as the explanatory factor" in American history. Recent scholarship sees the process not so much as mechanism, innovation, or in F. J. Turner's concepts on invention or change, but rather as "selected continuity and blending" and "the winnowing of traits and a concordant syncretism." See Jordan and Kaups, *The American Backwoods Frontier*, 67–68; Moss, "Dueling in Missouri History," 4. See also Louis Hartz, "A Comparative Study of Fragment Cultures," 107–12.

26. The southern penchant for violence is described in Franklin, *The Militant South*, introduction and chap. 1. Duty and honor did not produce radically different societies according to Marcus Cunliffe (*Soldiers and Civilians: The Martial Spirit in America, 1775–1865*, introduction). George Ogden, *Letters from the West*, 97; Bruce, Jr., *Violence and Culture*, 3–15; Frank E. Vandiver, "The Southerner as Extremist,"

43–44. For violence and slavery see Orlando Patterson, *Slavery and Social Death: A Comparative Study*, 77–101; Ingraham, *The South-West*, vol. 2, 259–60. See also Kenneth S. Greenberg, *Masters and Statesmen: The Political Culture of American Slavery*, 40; *Missouri Gazette*, April 21, 1819. For the same theme see Jordan and Kaups, *The American Backwoods Frontier*, 67. For the view that violence was equally dispersed across all regions and all American frontiers, see Jordan, *Frontier*, 65–69. Also see Francis S. Philbrick, *The Rise of the West*, 360. For a unique view of violence see Sheldon Hackney, "Southern Violence," *American Historical Review*, 909–18; *Goodspeed's History of Franklin, Jefferson, Washington, Crawford, and Gasconade Counties, Missouri*, 499; Gentry Family Scrapbook, collection no. 2294, scrapbook 5, folder 1, WHMC; W. B. Sappington to Erasmus Sappington, November 11, 1830, John Sappington Papers, collection no. 1027, folder 18, WHMC; Grady McWhiney, *Cracker Culture: Celtic Ways in the Old South*, xv; Bertram Wyatt-Brown, *Southern Honor: Ethics and Behavior in the Old South*, 32.

27. For a description of the violent heritage of this region, see William L. Montell, *Killings: Folk Justice in the Upper South*, chap. 1; Edward Pessen, *Jacksonian America: Society, Personality, and Politics*, chap. 1; Jerry L. Butcher, "A Narrative History of Selected Aspects of Violence in the New South, 1877–1920," see especially the introduction and chaps. 1–2. On unwritten law see Daniel J. Boorstin, *Hidden History: Exploring Our Secret Past*, 165.

28. For correspondence demonstrating this ethos, see Charles Lucas to Thomas Hart Benton, September 26, 1817, in John B. C. Lucas, *Communications and Letters of J. B. C. Lucas and T. H. Benton; Missouri Gazette*, October 4–11, 1817. For the most detailed study of the Benton-Lucas duel see Walter B. Stevens, *Missouri: The Center State 1821–1915*. Also, a beautifully written description of the duel can be found in van Ravenswaay, *The Arts and Architecture of German Settlements in Missouri*, 12–19.

29. For a flavor of the period see Henry M. Brackenridge, *Journal of a Voyage up the River Missouri, 1811*, 152, 161; Henry M. Brackenridge, *Views of Louisiana; Together with a Voyage up the Mississippi River, in 1811*, 144; Thomas Ashe, *Travels in America Performed in 1806*, 290–91; Rufus Babcock, ed., *Forty Years of Pioneer Life: Memoir of John Mason Peck*, 123; Henry R. Schoolcraft, *Journal of a Tour into the Interior of Missouri and Arkansaw, 1818–1819*, 46, 49–50. Also see Henry R. Schoolcraft, *Scenes and Adventures in Semi-Alpine Region of the Ozark Mountains of Missouri and Arkansas*, 77–79; Ingraham, *The South-West*, vol. 2, 47–50.

30. William E. Foley and C. David Rice, *The First Chouteaus: River Barons of Early St. Louis*, ix; Estwick Evans, *A Pedestrious Tour, 1818*, 309–10; WPA Historical Survey, collection 3551, folder 4289, WHMC; J. S. Buckingham, *The Eastern and Western States of America*, vol. 3, 214.

31. William S. Bryan and Robert Rose, *A History of Pioneer Families of Missouri*, 186; Fortescue Cuming, *Sketches of a Tour of the Western Country, 1808*, 281–82. See also Baron de Carondelet's description of New Madrid on November 24, 1794, in Robertson, *Louisiana*, 302.

32. John Mason Peck, *A New Guide for Emigrants to the West*, 110–11.

33. Charles Gibson, "Edward Bates," 66.

34. Robert S. Douglass, *History of Missouri Baptists*, 8.

35. Marie George Windell, "The Background of Reform on the Missouri Frontier," 157.

36. Flint, *Recollections,* 175–78.

37. *Missouri Gazette,* July 21, 1819; William F. English, *The Pioneer Lawyer and Jurist in Missouri,* 66–67.

38. Stoddard, *Sketches,* 214; Cape Girardeau *Southeast Missourian,* October 27, 1992. Conard maintained Ogle fell on first fire with a bullet in the brain. See Conard, ed., *Encyclopedia,* vol. 4, 260.

39. Frederick Bates to William Ogle, June 2, 1807, in Thomas M. Marshall, ed., *The Life and Papers of Frederick Bates,* 139; "Missouri History Not Found in Textbooks," *Missouri Historical Review* 25, no. 2 (January 1931): 375; Douglass, *History of Southeast Missouri,* 190.

40. Complaint, Breach of the Peace, *U.S. v. Richard Davis,* Cape Girardeau Court of Quarter Sessions, November 1808 Term, Missouri State Archives, Jefferson City, Missouri. Hereafter cited as MSA.

41. W. V. N. Bay, *Reminiscences of the Bench and Bar of Missouri,* 41, 50.

42. *Missouri Gazette,* November 30, 1808.

2. Pistols: Icons of Status in Early Missouri

1. Brackenridge, *Views of Louisiana,* 124; Monette, *History of the Discovery,* 547, 558. John F. Darby estimated the French population of St. Louis to be nearly two-thirds of the town as late as 1818. See John F. Darby, *Personal Recollections of Many Prominent People Whom I Have Known,* 5; Louise Callan, *Philippine Duchesne: Frontier Missionary of the Sacred Heart 1769–1852,* 255; Ekberg and Foley, *An Account,* 119; John F. McDermott, ed., *The Early Histories of St. Louis,* 31–45, 99–105, 131–64.

2. Gideon Granger to Rufus Easton, December 5, 1806, in Bay, *Reminiscences,* 87; van Ravenswaay, *The Arts and Architecture,* 8; William F. Switzler, *Switzler's Illustrated History of Missouri from 1541 to 1877,* 228–34.

3. For excellent descriptions of early Ste. Genevieve, see Ashe, *Travels,* 288–90; Firmin A. Rozier, "Address of Firmin A. Rozier Delivered before the Missouri Historical Society," November 13, 1879, Ste. Genevieve Papers, MHS; Floyd Shoemaker, *Missouri and Missourians: Land of Contrasts and People of Achievement,* 266; William E. Foley, "The American Territorial System: Missouri's Experience," 416. For Nicolas de Finiel's views on Ste. Genevieve see Ekberg and Foley, *An Account,* 119. Also see Neil H. Potterfield, "Ste. Genevieve, Missouri," in McDermott, ed., *Frenchmen and French Ways,* 141–48; Henry M. Brackenridge, *Recollections of Persons and Places in the West,* 213, 207, 236–37. For other observations see Schoolcraft, *Journal of a Tour,* 46; Ashe, *Travels,* 290–91. Also see Hattie M. Anderson, "The Evolution of a Frontier Society in Missouri, 1815–1828," 305–7. The exodus of "low standing" individuals, especially from Tennessee, continued unabated throughout the 1820s. See W. B. Sappington to Erasmus Sappington, November 11, 1830, John Sappington Papers, Collection 1027, folder 18, WHMC; Buckingham, *The Eastern and Western States of America,* vol. 3, 195; Logan, *Notes of a Journey,* 180–97.

4. Jerome O. Steffen, "William Clark: A New Perspective of Missouri Territorial Politics 1813–1820," 176–77; Lemont K. Richardson, "Private Land Claims in Missouri," 135–36.

5. Firmin A. Rozier, *Rozier's History of the Early Settlement of the Mississippi Valley,* 70–87; Note, John C. Fremont, n.d., Bryan O'Bear Collection, folder 5, WHMC.

6. William E. Foley, *The Genesis of Missouri: From Wilderness Outpost to Statehood,* 158; William E. Foley, *A History of Missouri, Volume 1: 1673 to 1820,* 103; Harry L. Coles, Jr., "Applicability of the Public Land System to Louisiana," 40–43.

7. Foley, *Genesis,* 144; Stoddard, *Sketches,* 243–67; William C. Carr to Moses Austin, August 6, 1807, Moses Austin Papers, vol. 1, pt. 1, 1765–1812, Barker Library, University of Texas, Austin. Unless otherwise noted, all citations of the Austin Papers will be in vol. 1.

8. David B. Gracy II, *Moses Austin: His Life,* 90–100; U.S. Congress, *American State Papers,* vol. 2, 389; James A. Gardner, "The Business Career of Moses Austin in Missouri, 1798–1821," 237–42.

9. Gracy, *Moses Austin,* 100; Donald J. Ambramoske, "The Federal Lead Leasing System in Missouri," 29–30; Carl J. Ekberg, *Colonial Ste. Genevieve,* 156; Joseph Brown to Thomas Jefferson, July 14, 1806, in Clarence E. Carter, ed., *The Territorial Papers of the United States,* vol. 13, 545–48. Hereafter cited as *Territorial Papers.*

10. Thomas Oliver to William C. Carr, July 29, 1805, William C. Carr Papers, MHS; Gracy, *Moses Austin,* 100–108, 113; Timothy Phelps to Moses Austin, August 6, 1807, Austin Papers; Fredrick Bates to Moses Austin, September 12, 1807, ibid.; Ekberg, *Colonial Ste. Genevieve,* 156; Legal Notes of J. B. C. Lucas, July 8, 1806, Lucas Collection, MHS. Austin maintained to Judge Lucas that it was Smith T who, while drunk, attacked Scott with a knife. Moses Austin to John Smith T, August 7, 1806, Austin Papers; Lucas Collection, Legal Notes, July 1806; William C. Carr to Moses Austin, August 12, 1806, Austin Papers; Moses Austin to Rufus Easton, August 14, 1805, Rufus Easton Papers, MHS.

11. Judge John B. C. Lucas to Albert Gallatin, February 13, 1806, *Territorial Papers,* vol. 13, 445–47. For an example of Hunt's posting, see Public Letter, William Keteltas, ibid., 253.

12. Challenge, John Smith T to Frederick Bates, December 22, 1811, Frederick Bates Papers, MHS; Response, Bates to Smith T, December 22, 1811, ibid.; Challenge, Smith T to Bates, December 24, 1811, ibid.; Response, Bates to Smith T, December 30, 1811, ibid. Also see Marshall, ed., *Bates,* 210–11.

13. For details on Austin's finances see Dick Steward, "Selection of a State Capital: Vagaries and Vicissitudes," 149–55; Foley, *Genesis,* 191. For a description of the mineral wars see Dick Steward, "'With the Scepter of a Tyrant': John Smith T and the Mineral Wars," 24–37; Jerome O. Steffen, *William Clark: Jeffersonian Man on the Frontier,* 105–8. For an account of the problem of Spanish land titles see Stoddard, *Sketches,* chap. 7.

14. Newspaper article, V. E. Phillips Papers, collection no. 25, folder 21, WHMC.

15. J. Beauchamp to Benjamin Reeves, January 6, 1818, Abiel Leonard Papers, collection no. 1013, folder 43, WHMC; Brackenridge, *Recollections,* 262; Wyatt-Brown, *Southern Honor,* 41, 56, 344–45.

16. Van Ravenswaay, *The Arts and Architecture*, 7.

17. Brackenridge, *Recollections*, 262. In relating this account the author mentioned that he had lost another friend, Tarleton Bates, in a duel on a similar point of honor. See ibid., 262–63; Notes and Scrapbook, Roy D. Williams Papers, collection no. 3769, folder 100, WHMC.

18. Brackenridge, *Recollections*, 265.

19. *Louisiana Gazette*, January 31, 1811.

20. Brackenridge, *Recollections*, 266.

21. Stephen Austin to Joshua Pilcher, June 1, 1817, Austin Papers.

22. *Missouri Gazette*, October 17, 1812.

23. Rozier, *Rozier's History*, 321–24.

24. *Missouri Gazette*, September 6, October 26, 1809; State Historical Society of Missouri, *This Week in Missouri History*, September 30–October 6, 1934.

25. Brackenridge, *Recollections*, 239; State Historical Society of Missouri, *This Week in Missouri History*, September 30–October 6, 1934; Douglass, *History of Southeast Missouri*, 190; Rozier, *Rozier's History*, 322; English, *The Pioneer Lawyer*, 61.

26. *Missouri Gazette*, March 15, 1810, February 6, 1813.

27. Van Ravenswaay, *The Arts and Architecture*, 7.

28. Bay, *Reminiscences*, 440; Van Ravenswaay, *The Arts and Architecture*, 7.

29. *Missouri Gazette*, August 12, 1815.

30. Bay, *Reminiscences*, 143; Moss, "Dueling in Missouri History," 8–10; Houck, *A History of Missouri*, vol. 3, 77.

31. For an excellent biographical sketch of Geyer see L. U. Reavis, *Saint Louis: The Future Great City of the World*, 311–20; *St. Louis Enquirer*, June 17, 1822, May 31, 1824.

32. J. Thomas Scharf, *History of Saint Louis City and County*, vol. 2, 1853; Conard, ed., *Encyclopedia*, 330. *Missouri Gazette*, August 7, 1818; Smith, "History of Dueling," 3.

33. *Missouri Gazette*, August 14, 1818.

34. This is more than likely the same man who John Smith T sent to see Governor James Wilkinson in 1805 to argue his case against Moses Austin. See Letter, Moses Austin to Rufus Easton, August 14, 1805, Easton Papers, MHS.

35. Indictment, *Territory of Missouri v. William Tharp*, Territorial Court Cases 1804–1820, case 61, record group 600, box 21, Missouri Supreme Court Cases, MSA; Roy Blunt, "The Smith-Tharp Incident and Dueling in Missouri," *Steelville Star*, September 27, 1989; J. B. C. Lucas to William Lucas, September 29, 1817, and October 3, 1818, in John B. C. Lucas, ed., *Letters of Hon. J. B. C. Lucas from 1815 to 1836*, 8, 27; *Missouri Gazette*, October 4, 1817; William Tharp to Thomas A. Smith, February 3, 1818, Thomas A. Smith Papers, collection no. 1029, folder 14, WHMC.

36. Observations and Notes, Byars Papers, Duels Files, MHS, 151. Born in 1857, Mr. Byars toiled in relative obscurity. This unpublished manuscript provided many insights into the violent world of antebellum Missouri. For a short biographical sketch of Byars see Alexander N. DeMenil, "A Century of Missouri Literature," 117.

37. Butcher, "A Narrative History," 119.

38. J. B. C. Lucas to William Lucas, October 3, 1818, in Lucas, *Letters*, 27; Butcher, "A Narrative History," 120.

39. Newton Bateman and Paul Selby, eds., *Historical Encyclopedia of Illinois, Vol. I*, 138. Timothy Flint maintained that Bennett twice shot Stuart. See Flint, *Recollections*, 181–82.

40. *Missouri Gazette*, February 17, 1819.

41. Ibid.; Baldick, *The Duel*, 124.

3. The Age of Political Dueling

1. For further details see chap. 11.

2. C. H. McClure, "A Century of Missouri Politics," 315; Viles, "Missouri in 1820," 50.

3. *Missouri Intelligencer and Boon's Lick Advertiser*, April 23, 1819. For examples of European hierarchy and dueling see Kiernan, *The Duel in European History*, 198; Gay, *The Cultivation of Hatred*, 20–25. On the issue of frontier violence see Francis Hall, *Travels in Canada and the United States in 1816 and 1817*. Hall's *Travels* was extensively reviewed in many journals. For an example see *The Western Review and Miscellaneous Magazine: A Monthly Publication Devoted to Literature and Science* 4 (March 1821): 129–54.

4. Thomas Shackleford, "Early Recollections of Missouri," *Missouri Historical Society Collection*, 5; Foley, "The American Territorial System," 415, 421; William N. Chambers, "Pistols and Politics: Incidents in the Career of Thomas H. Benton, 1816–1818," 6; Violette, "Early Settlements in Missouri," 48–50.

5. John R. Musick, *Stories of Missouri*, 83; *Missouri Gazette*, December 27, 1817; *Missouri Intelligencer*, November 27, 1821, March 25, 1823; Houck, *A History of Missouri*, vol. 3, 74–75; Brackenridge, *Views of Louisiana*, 140.

6. Peter H. Burnett, *Recollections and Opinions of an Old Pioneer*, 91; Kiernan, *The Duel in European History*, 51; Flint, *Recollections*, 180; Ronald L. F. Davis, "Community and Conflict in Pioneer Saint Louis, Missouri," 343–46.

7. Flint, *Recollections*, 179.

8. *Missouri Intelligencer*, March 25, 1823.

9. Ibid., December 3, 1822. For others who also saw these connections see Shoemaker, *Missouri and Missourians*, 264; L. U. Reavis, *The Life and Military Service of Gen. William Selby Harney*, 37–38; John C. O'Hanlon, *Life and Scenery in Missouri: Reminiscences of a Missionary Priest*, 75.

10. Flint, *Recollections*, 182–83; *Jackson Independent Patriot*, June 12, 1824.

11. *Missouri Intelligencer*, June 10, 1820; St. Louis *Missouri Argus*, July 17, 1840. The *Gazette* earlier made this connection. See *Missouri Gazette*, December 27, 1817.

12. Flint, *Recollections*, 214.

13. Steffen, "William Clark: A New Perspective," 183.

14. Joseph Charless to John Scott, August 10, 1816, Lucas Collection; Newspaper clippings, Roy D. Williams Papers, collection no. 3769, folder 100, WHMC. Dr. Walker had earlier volunteered to lead a mission with Scott to rescue Reuben Smith, the brother of John Smith T, from a Spanish prison. Pamphlet, Charles Lucas, "To the People of Missouri Territory: Charles Lucas' Exposition of a Late Difference between

John Scott and Himself," 5; Rozier, *Rozier's History,* 256; Thomas Wright to Charles Lucas, August 10, 1816, Lucas Collection.

15. Charles Lucas, "To the People," 7–9; Scharf, *History of Saint Louis City and County,* vol. 2, 1850.

16. Later, Andrew Scott killed an Arkansas general, Edmund Hogan, on March 31, 1828, with a walking cane spear. Scott weighed 130 pounds and Hogan between 250 and 300 pounds. See Subject File Duels, AHC. Also see *Arkansas Gazette,* June 1, 1824; WPA, Federal Writer's Project, "Early Days in Arkansas," chap. 2, AHC; *Missouri Intelligencer,* April 12, 1825; Alan S. Weiner, "John Scott, Thomas Hart Benton, David Barton and the Presidential Election of 1824," 481–83.

17. For similarities between American and medieval habits see Lynn White, Jr., "The Legacy of the Middle Ages in the American Wild West," 73–79, 95.

18. *Missouri Intelligencer,* December 3, 1822, March 25, 1823.

19. These exchanges can be found in "Rules . . . ," August 10–13, 1816, Thomas Hart Benton Papers, MHS; Moss, "Dueling in Missouri History," 10–11.

20. McArthur did own a tavern where fourteen years later John Smith T shot dead a young stranger named Samuel Ball, but no counterfeiting charges were ever proven. Testimony, William Oliver, August 30, 1816, Ste. Genevieve County Court Records, Ste. Genevieve, Missouri. These records have now been copied by the Missouri State Archives.

21. Franzwa, *Story of Old Ste. Genevieve,* 86; Testimony, John Scott, August 30, 1816, Ste. Genevieve County Court Records; Testimony, Thomas Watson, August 30, 1816, ibid; Goodspeed's *History of Southeast Missouri,* 312; Rozier, *Rozier's History,* 128–29.

22. Van Ravenswaay, *The Arts and Architecture,* 8–9.

23. Foley, *Genesis,* 291; Steffen, "William Clark: A New Perspective," 189–90; Van Ravenswaay, *The Arts and Architecture,* 9. Full details of the Benton-Lucas duels will be provided in chap. 4.

24. Rufus Pettibone to Henry R. Schoolcraft, September 26, 1819, in "Missouriana," November 1939, 412.

25. Ibid.

26. Smith, "History of Dueling," 3. Van Ravenswaay, *The Arts and Architecture,* 7.

27. *Washington Bee,* June 2, 1883.

28. William S. Bryan and Robert Rose, *A History of Pioneer Families of Missouri,* 186.

29. Charles Carroll to Mrs. Moses Tabbs, March 11, 1820, in Private Collection of Stuart Goldman, Randolph, Massachusetts. Located in WHMC. *Missouri Intelligencer,* March 4, 1820.

30. *Missouri Intelligencer,* January 24, July 17, July 3, 1821. For details of the shooting and trial see Gentry Family Scrapbook, collection no. 2294, folder 1, WHMC; Houck, *A History of Missouri,* vol. 3, 79.

31. Thomas Smith to Judge David Todd, May 30, 1820, Thomas A. Smith Papers, collection no. 1029, folder 19, WHMC; Gray Bynum to Judge David Todd, June 1, 1820, ibid.; Judge David Todd to Thomas Smith, May 29, 1820, ibid.; Charles Carroll to Thomas Smith, September 21, 1820, folder 20, ibid.

32. *Missouri Intelligencer,* June 26, 1824; William Lane to Mary Lane, August 31, July 31, 1824, William Carr Lane Collection, MHS.

33. Gentry Family Scrapbook, folder 1; W. R. Gentry, "The Missouri Soldier One Hundred Years Ago," 219; Joseph F. Gordon, "The Political Career of Lilburn W. Boggs," 117–18.

34. This information was provided by archivist Margaret Beggs. See Indictment, *State of Missouri v. Samuel Perry,* March Term, 1824, Washington County Circuit Court, Potosi, Missouri, 237.

35. State Historical Society of Missouri, *This Week in Missouri History,* June 28–July 4, 1931.

36. Van Ravenswaay, *The Arts and Architecture,* 19

37. *St. Louis Republican,* June 25, 1823; Smith, "History of Dueling," 2.

38. Van Ravenswaay, *The Arts and Architecture,* 20.

39. C. R. Barnes, *The Commonwealth of Missouri: A Centennial Record,* 487–88; van Ravenswaay, *The Arts and Architecture,* 20. State Historical Society of Missouri, *This Week in Missouri History,* June 28–July 4, 1931.

40. William Rector to James Monroe, July 25, 1823, vol. 38, Miscellaneous file, MSA, 278–81. See also Rector Correspondence, Missouri State Archives Collection, collection no. 2154, WHMC; Babcock, ed., *Forty Years of Pioneer Life,* 85; Moss, "Dueling in Missouri History," 16; *Missouri Intelligencer,* September 18, 1824; Speeches and Writings, Lilburn A. Kingsbury Papers, collection no. 3724, folder 443, WHMC.

41. *Missouri Intelligencer,* December 25, 1824.

4. Honor and Hubris: The Benton-Lucas Duel

1. Stevens, *Pistols,* chap. 10; van Ravenswaay, *The Arts and Architecture,* 9–19; Stevens, *Missouri,* vol. 1, chap. 6.

2. William N. Chambers, *Old Bullion Benton,* 65, 71; William M. Meigs, *The Life of Thomas Hart Benton,* 115. For the French influence see Callan, *Philippine Duchesne,* 255; Gabriel Franchere, *Narrative of a Voyage to the Northwest Coast of America, 1811–1814,* 403; Foley, *History of Missouri,* 204–5; Pitt-Rivers, "Honour and Social Status," 21–27.

3. John B. Wyeth, *Notes of 1832,* 45–47, 83; Hugh C. Cleland, "John B. C. Lucas, Physiocrat on the Frontier," *Western Pennsylvania Historical Magazine* 36, pt. 3, September–December 1953, 164; Stevens, *St. Louis,* 107; John K. Townsend, *Narrative of 1834,* 89; Van Ravenswaay, *The Arts and Architecture,* 10; Thomas J. C. Fagg, *Thomas Hart Benton: The Great Missourian and His Times Reviewed,* 2.

4. Foley, "The American Territorial System," 412.

5. Elbert B. Smith, *Magnificent Missourian: The Life of Thomas Hart Benton,* 55; Chambers, *Old Bullion Benton,* 66; Meigs, *Benton,* 85.

6. Chambers, *Old Bullion Benton,* 64; Meigs, *Benton,* 87.

7. Thomas H. Benton, *Auto-Biographical Sketch of Thomas H. Benton,* v. First printed in Benton, *Thirty Years' View,* vol. 1.

8. Chambers, *Old Bullion Benton,* 62, 63.

9. Smith, *Magnificent Missourian,* 21–22.

10. William N. Chambers, "As the Twig Is Bent: The Family and the North Carolina Years of Thomas Hart Benton, 1752–1801," 415.

11. Benton, *Auto-Biographical Sketch,* i–vi; van Ravenswaay, *The Arts and Architecture,* 10. See also Chambers, *Old Bullion Benton,* 63; Wyatt-Brown, *Honor and Violence,* 3; *New York Daily Times,* August 9, 1853; Ayers, *Vengeance and Justice,* 13–16; Bruce, Jr., *Violence and Culture,* 13–17; Stowe, "The Touchiness of the Gentleman Planter," 6–7.

12. Joseph M. Rogers, *Thomas H. Benton,* 22; Ernest Kirschten, *Catfish and Crystal,* 135; Stevens, *Missouri,* vol. 1, 75–76.

13. Thomas H. Benton to William B. Lewis, April 22, 23, 1813, Thomas H. Benton Papers, MHS. See also Posting, Thomas H. Benton of William B. Lewis, November 24, 1813, ibid. Benton may have come to Missouri as early as 1811. See Arrest Order, January 23, 1811, ibid; Statement, John C. Fremont, n.d., Bryan O'Bear Collection, folder 6, WHMC; Marshall D. Hier, "Lawyer Benton's Last Duel," 45–46.

14. William N. Chambers, "Young Man from Tennessee: First Years of Thomas H. Benton in Missouri," 204–6; John B. C. Lucas to William Carol, December 13, 1817 in Lucas, *Letters,* 26.

15. Richard Edwards, *Edwards' Great West and Her Commercial Metropolis,* 317.

16. Cleland, "John B. C. Lucas," 167, 165; Bay, *Reminiscences,* 53; Foley, *Genesis,* 160. Kenneth W. Keller, "Alexander McNair and John B. C. Lucas: The Background of Early Missouri Politics," 241; J. B. C. Lucas to Charles Lucas, November 12, 1807, John B. C. Lucas Collection, MHS; J. B. C. Lucas to Philip B. Barbour, January 15, 1820, Lucas, *Letters,* 95–96.

17. Charles Lucas to J. B. C. Lucas, June 1, 1811, Lucas Collection.

18. J. B. C. Lucas to William Lucas, August 10, 1817, Lucas, *Letters,* 4; J. B. C. Lucas to William Lucas, June 30, 1817, ibid., 14–15; J. B. C. Lucas to James Lucas, May 22, 1817, ibid., 12–13; *St. Louis Republican,* January 14, 1824.

19. Letter, J. B. C. Lucas to William Lucas, August 10, 1817, Lucas, *Letters,* 4.

20. "Rules of the Meeting. . ." and "Statement of Facts," August 10–13, 1816, Benton Papers.

21. Chambers, *Old Bullion Benton,* 65.

22. Van Ravenswaay, *The Arts and Architecture,* 12; Stevens, *Pistols,* 177–78.

23. James Neal Primm, *Lion of the Valley: St. Louis, Missouri,* 116; Memoir, August 11, 1817, Isaac H. Sturgeon Papers, MHS. A treatise by Venecian Girolamo Muzio in 1550 laid out these offenses. See Kiernan, *The Duel in European History,* 48. Challenge, Thomas H. Benton to Charles Lucas, October 15, 1816, Lucas Collection; Response to challenge, Charles Lucas to Thomas H. Benton, October 15, 1816, ibid. Also see Lucas, *Communications,* 7; Stevens, *Missouri,* vol. 1, 81; Houck, *A History of Missouri,* vol. 3, 77–79.

24. Lucas, *Communications,* 13–14.

25. J. G. Peristiany, "Introduction," in Peristiany, ed., *Honour and Shame: The Values of Mediterranean Society,* 16.

26. Burnett, *Old Pioneer,* 92.

27. Julio Caro Baroja, "Honour and Shame: A Historical Account of Several Conflicts," 84; Pitt-Rivers, "Honour and Social Status," 22–23, 35–38.

28. Van Ravenswaay, *The Arts and Architecture*, 12.

29. Lucas, *Communications*, "Origin and state of differences between Thos. H. Benton and Charles Lucas, St. Louis, Aug. 11, 1817, 9 o'clock at night," 6.

30. *Missouri Gazette*, September 6, 1817. For details on the entire affair of honor see Barnes, *The Commonwealth of Missouri*, 481–86.

31. Meigs, *Benton*, 113–14.

32. Van Ravenswaay, *The Arts and Architecture*, 12–13.

33. Stevens, *Missouri*, vol. 1, 81; *Missouri Gazette*, November 1, 1817; Lucas, *Communications*, 8; Stevens, *Pistols*, 178.

34. Smith, "History of Dueling," 3.

35. Lucas, *Communications*, 8–10.

36. J. B. C. Lucas to William Lucas, August 18, 1817, ibid., 6–7; Kirschten, *Catfish*, 137.

37. Charles Lucas to Thomas H. Benton, September 26, 1817, Benton Papers.

38. Stevens, *Missouri*, vol. 1, 83.

39. Ibid., 84; Stevens, *Pistols*, 178–79; Stevens, *Missouri*, vol. 1, 85.

40. Van Ravenswaay, *The Arts and Architecture*, 17.

41. Pitt-Rivers, "Honour and Social Status," 29.

42. Van Ravenswaay, *The Arts and Architecture*, 18.

43. Chambers, *Old Bullion Benton*, 75; Chambers, "Pistols and Politics," 14.

44. Benton, *Auto-Biographical Sketch*, v; Stevens, *Pistols*, 182–83.

45. Meigs, *Benton*, 113–14; Chambers, "Pistols and Politics," 12; Chambers, *Old Bullion Benton*, 74; David D. March, *The History of Missouri*, vol. 1, 224–25; Scharf, *History of Saint Louis City and County*, 1849, 1853; State Historical Society of Missouri, *This Week in Missouri History*, September 20–27, 1925; *Missouri Gazette*, November 8, 1817.

46. *Missouri Gazette*, January 15, 1819.

47. Perry McCandless, "The Political Philosophy and Political Personality of Thomas H. Benton," 146.

48. Senator Foote of Mississippi once pulled a pistol on Benton in the halls of Congress but did not fire. Benton did not challenge him. Also, Benton arranged for Senator Lewis Linn to serve as a second for Cilley in his duel with Graves of Kentucky. See Elizabeth Linn to David R. Atchison, February 19, 1844, David Rice Atchison Papers, collection no. 71, folder 1, WHMC.

49. Benton, *Auto-Biographical Sketch*, v.

50. This did not stop Benton from an occasional brawl. See Stevens, *Pistols*, 184–85. Pitt-Rivers, "Honour and Social Status," 35–38; A. W. Terrell, "Recollections of General Sam Houston," 129; Manuscript, William V. Byars, "Issues of the Civil War under the Pierce Administration as Illustrated in the Hostile Correspondence and Duel between B. Gratz Brown and Thomas C. Reynolds," n.d., William K. Bixby Collection, Duels File, MHS, 140. Hereafter cited as Manuscript, Byars.

51. *Missouri Gazette Extra*, n.d. This was located in the Thomas H. Benton Papers. Edward Bates, "Edward Bates against Thomas H. Benton," 3–12; Duane Meyer, *The*

Heritage of Missouri: A History, 176–77. Dr. Samuel Mery to Daniel Dunklin, August 6, 1835, Daniel Dunklin Papers, collection no. 97, folder 34, WHMC; Letter, Dunklin to F. A. Martin, August 11, 1835, ibid. Martin later reported to Governor Dunklin that Strother intended to go to Washington in the winter of 1835–1836 and challenge both Benton and Ashley. See Martin to Dunklin, August 30, 1835, ibid. J. B. C. Lucas to Robert Moore, October 27, 1820, Lucas, *Letters,* 30; Lucas, *Communications,* 18; Hyde and Conard, eds., *Encyclopedia of the History of St. Louis,* vol. 3, 1316.

5. The Press, Bar, and Pulpit: Institutional Opposition to the Code

1. Gardiner Spring, ed., *Memoirs of the Late Rev. Samuel J. Mills,* 73; Frances Lea McCurdy, *Stump, Bar, and Pulpit: Speechmaking on the Missouri Frontier,* ix, 5.

2. Timothy Flint, "The Bar, the Pulpit, and the Press," 639–42; Flint, "National Character of the Western People," 134; Samuel R. Brown, *The Western Gazetteer; or Emigrant's Dictionary,* 194; McCurdy, *Stump, Bar, and Pulpit,* 5–6.

3. Foley, *Genesis,* 210; State Historical Society of Missouri, *This Week in Missouri History,* July 12–19, 1930; William H. Lyon, *The Pioneer Editor in Missouri 1808–1860,* 13–17, 26, 33, 36. Charless opposed congressional restrictions on the admission of Missouri to statehood, but many suspected him of anti-slavery sentiments. Arvarh E. Strickland, "Aspects of Slavery in Missouri, 1821," 512–17, 519–23.

4. Perry McCandless, *A History of Missouri, Volume 2: 1820 to 1860,* 178.

5. McCurdy, *Stump, Bar, and Pulpit,* 12, 72, 80, 97–98; *Missouri Gazette,* April 19, 1820, November 8, 1817.

6. *Missouri Gazette,* July 12, 1820.

7. *Louisiana Gazette,* January 2, 1811.

8. A missionary priest to Missouri agreed with this assessment. See O'Hanlon, *Life and Scenery,* 75. Primm, *Lion of the Valley,* 91; Marshall, ed., *Bates,* 242.

9. *Missouri Gazette,* August 17, 1816, March 22, 1817, June 26, 1818.

10. Lyon, *The Pioneer Editor,* 157; *Jeffersonian Republican,* April 2, 1836.

11. William H. Taft, *Missouri Newspapers,* 10; *Missouri Gazette,* August 28, 1818, May 3, 17, 1820.

12. McCurdy, *Stump, Bar, and Pulpit,* 111; *Missouri Intelligencer,* February 8, 1825; John B. C. Lucas to Rufus King, November 20, 1823, John B. C. Lucas Collection, MHS.

13. *Jackson Independent Patriot,* August 11, 1821. For other reform articles in the same paper see May 17, 1823, October 7, 1826, and November 1, 1826; George B. Mangold, "Social Reform in Missouri 1820–1920," 191–203. Many controversial issues surfaced during the Constitutional Convention and the debate between the reservationists and their opponents. See *Missouri Gazette,* April 19, 1820, and October 10, 1821. Newspapers quoted reports from the *Arkansas Gazette* not only because of geographical proximity but also because so many Missourians had friends and relatives there. See *Missouri Intelligencer,* August 26, 1825; *Missouri Intelligencer and Boons Lick Advertiser,* April 23, 1819. On the distinctions of dueling and crime see the communication entitled "Amicus," ibid., November 27, 1821. See also ibid.,

January 29, February 5, 1821, January 7, 1823; *St. Charles Missourian,* March 17, 1821; McCurdy, *Stump, Bar, and Pulpit,* 73–75; *Hannibal Gazette,* August 26, 1847.

14. *Missouri Republican,* September 3, 1823; *St. Louis Herald of Religious Liberty,* January 15, 1846, June 12, 1824.

15. *Missouri Gazette,* September 17, 1810. At this time the paper was often called the *Louisiana Gazette.* Windell, "Background of Reform," 174; *St. Louis Republican,* February 10, 1824; *Missouri Gazette,* July 9, 1814, August 17, 1816.

16. *Missouri Intelligencer,* January 7, 1823.

17. *Jackson Independent Patriot,* February 22, 1823; *Bowling Green Salt River Journal,* December 13, 1837; Dabney, *Pistols and Pointed Pens,* chaps. 1–3; *Jeffersonian Republican,* April 2, 1836; McCurdy, *Stump, Bar, and Pulpit,* 132.

18. William F. Swindler, "The Southern Press in Missouri 1861–1864," 395; Taft, *Newspapers,* 50, 64–65; McCandless, *A History of Missouri,* 183.

19. Ervin H. Pollack, *Fundamentals of Legal Research,* 2–3; Oliver Wendell Holmes, *Collected Legal Papers,* 20–45; Wyatt-Brown, *Southern Honor,* 364; Jordan, *Frontier,* 1–7, 35; Richard B. Morris, "Foreword," vii–ix; Billias, "Editor's Introduction," xix–xx. For a good description of early-nineteenth-century Missouri see Francis A. Sampson, "Glimpses of Old Missouri by Explorers and Travelers," 247–67. Claiborne is quoted in Arnold, *Unequal Laws,* 131.

20. McCurdy, *Stump, Bar, and Pulpit,* 120; Roscoe Pound, *The Formative Era of American Law,* 8; W. Eugene Hollon, *Frontier Violence: Another Look,* viii; G. Gordon Post, *An Introduction to the Law,* 7–13; Wayne Gard, *Frontier Justice,* vi–vii.

21. John L. Harr, "Law and Lawlessness in the Lower Mississippi Valley, 1815–1860," 52–56; Pollack, *Fundamentals of Legal Research,* 1–2; Jordan, *Frontier,* 22–38, 159–61. David Brion Davis, *Homicide in American Fiction, 1798–1860: A Study in Social Values,* xv; McCurdy, *Stump, Bar, and Pulpit,* 107–38, 146; Edward J. White, *Legal Traditions and Other Papers,* 292.

22. North Todd Gentry, *The Bench and Bar of Boone County Missouri,* 114.

23. Pound, *The Formative Era,* 8; *Missouri Gazette,* October 12, 1808. Collection of articles, W. C. Breckenridge Papers, collection no. 1036, vol. 2, WHMC; Pessen, *Jacksonian America,* 14–15; Davis, *Homicide in American Fiction,* vii; Brackenridge, *Recollections,* 213.

24. Richard Maxwell Brown, *Strain of Violence: Historical Studies of American Violence and Vigilantism,* 22–26; *Missouri Gazette,* July 20, 13, 1816. For the position of the regulators see "Foe to Detraction" in the July 13, 1816, issue of the *Gazette.*

25. Houck, *A History of Missouri,* vol. 3, 12; McCurdy, *Stump, Bar, and Pulpit,* 125; Gibson, "Edward Bates," 66; Floyd C. Shoemaker, "Some Colorful Lawyers in the History of Missouri, 1804–1904," 126–31; William F. English, *The Pioneer Lawyer,* 120; Richard D. Heffner, ed., *Alexis de Tocqueville, Democracy in America,* 125.

26. English, *The Pioneer Lawyer,* 11–19; McCurdy, *Stump, Bar, and Pulpit,* 125–26. Boorstin, *Hidden History,* 159–65; Jordan, *Frontier,* 38, 157; Holmes, *Papers,* 27. One historian in particular argues that violence was a national, not just a sectional, characteristic. See Howard Zinn, *The Southern Mystique,* 238; McCandless, *A History of Missouri,* 180–81; Letter of Petition, George Shannon to Don Luis Lorimier, n.d.,

Correspondence and Petition, 1800–1804, Cape Girardeau County Records, WHMC. Other examples of personalized law can be found in Bryan and Rose, *A History of Pioneer Families of Missouri*, 90; Horace V. Redfield, *Homicide, North and South*, 161–64; Lillian H. Oliver, "Some Spanish Land Grants in the St. Charles District," WHMC; "Missouri History Not Found in Text Books," *Missouri Historical Review* 19, no. 2 (January 1925): 386–87; George Dargo, *Jefferson's Louisiana: Politics and the Clash of Legal Traditions*, 11.

27. Richard Maxwell Brown, *No Duty to Retreat: Violence and Values in American History and Society*, ii–iii, 15–25; Holmes, *Papers*, 187.

28. John N. Edwards, *Biography, Memoirs, Reminiscences and Recollections*, 293; Leonard Savitz, *Dilemmas in Criminology*, v, 13–15.

29. Thomas J. Kernan, "The Jurisprudence of Lawlessness," 55–60; McCurdy, *Stump, Bar, and Pulpit*, 132; Liberty *Weekly Tribune*, March 7, 1851.

30. Davis, *Homicide in American Fiction*, 61.

31. Roger D. McGrath, *Gunfighters, Highwaymen and Vigilantes: Violence on the Frontier*, 258–60; Louis Pelzer, *Henry Dodge*, 19–20; *St. Louis Republican*, March 15, 1824; Ingraham, *The South-West*, vol. 2, 187; Butcher, "A Narrative History," 120; *Missouri Intelligencer and Boons Lick Advertiser*, January 29, February 5, 1821. For examples of legal confusion well into the 1840s see Indictment, *Robert Rogers v. State of Missouri*, Polk County Circuit Court Records, vol. A, March 1841, MSA, 193; Indictment, *Joseph Young v. State of Missouri*, ibid., 223; Speeches and Writings, Kingsbury Manuscripts, collection no. 3724, folder 448, WHMC; Darby, *Personal Recollections*, 111, 113–16; English, *The Pioneer Lawyer*, 55; Pound, *The Formative Era*, 8; Trial, *Edward D. Worrell v. State of Missouri*, January 1857, in John D. Lawson, ed., *American State Trials*, 7; Laurance Hyde, *Historical Review of the Judicial System of Missouri*, 8; McCandless, *A History of Missouri*, 173; McCurdy, *Stump, Bar, and Pulpit*, 131–32; Bay, *Reminiscences*, 218–24; Savitz, *Dilemmas in Criminology*, 92; Daniel Breck, *Puke Lawin': Law Makin' and Law Breaken' in Missouri Especially*, 64.

32. English, *The Pioneer Lawyer*, 66–69; Robert K. Gilmore, *Ozark Baptizings, Hangings, and Other Diversions: Theatrical Folkways of Rural Missouri, 1885–1910*, 154–58; A. Loyd Collins and Georgia I. Collins, *Hero Stories from Missouri History*, 71–73; *Jefferson City Inquirer*, August 14, 1845, December 29, 1846. Houck, *A History of Missouri*, vol. 3, 73; Robert M. Ireland, "The Problem of Concealed Weapons in Nineteenth-Century Kentucky," 370–73; *Missouri Gazette*, February 24, 1819, July 6, 1816; Brackenridge, *Recollections*, 222.

33. English, *The Pioneer Lawyer*, 66, 79–80; David Brion Davis, "Violence in American Literature," 71. See also Walter M. Gerson, "Violence as an American Value Theme," 151–57; Joseph T. Klapper, "The Impact of Viewing 'Aggression': Studies and Problems of Extrapolation," 131–39; Brown, *Strain of Violence*, 15; Burnett, *Old Pioneer*, 90–91; William Blackstone, *Commentaries on the Laws of England*, 53–54; Jordan, *Frontier*, 168; Savitz, *Dilemmas in Criminology*, 10–13; *Missouri Gazette*, October 20, 1819.

34. State of Missouri, *Acts of the Second General Assembly of the State of Missouri, 1822*, chapter 30, "An Act More Effectually to Prevent Duelling," 53–56; *Missouri*

Intelligencer, December 3, 1822, February 8, 1827; Walter B. Davis and Daniel S. Durrie, *An Illustrated History of Missouri,* 89; James Q. Dealey, "Our State Constitutions," 60.

35. William B. Faherty, "The Personality and Influence of Louis William Valentine DuBourg," 43–55; J. J. Conway, "The Beginnings of Ecclesiastical Jurisdiction in the Archdiocese of St. Louis, 1764–1776," 8–12.

36. Leslie Gamblin Hill, "A Moral Crusade: The Influence of Protestantism on Frontier Society in Missouri," 16; Foley, *Genesis,* 276–77; Beecher, "Remedy for Duelling," 1–8.

37. Samuel Spring, *A Discourse in Consequence of the Late Duel,* 1–13; Alice F. Tyler, *Freedom's Ferment: Phases of Social History to 1860,* 32; Spring, ed., *Memoirs of the Late Rev. Samuel J. Mills,* 73; Flint, *Recollections,* 128–30, 178.

38. Spring, ed., *Memoirs of the Late Rev. Samuel J. Mills,* 59. See especially chap. 5, "His Missionary Tours into the Western and Southern Sections of the United States." Wyatt-Brown, *Southern Honor,* 351.

39. Weems, "God's Revenge," 1.

40. Ibid., 3–8; *Missouri Gazette,* August 17, 1816.

41. Weems, "God's Revenge," 47.

42. Ibid., 27–43.

43. Flint, "Duelling," 456; Flint, *Recollections,* 182; Lucy Simmons, "The Rise and Growth of Protestant Bodies in the Missouri Territory," 296–305.

44. Colin B. Goodykoontz, *Home Missions on the American Frontier,* 18; Samuel S. Hill, *The South and the North in American Religion,* 36–37; Edwin S. Gaustad, *A Religious History of America,* 132–36; Walter B. Posey, *Religious Strife on the Southern Frontier,* 77, xiii; Robert T. Handy, *A Christian America: Protestant Hopes and Historical Realities,* 65–94; Ference M. Szasz, *The Protestant Clergy in the Great Plains and Mountains West, 1865–1915,* 13–14; Spring, ed., *Memoirs of the Late Rev. Samuel J. Mills,* 69, 73; Foley, *Genesis,* 275.

45. Ray V. Denslow, *Territorial Masonry,* 75–92.

46. William W. Sweet, *The Story of Religion in America,* 316; Whitney R. Cross, *The Burned-Over District: The Social and Intellectual History of Enthusiastic Religion in Western New York, 1800–1850,* 3; Tyler, *Freedom's Ferment,* 34.

47. William W. Sweet, *Religion on the American Frontier: The Baptists 1783–1830,* 43; Violette, *A History of Missouri,* 85–86; Tyler, *Freedom's Ferment,* 35; Lawrence E. Murphy, "Beginnings of Methodism in Missouri, 1798–1824," 387–94; John Mason Peck, *A Guide for Emigrants Containing Sketches of Illinois, Missouri, and the Adjacent Parts,* 70; Babcock, *Forty Years,* 88, 120.

48. John Mason Peck, ed., *The Serpent Uncoiled: Or a Full Length Picture of Universalism by a Western Layman,* Introduction and Notes by J. M. Peck, 1–20; William Henry Milburn, *The Rifle, Axe, and Saddlebags, and Other Lectures,* 116; Spring, *Memoirs of the Late Rev. Samuel J. Mills,* 7, 22, 26.

49. Posey, *Religious Strife,* 35; Schoolcraft, *Scenes and Adventures,* 100; Foley, *Genesis,* 276; Tyler, *Freedom's Ferment,* 16; *Goodspeed's History of Franklin, Jefferson, Washington, Crawford, and Gasconade Counties, Missouri,* 220; Speeches and Writings, Lilborn A. Kingsbury Manuscripts, collection no. 3724, folder 448, WHMC; McCurdy, *Stump,*

Bar, and Pulpit, 150–52; John E. Rothensteiner, "The Missouri Priest One Hundred Years Ago," 565; Babcock, *Forty Years,* 85–86; Tyler, *Freedom's Ferment,* 45.

50. Adolph Schroeder, *Bethel German Colony, 1844–1879: Religious Beliefs and Practices,* 4–14. Patrick J. Harris, "William Keil and the Aurora Colony: A Communal Society Crosses the Oregon Trail," 425–29; Baptist Minutes and Pamphlets, 1820–1850, St. Louis Mercantile Bank and Library, St. Louis, Missouri; Miscellaneous Notes, John Mason Peck Collection, St. Louis Mercantile Bank and Library; Hill, *The South and the North in American Religion,* 22–28.

51. William W. Sweet, *Religion in the Development of American Culture 1765–1840,* 57, 137–46; T. Scott Miyakawa, *Protestants and Pioneers: Individualism and Conformity on the American Frontier,* 3–9, 174–79; Donald G. Mathews, *Religion in the Old South,* xv–xvi, 87–90; Nathan O. Hatch, *The Democratization of American Christianity,* 3–9.

52. Charles R. Wilson, *Baptized in Blood: The Religion of the Lost Cause, 1865–1920,* 1–5; Martin E. Marty, *Righteous Empire: The Protestant Experience in America,* 62–69; Harrison A. Trexler, *Slavery in Missouri: 1804–1856,* 106, 126–27; Foley, *Genesis,* 277–78; Frank C. Tucker, *The Methodist Church in Missouri 1798–1939: A Brief History,* 97–101, 102–4; James K. Folsom, *Timothy Flint,* 51; Flint, *Recollections,* 139. For Catholic racism see Callan, *Philippine Duchesne,* 277–84, 289–92.

53. O'Hanlon, *Life and Scenery,* 76; Flint, "The Bar, the Pulpit, and the Press," 639–42; *Jeffersonian Republican,* July 27, 1833.

54. Milburn, *The Rifle,* xii, 37–38, 55.

55. John Mason Peck, *Father Clark on the Pioneer Preacher,* 256–73; Peck, *A Guide for Emigrants,* 70–76, 212–15; North Todd Gentry, "David Todd," 527–31. The whipping bill will be examined in greater detail in the next chapter.

56. Burnett, *Old Pioneer,* 18–19, 41, 81–82, 92–94; *Missouri Gazette,* August 17, 1816.

6. Shame and Vengeance on the Missouri Frontier

1. William Carr Lane to Mary Lane, August 31, 1824, William Carr Lane Collection, MHS.

2. John F. Philips, "Reminiscences of Some Deceased Lawyers of Central Missouri," address delivered to the Missouri State Bar Association, St. Louis, September 24, 1914. Located in the State Historical Society of Missouri, Columbia; John W. Henry, "Personal Recollections," in A. J. D. Stewart, ed., *The History of the Bench and Bar of Missouri,* 390.

3. Wyatt-Brown, *Southern Honor,* 48.

4. Hugh P. Williamson, "Abiel Leonard, Lawyer and Judge," 268.

5. *History of Howard and Chariton Counties, Missouri,* 246.

6. Bradbury, *Travels,* 51; Walter A. Schroeder, "Spread of Settlement in Howard County, Missouri: 1810–1859," 10–14; Robert C. Dyer, *Boonville: An Illustrated History,* chap. 2; Thomas Smith to David Todd, May 30, 1820, Thomas A. Smith Papers, collection 1029, folder 19, WHMC; Gray Bynum to David Todd, June 1, 1820, ibid.

7. *Missouri Intelligencer,* December 4, 1824.

8. English, *The Pioneer Lawyer,* 108.

9. Nathaniel Leonard to Abiel Leonard, January 14, 1820, Abiel Leonard Papers, collection 1013, folder 44, WHMC; English, *The Pioneer Lawyer,* 108.

10. Daniel M. Grissom, "Personal Recollections of Distinguished Missourians—Abiel Leonard," 400–402; L. Langeant to Abiel Leonard, April 24, 1826, Leonard Papers, folder 61.

11. Williamson, "Abiel Leonard," 267.

12. Moss, "Dueling in Missouri History," 17; *Missouri Intelligencer,* November 6, 1824; W. Christry to Thomas Smith, March 12, 1824, Thomas A. Smith Papers, folder 24; W. Christry to John Miller, March 12, 1824, ibid., folder 24.

13. Bourdieu, "The Sentiment of Honour in Kabyle Society," 197–98.

14. Pitt-Rivers, "Honour and Social Status," 26; Boorstin, *Hidden History,* 159–62. A cowhiding in Richmond, Kentucky, in 1823 had also resulted in the death of the assailant in a duel. See *Missouri Intelligencer,* January 21, 1823.

15. Quoted in Columbia *Missouri Statesman* (weekly), May 21, 1875; *Missouri Gazette,* July 15, 1815.

16. Alfred Arrington, *Illustrated Lives and Adventures of the Desperadoes of the New World,* 82–83.

17. Brackenridge, *Recollections,* 222–23; Smith, "History of Dueling," 1; Violette, *A History of Missouri,* 83; Switzler, *Switzler's Illustrated History,* 197; Ayers, *Vengeance and Justice,* 13–14; *Bulletin of the Missouri Historical Society* 2, no. 1 (January 1900): 76; Foley, *Genesis,* 241. For a description of mid-Missouri people during this period, see Monette, *History of the Discovery,* 547–58; Samuel Brown, *The Western Gazetteer,* 194. For a descriptive analysis of frontier institutions and northern adaptations, see James F. Keefe and Lynn Morrow, eds., *A Connecticut Yankee in the Frontier Ozarks: The Writings of Theodore Pease Russell,* chap. 8.

18. Floyd Shoemaker, ed., *Missouri—Day by Day,* vol. 2, 145; Stevens, *Missouri,* 94; Walter B. Stevens, *Centennial History of Missouri: (The Center State),* vol. 1, 289; *History of Howard and Cooper Counties Missouri,* 247–48.

19. For details and correspondence on the duel see *History of Howard and Cooper Counties Missouri,* 247–49.

20. *Missouri Farm and Home* (Columbia), March 30, 1955; Frederic A. Culmer, "The Leonard-Berry Duel of 1824," 358–59; Moss, "Dueling in Missouri History," 17–18; State Historical Society, *This Week in Missouri History,* August 31–September 6, 1930; *Fulton Telegraph,* February 17, 1882; *History of Howard and Cooper Counties, Missouri,* 248–49. For a complete detail of the terms of the meeting see letter, Edward Dobyns to Colonel Switzler, 1882, Francis A. Sampson Papers, collection no. 3813, folder 396, WHMC.

21. Columbia *Missouri Statesman* (weekly), May 21, 1875; *Missouri Intelligencer,* September 18, 1824.

22. *Missouri Intelligencer,* November 6, 1824; Indictment, Howard County Circuit Court Records, vols. 3–4, index no. C2821 in MSA. Ironically, the prosecutor, John Ryland, later served with Leonard on the Missouri Supreme Court. State of Missouri, *Laws of the State of Missouri up to the Year 1824,* chap. 410, 1822, vol. 1, 978–80.

Boggs, Leonard's second, "took legal immunity and was discharged." See "Missouriana," *Missouri Historical Review* 35, no. 3 (April 1941): 442–43. Receipt, Abiel Leonard from Sheriff Benjamin Ray, June 28, 1825, Leonard Papers, folder 57; Bay, *Reminiscences*, 362–63.

23. State of Missouri, *Acts of the Second General Assembly of the State of Missouri, 1822*, chap. 21, "An Act More Effectually to Prevent Duelling," 53–56; Anderson, "The Evolution of a Frontier Society," 310.

24. State of Missouri, *Acts of the Second General Assembly*, 53–56; Smith, "History of Dueling," 3–4.

25. *Missouri Intelligencer*, February 1, 1825 (reprinted from the *Missouri Advocate*); *Missouri Intelligencer*, December 3, 1822.

26. State of Missouri, *Journal of the House of the General Assembly of the State of Missouri at the Session Begun and Held at the Town of St. Charles on the 2nd Monday of November in the Year One Thousand Eight Hundred and Twenty Four*, 144; State of Missouri, *Journal of the Senate of the General Assembly of the State of Missouri at the Session Begun and Held at the Town of St. Charles on the 2nd Monday of November in the Year One Thousand Eight Hundred and Twenty Four*, 122; *Missouri Intelligencer*, February 1, 1825.

27. For details on the original bill and the debate, see *Missouri Intelligencer*, December 3, 1822.

28. Ibid., January 25, 1825, December 25, 1824.

29. For Barton's view of the Conway duel see ibid., August 21, 1824.

30. Ibid., March 25, 1823; February 8, 1825; *Missouri Gazette*, August 17, 1816.

31. On evangelicalism see "Speeches and Writings," Lilburn A. Kingsbury Manuscript, collection no. 3724, folder 448, WHMC.

32. *Missouri Intelligencer*, February 8, 1825.

33. Many valuable insights into honor were gained from Bruce, Jr., *Violence and Culture*, 14–15; Wyatt-Brown, *Honor and Violence*, 27, 39; Ayers, *Vengeance and Justice*, 13–16; Indictments, *State of Missouri v. Green M. Davis, Robert Green, Samuel McFarland, John Payne, and Nathaniel Watkins*, Fourth Judicial Circuit, Cape Girardeau County, February 21, 1824. These records are also available at the Missouri State Archives. Thomas Shackelford, "Reminiscences of the Bench and Bar in Central Missouri," 394.

34. Williamson, "Abiel Leonard," 270–71. In many ways Leonard built upon a reputation of good character. See John Thorton to Doctor Joseph Ormerod, November 8, 1822, Joseph Ormerod Collection, MHS; David Barton to Abiel Leonard, January 1825, Leonard Papers, folder 55; Rufus Easton to Abiel Leonard, August 6, 1825, ibid., folder 58; English, *The Pioneer Lawyer*, 109–12.

35. Dr. L. Cooper to Abiel Leonard, October 1826, Leonard Papers, folder 57.

36. English, *The Pioneer Lawyer*, 111. For details on Oakwood see James M. Denny, "Oakwood," June 10, 1982, National Register of Historic Places—Inventory Nomination Form, Division of Parks, Recreation, and Historic Preservation, Missouri Department of Natural Resources, Jefferson City; *Missouri Republican*, April 6, 1863.

37. Walter B. Stevens, "The Missouri Tavern," 246–48.

38. Bay, *Reminiscences*, 367–69; Abiel Leonard to Dr. Scott, September 15, 1840,

Leonard Papers, folder 156; Henry, "Personal Recollections," 385; Shackelford, "Early Recollections of Missouri," 7; *Missouri Farm and Home* (Columbia), March 30, 1955.

39. These papers and the story of Bloody Bill are located in the State Historical Society, but the exact dates of publication were not available.

40. Bay, *Reminiscences,* 363.

41. Abiel Leonard to Benjamin Bowles, July 9, 1825, Leonard Papers, folder 58; Bay, *Reminiscences,* 368.

7. Dueling in Jacksonian Missouri

1. Rudolph E. Forderhase, "Jacksonianism in Missouri, from Predilection to Party 1820–1836," 3, 483–84.

2. Windell, "Background of Reform," 182.

3. Indictment, *State of Missouri v. William Webster,* November term, 1827, no. 28, box 9133, Madison County Circuit Court Records, Madison County, Fredericktown, Missouri. These records are also located in MSA.

4. Anderson, "The Evolution of a Frontier Society," 310; *Missouri Intelligencer,* September 12, 1828.

5. *Jeffersonian Republican,* June 25, 1831; Gentry, *The Bench and Bar of Boone County Missouri,* 117; *New York Daily Times,* August 4, 1857; *St. Louis Republican,* July 30, 1857.

6. *Missouri Intelligencer,* November 30, 1827. It should also be noted that Colonel John C. Moore, second to General John S. Marmaduke in his duel with General L. M. Walker, had left Missouri and become mayor of Denver. "I introduced the duello" and "systematized the shooting game," he wrote. He always believed that dueling curtailed violence and saved the lives of many innocent bystanders. See the *Kansas City Star,* February 21, 1915.

7. Mrs. William Clark, "The Intimate View," 4, no. 3 (April 1948): 163.

8. *St. Louis Beacon,* January 27, 1830.

9. Indictment, *State of Missouri v. James Boles,* October term, 1858, *Howell County Circuit Court,* MSA.

10. *Sedalia Central Missouri News,* December 27, 1989.

11. *The History of Cass and Bates Counties,* 803; *Nevada Post,* December 3, 1915.

12. *St. Louis Republican,* September 3, 1823; Notes and Vignettes, V. E. Phillips Papers, collection no. 25, folder 21, WHMC.

13. John C. Crighton, *A History of Columbia and Boone County,* 104, 135; Notes and Vignettes, V. E. Phillips Papers, collection no. 25, folder 21; Indictment, *State of Missouri v. Ira Nash,* circa August 1831, vol. A, 426, 428–29, 443. See also vol. B, 82, Boone County Circuit Court Records, MSA; *Missouri Farm and Home,* March 30, 1955; William F. Switzler, *History of Boone County, Missouri,* 134, 147, 639. For the note sent to Tuttle and a short biographical sketch of Nash see Notes, Walter Williams, in Sara Lockwood Williams Scrapbook, collection no. 2533, folder 494, WHMC.

14. Moss, "Dueling in Missouri History," 7. Linn is quoted in *Missouri Farm and Home,* March 30, 1955. Stevens, *Missouri,* vol. 1, 90–91.

15. *New York Daily Times,* July 21, 1856. This was reprinted from Benton's *Thirty Years' View,* Vol. 2, 120–21.

16. Benton's defense was also printed in Stevens, *Missouri,* vol. 1, 89–90.

17. State Historical Society of Missouri, *This Week in Missouri History,* August 24–30, 1930. Also see Biddle's obituary in the *St. Louis Beacon,* September 8, 1831.

18. *Missouri Intelligencer and Boon's Lick Advertiser,* September 3, 1831; *Sedalia Capital,* February 9, 1916.

19. *Sedalia Capital,* February 9, 1916; Stevens, *Missouri,* vol. 1, 91; *Kansas City Star,* January 28, 1915.

20. Stevens, *Missouri,* vol. 1, 92.

21. *St. Louis Beacon,* September 17, 1831; State Historical Society of Missouri, *This Week in Missouri History,* August 24–30, 1930; Stevens, *Missouri,* vol. 1, 93; Scharf, *History of Saint Louis City and County,* vol. 2, 1854.

22. Darby, *Personal Recollections,* 197–98.

23. *St. Louis Beacon,* September 8, 1831; Letter, A. L. Langham to Thomas A. Smith, September 1, 1831, Thomas A. Smith Papers, collection no. 1029, folder 34, WHMC; "Missouriana," *Missouri Historical Review* 26, no. 4 (July 1932): 389–91; George R. Brooks, "Duels in St. Louis."

24. *Missouri Intelligencer,* September 3, 1831, June 21, November, 1, 1834; Warrant, *State of Missouri v. Patrick W. Davis,* January 24, 1833, Cape Girardeau Circuit Court Records, Cape Girardeau, Missouri; Indictment, *Gordon v. the State of Missouri,* November 7, 1835, Franklin County Circuit Court, MSA; Windell, "Background of Reform," 182; Convictions, *State of Missouri v. Joseph Ferguson,* circa August 1833, St. Louis Circuit Court, MSA. Ferguson had killed Jacob Sigler earlier that year in Polk County. Convictions, *State of Missouri v. George F. Strother,* October 3, 1835, St. Louis Circuit Court, MSA; Letter, Dr. Samuel Merry to Daniel Dunklin, August 6, 1835, Daniel Dunklin Papers, collection no. 97, folder 34, WHMC; Letter, Daniel Dunklin to F. A. Martin, August 11, 1835, ibid.; Letter, F. A. Martin to Daniel Dunklin, August 30, 1835, ibid., folder 35.

25. Indictment, *Rogers v. State of Missouri,* circa March 1841, vol. A, 156, 193–95, 223, Polk County Circuit Court Records, MSA; Indictment, *Young v. State of Missouri,* ibid.; "Historical Notes and Comments," *Missouri Historical Review* 31, no. 4 (July 1937): 451; Gill, *St. Louis Duels,* 9–10; Stevens, *Missouri,* vol. 1, 93; *St. Louis Republic,* November 23, 1837; St. Louis *Missouri Argus,* November 11, 1837; Ste. Genevieve Archives, 1756–1930, collection no. 3636, folder 1269, WHMC.

26. Smith, "History of Dueling," 5.

27. Van Ravenswaay, *The Arts and Architecture,* 34. See also William G. Bek, "The Followers of Duden," 684. Note, George W. Jones, n.d., Bryan O'Bear Collection, collection no. 1387, folder 5, WHMC; Letter, Abiel Leonard to Dr. Scott, September 15, 1840, Abiel Leonard Papers, collection no. 1013, folder 156, WHMC; Stevens, *Missouri,* vol. 1, 94. For the full correspondence in this affair of honor see *History of Howard and Chariton Counties,* 316–19.

28. For an excellent interpretation of these events see Thomas Verdot, "St. Louis and the Political Duelists of 1840."

29. *Missouri Argus,* May 30, June 1, 22, July 17–20, 1840; Daniel M. Grissom,

"Personal Recollections of Distinguished Missourians—Thomas H. Benton," 135; *Missouri Republican,* July 13, 18, 1840; Verdot, "St. Louis and the Political Duelists," 5–7; Thomas S. Nelson, *A Full and Accurate Record of the Trial of William P. Darnes . . .* , 4; Bay, *Reminiscences,* 193–94.

30. *Boon's Lick Times,* July 25, 1840. The names of all penitentiary inmates and offenses in the mid-1840s showed that no one had been convicted under the anti-dueling laws. See State of Missouri, *Senate Journal 1844,* 163.

31. *Missouri Statesman,* November 29, 1878.

32. *Jefferson City Inquirer,* April 28, 1849.

33. *Missouri Republican,* September 5, 1849.

34. *St. Joseph Gazette,* May 16, 18, June 6, 13, 1845; Moss, "Dueling in Missouri History," 20; Smith, "History of Dueling," 5; Columbia *Missouri Herald,* December 23, 1904; Thomas J. McCormack, ed., *Memoirs of Gustave Koerner 1809–1896,* vol. 1, 136.

35. *Jefferson City Inquirer,* September 18, 1845.

36. *Kansas City Star,* April 22, 1990; R. I. Holcombe, *History of Marion County Missouri 1884,* 276–80. For comments dealing with other aspects of Glover's life see the *Jefferson City State Times,* December 8, 1865.

37. For the tone of this new reform impetus see its first volume, *The Western Miscellany,* vol. 1, July 1848–1849, 279–80. *Hannibal Gazette,* September 2, 1847; Holcombe, *History of Marion County,* 282; *Jefferson City Inquirer,* June 17, 1846; *Kansas City Star,* April 22, 1990.

38. Columbia *Missouri Statesman,* January 8, 1847. It was also reported in the *Boonville Observer* earlier that month.

39. Trial and Proceedings, *State of Missouri v. Sullivan Phillips, Presley Phillips, and Dr. John L. Ross,* Madison County Circuit Court Records, Spring term, 1856, Madison County, Fredericktown, Missouri. These records are on loan to the Missouri State Archives for microfilming. Appeal, *State of Missouri, St. Louis District v. Presley Phillips and Dr. John L. Ross,* October term, 1859, State Supreme Court Records, box 586, folder 13, MSA.

40. Leonard B. Wurthman, Jr., "Frank Blair: Lincoln's Congressional Spokesman," 266–67. Stevens, *Missouri,* vol. 1, 96.

41. Scharf, *History of St. Louis City and County,* vol. 2, 1855; Stevens, *Missouri,* vol. 1, 94–95; William E. Parrish, *Frank Blair: Lincoln's Conservative,* 41; "From the Director's Note Book," *Bulletin of the Missouri Historical Society* 5, no. 2 (January 1949): 135. Primm, *Lion of the Valley,* 181.

8. The Duel as a Changing Metaphor

1. *New York Daily Times,* June 7, 1856.

2. Helen K. Harr, "Duelling," 1; Graham and Gurr, "Conclusion," in Graham and Gurr, eds., *The History of Violence,* 790–91; Davis, *Homicide in American Fiction,* 272–80; *Missouri Gazette,* April 12, 1817.

3. Harr, "Duelling," 1; *New York Daily Times,* July 21, 1856, reprinted from Benton's *Thirty Years' View.* Henry, "Personal Recollections," 389–90; *Kansas City Star,*

February 21, 1915; Williams, *Dueling in the Old South,* 89–90. Modern historians have also been charmed by the duel. See Kiernan, *The Duel in European History,* 206; Stevens, *Pistols,* 276–77.

4. Reavis, *The Life and Military Service of Gen. William Selby Harney,* 38.

5. Burnett, *Old Pioneer,* 89–91. For abusive language that would earlier have provoked a challenge see Public Letter, Mason S. Peters to Moses Shoemaker, circa 1878, David Rice Atchison Papers, collection no. 71, folder 1, WHMC.

6. Eaton, "Mob Violence," 352.

7. Joe B. Frantz, "The Frontier Tradition: An Invitation to Violence," 128–29.

8. Stevens, *Pistols,* 109; Brown, *Strain of Violence,* 11–12; Mary Hartman and Elmo Ingenthron, *Bald Knobbers: Vigilantes on the Ozark Frontier,* 5; Lynn Morrow, "Where Did All the Money Go? War and the Economics of Vigilantism in Southern Missouri," 3. For an excellent portrayal of these early days see J. B. Jones, *Life and Adventures of a Country Merchant,* chaps. 1–6.

9. Stevens, *Centennial History of Missouri,* vol. 2, 235–40.

10. Hickory County was actually organized after the Slicker War from former lands in Benton and Polk Counties. See Clarke Thomas and Jack Glendenning, *The Slicker War,* 15; Richard Maxwell Brown, "Historical Patterns of Violence in America," in Graham and Gurr, eds., *The History of Violence,* 45–76.

11. McCurdy, *Stump, Bar, and Pulpit,* 7; Everett Dick, *The Dixie Frontier,* 336.

12. McWhiney, *Cracker Culture,* 159–66; McCurdy, *Stump, Bar, and Pulpit,* 128–30; Chambers, "Young Man from Tennessee," 205. Also see Chambers, *Old Bullion Benton,* 64; Dick, *The Dixie Frontier,* 140; Shoemaker, *Missouri and Missourians,* vol. 1, 267; *Missouri Intelligencer,* July 31, 1824.

13. Gilmore, *Ozark Baptizings, Hangings, and Other Diversions,* 154–58.

14. Ibid., 158–60.

15. *History of Caldwell and Livingston Counties, Missouri,* 728–29; Buckingham, *The Eastern and Western States of America,* vol. 2, 295–96; Dick, *The Dixie Frontier,* 140, 269–70; Switzler, *History of Boone County, Missouri,* 344–45; Windell, "Background of Reform," 107; John G. Westover, "The Evolution of the Missouri Militia 1804–1919," 58.

16. Burnett, *Old Pioneer,* 18–19.

17. Ibid., 19.

18. Westover, "The Evolution of the Missouri Militia," 60.

19. Notes and Vignettes, V. E. Phillips Papers, collection no. 25, folder 21, WHMC.

20. Buckingham, *The Eastern and Western States of America,* vol. 2, 117; *Missouri Gazette,* July 27, 1816.

21. Buckingham, *The Eastern and Western States of America,* vol. 2, 509.

22. Brackenridge, *Views of Louisiana,* 144; Jerena East Giffen, "'Add a Pinch and a Lump' Missouri Women in the 1820," 483–85; Buckingham, *The Eastern and Western States of America,* vol. 3, 28.

23. William R. Taylor, *Cavalier and Yankee: The Old South and American National Character,* 173.

24. *Missouri Gazette,* September 6, 1817. For an opposing view see "The Destiny of Women," *Western Monthly Magazine* 2 (January 1834): 137.

25. For the full flavor of this aspect of Anglo-Saxon superiority, see the Brown-Reynolds Duels Collection, MHS.

26. Historian Richard Slotkin believed this to be typically Jeffersonian. Although some commoners might achieve status, the frontier aristocrat believed that he would breed true. Theoretical equality in fact produced traditional inequalities. See Richard Slotkin, *The Fatal Environment: The Myth of the Frontier in the Age of Industrialization, 1800–1890,* 103.

27. Charles P. Johnson, "Personal Recollections," Address to the State Historical Society and Press Association of Missouri, January 22, 1903, *Missouri Historical Society Collection* 2, no. 2 (April 1903): pp. 1–6; *Missouri Intelligencer,* April 12, 26, May 7, 1825; *Missouri Gazette,* March 1, 1817; Notes, Byars Papers, Duels Files, MHS, 136.

28. Bruce, Jr., *Violence and Culture,* 12; Stowe, *Intimacy and Power,* 11; Flint, *Recollections,* 180; *Missouri Intelligencer,* June 25, 1825.

29. This sense of history and life produced much of the pessimism and fatalism that characterized antebellum life in the South. For the western perspective see "Progress of Civilization," *Western Monthly Magazine* 3 (October 1835): 351–52.

30. Notes, Byars Papers, Duels File, MHS, 148.

31. Stowe, *Intimacy and Power,* 21.

32. Brackenridge, *Views of Louisiana,* 144.

33. Ibid., 135; Westover, "The Evolution of the Missouri Militia," 45; Dick, *The Dixie Frontier,* 333; J. G. Peristiany, "Introduction," in Peristiany, ed., *Honour and Shame,* 16.

34. Challenge, Stephen Austin to Joshua Pilcher, May 14, 1817, Moses Austin Papers, vol. 1, pt. 2, 1812–1820; Letter, Stephen Austin to Joshua Pilcher, June 1, 1817, ibid.; Apology, Pilcher to Austin, June 7, 1817, ibid.

35. Darby, *Personal Recollections,* 402. See also James W. Goodrich and Lynn Wolf Gentzler, eds., "'I Well Remember': David Holmes Conrad's Recollections of St. Louis, 1819–1823," 162–65; *Missouri Republican,* September 24, 1822.

36. Charles S. Sydnor, "The Southerner and the Laws," 12; Notes, Byars Papers, 108; Terrell, "Recollections of General Sam Houston," 128; Miscellaneous File, Tennessee State Library and Archives, Nashville, Tennessee; Historical Sketches, Frank Laren Collection, ibid.

37. "Notes on John Smith T," Harry R. Burke Papers, MHS, 1; *Kansas City Journal,* August 7, 1896; Letter, Dr. L. Cooper to Abiel Leonard, October 1826, Abiel Leonard Papers, collection no. 1013, folder 57, WHMC; Randolph B. Campbell, *Sam Houston and the American Southwest,* 14–15; Terrell, "Recollections of General Sam Houston," 129.

9. Sectionalism and Sacrifice: The Duel as a New Rationale for Old Violence

1. Stevens, *Pistols,* 81–82.

2. Cochran, *Noted American Duels,* 141.

3. Letter, Elizabeth Linn to David Atchison, February 19, 1844, David Rice

Atchison Papers, collection no. 71, folder 1, WHMC; Letter, George G. Vest to David Atchinson, December 30, 1844, ibid.

4. Seitz, *Famous American Duels,* 251–82.

5. Taylor, *Cavalier and Yankee,* 19, 21–22, 147.

6. *New York Daily Times,* August 9, 1853, June 7, 1856. Cunliffe, introduction to *Soldiers and Civilians.*

7. Frank E. Vandiver, "The Southerner as Extremist," 43–46; Wyatt-Brown, *Honor and Violence,* 27; Ayers, *Vengeance and Justice,* 13–16; Seitz, *Famous American Duels,* 277.

8. William J. Cooper, *The South and the Politics of Slavery 1828–1856,* 69–75; Patterson, *Slavery and Social Death,* 77–101; Greenberg, *Masters and Statesmen,* 40; Gay, *The Cultivation of Hatred,* 12–33.

9. Franklin, *The Militant South,* 58–62; Sheldon Hackney, "Southern Violence," and Richard Maxwell Brown, "Historical Patterns of Violence in America," both in Graham and Gurr, eds., *The History of Violence in America,* 505–6, 62–64. Wyatt-Brown, *Honor and Violence,* 145–46; Bruce, Jr., *Violence and Culture,* 6; Stowe, *Intimacy and Power,* chap. 1.

10. Manuscript, Byars, 136–42, 150–54; Stowe, *Intimacy and Power,* 17–18.

11. Allen Johnson, ed., *Dictionary of American Biography,* vol. 2, 105; *The National Cyclopedia of American Biography,* vol. 20, 318; Norma L. Peterson, *Freedom and Franchise: The Political Career of B. Gratz Brown,* 29–30; Conard, ed., *Encyclopedia of the History of Missouri,* vol. 5, 339–40; Stevens, *The Brown-Reynolds Duel,* 9–15.

12. Note, Bryan O'Bear Collection, collection no. 1387, folder 4, WHMC; Note, John B. Clark, n.d., ibid., folder 12; Note, Judge Nathaniel W. Watkins, n.d., ibid., folder 6; State Historical Society of Missouri, *This Week in Missouri History, October 8–14, 1939.*

13. Peterson, *Freedom and Franchise,* 29–30; George H. Kellner, "The German Element on the Urban Frontier: St. Louis, 1830–1860," 168–70, 208, 227–28, 214; Hans L. Trefousse, *Carl Schurz: A Biography;* McCandless, *A History of Missouri,* 247–53; Norma L. Peterson, "B. Gratz Brown, The Rise of a Radical, 1850–1863," 10–12; Stevens, *The Brown-Reynolds Duel,* 39.

14. *Missouri Democrat,* April 21, 24, 25, 1854; Stevens, *Missouri,* vol. 1, 229.

15. Stevens, *The Brown-Reynolds Duel,* 22–23.

16. Ibid., 17–19, 41–43, 33; McCandless, *A History of Missouri,* 268.

17. Entry, February 2, 1855, Diary of James Edgar McHenry, MSA; Entry, February 3, 1855, ibid; Peterson, *Freedom and Franchise,* 39–40; Indictment, *State of Missouri v. B. Gratz Brown,* Cole County Circuit Court, February 1855 term, B. Gratz Brown Papers, accession no. 56, folder 1, WHMC.

18. Jay Monaghan, *Civil War on the Western Border 1854–1865,* 32–34.

19. Swindler, "The Southern Press in Missouri," 395; Jonas Viles, *The University of Missouri: A Centennial History,* 76–78. *Eleventh Annual Catalogue of the Officers and Students of the Missouri University, 1853* (Columbia: E. C. Davis, 1853), p. 7, Vertical File, State Historical Society of Missouri.

20. Stevens, *The Brown-Reynolds Duel,* 9; Stevens, *Missouri,* 232, 229, 230; McCandless, *A History of Missouri,* 265–70.

21. State Historical Society of Missouri, *This Week in Missouri History,* December 9–15, 1928; A. A. Dunson, "Notes on the Missouri Germans on Slavery," 355–60; Douglas D. Hale, Jr., "Friedrich Adolph Wislizenus: From Student Rebel to Southwestern Explorer," 260–73; Stevens, *The Brown-Reynolds Duel,* 44–46, 81; Stevens, *Missouri,* 230–31; Peterson, *Freedom and Franchise,* 41–43.

22. Stevens, *Missouri,* 231. See also Note, Thomas Reynolds to B. Gratz Brown, March 25, 1855, in Stevens, *The Brown-Reynolds Duel,* 56–60.

23. Stevens, *The Brown-Reynolds Duel,* 47; 62, Manuscript, Byars, 139–50.

24. Sabine, *Notes on Duels and Duelling,* 16; Stevens, *The Brown-Reynolds Duel,* 61–65.

25. Stevens, *The Brown-Reynolds Duel,* 59–61.

26. Writ, State of Missouri to Cole County Sheriff, June 23, 1855, Brown Papers; *Jefferson City Tribune,* February 22, 1888; Indictment, *State of Missouri v. B. Gratz Brown,* and Receipt for $500, State of Missouri to County of St. Louis, August 7, 1855, Brown Papers.

27. Stevens, *The Brown-Reynolds Duel,* 80. Stevens, *Missouri,* 231–32.

28. The *Pilot* was the afternoon edition of the *Missouri Republican. Pilot,* July 29, 1856. Challenge, B. Gratz Brown to Thomas C. Reynolds, August 18, 1856, Brown-Reynolds Duel Collection, MHS. The peremptory challenge was probably destroyed by Brown after drafting the second note. Letter, Isaac H. Sturgeon to Louise Dalton, May 27, 1906, Isaac Sturgeon Papers, MHS. Sturgeon maintained that all of the arrangements were made at his home.

29. Stevens, *Missouri,* 232.

30. Ibid., 233; Zoe B. Rutledge, *Our Jefferson County Heritage,* 134.

31. Stevens, *Missouri,* 235.

32. The Columbia *Missourian Magazine,* October 4, 1987; Note, Colonel David P. Mitchell to Ferdinand Kennett, August 26, 1856, Brown-Reynolds Duel Collection, MHS; Letter, Ferdinand Kennett to Thomas Reynolds, August 31, 1856, Thomas Reynolds Papers, MHS. For numerous newspaper accounts printed then and later concerning the duel see Scrapbook, Mrs. John Green, vol. 1, pp. 21A–E, MHS.

33. The *Morning Herald,* August 27, 1856. For other newspaper accounts see the Brown-Reynolds Duel Collection.

34. Manuscript, Byars, 126.

35. *St. Louis Leader,* August 27, 1856.

36. Manuscript, Byars, 153.

37. McCandless, *A History of Missouri,* 282.

38. Letter, John N. Edwards to Thomas C. Reynolds, December 9, 1871, Brown-Reynolds Duel Collection, MHS. Reynolds's life is detailed in many state histories, but Edwards grasped the significance of the duel early on.

39. *New York Times,* July 9, 1858.

40. McCormack, ed., *Memoirs of Gustave Koerner,* vol. 1, 27–29, 85, 107, 128, 133, 136, 163–65; Stevens, *Pistols,* 245.

41. Letter, John N. Edwards to Thomas C. Reynolds, December 9, 1871, Brown-Reynolds Duel Collection.

42. Carl Schurz, *The Reminiscences of Carl Schurz,* vol. 1, 1829–1852, 95–96 and vol. 2, 1852–1863, 167; James P. Terzian, *Defender of Human Rights: Carl Schurz,*

9–16; Clara M. Lovett, *Carl Schurz: 1829–1906*, 3; Claude M. Fuess, *Carl Schurz: Reformer (1829–1906)*, 17–30; Letter, Carl Schurz to His Parents and Sisters, July 21, 1849, in Joseph Schafer, ed., *Intimate Papers of Carl Schurz 1841–1869*, vol. 30, 60–61; Letter, Carl Schurz to Henry Meyer, November 20, 1856, ibid., 174; Carl Schurz, *Speeches of Carl Schurz*, 11. There appears to be no evidence, however, that Schurz knew of or understood the ramifications of the Brown-Reynolds duel.

43. Sydnor, "The Southerner and the Laws," 22; David H. Donald, *Charles Sumner and the Coming of the Civil War*, 290–94.

44. *New York Daily Times*, June 7, 1856; James Sterling, "Letters from the Slave States," in Bertram Wyatt-Brown, ed., *The American People in the Antebellum South*, 110; McWhiney, *Cracker Culture*, 155. Schurz wrote at length on Sumner and the southern slave mentality. See Arthur Hogue, ed., *Charles Sumner: An Essay by Carl Schurz*, 61–65.

45. Letter, Carl Schurz to J. R. Doolittle, April 12, 1860, in Frederic Bancroft, ed., *Speeches, Correspondence, and Political Papers of Carl Schurz*, vol. 1, 114.

46. Letter, Carl Schurz to J. F. Potter, April 7, 1860, in Bancroft, ed., *Speeches*, 115; Joseph Schafer, *Carl Schurz: Militant Liberal*, 122; McWhiney, *Cracker Culture*, 155; Schurz, *Reminiscences*, vol. 2, 168. Chester V. Easum, *The Americanization of Carl Schurz*, 315.

47. Easum, *The Americanization of Carl Schurz*, 169.

10. Myths and Legends of Dueling

1. Kathryn C. Esselman, "From Camelot to Monument Valley," 11; Kent L. Steckmesser, *The Western Hero in History and Legend*, 139.

2. B. A. Botkin, *A Treasury of American Folklore*, 1.

3. Richard Slotkin, *Gunfighter Nation: The Myth of the Frontier in Twentieth-Century America*, 5–7; Richard Maxwell Brown, "Historiography of Violence in the American West," 235.

4. Tristram P. Coffin and Henning Cohen, *The Parade of Heroes: Legendary Figures in American Lore*, xix–xxvi; Collins and Collins, *Hero Stories from Missouri History*, 1–25; Joseph G. Rosa, *They Called Him Wild Bill: The Life and Adventures of James Butler Hickok*, 338; Philip A. Rollins, *The Cowboy*, 347–49; David Brion Davis, "Ten-Gallon Hero," 112–16.

5. Joseph G. Rosa, *The Gunfighter: Man or Myth?* 209, 13; Michael T. Marsden, "Savior in the Saddle: The Sagebrush Testament," 94; Peter Homans, "Puritanism Revisited: An Analysis of the Contemporary Screen-Image Western," 87.

6. For his views on violence, see Flint, *Recollections*, 175–83; Rozier, *Rozier's History*, 312–13. Schoolcraft, *Journal of a Tour*, 44; Brackenridge, *Recollections*, 266.

7. Rosa, *Gunfighter*, 29; *Missouri Intelligencer*, February 8, 1825; Everett Dick, *Vanguards of the Frontier: A Social History of the Northern Plains and Rocky Mountains from the Fur Traders to the Sod Busters*, 514.

8. Reavis, *The Life and Military Service of Gen. William Selby Harney*, 37–38.

9. Letter, General James Wilkinson to Secretary of State James Madison, July 28, 1805, in Carter, ed., *The Territorial Papers*, vol. 13, 173–74.

10. Slotkin, *The Fatal Environment*, 15–22.

11. Historian Louise Davis quoted an earlier unnamed historian who made the analogy to Boone. See her article in the *Tennessean* (Nashville), March 20, 1983.

12. *Goodspeed's History of Southeast Missouri*, 313.

13. John Mack Faragher, *Daniel Boone: The Life and Legend of an American Pioneer*, 6; Dale Van Every, *A Company of Heroes: The American Frontier 1775–1783*, 17–46; Slotkin, *The Fatal Environment*, 16–19; Steckmesser, *The Western Hero in History and Legend*, 241.

14. Steckmesser, *The Western Hero in History and Legend*, vii–viii; Slotkin, *Gunfighter*, 5–8; Richard Slotkin, *Regeneration through Violence: The Mythology of the American Frontier, 1600–1860*, 7–13.

15. Henry Steele Commager, "The Search for a Usable Past," 90–94.

16. State Historical Society of Missouri, *This Week in Missouri History*, April 30–May 6, 1933.

17. *Tennessean* (Nashville), March 20, 1983; Ray Allen Billington, *Westward Expansion: A History of the American Frontier*, 410; William B. Napton, *Past and Present of Saline County Missouri*, 351.

18. Letter, Moses Austin to Rufus Easton, August 14, 1805, Rufus Easton Papers, MHS.

19. William F. Keller, *The Nation's Advocate: Henry Marie Brackenridge and Young America*, ix.

20. Dale Van Every, *Forth to the Wilderness: The First American Frontier 1754–1774*, 101.

21. Rozier, *Rozier's History*, 313–17; Rozier, "Address of Firmin A. Rozier."

22. Brackenridge, *Recollections*, 217–21; Brackenridge, *Views of Louisiana*, 140, 143.

23. Darby, *Personal Recollections*, 85, 97; Dick Steward, "Western Myth: History versus the Legends and Lore of John Smith T," 1–12.

24. Arrington, *Desperadoes of the New World*, 9; Alfred Arrington, *The Lives and Adventures of the Desperadoes of the South-West*, 54–55, 58.

25. Arrington, *Desperadoes of the South-West*, 55–56.

26. *Goodspeed's History of Southeast Missouri*, 313–14; *History of Saline County, Missouri*, 507–9; Napton, *Past and Present of Saline County*, 350.

27. Stevens, *Missouri*, vol. 2, 689–90; Douglas, *History of Southeast Missouri*, vol. 1, 60; State Historical Society of Missouri, *This Week in Missouri History*, April 30–May 6, 1933; Shoemaker, *Missouri and Missourians*, vol. 1, 139–43, 237, 260.

28. Statement, Bryan Obear, n.d., Bryan Obear Collection, folder 4, WHMC.

29. Ibid.

30. Note, Nathaniel W. Watkins, n.d., ibid; Note, John B. Clark, Sr., n.d., ibid., folder 6; Note, Thomas L. Snead, n.d., ibid., folder 5; Note, William T. Hord, n.d., ibid; Note, Andrew F. Casey, n.d., ibid., folder 15.

31. Note, Thomas Fletcher, n.d., ibid., folder 6; Note, Nathaniel W. Watkins, n.d., ibid., folder 4; Note, Thomas Wiley, n.d., ibid., folder 7; Note, Edward Bredell, n.d., ibid., folder 15.

32. Eulogy, William H. Swift, n.d., ibid., folder 16; Note, John S. Brickey, n.d., ibid., folder 17.

33. Note, George Knapp, n.d., ibid., folder 5; Note, Henry C. Brockmeyer, n.d., ibid.; Note, Joseph N. McDowell, n.d., ibid.; Note, George M. Wilson, n.d., ibid., folder 7. Wilson also credited Bryan with seeing to it that Mason Brown, Mike Fink, Thomas Waller, Henry Renshaw, and Curt Forbis, all unsavory characters in early Missouri history, left the state.

34. Hyde and Conard, eds., *Encyclopedia of the History of St. Louis,* 261–62.

35. Slotkin, *Regeneration through Violence,* 12–14, 269; Slotkin, *Gunfighter,* 22–33, 55–61; G. Edward White, *The Eastern Establishment and the Western Experience: The West of Frederic Remington, Theodore Roosevelt, and Owen Wister,* 1–3; John Clay, "Justice on the Range," 168–77; Emerson Hough, *The Story of the Cowboy,* 339. This book was copyrighted in 1897. Botkin, *A Treasury of American Folklore,* 74–78.

36. Rosa, *They Called Him Wild Bill,* 72–81. In 1870 another legend, Wyatt Earp, was elected constable of Lamar, Missouri.

37. Richard O'Connor, *Wild Bill Hickok,* 79; Frank J. Wilstach, *Wild Bill Hickok: The Prince of Pistoleers,* 118; E. F. Perkins and T. M. Horne, *History of Greene County, Missouri,* 498–99; William L. Roper, "When the Clock Struck Twelve: A Famous Ozark Duel," Subject File, Duels, AHC; Botkin, *A Treasury of American Folklore,* 72–93.

38. O'Connor, *Wild Bill Hickok,* 92.

39. Davis, "Ten-Gallon Hero," 116–25; O'Connor, *A Treasury of American Folklore,* 10.

40. White, *The Eastern Establishment and the Western Experience,* 16–20.

41. Ibid., 31–40, 45–56, 50; Slotkin, *Gunfighter,* 33; David Dary, *Cowboy Culture: A Saga of Five Centuries,* 124.

42. Slotkin, *Gunfighter,* 55.

43. Theodore Roosevelt, *The Strenuous Life,* 3–22; Theodore Roosevelt, *The Winning of the West,* vol. 4, 265; Theodore Roosevelt, *The Rough Riders,* 219–23.

44. Esselman, "From Camelot to Monument Valley," 24; Slotkin, *Gunfighter,* 92–95, 37–55.

45. Slotkin, *Gunfighter,* 127–35; Frank R. Prassel, *The Great American Outlaw: A Legacy of Fact and Fiction,* 136, xi–xii; Steckmesser, *The Western Hero in History and Legend,* 61; Margaret Baldwin and Pat O'Brien, *Wanted: Frank and Jesse James: The Real Story,* 13; David Thelen, *Paths of Resistance: Tradition and Democracy in Industrializing Missouri,* 70–77.

46. For the connection between crime and war in the mid to late nineteenth century see Edith Abbot, "The Civil War and the Crime Wave of 1865–70," 212–34; Gard, *Frontier Justice,* 195–205; Betty B. Rosenbaum, "The Relationship between War and Crime in the United States," 722–40, 929; Steckmesser, *The Western Hero in History and Legend,* 247–55.

47. Davis, *Homicide in American Fiction,* 272.

48. Steckmesser, *The Western Hero in History and Legend,* 139; John Cawelti, *The Six-Gun Mystique,* 35–42; Brown, *No Duty to Retreat,* 43–53; Baldwin and O'Brien, *Wanted: Frank and Jesse James,* 13–21.

49. Prassel, *The Great American Outlaw,* xi–xii, 324, 328; Paul F. Angiolillo, *A Criminal as Hero: Angelo Duca,* 3–4; Rosa, *Gunfighter,* 209.

50. O'Connor, *A Treasury of American Folklore,* 10.

51. Ibid., 198, 133, 236.

11. Dueling and Transitional Violence

1. Davis, *Homicide in American Fiction,* 271.

2. Paul Fatout, *Mark Twain in Virginia City,* 212.

3. Mark Twain, *Mark Twains's Autobiography,* vol. 2, 7.

4. Quoted in Arthur G. Pettit, *Mark Twain and the South,* 51. Also see Cyril Clemens, *My Cousin Mark Twain,* 44; James P. Wood, *Spunkwater, Spunkwater: A Life of Mark Twain,* 33–34; DeLancey Ferguson, "Mark Twain's Comstock Duel: The Birth of a Legend," 69; Cyril Clemens, "'The Birth of a Legend' Again," 64–65.

5. *Columbia, Missouri Farm and Home,* March 30, 1955; Moss, "Dueling in Missouri History," 27–28.

6. Eugene Field, "The Duel," 182; Eugene Field, *Poems of Childhood,* 117–18.

7. DeMenil, "A Century of Missouri Literature," 108.

8. Charles H. Dennis, *Eugene Field's Creative Years,* 14–15, 29–30.

9. Ibid., 28.

10. Gard, *Frontier Justice,* 41.

11. Some have argued the duel took place on Bloody Island. See Hyde and Conard, eds., *Encyclopedia of the History of St. Louis,* vol. 1, 614; *Liberty Tribune,* December 28, 1860.

12. *Jefferson City Inquirer,* December 22, 1860.

13. Hyde and Conard, eds., *Encyclopedia of the History of St. Louis,* vol. 1, 614; *Liberty Tribune,* December 28, 1860; Convictions, *State of Missouri v. E. B. Sayers,* St. Louis Circuit Court, circa December 20–28, 1860, MIA.

14. Smith, "History of Dueling," 6.

15. WPA, "Duels and Feuds," Research File, AHC; Leo E. Huff, "The Last Duel in Arkansas: The Marmaduke-Walker Duel," 36.

16. Conard, ed., *Encyclopedia of the History of Missouri,* vol. 4, 199; *Marshall Democrat-News,* April 17, 1961; *Arkansas Democrat,* July 6, 26, 1952; Huff, "The Last Duel in Arkansas," 37–45; *Kansas City Star,* February 21, 1915; *Kansas City Times,* February 16, 1915; *Houston Chronicle,* September 16, 26, 1920; Hyde and Conard, eds., *Encyclopedia of the History of St. Louis,* vol. 1, 615; Letter, Major General Sterling Price to Colonel Archibald S. Dobbin, November 25, 1863, *The War of the Rebellion: A Compilation of the Official Records of the Union and Confederate Armies,* vol. 22, pt. 1, 525; *Civil War Times Illustrated* 26, no. 9 (January 1988): 22–23.

17. Michael Fellman, *Inside War: The Guerrilla Conflict in Missouri during the American Civil War,* 16.

18. Ibid., 183–84.

19. U. S. Grant, *Personal Memoirs of U.S. Grant,* vol. 1, 59.

20. Hyde and Conard, eds., *Encyclopedia of the History of St. Louis,* vol. 1, 615.

21. *Kansas City Times,* March 18, 1940.

22. Ibid; Cochran, *Noted American Duels,* 97.

23. Baldwin and O'Brien, *Wanted: Frank and Jesse James*, 13–14.

24. *Sedalia Daily Bazoo*, July 14, 1870.

25. Edwards, *Biography*, 18–19.

26. William A. Settle, Jr., *Jesse James Was His Name*, 21; Moss, "Dueling in Missouri History," 26–27; Edwards, *Biography*, 19–23; Hyde and Conard, eds., *Encyclopedia of the History of St. Louis*, vol. 1, 615; *Jefferson City Tribune*, September 7, 1875; Smith, "History of Dueling," 6.

27. *Kansas City Times*, September 5, 1875.

28. *Columbia Herald*, May 4, 1882.

29. Jordan, *Frontier*, 67, 36; Lynn Morrow, "The Sons of Honor and Gen. George Caleb Bingham," 1–16.

30. *Jefferson City Tribune*, November 5, 1873.

31. Letter, Johann Bauer to his mother, December 4, 1875, in Walter D. Kamphoefner et al., *News from the Land of Freedom: German Immigrants Write Home*, 175.

32. Lewis Larkin, *Missouri Heritage*, 10; "Convictions," Lawrence County Circuit Court, *State of Missouri v. Doctor McBride*, circa May 1881, MSA; "Missourians," *Missouri Historical Review* 20, no. 3 (April 1936): 294.

33. *Washington Bee*, January 27, 1883.

34. Henry R. Schoolcraft, *A View of the Lead Mines of Missouri*, 75–76.

35. *Milan Republican*, October 6, 1892; Davis, *Homicide in American Fiction*, 271.

36. *Kansas City Call*, September 15, 1922; March 23, November 23, 1923; January 28, 1927.

37. Ibid., January 28, 1927.

38. "Convictions," *State of Missouri v. Americus Farmer*, Ralls County Circuit Court, circa May 1886, MSA.

39. *Carthage Evening Press*, July 12, 1886.

40. *St. Louis Sunday Post Dispatch*, June 19, 1898; Brunswick-Heisel File, Benecke Family Papers, collection no. 3825, folder 501, WHMC.

41. *Davis et al. v. Modern Woodmen of America, The Southwestern Reporter*, vol. 73, April 22–May 27, 1903, 923–26.

42. *Joplin Daily Globe*, November 16, 1902.

43. Davis, *Homicide in American Fiction*, 272; *Higbee Weekly News*, February 12, 1909.

44. *Branson Echo*, November 27, 1908.

45. Ibid.

Bibliography

A. Books

Abernethy, Thomas P. *The South in the New Nation 1789–1819.* Vol. 4. Baton Rouge: Louisiana State University Press, 1961.

Alvord, Clarence W. *The Illinois Country 1673–1818.* Urbana and Chicago: University of Illinois Press, 1965.

An Amateur, Down the River; or, Practical Lessons Under the Code Duello. New York: E. J. Hale and Son, Publishers, 1874.

Angiolillo, Paul F. *A Criminal as Hero: Angelo Duca.* Lawrence: Regents Press of Kansas, 1979.

Anthony, Allen. *River at the Door: Unusual Experiences in Isolated Areas.* Fort Davis, Texas: River Microstudies, 1987.

Arnold, Morris S. *Unequal Laws unto a Savage Race: European Legal Traditions in Arkansas, 1686–1836.* Fayetteville: University of Arkansas Press, 1985.

Arpy, Jim. *The Magnificent Mississippi.* Grinnell, Iowa: Iowa Heritage Gallery, 1983.

Arrington, Alfred. *Duelists and Dueling in the Southwest: With Sketches of Southern Life.* New York: W. H. Graham, 1847.

———. *Illustrated Lives and Adventures of the Desperadoes of the New World.* Philadelphia: T. B. Peterson, 1849.

———. *The Lives and Adventures of the Desperadoes of the South-West.* New York: W. H. Graham, 1849.

Ashe, Thomas. *Travels in America Performed in 1806.* London: William Sawyer and Co., 1808.

Ayers, Edward L. *Vengeance and Justice: Crime and Punishment in the 19th Century American South.* New York: Oxford University Press, 1984.

Babcock, Rufus, ed. *Forty Years of Pioneer Life: Memoir of John Mason Peck.* Philadelphia: American Baptist Publication Society, 1864.

Baker, Jean H. *Mary Todd Lincoln: A Biography.* New York: W. W. Norton and Co., 1987.

Baldick, Robert. *The Duel: A History of Duelling.* New York: Clarkson N. Potter, Inc., 1965.

Baldwin, Leland D. *The Keelboat Age on Western Waters.* Pittsburgh: University of Pittsburgh Press, 1941.

Baldwin, Margaret, and Pat O'Brien. *Wanted: Frank and Jesse James: The Real Story.* New York: MacMillan Publishing Co., 1982.

Ballagh, James C., ed. *The South in the Building of the Nation.* Vol. 3. Richmond: Southern Historical Publication Society, 1909.

Bancroft, Frederic, ed. *Speeches, Correspondence, and Political Papers of Carl Schurz.* Vols. 1–2. New York: G. P. Putnam's Sons, 1913.

Bannon, John F. *The Spanish Borderlands Frontier, 1513–1821.* New York: Holt, Rinehart, and Winston, 1970.

Barker, Eugene C., ed. *The Austin Papers.* Vols. 1–2. Washington, D.C.: Government Printing Office, 1924.

Barnes, C. R. *The Commonwealth of Missouri: A Centennial Record.* St. Louis: Bryan, Brand and Co., 1877.

Bateman, Newton, and Paul Selby, eds. *Historical Encyclopedia of Illinois.* Vol. 1. Chicago: Munsell Publishing Co., 1907.

Bay, W. V. N. *Reminiscences of the Bench and Bar of Missouri.* St. Louis: F. H. Thomas and Co., 1878.

Benson, Ivan. *Mark Twain: Western Years.* Palo Alto, Calif.: Stanford University Press, 1938.

Benton, Thomas Hart. *Auto-Biographical Sketch of Thomas H. Benton.* Columbia: State Historical Society, n.d.

———. *Thirty Years' View.* Vols. 1–2. New York and London: D. Appleton and Co., 1854.

Billington, Ray Allen. *Westward Expansion: A History of the American Frontier.* 5th ed. New York: MacMillan Publishing Co., 1982.

Blackstone, William. *Commentaries on the Laws of England.* Vol. 1, books 1 and 2. New York: W. E. Dean, 1846.

Boorstin, Daniel J. *The Americans: The Democratic Experience.* New York: Random House, 1973.

———. *Hidden History: Exploring Our Secret Past.* New York: Vintage Books, 1989.

Botkin, B. A. *A Treasury of American Folklore.* New York: Crown Publishers, 1944.

Boyd, Julian, ed. *The Papers of Thomas Jefferson.* Vol. 9. Princeton: Princeton University Press, 1954.

Brackenridge, Henry M. *Journal of a Voyage up the River Missouri, 1811.* In Reuben Gold Thwaites, ed., *Early Western Travels,* vol. 6. Cleveland: Arthur H. Clark Co., 1905.

———. *Recollections of Persons and Places in the West.* 2d ed. Philadelphia: J. B. Lippincott and Co., 1868.

———. *Views of Louisiana; Together with a Voyage up the Mississippi River in 1811.* Pittsburgh: Cramer, Spear and Eichbaum, 1814.

Bradbury, John. *Travels, 1809.* In Reuben Gold Thwaites, ed., *Early Western Travels, 1748–1846.* Vol. 5. Cleveland: Arthur H. Clark, 1905.

Breck, Daniel. *Puke Lawin': Law Makin' and Law Breaken' in Missouri Especially.* St. Louis: Mound City Press, Inc., 1933.

Bridenbaugh, Carl. *Myths and Realities: Societies of the Colonial South.* New York: Atheneum, 1963.

Brown, Richard Maxwell. *No Duty to Retreat: Violence and Values in American History and Society.* Oxford and New York: Oxford University Press, 1991.

———. *Strain of Violence: Historical Studies of American Violence and Vigilantism.* Oxford and New York: Oxford University Press, 1975.

Brown, Samuel R. *The Western Gazetteer; or Emigrant's Dictionary.* Auburn, New York: H. S. Southwick, 1817.

Bruce, Dickson D., Jr. *Violence and Culture in the Antebellum South.* Austin: University of Texas Press, 1979.

Bryan, William S., and Robert Rose. *A History of Pioneer Families of Missouri.* St. Louis: Bryan, Brand, and Co., 1876.

Buckingham, J. S. *The Eastern and Western States of America.* Vols. 1–3. Newgate St. London: Fisher, Son, and Co., 1842.

Bud, Louis J., ed. *Mark Twain: Collected Tales, Sketches, Speeches, and Essays 1852–1890.* New York: Literary Classics of the United States and the Library of America, 1984.

Burnett, Peter H. *Recollections and Opinions of an Old Pioneer.* New York: D. Appleton and Co., 1880.

Butterfield, Fox. *All God's Children: The Bosket Family and the American Tradition of Violence.* New York: Alfred A. Knopf, 1995.

Callan, Louise. *Philippine Duchesne: Frontier Missionary of the Sacred Heart 1769–1852.* Westminister, Md.: Newman Press, 1957.

Campbell, Randolph B. *Sam Houston and the American Southwest.* New York: Harper Collins College Publishers, 1993.

Campbell, Robert A. *Campbell's Gazetteer of Missouri.* St. Louis: R. A. Campbell, 1874.

Cash, W. J. *The Mind of the South.* New York: Alfred A. Knopf, 1941.

Cawelti, John. *The Six-Gun Mystique.* 2d ed. Bowling Green, Ohio: Bowling Green University Press, 1984.

Chambers, William N. *Old Bullion Benton.* Boston: Little, Brown, and Co., 1956.

Clark, John. *"Father Clark" or the Pioneer Preacher: Sketches and Incidents of Rev. John Clark.* New York: Sheldon, Lamport and Blakeman, 1855.

Clemens, Cyril. *My Cousin Mark Twain.* Emmaus, Pa.: Rodale Press, 1939.

Clokey, Richard M. *William A. Ashley: Enterprise and Politics in the Trans-Mississippi West.* Norman: University of Oklahoma Press, 1980.

Cochran, Hamilton. *Noted American Duels and Hostile Encounters.* Philadelphia: Chilton Co., 1963.

Cockburn, John. *The History and Examination of Duels.* London: G. Strahan, 1720.

Coffin, Tristram P., and Henning Cohen. *The Parade of Heroes: Legendary Figures in American Lore.* Garden City, N.Y.: Anchor Press/Doubleday, 1978.

Coleman, J. Winston, Jr. *Famous Kentucky Duels.* Lexington: Henry Clay Press, 1969.

Collins, A. Loyd, and Georgia I. Collins. *Hero Stories from Missouri History.* Kansas City: Burton Publishing Co., 1956.

Conard, Howard L., ed. *Encyclopedia of the History of Missouri.* Vols. 1–5. New York: Southern History Co., 1901.

Cooper, William J. *The South and the Politics of Slavery 1828–1856.* Baton Rouge: Louisana State University Press, 1978.

Crighton, John C. *A History of Columbia and Boone County.* Columbia: Computer Color Graphics, Inc., 1987.

Cross, Whitney R. *The Burned-Over District: The Social and Intellectual History of Enthusiastic Religion in Western New York, 1800–1850.* Ithaca: Cornell University Press, 1950.

Cuming, Fortescue. *Sketches of a Tour of Western Country, 1808.* In Reuben Gold Thwaites, ed., *Early Western Travels,* vol. 4. Cleveland: Arthur H. Clark Co., 1905.

Cunliffe, Marcus. *Soldiers and Civilians: The Martial Spirit in America, 1775–1865.* 2d ed. New York: Free Press, 1973.

Dabney, Virginius. *Pistols and Pointed Pens: The Dueling Editors of Old Virginia.* Chapel Hill, N.C.: Algonquin Books, 1987.

Darby, John F. *Personal Recollections of Many Prominent People Whom I Have Known.* St. Louis: G. I. Jones and Co., 1880.

Dargo, George. *Jefferson's Louisiana: Politics and the Clash of Legal Traditions.* Cambridge: Harvard University Press, 1975.

Dary, David. *Cowboy Culture: A Saga of Five Centuries.* Lawrence: University of Kansas Press, 1989.

Davis, David Brion. *Homicide in American Fiction, 1798–1860: A Study in Social Values.* Ithaca: Cornell University Press, 1957.

Davis, Walter B., and Daniel S. Durrie. *An Illustrated History of Missouri.* St. Louis: A. J. Hill and Co., 1876.

Dennis, Charles H. *Eugene Field's Creative Years.* Garden City, N.Y.: Doubleday, Page and Co., 1924.

Denslow, Ray V. *Territorial Masonry.* Washington, D.C.: Masonic Service Association, 1925.

Devol, George H. *Forty Years a Gambler on the Mississippi.* 2d ed. New York: Devol Publisher, 1892.

Dick, Everett. *The Dixie Frontier.* New York: Alfred A. Knopf, 1948.

———. *Vanguards of the Frontier: A Social History of the Northern Plains and Rocky Mountains from the Fur Traders to the Sod Busters.* Lincoln: University of Nebraska Press, 1941.

Dictionary of American History. Vol. 1, 2d ed. New York: Charles Scribner's Sons, 1940.

Donald, David H. *Charles Sumner and the Coming of the Civil War.* New York: Fawcett Columbine, 1960.

———. *Lincoln.* New York: Simon and Schuster, 1995.

Douglass, Robert S. *History of Missouri Baptists.* Kansas City: Western Baptist Publishing Co., 1934.

———. *History of Southeast Missouri.* New York: Lewis Publishing Co., 1912.

Dyer, Robert C. *Boonville: An Illustrated History.* Marceline, Mo.: Walsworth Press Co., 1987.

Easum, Chester V. *The Americanization of Carl Schurz.* Chicago: University of Chicago Press, 1929.

Edwards, John N. *Biography, Memoirs, Reminiscences and Recollections.* Kansas City: Jennie Edwards Publisher, 1889.

Edwards, Richard. *Edwards' Great West and Her Commercial Metropolis.* St. Louis: Edwards' Monthly, 1860.

Ekberg, Carl J. *Colonial Ste. Genevieve.* Gerald, Mo.: Patrice Press, 1985.

Ekberg, Carl J., and William E. Foley. *An Account of Upper Louisiana by Nicolas de Finiels.* Columbia: University of Missouri Press, 1989.

Eleventh Annual Catalogue of the Officers and Students of the Missouri University, 1853. Columbia: E. C. Davis, 1853.

English, William F. *The Pioneer Lawyer and Jurist in Missouri.* Columbia: University of Missouri, 1947.

Evans, Estwick. *A Pedestrious Tour, 1818.* In Reuben Gold Thwaites, ed., *Early Western Travels,* vol. 8. Cleveland: Arthur H. Clark Co., 1905.

Fagg, Thomas J. C. *Thomas Hart Benton: The Great Missourian and His Times Reviewed.* Columbia: State Historical Society, 1905.

Faragher, John Mack. *Daniel Boone: The Life and Legend of an American Pioneer.* New York: Henry Holt and Co., 1992.

Fatout, Paul. *Mark Twain in Virginia City.* Bloomington: Indiana University Press, 1964.

Faust, Drew Gilpin. *A Sacred Circle: The Dilemma of the Intellectual in the Old South, 1840–1860.* Baltimore: Johns Hopkins Press, 1977.

Fellman, Michael. *Inside War: The Guerrilla Conflict in Missouri during the American Civil War.* New York: Oxford University Press, 1989.

Field, Eugene. *Poems of Childhood.* New York: Charles Scribner's Sons, 1904.

Fischer, David H., and James C. Kelley. *Away I'm Bound Away: Virginia and the Westward Movement.* Richmond: Virginia Historical Society, 1993.

Flint, Timothy. *Recollections of the Last Ten Years.* Boston: Cummings, Hilliard and Co., 1826.

Foley, William E. *The Genesis of Missouri: From Wilderness Outpost to Statehood.* Columbia: University of Missouri Press, 1989.

———. *A History of Missouri, Volume 1: 1673 to 1820.* Columbia: University of Missouri Press, 1971.

Foley, William E., and C. David Rice. *The First Chouteaus: River Barons of Early St. Louis.* Urbana: University of Illinois Press, 1983.

Folsom, James K. *Timothy Flint.* New York: Twayne Publishers, Inc., 1965.

Foner, Philip S., ed. *Basic Writings of Thomas Jefferson.* Garden City, N.Y.: Halcyon House, 1944.

Franchere, Gabriel. *Narrative of a Voyage to the Northwest Coast of America, 1811–1814.* In Reuben Gold Thwaites, ed., *Early Western Travels,* vol. 6. Cleveland: Arthur H. Clark Co., 1905.

Franklin, John Hope. *The Militant South, 1800–1861.* Cambridge: Harvard University Press, 1956.

Franzwa, Gregory M. *The Story of Old Ste. Genevieve.* St. Louis: Patrice Press, Inc., 1967.

Fuess, Claude M. *Carl Schurz: Reformer 1829–1906.* Port Washington, N.Y.: Kennikat Press, Inc., 1963.

Gamble, Thomas. *Savannah Duels and Duelists, 1733–1877.* Savannah, Ga.: Review Publishing and Printing Co., 1923.

Gard, Wayne. *Frontier Justice.* Norman: University of Oklahoma Press, 1949.

Gardner, James A. *Lead King: Moses Austin.* St. Louis: Sunrise Publishing Co., 1980.

Gaustad, Edwin S. *A Religious History of America.* New York: Harper and Row Publishers, 1966.

Gay, Peter. *The Cultivation of Hatred: The Bourgeois Experience Victoria to Freud.* Vol. 3. New York: W. W. Norton and Co., 1993.

Gaylord, Irving C. *The Burr-Hamilton Duel.* New York: n.p., 1889.

Gentry, North Todd. *The Bench and Bar of Boone County Missouri.* Columbia: E. W. Stephens Publishing Co., 1916.

Gibson, Charles. *Spain in America.* New York: Harper and Row, 1966.

Gill, McCune. *St. Louis Duels.* St. Louis: n.p., n.d.

Gillis, William R. *Gold Rush Days with Mark Twain.* New York: Albert and Charles Boni, 1930.

Gilmore, Robert K. *Ozark Baptizings, Hangings, and Other Diversions: Theatrical Folkways of Rural Missouri, 1885–1910.* Norman: University of Oklahoma Press, 1984.

Gladstone, T. H. *The Englishman in Kansas.* New York: Miller and Co., 1857.

Glenn, Myra C. *Campaigns against Corporal Punishment: Prisoners, Sailors, Women, and Children in Antebellum America.* Albany: State University of New York Press, 1984.

Goodspeed's History of Franklin, Jefferson, Washington, Crawford, and Gasconade Counties, Missouri. Chicago: Goodspeed Publishing Co., 1888.

Goodspeed's History of Southeast Missouri. Chicago: Goodspeed Publishing Co., 1888.

Goodykoontz, Colin B. *Home Missions on the American Frontier.* Caldwell, Idaho: Caxton Printers, Ltd., 1939.

Gracy, David B., II. *Moses Austin: His Life.* San Antonio: Trinity University Press, 1987.

Graham, Hugh Davis, and Ted Robert Gurr, eds. *The History of Violence in America: Historical and Comparative Perspectives—A Report Submitted to the National Commission on the Causes and Prevention of Violence.* New York: Frederick A. Praeger, 1969.

Grant, U. S. *Personal Memoirs of U. S. Grant.* Vol. 1. New York: Charles L. Webster and Co., 1885.

Green, Karen M. *The Kentucky Gazette 1801–1820.* Baltimore: Gateway Press, Inc., 1985.

Greenberg, Kenneth S. *Masters and Statesmen: The Political Culture of American Slavery.* Baltimore: Johns Hopkins Press, 1985.

Hall, Francis. *Travels in Canada and the United States in 1816 and 1817.* London: Longman, Hurst, Rees, Orme, and Brown, c. 1818.

Hall, James. *Letters from the West: Containing Sketches of Scenery, Manners, and Customs; and Anecdotes Connected with the First Settlements of the Western Sections of the United States.* London: Henry Colburn, 1828.

————. *Sketches of History, Life, and Manners, in the West.* Vol. 2. Philadelphia: Harrison Hall, 1835.

Handy, Robert T. *A Christian America: Protestant Hopes and Historical Realities.* New York: Oxford University Press, 1971.

Hart, Henry C. *The Dark Missouri.* Madison: University of Wisconsin Press, 1957.

Hartman, Mary, and Elmo Ingenthron. *Bald Knobbers: Vigilantes on the Ozark Frontier.* Gretna, La.: Pelican Publishing Co., 1988.

Hartz, Louis. *The Founding of New Societies.* New York: Harcourt, Brace and World, Inc., 1964.

Hatch, Nathan O. *The Democratization of American Christianity.* New Haven: Yale University Press, 1989.

Higginbotham, Vallé. *John Smith T: Missouri Pioneer.* N.p.: n.p., 1968.

Hill, Hamlin. *Mark Twain: God's Fool.* New York: Harper and Row, 1973.

Hill, Samuel S. *The South and the North in American Religion.* Athens: University of Georgia Press, 1980.

History of Caldwell and Livingston Counties, Missouri. St. Louis: National History Co., 1886.

History of Cass and Bates Counties. St. Joseph: National Historical Co., 1883.

History of Howard and Chariton Counties, Missouri. St. Louis: National Publishing Co., 1883.

History of Saline County, Missouri. St. Louis: Missouri Historical Co., 1881.

Hogue, Arthur, ed. *Charles Sumner: An Essay by Carl Schurz.* Urbana: University of Illinois Press, 1951.

Holcombe, R. I. *History of Marion County Missouri 1884.* St. Louis: E. F. Perkins, 1884.

Hollon, W. Eugene. *Frontier Violence: Another Look.* New York: Oxford University Press, 1974.

Holmes, Oliver Wendell. *Collected Legal Papers.* New York: Peter Smith, 1952.

Houck, Louis. *A History of Missouri.* Vols. 1–3. Chicago: R. R. Donnelley and Sons Co., 1908.

————. *The Spanish Regime in Missouri.* Vols. 1–2. Chicago: R. R. Donnelley and Sons Co., 1909.

Hough, Emerson. *The Story of the Cowboy.* New York: D. Appleton and Co., 1930.

Howard, Oliver. *The Mark Twain Book.* Marceline, Mo.: Walsworth Co., 1985.

Hyde, Laurance. *Historical Review of the Judicial System of Missouri.* Kansas City: Vernon Law Book Co., 1952.

Hyde, William, and Howard L. Conard, eds. *Encyclopedia of the History of St. Louis.* Vols. 1–3. New York: Southern History Co., 1899.

Ingraham, Joseph Holt. *The South-West By a Yankee.* Vols. 1–2. New York: Harper and Brothers, 1835.

Johnson, Allen, ed. *Dictionary of American Biography.* Vol. 2. New York: Charles Scribner's Sons, 1929.

Jones, J. B. *Life and Adventures of a Country Merchant.* Philadelphia: J. B. Lippincott and Co., 1882.

Jordan, Philip. *Frontier Law and Order.* Lincoln: University of Nebraska Press, 1970.

Jordan, Terry G., and Matti Kaups. *The American Backwoods Frontier: An Ethnic and Ecological Interpretation.* Baltimore: Johns Hopkins University Press, 1989.

Kamphoefner, Walter D., et al. *News from the Land of Freedom: German Immigrants Write Home.* Ithaca: Cornell University Press, 1991.

Kane, Harnett T. *Gentlemen, Swords and Pistols.* New York: William Morrow and Co., 1951.

Keefe, James F., and Lynn Morrow, eds. *A Connecticut Yankee in the Frontier Ozarks: The Writings of Theodore Pease Russell.* Columbia: University of Missouri Press, 1988.

———. *The White River Chronicles of S. C. Turnbo.* Fayetteville: University of Arkansas Press, 1994.

Keller, William F. *The Nation's Advocate: Henry Marie Brackenridge and Young America.* Pittsburgh: University of Pittsburgh Press, 1965.

Kiernan, V. G. *The Duel in European History: Honour and the Reign of Aristocracy.* Oxford: Oxford University Press, 1988.

Kirschten, Ernest. *Catfish and Crystal.* 3d ed. St. Louis: Patrice Press, 1989.

Larkin, Lewis. *Missouri Heritage.* Vol. 2. Point Lookout, Mo.: School of the Ozarks Press, 1971.

Lawson, John D., ed. *American State Trials.* Vol. 10. St. Louis: F. H. Thomas Law Book Co., 1918.

Logan, James. *Notes of a Journey through Canada, the United States of America, and the West Indies.* Edinburgh: Fraser and Co., 1838.

Logan, Sheridan A. *Old Saint Jo: Gateway to the West, 1799–1932.* St. Joseph: Stinehour Press, 1979.

Lovett, Clara M. *Carl Schurz: 1829–1906.* Washington, D.C.: Library of Congress, 1983.

Lucas, John B. C. *Communications and Letters of J. B. C. Lucas and T. H. Benton.* Columbia: State Historical Society of Missouri, n.d.

————, ed. *Letters of Hon. J. B. C. Lucas from 1815 to 1836.* St. Louis: Lippincott and Co., 1905.

Lyon, William H. *The Pioneer Editor in Missouri 1808–1860.* Columbia: University of Missouri Press, 1965.

McCandless, Perry. *A History of Missouri, Volume 2: 1820 to 1860.* Columbia: University of Missouri Press, 1972.

McCormack, Thomas J., ed. *Memoirs of Gustave Koerner 1809–1896.* Vol. 1. Cedar Rapids, Iowa: Torch Press, 1909.

McCurdy, Frances Lea. *Stump, Bar, and Pulpit: Speechmaking on the Missouri Frontier.* Columbia: University of Missouri Press, 1969.

McDermott, John F., ed. *The Early Histories of St. Louis.* St. Louis Historical Documents Foundation, 1952.

————. *Frenchmen and French Ways in the Mississippi Valley.* Urbana: University of Illinois Press, 1969.

McGrath, Roger D. *Gunfighters, Highwaymen and Vigilantes: Violence on the Frontier.* Berkeley: University of California Press, 1984.

Mack, Effie Mona. *Mark Twain in Nevada.* New York: Charles Scribner's Sons, 1947.

McWhiney, Grady. *Cracker Culture: Celtic Ways in the Old South.* Tuscaloosa: University of Alabama Press, 1988.

Malone, Dumas. *Jefferson the President: Second Term, 1805–1809.* Vol. 5 of *Jefferson and His Time.* Boston: Little, Brown and Co., 1974.

Marbois, Barbé. *The History of Louisiana.* Philadelphia: Corey and Lea, 1830.

March, David D. *The History of Missouri.* 2 vols. New York: Lewis Historical Publishing Co., 1967.

Marjoribanks, Alexander. *Travel in South and North America.* London: Simpkin, Marshall and Co., 1853.

Marshall, Thomas M., ed. *The Life and Papers of Frederick Bates.* Vol. 1. St. Louis: Missouri Historical Society, 1926.

Marty, Martin E. *Righteous Empire: The Protestant Experience in America.* New York: Dial Press, 1970.

Mason, Edward G., ed. *Early Chicago and Illinois.* Chicago: Fergus Printing Co., 1890.

Mathews, Donald G. *Religion in the Old South.* Chicago: University of Chicago Press, 1977.

Meigs, William M. *The Life of Thomas Hart Benton.* Philadelphia: J. B. Lippincott Co., 1904.

Meltzer, Milton. *Mark Twain: A Writer's Life.* New York: Franklin Watts, 1985.

Merrick, George B. *Old Times on the Upper Mississippi: The Recollections of a*

Steamboat Pilot from 1854 to 1863. St. Paul: Minnesota Historical Society Press, 1987.

Meyer, Duane. *The Heritage of Missouri: A History.* Rev. ed. St. Louis: State Publishing Co., 1973.

Milburn, William Henry. *The Rifle, Axe, and Saddlebags, and Other Lectures.* London: Sampson, Low, Son and Co., 1857.

Miyakawa, T. Scott. *Protestants and Pioneers: Individualism and Conformity on the American Frontier.* Chicago: University of Chicago Press, 1964.

Monaghan, Jay. *Civil War on the Western Border 1854–1865.* New York: Bonanza Books, 1955.

Monette, John W. *History of the Discovery and Settlement of the Valley of the Mississippi.* Vol. 2. New York: Harper and Brothers, 1846.

Montell, William L. *Killings: Folk Justice in the Upper South.* Lexington: University of Kentucky Press, 1968.

Moser, Harold D., et al., eds. *The Papers of Andrew Jackson, 1814–1815.* Vol. 3. Knoxville: University of Tennessee Press, 1991.

Murray, Ellen N. *The Code of Honor: Dueling in America.* Bryan, Texas: Newman Printing Co., 1984.

Musick, John R. *Stories of Missouri.* New York: American Book Co., 1897.

Napton, William B. *Past and Present of Saline County Missouri.* Indianapolis: B. F. Bowen and Co., 1910.

National Cyclopedia of American Biography, The. Vols. 1–20. New York: James T. White and Co., 1929.

Nelson, Thomas S. *A Full and Accurate Record of the Trial of William P. Darnes.* Boston: Saxton and Pierce, 1841.

O'Connor, Richard. *Wild Bill Hickok.* Garden City, N.Y.: Doubleday and Co., Inc., 1959.

Ogden, George. *Letters from the West, 1821–1823.* In Reuben Gold Thwaites, ed., *Early Western Travels,* vol. 19. Cleveland: Arthur H. Clark Co., 1905.

O'Hanlon, John C. *Life and Scenery in Missouri: Reminiscences of a Missionary Priest.* Dublin: James Duffy and Co., 1890.

Owsley, Frank L. *Plain Folk of the Old South.* Chicago: Quadrangle Books, 1965.

Parmet, Herbert S., and Marie B. Hecht. *Aaron Burr: Portrait of an Ambitious Man.* New York: MacMillan Co., 1967.

Parrish, William E. *Frank Blair: Lincoln's Conservative.* Columbia: University of Missouri Press, 1998.

———, et al. *Missouri: The Heart of the Nation.* St. Louis: Forum Press, 1980.

Patterson, Orlando. *Slavery and Social Death: A Comparative Study.* Cambridge: Harvard University Press, 1982.

Paxson, Frederic L. *History of the American Frontier 1763–1893.* Boston: Houghton Mifflin Co., 1924.

Peck, John Mason. *Father Clark on the Pioneer Preacher.* New York: Sheldon, Lamport and Blakeman, 1855.

————. *A Guide for Emigrants Containing Sketches of Illinois, Missouri, and the Adjacent Parts.* Boston: Lincoln and Edmands, 1931.

————. *A New Guide for Emigrants to the West.* Boston: Gould, Kendall and Lincoln, 1836.

————, ed. *The Serpent Uncoiled: Or a Full Length Picture of Universalism by a Western Layman, Introduction and Notes by J. M. Peck.* Philadelphia: American Baptist Publication Society, 1846.

Pelzer, Louis. *Henry Dodge.* Iowa City: State Historical Society of Iowa, 1911.

Perkins, E. F., and T. M. Horne. *History of Greene County, Missouri.* St. Louis: Western Historical Co., 1883.

Perkins, James H. *Annals of the West: Embracing a Concise Account of Principal Events Which Have Occurred in the Western States and Territories.* St. Louis: James R. Alback, 1850.

Pessen, Edward. *Jacksonian America: Society, Personality, and Politics.* Homewood, Ill.: Dorsey Press, 1969.

Peterson, Charles E. *Colonial St. Louis: Building a Creole Capital.* St. Louis: Missouri Historical Society, 1949.

Peterson, Norma L. *Freedom and Franchise: The Political Career of B. Gratz Brown.* Columbia: University of Missouri Press, 1965.

Pettit, Arthur G. *Mark Twain and the South.* Lexington: University of Kentucky Press, 1974.

Philbrick, Francis. *The Rise of the West.* New York: Harper and Row, 1966.

Pollack, Ervin H. *Fundamentals of Legal Research.* 3d ed. Brooklyn: Foundation Press, Inc., 1967.

Posey, Walter B. *Religious Strife on the Southern Frontier.* Baton Rouge: Louisiana State University Press, 1965.

Post, G. Gordon. *An Introduction to the Law.* Englewood Cliffs, N.J.: Prentice-Hall, 1965.

Pound, Roscoe. *The Formative Era of American Law.* Gloucester, Mass.: Peter Smith, 1938.

Prassel, Frank R. *The Great American Outlaw: A Legacy of Fact and Fiction.* Norman: University of Oklahoma Press, 1972.

Primm, James Neal. *Lion of the Valley: St. Louis, Missouri.* Boulder, Colo.: Pruett Publishing Co., 1981.

Prucha, Francis P. *The Sword of the Republic: The United States Army on the Frontier 1783–1846.* Lincoln: University of Nebraska Press, 1960.

Reavis, L. U. *The Life and Military Service of Gen. William Selby Harney.* St. Louis: Bryan, Brand, and Co., 1878.

———. *Saint Louis: The Future Great City of the World.* St. Louis: Gray, Baker and Co., 1875.

Redfield, Horace V. *Homicide, North and South.* Philadelphia: J. P. Lippincott and Co., 1880.

Reilly, Kevin. *The West and the World.* New York: Harper and Row, 1980.

Robertson, James A., ed. *Louisiana under the Rule of Spain, France, and the United States 1785–1807.* Vol. 1. Cleveland: Arthur A. Clark Co., 1911.

Rodemyre, Edgar T. *History of Centralia Missouri.* Centralia: The Centralia Fireside Guard, 1936.

Rogers, Joseph M. *Thomas H. Benton.* Philadelphia: George W. Jacobs and Co., 1905.

Rollins, Philip A. *The Cowboy.* New York: Charles Scribner's Sons, 1922.

Roosevelt, Theodore. *The Rough Riders.* New York: Review of Reviews Co., 1904.

———. *The Strenuous Life.* New York: Review of Reviews Co., 1899.

———. *The Winning of the West.* New York: Review of Reviews Co., 1904.

Rosa, Joseph G. *The Gunfighter: Man or Myth?* Norman: University of Oklahoma Press, 1969.

———. *They Called Him Wild Bill: The Life and Adventures of James Butler Hickok.* 2d ed. Norman: University of Oklahoma Press, 1974.

Rozier, Firmin A. *Rozier's History of the Early Settlement of the Mississippi Valley.* St. Louis: G. A. Pierrot and Son, 1890.

Rush, Philip. *The Book of Duels.* London: George E. Harrap and Co., Ltd., 1964.

Rutledge, Zoe B. *Our Jefferson County Heritage.* Cape Girardeau, Mo.: Ramfre Press, 1970.

Sabine, Lorenzo. *Notes on Duels and Duelling.* Boston: Crosby, Nichols, and Co., 1855.

Sahlins, Marshall. *Historical Metaphors and Mythical Realities.* Ann Arbor: University of Michigan Press, 1981.

Savitz, Leonard. *Dilemmas in Criminology.* New York: McGraw Hill Book Co., 1967.

Schafer, Joseph. *Carl Schurz: Militant Liberal.* Evansville, Wisc.: Antes Press, 1930.

———, ed. *Intimate Papers of Carl Schurz 1841–1869.* Vol. 30. Madison: State Historical Society of Wisconsin, 1928.

Scharf, J. Thomas. *History of Saint Louis City and County.* Vols. 1–2. Philadelphia: Louis H. Everts and Co., 1883.

Schoolcraft, Henry R. *Journal of a Tour into the Interior of Missouri and Arkansaw, 1818–1819.* London: Sir Richard Phillips and Co., 1821.

———. *Scenes and Adventures in the Semi-Alpine Region of the Ozark Mountains of Missouri and Arkansas.* Philadelphia: Lippincott, Grambo and Co., 1853.

———. *A View of the Lead Mines of Missouri.* Reprt., New York: Charles Wiley and Co., 1819.

Schroeder, Adolph. *Bethel German Colony, 1844–1879: Religious Beliefs and Practices.* Bethel, Mo.: Historic Bethel German Colony, 1990.

Schurz, Carl. *The Reminiscences of Carl Schurz.* Vols. 1–2. New York: McClure Co., 1907.

———. *Speeches of Carl Schurz.* Philadelphia: J. B. Lippincott and Co., 1865.

Seitz, Don C. *Famous American Duels.* New York: Thomas Y. Crowell Co., 1929.

Settle, William A., Jr. *Jesse James Was His Name.* Lincoln: University of Nebraska Press, 1977.

Shepard, Elihu. *The Early History of St. Louis and Missouri.* St. Louis: Southwestern Book and Publishing Co., 1870.

Shoemaker, Floyd. *Missouri and Missourians: Land of Contrasts and People of Achievement.* Vol. 1. Chicago: Lewis Publishing Co., 1943.

———. *Missouri—Day by Day.* Vols. 1–2. Columbia: State Historical Society of Missouri, 1943.

———. *Missouri's Struggle for Statehood, 1804–1821.* Jefferson City: Hugh Stephens Printing Co., 1916.

Skolnick, Jerome H. *Justice without Trial: Law Enforcement in Democratic Society.* New York: John Wiley and Sons, Inc., 1966.

Slotkin, Richard. *The Fatal Environment: The Myth of the Frontier in the Age of Industrialization, 1800–1890.* New York: Atheneum, 1985.

———. *Gunfighter Nation: The Myth of the Frontier in Twentieth-Century America.* New York: Atheneum, 1992.

———. *Regeneration through Violence: The Mythology of the American Frontier, 1600–1860.* Middletown, Conn.: Wesleyan University Press, 1973.

Smith, Elbert B. *Magnificent Missourian: The Life of Thomas Hart Benton.* Philadelphia: J. B. Lippincott Co., 1958.

Smith, Sam B., and Harriet C. Owsley, eds. *The Papers of Andrew Jackson, 1770–1803.* Vols. 1–3. Knoxville: University of Tennessee Press, 1980.

Spring, Gardiner, ed. *Memoirs of the Late Rev. Samuel J. Mills.* Philadelphia: Missionary Society Publication, 1820.

Steckmesser, Kent L. *The Western Hero in History and Legend.* Norman: University of Oklahoma Press, 1965.

Steffen, Jerome O. *William Clark: Jeffersonian Man on the Frontier.* Norman: University of Oklahoma Press, 1977.

Stevens, Walter B., ed. *The Brown-Reynolds Duel: A Complete Documentary Chronicle of the Last Bloodshed under the Code between St. Louisians.* St. Louis: Franklin Club, 1911.

————. *Centennial History of Missouri (The Center State).* Vols. 1–2. St. Louis: S. J. Clarke Publishing Co., 1921.

————. *Missouri: The Center State 1821–1915.* Vols. 1–2. Chicago: S. J. Clarke Publishing Co., 1915.

————. *St. Louis: The Fourth City 1764–1909.* St. Louis–Chicago: S. J. Clarke Publishing Co., 1909.

Stevens, William O. *Pistols at Ten Paces: The Story of the Code of Honor in America.* Boston: Houghton Mifflin Co., 1940.

Stewart, A. J. D., ed. *The History of the Bench and Bar of Missouri.* St. Louis: Legal Publishing Co., 1898.

Stoddard, Amos. *Sketches, Historical and Descriptive, of Louisiana.* Philadelphia: Mathew Carey, 1812.

Stowe, Steven M. *Intimacy and Power in the Old South: Ritual in the Lives of the Planters.* Baltimore: Johns Hopkins University Press, 1987.

Sweet, William W. *Religion in the Development of American Culture 1765–1840.* New York: Charles Scribner's Sons, 1952.

————. *Religion on the American Frontier: The Baptists 1783–1830.* New York: Henry Holt and Co., 1931.

————. *The Story of Religion in America.* New York and London: Harper and Brothers Publishers, 1930.

Switzler, William F. *History of Boone County, Missouri.* St. Louis: Western Publishing Co., 1882.

————. *Switzler's Illustrated History of Missouri from 1541 to 1877.* St. Louis: C. R. Barnes, 1879.

Szasz, Ference M. *The Protestant Clergy in the Great Plains and Mountains West, 1865–1915.* Albuquerque: University of New Mexico Press, 1988.

Taft, William H. *Missouri Newspapers.* Columbia: University of Missouri Press, 1964.

Taylor, William R. *Cavalier and Yankee: The Old South and American National Character.* New York: Oxford University Press, 1957.

Terzian, James P. *Defender of Human Rights: Carl Schurz.* New York: Julian Messner, 1965.

Thelen, David. *Paths of Resistance: Tradition and Democracy in Industrializing Missouri.* Columbia: University of Missouri Press, 1991.

Thomas, Clarke, and Jack Glendenning. *The Slicker War.* Aldrich, Mo.: Bona Publishing Co., 1984.

Thwaites, Reuben Gold, ed. *Early Western Travels 1748–1846.* Vols. 1–22. Cleveland: Arthur H. Clark Co., 1905.

Tocqueville, Alexis de. *Democracy in America.* Richard D. Heffner, ed. New York: Mentor Books, 1956.

Townsend, John. *Narrative of 1834.* In Reuben Gold Thwaites, eds., *Early Western Travels,* vol. 21. Cleveland: Arthur H. Clark Co., 1905.

Trefousse, Hans L. *Carl Schurz: A Biography.* Knoxville: University of Tennessee Press, 1982.

Trexler, Harrison A. *Slavery in Missouri: 1804–1865.* Baltimore: Johns Hopkins University Press, 1914.

Truman, Ben C. *The Field of Honor.* New York: Fords, Howard and Hulbert, 1884.

Tucker, Frank C. *The Methodist Church in Missouri 1798–1939: A Brief History.* Nashville: Parthenon Press, 1966.

Turner, Frederick Jackson. "The Significance of the Frontier in American History." In Turner, ed., *The Frontier in American History.* New York: Henry Holt and Co., 1920.

Twain, Mark. *The Adventures of Huckleberry Finn.* New York: Bantam Books, Inc., 1981.

———. *The Autobiography of Mark Twain.* New York: Harper and Brothers, 1959.

———. *Mark Twain's Autobiography.* Vols. 1–2. New York: P. F. Collier and Son Co., 1925.

Tyler, Alice F. *Freedom's Ferment: Phases of Social History to 1860.* Freeport, N.Y.: Books for Libraries Press, 1944.

Vandiver, Frank E., ed. *The Idea of the South: Pursuit of a Central Theme.* Chicago: University of Chicago Press, 1964.

Van Every, Dale. *A Company of Heroes: The American Frontier 1775–1783.* New York: William Morrow and Co., 1962.

———. *Forth to the Wilderness: The First American Frontier 1754–1774.* New York: William Morrow and Co., 1961.

Van Ravenswaay, Charles. *The Arts and Architecture of German Settlements in Missouri.* Columbia: University of Missouri Press, 1977.

Vaugh, Alden T. *American Genesis: Captain John Smith and the Founding of Virginia.* Boston: Little, Brown and Co., 1975.

Viles, Jonas. *The University of Missouri: A Centennial History.* Columbia: University of Missouri Press, 1939.

Violette, E. M. *A History of Missouri.* St. Louis: State Publishing Co., 1954.

Wandell, Samuel H., and Meade Minnigerode. *Aaron Burr: A Biography Written, in Large Part, from Original and Hitherto Unused Material.* Vols. 1–2. New York: G. P. Putnam's Sons, 1927.

White, Edward J. *Legal Traditions and Other Papers.* St. Louis: Thomas Law Book Co., 1929.

White, G. Edward. *The Eastern Establishment and the Western Experience: The West of Frederic Remington, Theodore Roosevelt, and Owen Wister.* New Haven: Yale University Press, 1968.

Williams, Jack K. *Dueling in the Old South: Vignettes of Social History.* College Station: Texas A&M University Press, 1980.

————. *Vogues in Villainy.* Columbia: University of South Carolina Press, 1959.

Wilson, Charles R. *Baptized in Blood: The Religion of the Lost Cause, 1865–1920.* Athens: University of Georgia Press, 1980.

Wilson, John Lyde. *The Code of Honor or, Rules for the Government of Principals and Seconds in Duelling.* Charleston: n.p., 1838.

Wilstach, Frank J. *Wild Bill Hickok: The Prince of Pistoleers.* Garden City, N.Y.: Doubleday, Page and Co., 1926.

Wood, James P. *Spunkwater, Spunkwater: A Life of Mark Twain.* New York: Pantheon Books, 1968.

Wood, Tim. *What They Don't Teach You about History.* New York: Dorsett Press, 1992.

Wyatt-Brown, Bertram. *Honor and Violence in the Old South.* New York: Oxford University Press, 1986.

————. *Southern Honor: Ethics and Behavior in the Old South.* Oxford and New York: Oxford University Press, 1982.

————, ed. *The American People in the Antebellum South.* West Haven, Conn.: Pendulum Press, 1973.

Wyeth, John B. *Notes of 1832.* In Reuben Gold Thwaites, ed., *Early Western Travels,* vol. 21. Cleveland: Arthur H. Clark Co., 1905.

Zinn, Howard. *The Southern Mystique.* New York: Alfred A. Knopf, 1964.

B. Articles, Essays

Abbott, Edith. "The Civil War and the Crime Wave of 1865–70." *Social Service Review* 1 (June 1927).

Ambramoske, Donald J. "The Federal Lead Leasing System in Missouri." *Missouri Historical Review* 64, no. 1 (October 1959).

Anderson, Hattie M. "The Evolution of a Frontier Society in Missouri, 1815–1828." *Missouri Historical Review* 32, no. 3, pt. 1 (April 1938).

Baroja, Julio Caro. "Honour and Shame: A Historical Account of Several Conflicts." In J. G. Peristiany, ed., *Honour and Shame: The Values of Mediterranean Society.* Chicago: University of Chicago Press, 1966.

Bek, William G. "The Followers of Dudan." *Missouri Historical Review* 15, no. 4 (July 1921).

Billias, George A. "Editor's Introduction." In George A. Billias, ed., *Law and Authority in Colonial America.* New York: Dover Publications, Inc., 1970.

Blunt, Roy. "The Smith–Tharp Incident and Dueling in Missouri." *Steelville* (Mo.) *Star,* September 27, 1989.

Bourdieu, Pierre. "The Sentiment of Honour in Kabyle Society." In J. G. Peristiany, ed., *Honour and Shame: The Values of Mediterranean Society.* Chicago: University of Chicago Press, 1966.

Bowman, Shearer Davis. "Honor and Martialism in the U.S. South and Prussian East Elbia during the Mid-Nineteenth Century." In Kees Gispen, ed., *What Made the South Different?* Jackson: University of Mississippi Press, 1990.

Boyle, Susan C. "Did She Generally Decide? Women in Ste. Genevieve, 1750–1805." *William and Mary Quarterly* 44, no. 3 (October 1987).

Brooks, George R. "Duels in St. Louis." *St. Louis Globe-Democrat Sunday Magazine,* June 7, 1964.

Brown, Richard Maxwell. "Historical Patterns of Violence in America." In Graham and Gurr, eds., *The History of Violence in America.* New York: Frederick A. Praeger, 1969.

———. "Historiography of Violence in the American West." In Michael P. Malone, ed., *Historians and the American West.* Lincoln: University of Nebraska Press, 1987.

Chambers, William N. "As the Twig Is Bent: The Family and the North Carolina Years of Thomas Hart Benton, 1752–1801." *North Carolina Historical Review* 26, no. 4 (October 1949).

———. "Pistols and Politics: Incidents in the Career of Thomas H. Benton, 1816–1818." *Bulletin of the Missouri Historical Society* 5, no. 1 (October 1948).

———. "Young Man from Tennessee: First Years of Thomas H. Benton in Missouri." *Bulletin of the Missouri Historical Society* 4, no. 4 (July 1948).

Clark, Mrs. William. "The Intimate View." *Bulletin of the Missouri Historical Society* 4, no. 3 (April 1948).

Clay, John. "Justice on the Range." In Ramon F. Adams, ed., *The Best of the American Cowboy.* Norman: University of Oklahoma Press, 1957.

Cleland, Hugh C. "John B. C. Lucas, Physiocrat on the Frontier." *Western Pennsylvania Historical Magazine* 36, pt. 3 (September–December 1953).

Clemens, Cyril. "'The Birth of a Legend' Again." *American Literature* 15, no. 1 (March 1943).

Coles, Harry L., Jr. "Applicability of the Public Land System to Louisiana." *Mississippi Valley Historical Review* 43, no. 1 (June 1956).

Commager, Henry Steele. "The Search for a Usable Past." *American Heritage Magazine* 16, no. 2 (February 1965).

Conway, J. J. "The Beginnings of Ecclesiastical Jurisdiction in the Archdiocese of St. Louis, 1764–1776." *Missouri Historical Society Collection* 1, no. 14 (1897).

Culmer, Frederic A. "The Leonard-Berry Duel of 1824." *Missouri Historical Review* 49, no. 4 (July 1955).

Davis, David Brion. "Ten-Gallon Hero." *American Quarterly* 6, no. 2 (summer 1954).

———. "Violence in American Literature." In Otto N. Larsen, ed., *Violence and the Mass Media.* New York: Harper and Row, 1968.

Davis, Ronald L. F. "Community and Conflict in Pioneer Saint Louis, Missouri." *Western Historical Quarterly* 10, no. 3 (July 1979).

Dealey, James Q. "Our State Constitutions." *Annals of American Academy of Political and Social Science,* March Supplement, 1907.

DeMenil, Alexander N. "A Century of Missouri Literature." *Missouri Historical Review* 15, no. 1 (October 1920).

Din, Gilbert C. "The Immigration Policy of Governor Esteban Miró in Spanish Louisiana." *Southwestern Historical Quarterly* 73, no. 3 (October 1969).

———. "Spain's Immigration Policy in Louisiana and the American Penetration, 1792–1803." *Southwestern Historical Quarterly* 76, no. 4 (January 1973).

Dunson, A. A. "Notes on the Missouri Germans on Slavery." *Missouri Historical Review* 59, no. 3 (April 1965).

Eaton, Clement. "Mob Violence in the Old South." *Mississippi Valley Historical Review* 29, no. 3 (December 1942).

Esselman, Kathryn C. "From Camelot to Monument Valley." In Jack Nachbar, ed., *Focus on the Western.* Englewood Cliffs, N.J.: Prentice-Hall, Inc., 1974.

Faherty, William B. "The Personality and Influence of Louis William Valentine DuBourg." In John F. McDermott, ed., *Frenchmen and French Ways in the Mississippi Valley.*

Ferguson, DeLancey. "Mark Twain's Comstock Duel: The Birth of a Legend." *American Literature* 14, no. 1 (March 1942).

Field, Eugene. "The Duel." *Childcraft Books.* Vol. 1. Chicago: World Book, Inc., 1948.

Field, Roswell. "Eugene Field: A Memory." *Missouri Historical Review* 44, no. 2 (January 1950).

Flint, Timothy. "The Bar, the Pulpit, and the Press." *Western Monthly Review* 3 (June 1830).

———. "Duelling." *Western Monthly Review* 1 (April 1828).

———. "National Character of the Western People." *Western Monthly Review* 1 (May 1827).

Foley, William E. "The American Territorial System: Missouri's Experience." *Missouri Historical Review* 65, no. 4 (July 1971).

———. "Antebellum Missouri in Historical Perspective." *Missouri Historical Review* 82, no. 2 (January 1988).

Frantz, Joe B. "The Frontier Tradition: An Invitation to Violence." In Graham and Gurr, eds., *The History of Violence in America: Historical and Comparative Perspectives—A Report Submitted to the National Commission on the Causes and Prevention of Violence.* New York: Frederick A. Praeger, 1969.

"From the Director's Note Book." *Bulletin of the Missouri Historical Society* 5, no. 2 (January 1949).

Gardner, James A. "The Business Career of Moses Austin in Missouri, 1798–1821." *Missouri Historical Review* 50, no. 3 (April 1956).

Gentry, North Todd. "David Todd." *Missouri Historical Review* 21, no. 4 (July 1927).

Gentry, W. R. "The Missouri Soldier One Hundred Years Ago." *Missouri Historical Review* 12, no. 4 (July 1918).

Gerson, Walter M. "Violence as an American Value Theme." In Otto N. Larsen, ed., *Violence and the Mass Media.* New York: Harper and Row, 1968.

Gibson, Charles. "Edward Bates." *Bulletin of the Missouri Historical Society* 2, no. 1 (January 1900).

Giffen, Jerena East. "'Add a Pinch and a Lump': Missouri Women in the 1820s." *Missouri Historical Review* 65, no. 4 (July 1971).

Godkin, E. L. "The Probative Force of the Duel." *Nation* 33 (October 20, 1881).

———. "Southern and Other Duelling." *Nation* 36 (May 10, 1883): 397–98.

Goodrich, James W., and Lynn Wolf Gentzler, eds. "'I Well Remember': David Holmes Conrad's Recollections of St. Louis, 1819–1823." Pt. 2. *Missouri Historical Review* 90, no. 2 (January 1996).

Gordon, Joseph F. "The Political Career of Lilburn W. Boggs." *Missouri Historical Review* 52, no. 2 (January 1958).

Gorn, Elliott J. "'Gouge and Bite, Pull Hair and Scratch': The Social Significance of Fighting in the Southern Backcountry." *American Historical Review* 90, no. 1 (February 1985).

Greenberg, Kenneth S. "The Nose, the Lie, and the Duel in the Antebellum South." *American Historical Review* 95 (February 1990).

Grimes, Absalom, and M. M. Quaife, ed. "Campaigning with Mark Twain." *Missouri Historical Review* 21, no. 2 (January 1927).

Grissom, Daniel M. "Personal Recollections of Distinguished Missourians— Thomas H. Benton." *Missouri Historical Review* 18, no. 2 (January 1924).

———. "Personal Recollections of Distinguished Missourians—Abiel Leonard." *Missouri Historical Review* 18, no. 3 (April 1924).

Hackney, Sheldon. "Southern Violence." *American Historical Review* 74, no. 3 (February 1969).

Hale, Douglas D., Jr. "Friedrich Adolph Wislizenus: From Student Rebel to Southwestern Explorer." *Missouri Historical Review* 62, no. 3 (April 1968).

Harr, Helen K. "Duelling." In *Bushwhacker's Annual Calendar.* St. Joseph: n.p., 1981.

Harr, John L. "Law and Lawlessness in the Lower Mississippi Valley, 1815–1860." *Northwest Missouri State College Studies* 19, no. 1 (June 1, 1955).

Harris, Patrick J. "William Keil and the Aurora Colony: A Communal Society Crosses the Oregon Trail." In Carl Guarner et al., eds., *Religion and Society in the American West: Historical Essays.* Laham: University Press of America, 1987.

Hartz, Louis. "A Comparative Study of Fragment Cultures." In Hugh Davis Graham and Ted Robert Gurr, eds., *The History of Violence in America: Historical and Comparative Perspectives—A Report Submitted to the National Commission on the Causes and Prevention of Violence.* New York: Frederick A. Praeger, 1969.

Henry, John W. "Personal Recollections." In A. J. D. Stewart, ed., *The History of the Bench and Bar of Missouri.* St. Louis: Legal Publishing Co., 1898.

Hier, Marshall D. "Lawyer Benton's Last Duel." *St. Louis Bar Journal* 36, no. 1 (summer 1989).

Hill, Leslie Gamblin. "A Moral Crusade: The Influence of Protestantism on Frontier Society in Missouri." *Missouri Historical Review* 45, no. 1 (October 1950).

"Historical Notes and Comments." *Missouri Historical Review* 31, no. 4 (July 1937).

Homans, Peter. "Puritanism Revisited: An Analysis of the Contemporary Screen-Image Western." In Jack Nachbar, ed., *Focus on the Western.* Englewood Cliffs, N.J.: Prentice Hall, Inc., 1974.

Huff, Leo E. "The Last Duel in Arkansas: The Marmaduke-Walker Duel." *Arkansas Historical Quarterly* 23, no. 1 (spring 1964).

Ireland, Robert M. "The Problem of Concealed Weapons in Nineteenth-Century Kentucky." *Register of the Kentucky Historical Society* 3 (spring 1993).

Jones, W. A. Burt. "Rice Jones: A Brief Memoir . . ." In Edward G. Mason, ed., *Early Chicago and Illinois.* Chicago: Fergus Printing Co., 1890.

Kalen, Kristen, and Lynn Morrow. "A Bald Knobber Sues Springfield!" *White River Valley Historical Quarterly* (July 1993).

Keller, Kenneth W. "Alexander McNair and John B. C. Lucas: The Background of Early Missouri Politics." *Bulletin of the Missouri Historical Society* 33, no. 2 (July 1977).

Kernan, Thomas J. "The Jurisprudence of Lawlessness." *American Bar Association Report* 29 (1906).

Kirkpatrick, R. L. "Professional, Religious, and Social Aspects of St. Louis Life, 1804–1816." *Missouri Historical Review* 44, no. 4 (July 1950).

Klapper, Joseph T. "The Impact of Viewing 'Aggression': Studies and Problems of Extrapolation." In Otto N. Larsen, ed., *Violence and the Mass Media.* New York: Harper and Row, 1968.

McCandless, Perry. "The Political Philosophy and Political Personality of Thomas H. Benton." *Missouri Historical Review* 50, no. 1 (October 1955).

McClure, C. H. "A Century of Missouri Politics." *Missouri Historical Review* 15, no. 2 (January 1921).

McDermott, John F. "Auguste Chouteau: First Citizen of Upper Louisiana." In John F. McDermott, ed., *Frenchmen and French Ways in the Mississippi Valley.* Urbana: University of Illinois Press, 1969.

———. "The Confines of a Wilderness." *Missouri Historical Review* 29, no. 1 (October 1934).

McKee, Christopher. "The Pathology of a Profession: Death in the United States Navy Officer Corps." *War and Society* 3, no. 1 (May 1985).

Mangold, George B. "Social Reform in Missouri 1820–1920." *Missouri Historical Review* 15, no. 1 (October 1920).

March, David D. "The Admission of Missouri." *Missouri Historical Review* 65, no. 4 (July 1971).

Marsden, Michael T. "Savior in the Saddle: The Sagebrush Testament." In Jack Nachbar, ed., *Focus on the Western.* Englewood Cliffs, N.J.: Prentice-Hall, Inc., 1974.

"Missouri History Not Found in Textbooks." *Missouri Historical Review* 19, no. 2 (January 1925).

"Missouri History Not Found in Textbooks." *Missouri Historical Review* 25, no. 2 (January 1931).

"Missouriana." *Missouri Historical Review* 26, no. 4 (July 1932).

———. *Missouri Historical Review* 33, no. 3 (April 1939).

———. *Missouri Historical Review* 33, no. 3 (November 1939).

———. *Missouri Historical Review* 35, no. 3 (April 1941).

Morris, Richard B. "Foreword." In George A. Billias, ed., *Law and Authority in Colonial America*. New York: Dover Publication, Inc., 1970.

Morrow, Lynn. "The Sons of Honor and Gen. George Caleb Bingham." *White River Valley Historical Quarterly* (fall 1996).

———. "Where Did All The Money Go? War and the Economics of Vigilantism in Southern Missouri." *White River Valley Historical Quarterly* (fall 1994).

Moss, James E. "Dueling in Missouri History: The Age of Dirk Drawing and Pistol Snapping." *Trail Guide* 11, no. 4 (December 1966).

Murphy, Lawrence, E. "Beginnings of Methodism in Missouri, 1798–1824." *Missouri Historical Review* 21, no. 3 (April 1927).

Oliver, Lillian H. "Some Spanish Land Grants in the St. Charles District." Miscellaneous file 1965, collection no. 2904, WHMC.

Owen, Mary Alicia. "Social Customs and Usages in Missouri during the Last Century." *Missouri Historical Review* 15, no. 1 (October 1920).

Pelzer, Louis. "The Spanish Land Grants." *Iowa Journal of History and Politics* 11, no. 1 (January 1913).

Peristiany, J. G. "Introduction." In J. G. Peristiany, ed., *Honour and Shame: The Values of a Mediterranean Society.* Chicago: University of Chicago Press, 1966.

Pitt-Rivers, Julian. "Honour and Social Status." In J. G. Peristiany, ed., *Honour and Shame: The Values of Mediterranean Society.* Chicago: University of Chicago Press, 1966.

Potterfield, Neil H. "Ste. Genevieve, Missouri." In John F. McDermott, ed., *Frenchmen and French Ways in the Mississippi Valley.* Urbana: University of Illinois Press, 1969.

Richardson, Lemont K. "Private Land Claims in Missouri." *Missouri Historical Review* 50, no. 1 (October 1955).

Roper, William L. "When the Clock Struck Twelve: A Famous Ozark Duel." Subject File, Duels, AHC.

Rorabaugh, W. J. "The Political Duel in the Early Republic: Burr V. Hamilton." *Journal of the Early Republic* 15 (spring 1995).

Rosenbaum, Betty B. "The Relationship between War and Crime in the United States." *Journal of Criminal Law and Criminology* 30 (January 1940).

Rothensteiner, John E. "The Missouri Priest One Hundred Years Ago." *Missouri Historical Review* 21, no. 4 (July 1927).

Sampson, Francis A. "Glimpses of Old Missouri by Explorers and Travelers." *Missouri Historical Review* 1, no. 4 (July 1907).

Schroeder, Walter A. "Spread of Settlement in Howard County, Missouri: 1810–1859." *Missouri Historical Review* 53, no. 1 (October 1968).

Shackleford, Thomas. "Early Recollections of Missouri." *Missouri Historical Society Collection* 2, no. 2 (April 1903).

———. "Reminiscences of the Bench and Bar in Central Missouri." In A. J. D. Stewart, ed., *The History of the Bench and Bar of Missouri*. St. Louis: Legal Publishing Co., 1898.

Shoemaker, Floyd C. "Some Colorful Lawyers in the History of Missouri, 1804–1904." Pt. 1. *Missouri Historical Review* 53, no. 2 (January 1959).

Simmons, Lucy. "The Rise and Growth of Protestant Bodies in the Missouri Territory." *Missouri Historical Review* 22, no. 3 (April 1928).

Steffen, Jerome O. "William Clark: A New Perspective of Missouri Territorial Politics 1813–1820." *Missouri Historical Review* 67, no. 2 (January 1973).

Sterling, James. "Letters from the Slave States." In Bertram Wyatt-Brown, ed., *The American People in the Antebellum South*. West Haven, Conn.: Pendulum Press, Inc., 1973.

Stevens, Walter B. "The Missouri Tavern." *Missouri Historical Review* 15, no. 1 (January 1921).

Steward, Dick. "The Bitter Sport of Gentlemen: The Leonard-Berry Duel of 1824." *Gateway Heritage* 12, no. 2 (fall 1991).

———. "John Smith T and the Way West: Filibustering and Expansion on the Missouri Frontier." *Missouri Historical Review* 89, no. 1 (October 1994).

———. "Selection of a State Capital: Vagaries and Vicissitudes." *Pioneer Times* 14, no. 4 (July 1990).

———. "Western Myth: History versus the Legends and Lore of John Smith T." *Missouri Folklore Society Journal* 15 (1993).

———. "'With the Sceptor of a Tyrant': John Smith T and the Mineral Wars." *Gateway Heritage* 14, no. 2 (fall 1993).

Stowe, Steven M. "The Touchiness of the Gentleman Planter: The Sense of Esteem and Continuity in the Ante-Bellum South." *Psychohistory Review* 8 (winter 1979).

Strickland, Arvarh E. "Aspects of Slavery in Missouri, 1821." *Missouri Historical Review* 65, no. 4 (July 1971).

Swindler, William F. "The Southern Press in Missouri 1861–1864." *Missouri Historical Review* 35, no. 3 (April 1941).

Sydnor, Charles S. "The Southerner and the Laws." *Journal of Southern History* 6, no. 1 (February 1940).

Terrell, A. W. "Recollections of General Sam Houston." *Southwestern Historical Quarterly* 16, no. 2 (October 1912).

Trexler, Harrison A. "Slavery in Missouri Territory." *Missouri Historical Review* 3, no. 3 (April 1909).

Turner, Frederick J. "The Significance of the Frontier in American History." In Frederick J. Turner, ed., *The Frontier in American History*. New York: Henry Holt and Co., 1920.

Van Ravenswaay, Charles. "Bloody Island: Honor and Violence in Early Nineteenth-Century St. Louis." *Gateway Heritage* 10, no. 4 (spring 1990).

Vandiver, Frank E. "The Southerner as Extremist." In Vandiver, ed., *The Idea of the South: Pursuit of a Central Theme*. Chicago: University of Chicago Press, 1964.

Viles, Jonas. "Missouri in 1820." *Missouri Historical Review* 15, no. 1 (October 1920).

Violette, E. M. "Early Settlements in Missouri." *Missouri Historical Review* 1, no. 1 (October 1906).

Weiner, Alan S. "John Scott, Thomas Hart Benton, David Barton and the Presidential Election of 1824." *Missouri Historical Review* 60, no. 4 (July 1966).

White, Edward J. "A Century of Transportation in Missouri." *Missouri Historical Review* 15, no. 1 (October 1920).

White, Lynn, Jr. "The Legacy of the Middle Ages in the American Wild West." *Speculum* 40 (April 1965).

Williamson, Hugh P. "Abiel Leonard, Lawyer and Judge." *Benchmarks, Journal of the Missouri Bar* (June 1959).

Windell, Marie George. "The Background of Reform on the Missouri Frontier." *Missouri Historical Review* 39, no. 2 (January 1945).

Wurthman, Leonard B., Jr. "Frank Blair: Lincoln's Congressional Spokesman." *Missouri Historical Review* 64, no. 3 (April 1970).

C. Newspapers and Journals

American Pioneer, The: A Monthly Periodical
Arkansas Gazette
Boon's Lick Times
Boonville Observer

Bowling Green Salt River Journal
Branson Echo
Carthage Evening Press
Central Missouri News (Sedalia)
DeSoto Press
Fulton Telegraph
Hannibal Gazette
Harper's New Monthly Magazine
Jackson Independent Patriot
Jefferson City Inquirer
Jefferson City State Times
Jefferson City Tribune
Jeffersonian Republican
Joplin Daily Globe
Kansas City Journal
Kansas City Star
Louisiana Gazette
Missouri Argus (St. Louis)
Missouri Democrat
Missouri Farm and Home (Columbia)
Missouri Gazette (St. Louis)
Missouri Herald (Columbia)
Missouri Intelligencer and Boon's Lick Advertiser (Boonville)
Missourian Magazine (Columbia)
Missouri Republican
Missouri Statesman (Columbia)
Morning Herald
Nevada Post
New York Daily Times
Pilot, The
St. Joseph Gazette
St. Louis Beacon
St. Louis Enquirer
St. Louis Globe-Democrat
St. Louis Globe-Democrat Magazine
St. Louis Herald of Religious Liberty
St. Louis Leader
St. Louis Post-Dispatch
St. Louis Republic
St. Louis Republican

Sedalia Capital
Southeast Missourian (Cape Girardeau)
Southern Literary Messenger
Southwestern Reporter
Springfield Leader-Democrat
Steelville Star
Tennessean, The (Nashville)
Washington Bee
Weekly Tribune (Liberty)
Western Miscellany, The
Western Monthly Magazine
Western Monthly Review
Western Review and Miscellaneous Magazine: A Monthly Publication Devoted to Literature and Science

D. Addresses, News Releases, Speeches, and Papers

Denny, James M. "Oakwood." Inventory Nomination Form, National Register of Historic Places, June 10, 1982. Located in Division of Parks, Recreation, and Historic Preservation, Missouri Department of Natural Resources, Jefferson City, Missouri.

Johnson, Charles P. "Personal Recollections." Address to the State Historical Society and Press Association of Missouri, January 22, 1903. Located in the Missouri Historical Society Collection, vol. 11, no. 2, April 1903.

Muenks, Janice. "Frontier Society and the Missouri Duel." Paper read at Lincoln University, Jefferson City, Missouri, fall 1989.

Philips, John F. "Reminiscences of Some Deceased Lawyers of Central Missouri." Address to the Missouri State Bar Association, St. Louis, Missouri, September 24, 1914. Located in the State Historical Society, Columbia, Missouri.

Rozier, Firmin A. "Address of Firmin A. Rozier." Address to the Missouri Historical Society, November 13, 1879. Located in the Ste. Genevieve Papers, MHS, St. Louis, Missouri.

Smith, W. R. "History of Dueling in the State of Missouri." Paper read before the State Historical Society, December 9, 1904. Located in the State Historical Society, Columbia, Missouri.

State Historical Society of Missouri. *This Week in Missouri History.* September 20–27, 1925.

———. December 9–15, 1928.

———. August 11–17, 1929.

————. July 12–19, 1930.

————. August 24–30, 1930.

————. August 31–September 6, 1930.

————. June 28–July 4, 1931.

————. September 20–26, 1931.

————. April 30–May 6, 1933.

Verdot, Thomas. "St. Louis and the Political Duelists of 1840." Paper read at Lincoln University, Jefferson City, Missouri, fall 1989.

E. Interviews

Frank Magre, June 7, 1993.

Anna Price, June 15, 1990.

Frank Showalter, April 3, 1991.

F. Pamphlets

Bates, Edward. "Edward Bates against Thomas H. Benton." St. Louis: Charles and Paschall Printers, 1828.

Beecher, Lyman. "Remedy for Duelling." Boston: n.p., April 16, 1806.

Dana, W. C. "The Sense of Honor: A Discourse." Charlestown: Steam Power Press, 1857.

Kendrick, James. "Dueling: A Sermon Preached at the First Baptist Church, Charlestown, South Carolina, August 7, 1853." Charlestown: A. J. Burke, 1853.

Lucas, Charles. "To the People of Missouri Territory: Charles Lucas' Exposition of a Late Difference Between John Scott and Himself." St. Louis: Missouri Gazette Office, 1816.

Spring, Samuel. "A Discourse in Consequence of the Late Duel." Newbury, Ma.: E. W. Allen, 1804.

Weems, Mason L. "God's Revenge against Duelling, or the Duellist's Looking Glass." District of Pennsylvania: n.p., 1816.

G. Unpublished Theses and Dissertations

Butcher, Jerry L. "A Narrative History of Selected Aspects of Violence in the New South, 1877–1920." Ph.D. diss., University of Missouri–Columbia, 1977.

Forderhase, Rudolph E. "Jacksonianism in Missouri, from Predilection to Party 1820–1836." Ph.D. diss., University of Missouri–Columbia, 1968.

Kellner, George H. "The German Element on the Urban Frontier: St. Louis, 1830–1860." Ph. D. diss., University of Missouri–Columbia, 1973.

Peterson, Norma L. "B. Gratz Brown, The Rise of a Radical, 1850–1863." Ph.D. diss., University of Missouri–Columbia, 1953.

Westover, John G. "The Evolution of the Missouri Militia 1804–1919." Ph.D. diss., University of Missouri–Columbia, 1948.

H. Manuscripts, Diaries, Letters, Testimonies, Case Files

Arkansas History Commission, Little Rock, Arkansas
    Federal Writers Project, "Early Days in Arkansas"
    Research File
    Subject File, Duels
Barker Library, University of Texas, Austin, Texas
    Moses Austin Papers
Cape Girardeau Circuit Court Records
Madison County Circuit Court Records, 1827–1855, Fredericktown, Missouri
Frank Magre Collection, Herculaneum, Missouri
Missouri Historical Society, St. Louis, Missouri
    Frederick Bates Papers
    Thomas Hart Benton Papers
    William K. Bixby Collection
    Brown-Reynolds Duels Collection
    Harry R. Burke Papers
    William V. Byars Papers
    William C. Carr Papers
    Duels Files
    Rufus Easton Papers
    Mrs. John Green Scrapbook
    William Carr Lane Collection
    J. B. C. Lucas Collection
    David Murphy Papers
    Joseph Ormerod Collection
    Thomas Reynolds Papers
    Ste. Genevieve Papers
    Isaac H. Sturgeon Papers
    Vertical File

Missouri State Archives, Jefferson City, Missouri
    Boone County Circuit Court Records
    Cape Girardeau Court of Quarter Sessions
    Cape Girardeau Fourth Judicial Circuit Court Records
    Franklin County Circuit Court Records
    Howard County Circuit Court Records
    Howell County Circuit Court Records
    Lawrence County Circuit Court Records
    James Edgar McHenry Diary
    Missouri Supreme Court Cases, Territorial Court Cases,1804–1820
    Polk County Circuit Court Records
    Ralls County Circuit Court Records
    St. Louis Circuit Court Records
    State Supreme Court Records
St. Louis Mercantile Bank and Library, St. Louis, Missouri
    Baptist Minutes and Pamphlets, 1820–1850
    John Mason Peck Collection
Ste. Genevieve County, Ste. Genevieve, Missouri
    County and Circuit Court Records
Tennessee State Library and Archives, Nashville, Tennessee
    Frank Laren Collection
    Legislative Material, Record Group 60
    Miscellaneous File
Washington County, Potosi, Missouri
    Circuit Court Records
    Probate and Deeds Records
Western Historical Manuscript Collection, State Historical Society,
Columbia, Missouri
    David Rice Atchison Papers
    Benecke Family Papers
    W. C. Breckenridge Papers
    B. Gratz Brown Papers
    Cape Girardeau County Court Records, 1800–1804
    Daniel Dunklin Papers
    Gentry Family Scrapbook
    Stuart Goldman Collection
    Lilborn A. Kingsbury Manuscripts
    Abiel Leonard Papers
    Miscellaneous File
    Missouri State Archives Collection

Bryan Obear Collection
V. E. Phillips Papers
Ste. Genevieve Archives, 1756–1930
Francis A. Sampson Papers
John Sappington Papers
Thomas A. Smith Papers
Robert M. Synder, Jr., Papers
Roy D. Williams Papers
Sarah Lockwood Williams Scrapbook
Vertical File
WPA Historical Survey

I. Government Documents

Carter, Clarence E., ed. *The Territorial Papers of the United States*. Vols. 4–13. Washington, D.C.: Government Printing Office, 1936–1948.

State of Missouri. *Acts of the Second General Assembly of the State of Missouri, 1822*. St. Charles: Nathaniel Paschall, 1823.

———, Department of Public Safety. *Missouri Crime Summary, 1994*. Jefferson City: Missouri Highway Patrol, 1995.

———. *Journal of the House of the General Assembly of the State of Missouri, 1824*. St. Louis: Duff Green, 1825.

———. *Journal of the Senate of the General Assembly of the State of Missouri, 1824*. St. Louis: Duff Green, 1825.

———. *Laws of the State of Missouri Up to the Year 1824*. Jefferson City: W. Lusk and Son, 1842.

———. *Senate Journal 1844*. Jefferson City: Gunn, Hammond, and Main, 1845.

———. Treaty of Cession. *Laws of a Public and General Nature of the District of Louisiana, of the Territory of Louisiana, of Territory of Missouri and of the State of Missouri up to 1824*. Vol 1. Jefferson City: Duff Green Publishing Co., 1842.

U.S. Congress. *American State Papers, Documents, Legislative and Executive, of the Congress of the United States in Relation to the Public Lands*. Vol. 2. Washington, D.C.: Duff Green, 1834.

———. *The War of the Rebellion: A Compilation of the Official Records of the Union and Confederate Armies*, 22, pt 1. Washington, D.C.: Government Printing Office, 1888.

———, Department of Justice. *FBI Uniform Crime Report, January–June, 1995.* Washington, D.C.: Government Printing Office, 1996.

———, Secretary of War. *The War of the Rebellion: A Compilation of the Official Records of the Union and Confederate Armies.* Vol. 22, pt. 1. Washington, D.C.: Government Printing Office, 1888.

Index